WORKERS ON THE EDGE

Columbia History of Urban Life
KENNETH T. JACKSON, GENERAL EDITOR

Workers On the Edge

WORK, LEISURE, AND POLITICS IN INDUSTRIALIZING CINCINNATI, 1788 – 1890

Steven J. Ross

New York
Columbia University Press
1985

Columbia University Press
New York   Guildford, Surrey

Copyright © 1985 Columbia University Press

Printed in the United States of America

Library of Congress Cataloging in Publication Data

Ross, Steven Joseph.
  Workers on the edge.

  (Columbia history of urban life.)
  Bibliography: p.
  Includes index.
  1. Cincinnati—Industries—History.   2. Labor and
laboring classes—Ohio—Cincinnati—History.
3. Industrial relations—Ohio—Cincinnati—History.
I. Title.   II. Series.
HC108.C5R67   1985   331'.09771'78   84-21376
ISBN 0-231-05520-X (alk. paper)
ISBN 0-231-05521-8 (pbk.)

Clothbound editions of Columbia University Press Books are Smyth-sewn and printed on permanent and durable acid-free paper.

To My Mother and Father
Esther and Ben Ross

The Columbia History of Urban Life

Kenneth T. Jackson, General Editor

Contents

PART III: The Age of Modern Industry (1873 –1890)

Tables

Illustrations

Acknowledgments

Acknowledgments are the legal tender of the academic world. Consequently, I would like to pay off some debts by thanking the many people and institutions that have helped me during the course of this project. My research efforts were materially aided by grants from the National Endowment for the Humanities, the Haynes Foundation, Princeton University, and the University of Southern California. The often arduous tasks of daily research were greatly eased by the kindness and help of the staff of the University of Cincinnati Library, the Public Library of Hamilton County and Cincinnati, the Ohio Historical Society, the New York Public Library, the New York University Library, the Princeton University Library, the U.C.L.A. Library, and the University of Southern California Library.

I want to extend a special acknowledgment to the staff of the Cincinnati Historical Society. Laura Chace, Frances Forman, Gale Peterson, and the rest of the crew made it an absolute delight to do research each day. In addition to their cheerful assistance in locating archival material, they, with the aid of the employees of the City View Tavern, helped an historian writing about the links between work and leisure put his theories into practice.

Many people have given their time and energy to read and comment on portions of this study. My thanks go to Ed Berenson, David Brody, Bob Byer, Chris Covert, Geoff Eley, Bill Hirsch, Rudy Koshar, Dick Miller, Frank Mitchell, Judy Newton, Doyce Nunis, Roy Rosenzweig, and James Shenton. I want to give a special thanks to Eric Foner, Ed Perkins,

and Danny Walkowitz for their help, advice, and encouragement through-
out the project. To those who claim that intellectual life wanes west of the
Hudson River, I want to say that the Los Angeles Social History Study
Group has served as a beacon of creative energy and critical thought over
the past several years. My deepest gratitude goes to Dave Brundage, Jackie
Greenberg, John Laslett, Terrry Meade, Gary Nash, Jim Prickett, Ron
Schultz, Peter Seixas, Cindy Shelton, Deborah Schopp, Frank Stricker, and
Devra Weber. I also want to thank my students at U.S.C. for continually
forcing me to rethink my ideas and assumptions.

Five more acknowledgments and most of my IOUs should be
paid off. Since our early years at graduate school, Gary Kornblith has
repeatedly shared with me his profound — and I do not use that word
lightly — knowledge of the contours and complexities of American history.
His friendship, constant encouragement, and willingness to read and reread
the manuscript several times, has impoved this book and its author in
innumerable ways. Similarly, I want to thank Herbert Gutman for gener-
ously giving me — as he has done for so many young scholars — his time,
smart advice, and critical thoughts about working-class history. A very
special debt is also owed to the two people who have shepherded this study
from its inception to its completion. James McPherson has offered his
shrewd advice, criticism, and kind support at all stages of this project.
Arthur S. Link has improved the quality of this book in more ways than I
can begin to mention. I am deeply grateful for his steadfast dedication,
encouragement, and friendship. Finally, I want to thank Linda Kent. Her
support, love, and comments made the task of completing the manuscript
more enjoyable and fulfilling.

Introduction

On September 5, 1883, Cincinnati's leading citizens gathered at the opening day ceremonies of an industrial exposition intended to honor the advancements brought by industrialization. The growth of industry and the development of new labor-saving machinery, various speakers remarked, had created more jobs, more opportunities, and greater prosperity for countless numbers of local residents. Yet, these views of the beneficent aspects of industrialization were not shared by all of Cincinnati's citizens.

Less than seven months later, on the evening of March 28, 1884, several thousand Cincinnati workers, shouting demands for justice, burned down the county jail and courthouse. For three nights, the streets of Cincinnati were turned into a bloody battleground while local citizens clashed with the 7,000 militiamen sent in to restore order. By the time the riots were quelled on the morning of March 31, thirty-five men had been killed, nearly 200 lay wounded, and property damage approached $1 million.

Two years later, on May 1, 1886, 32,000 men and women walked off their jobs and launched the city's first general strike. When manufacturers and municipal authorities attempted to intimidate strikers by calling in government troops, Cincinnati workers, angered by what they insisted was an unjustifiable use of military force against law-abiding citizens, united to seize the reins of government from the hands of capitalists and mainstream politicians friendly to capitalistic interests. During the course of their ensuing political crusade, the United Labor Party — the party of this working-class alliance — developed a political program which, if adopted, might have changed the course of industrial development and of American society.

To students of American history accustomed to the generalization that the United States lacked the rigid class structures and class struggles that characterized most European nations, these episodes of violence may seem surprising. Yet the contrasts and conflicts they reveal were central to American life in the late nineteenth century. In the two decades after the Centennial Exhibition of 1876, with its grand celebration of American industry and progress, there were more strikes and more people killed or wounded in labor demonstrations in the United States than in any other country in the world.[1] The disjunction between manufacturers' rhetoric and mass violence demands a careful reconsideration of the nature of industrialization in the United States and its impact upon the lives of ordinary men and women.

Fortunately, this reevaluation has already begun. In recent years, a number of social historians have endeavored to trace the process of industrialization and the evolution of working-class consciousness by studying in great depth various American communities. Most of these studies have been confined to towns and cities in New England and the mid Atlantic region.[2] Yet, we cannot assume, given the great diversity of regional economies and cultures in the nineteenth century, that industrialization proceeded in the same way for all areas. Consequently, we need to turn our attention westward and examine the ways in which industrialization affected the lives of those Americans who inhabited the booming new cities of the western frontier.

Cincinnati, Ohio, is a particularly appropriate setting for illuminating the complex process of industrial development and the formation of working-class consciousness in the nineteenth-century Midwest. As the first great metropolis of the West, its pattern of economic growth, conflict, and consensus anticipated the experiences of, for example, Chicago, Cleveland, Kansas City, and Omaha. Indeed, few American cities exhibited a faster rate of growth during the first half of the nineteenth century than did Cincinnati. Founded in 1788 and inhabited by a mere 750 people in 1800, Cincinnati grew to 24,831 residents in 1830, and to 161,044 in 1860. This meteoric expansion in population was accompanied by an equally dramatic change in the city's ethnic and religious composition. Whereas in 1800 the vast majority of Cincinnatians were native-born, by 1860 nearly one-half of its residents were foreign-born. Similarly, the predominantly Protestant character of early religious activity was altered by the influx of large numbers of German and Irish Catholics and English and German Jews.

The rapid development and diversification of the city's economy was no less astounding than the growth of its population. In the years after 1800, Cincinnati quickly evolved from a small frontier settlement engaged in simple transactions with the immediate hinterlands to the reigning commercial and manufacturing center of the West. By 1860, the scope and value of its industrial production were superseded only by New York and Philadelphia. During the next thirty years, although falling to seventh in overall manufacturing, Cincinnati either led or was among the top five national producers of carriages, furniture, glycerine, coffins, plug tobacco, whiskey, safes, clothing, boots and shoes, beer, printed materials, pork and pork byproducts, sawed lumber, harnesses, and various leather goods.

Industrialization did not take place all at once. The settings and conditions of production were not transformed in one revolutionary moment. Small artisan shops were not suddenly or unexpectedly replaced by large factories; artisans were not abruptly swept away by the tide of unskilled factory laborers; happy and content workers were not instantly transformed into discontented radicals. Instead, industrialization took place gradually and at an uneven rate, affecting different workers at different times and in different ways. Despite the explosion of class conflict in the 1880s, Cincinnati was not a city constantly gripped by battles between employers and employees. Rather, it was marked by both periods of working-class resistance and acquiesence; of rejection and acceptance of new forms of production. Consequently, in order to understand the full complexity of the industrial revolution in Cincinnati, to understand the diverse ways it changed people's lives, we need to begin our study before the drama of the 1880s, and examine the process of industrialization from the start.

For the sake of analytical clarity, it is useful to divide the city's evolution from frontier town to midwestern metropolis into three eras: the Age of the Artisan (1788 to the early 1840s), the Age of Manufacturing (early 1840s to 1873), and the Age of Modern Industry (1873 to the end of the century). During the first of these eras, work was generally conducted in small establishments by masters, journeymen, and apprentices who were skilled in all aspects of their trade and made products in their entirety with the help of hand-powered tools and according to craft traditions. During the Age of Manufacturing, production was centralized into large manufactories where journeymen and apprentices labored under the control of individual employers. Handicraft traditions were altered by the division of labor and the introduction of steam-powered machinery. Instead of making a complete product, factory workers labored on only a small number of specialized tasks. Prior systems of training were eroded during this era as employers taught their apprentices a few specific operations rather than the entire workings of the craft. In the Age of Modern Industry, the centralization of production intensified, while the division and specialization of labor increased and traditional techniques gave way to new skills and large numbers of unskilled laborers. It was also during this era that highly capitalized corporations began to supersede family firms and partnerships as the most important form of industrial organization.

While any effort at periodization raises problems of oversimplification, these three eras provide a conceptual model for delineating the major stages in the development of industrial capitalism in Cincinnati. It should be emphasized, however, that these were evolutionary and not discontinuous stages of development. One era did not so much replace the former as to envelop and expand upon its previous character. Thus, the beginning of one stage of production resembled the end of the prior stage.

While industrialization is often associated simply with changes in technology, it was a much broader process that affected not only the nature of work, but the nature of family life, social activities, politics, and ideology. This study focuses upon three of the main areas of daily life: work, leisure, and politics. In none of these were the experiences of workers uniform. The uneven development of the city's numerous trades and industries created a wide variety of workers and working-class concerns, conditions, and needs. By the 1860s, industrialization had fragmented workers into four main categories: small shop artisans, factory artisans, factory laborers and outworkers. During most of the century, these workers remained divided by concerns peculiar to their skill, craft, or industry. Yet, as greater numbers of wage earners found themselves working under similar conditions and experiencing similar hardships in the late 1870s and 1880s, Cincinnati workers joined together in a number of common struggles to redirect the course of industrialization. Although the artisan has been the central focus of recent working-class historiography, it was ultimately the factory worker — especially the factory artisan — who led the major working-class challenges of the 1880s.

The arena of work, however, provided only one of many perspectives from which men and women viewed the world. The formation of working-class consciousness was as much a social phenomenon as it was an economic one. The experiences gained in saloons, voluntary associations, ethnic societies, and churches were often as important, if not more so, than those gained in the shop, factory, or labor union. Leisure activities, while at times reinforcing the common bonds forged at the point of production, also acted at other moments to divide men and women and turn their attention away from the immediate concerns of the workplace. Ethnic and religious loyalties often proved stronger than common class identities. Indeed, the major public battles between the 1830s and 1885 were not fought over economic matters, but over issues directly related to the social sphere: temperance, Sunday-closing laws, Bible reading in public schools, and a wide array of other ethnocultural concerns.

Politics and ideology served both to unite and to fragment Cincinnati workers. Like other U.S. citizens, Cincinnati workers took seriously the republican heritage of the American Revolution — a heritage which both encouraged and restrained the development of a radical class consciousness. Because the United States experienced its political revolution before its industrial revolution, wage earners saw themselves as holding two identities: *workers* who operated in a highly stratified economic sphere and *citizens* who participated in what they believed was an egalitarian political sphere. Their conviction that government served as a neutral arbiter between labor and capital and would act to correct the inequities of economic life led many workers to reject class oriented workingmen's parties in favor of pursuing their aims within mainstream organizations. Democratic, Whig, and Republican party leaders also pledged their loyalty to republican ideals and promised to represent the interests of all members of society regardless of economic or social condition. Yet, while mainstream parties often succeeded in absorbing working-class leaders and programs into their organization, party politics did, on occasion, serve as an important means of unifying a fragmented working class in a common series of struggles. On several occasions, most particularly in the 1880s, Cincinnati workers organized political campaigns which sought to redirect industrialization along a more just and equitable path of development; campaigns which at times led them to challenge the very foundation of industrial capitalism — the sanctity of private property.

Workers On the Edge, then, is an attempt to assess the development of industrialization, its impact upon working-class life, and the ways in which ordinary men and women attempted to respond to and reshape their changing world. The class consciousness and struggles which gripped Cincinnati in the 1880s were not the automatic products of industrial development. They were part of a continually evolving economic, social, and political process which, while prompting periodic outbursts of radicalism, also led to compromise or acquiescence. To understand the making of the Cincinnati working class, we need also to understand the extent to which it remained unmade throughout the nineteenth century.

PART 1

The Age
of the Artisan
(1788 – 1843)

CHAPTER ONE

Forging
a Republican World

From its settlement in 1788 until the mid 1820s, Cincinnati seemed to be the realization of an American dream for a more egalitarian and cooperative world. Founded in the wake of the American Revolution, in a transmontane wilderness free of the entrenched elites and class divisions that already characterized older eastern cities, Cincinnati stood out as the republican City on a Hill — not a moral settlement, but a representation of the harmonious workings of a republican economic, social, and political system. While the rest of the nation debated the manner in which the goals of the Revolution would be implemented, Cincinnati's artisans, merchants, and nearby farmers acted together in the pursuit of individual and collective prosperity. Ideology and material conditions in this young society seemed mutually reinforcing. There was no perceived clash, as in eastern communities, between republican professions of loyalty to the commonwealth and the expansion of the market economy. The economy appeared to work on behalf of the commonwealth of all citizens. Independence, cooperation, and harmony of interest — linchpins of republican ideology — seemed deeply embedded in the foundation of Cincinnati society.

Despite their claims to the contrary, the people of Cincinnati were probably no more virtuous than their eastern counterparts. Practical necessity, not idealism, dictated their early republican development. The demands of frontier life obscured the tensions and inequities that lay beneath outward appearances of harmony. The task of turning a wilderness into a bustling city required a high degree of cooperation and daily contact among Cincinnati residents. Although city boosters would later idealize the camaraderie and egalitarian spirit of these early years, there was more than a grain of truth to their boasts that independence, opportunity, and mutuality — not dependence and class conflict — were the ruling forces of daily life. When compared with life in eastern cities, this *was* a relatively republican world. Artisans as a class appeared to enjoy greater opportunities and to suffer fewer inequalities in all areas of life than did their eastern counterparts. Indeed, although it was by no means a golden age, rarely were the economic, social, and political lives of all classes so closely integrated as in the first quarter of the nineteenth century.

The early experiences of cooperation and harmony, whatever their root causes, helped shape the ways in which workers, manufacturers, and merchants alike responded to industrialization. Indeed, long after the relative harmony of this republican world had disappeared and Cincinnati found itself beset by the same tensions which plagued eastern cities, the beliefs, hopes, and dreams of this age continued to shape civic language, ideology, and class relationships. For the workers of Cincinnati, the lingering influence of this early republican world both provoked and defused working-class radicalism.

Prosperous Artisans

On the morning of September 16, 1802, Thomas Carter, his wife and eight children — frustrated by the adverse conditions and limited opportunites in Reading, Massachusetts — loaded the last of their goods on to their Conestoga wagon and set off with nine friends in search of a more prosperous life in Ohio. For the next several months, Carter and his entourage braved the hazards of nature and traveled some 700 miles across poor roads and 400 miles down often dangerous rivers. In early January 1803, the pioneers finally arrived in Cincinnati.

Although the city was scarcely more than a dozen years old, Carter found it much to his liking. "This country is the best land I ever saw," he wrote back to his sister that spring. Land was cheap and opportunites for artisans and merchants plentiful. "A shoemaker may earn more in one day here," he marveled, "than in three days there [Lynn, Massachusetts]." Commerce, however, seemed to offer even greater opportunites than the crafts. Carter soon opened a small grocery store and sold produce — which his sons purchased at low prices from farmers in the surrounding hinterlands — at a profit of 50 to 100 percent. "I have twenty dollars here," he wrote his family, "where I had one in Reading."[1]

By April 1808, Carter had achieved all that he had hoped for: he was in good health, he owned his own home, and his store was "making money very fast." His only frustration was that he could not persuade his old friends, particularly those trying to eke out a living by farming and making shoes, to migrate west. "If the people of New England would believe the truth," he lamented some years later, "they would flock to this country in the thousands; but they will stay and starve; though a man would come from the dead they would not believe him."[2] The Revolution may well have begun in New England, but Cincinnati was where its dreams were being realized.

Carter's experiences were by no means unique. Similar tales of success were told by hundreds of other early pioneers—by cabinetmaker Benjamin Mason who arrived in Cincinnati in 1802 and gradually worked his way up from journeyman to master to merchant capitalist; by Irish tailor George Valentine who came to the city in 1819 via Philadelphia and soon saved enough money to buy a house and a cow.[3] These early settlers had chosen wisely in coming to Cincinnati, for its natural resources and strategic location made it a most favorable area for launching a new "republican" settlement.

Lying in the midst of an enormous valley basin that spread over parts of Ohio, Kentucky, and Indiana, Cincinnati was the center of one of the wealthiest inland agricultural and mineral areas in the new nation. The region's rich alluvial soil, abundant forests, and nearby mines yielded sufficient food and raw materials to meet the basic needs of future generations of settlers.[4] The valleys and waterways that surrounded the town provided a natural transportation network that connected Cincinnati to expanding regional and national markets. Its location on the northern banks of the Ohio River and its proximity to the Mississippi River afforded settlers easy access to the region's main east-west and north-south trade routes. The Licking and Miami Rivers and the Deer and Mill Creeks provided additional routes into western and northern farm lands.[5]

Early settlers were attracted, as one early resident suggested, by the "fertility of its soil; the low prices of lands, and the entire security of titles; the high price of labor, and the exclusion of slavery."[6] The frontier outpost of 1788 was transformed by 1820 into the West's largest and the nation's seventh most populous city. The 500 daring souls of 1795 had grown to 750 by 1800, 2,540 by 1810, 9,642 by 1820, and 16,230 by 1826. Cincinnati's legal status quickly changed from village (1788), to town (1802), and finally to city (1819).

Until the 1840s, Cincinnati remained a relatively homogeneous world of white, native-born Protestants with few foreigners and fewer Catholics and blacks. The City Directory of 1825, published just after the first influx of foreign immigrants, noted that nearly four fifths of the city's population were native-born Americans. Of the city's foreign-born residents, 10.8 percent were from Great Britain, 7.0 percent from Ireland, 2.6 percent from Germany, and 1.5 percent from various other nations. The city's black residents, driven out by a strongly racist citizenry, declined from 5.0 percent of the population in 1815 to 4.3 percent in 1830. Thus, even as late as 1825, over 95 percent of the city's residents were white and either American-born or native English-speaking people.[7]

Religious cleavages in this overwhelmingly Protestant community were minimal. By 1815, only the Presbyterians, Methodists, Baptists, Friends, and Swedenborgians had erected permanent churches. Catholics and Jews made up but a small percentage of the early settlers, the former numbering only 100 by 1820, and the latter not even arriving until after 1817. Nevertheless, local antipathy toward Catholics was so great that until 1822 they were proscribed from building any house of worship within the city limits. Even as late as 1833, one itinerant traveler remarked that the Cincinnati's Catholics were "so obsure as to be quite unknown to the citizens generally."[8]

From its very beginnings, Cincinnati was a city built and populated predominantly by artisans. "By far the greatest number" of inhabitants, local chronicler Daniel Drake wrote in 1810, "are mechanics. The rest are chiefly merchants, professional men, and teachers."[9] The first local survey, taken in 1805, reported that artisans and laborers, the backbone of the producing classes, constituted 60.9 percent of the working population, merchants 18.1 percent, professionals 12.7 percent, and innkeepers 8.3 percent. These occupational percentages remained fairly constant during the next quarter century. In 1825, artisans still accounted for 49 percent of the workforce, laborers 17 percent, manufacturers 1 percent, merchants 23 percent, professionals 7 percent, and miscellaneous others 3 percent.[10]

Visitors, particularly traveling artisans, were impressed by the wide range of crafts practiced in Cincinnati. After touring the city's various shops in the fall of 1811, British traveler Henry Melish postulated that Cincinnati was the "greatest place for manufactures and mechanical operations on the river, and the professions exercised are nearly as numerous as Pittsburgh." During his brief inspection of the city's productive sector, Melish observed at least 38 different trades in operation. More importantly, he concluded, the "branches of all trades are mostly increasing and afford good wages to the journeymen."[11] Melish's description of a prosperous and expanding artisanal sector was echoed by countless other visitors and residents. In 1819, local statisticians counted at least 55 trades being practiced; by 1826 the number had grown to 76.[12]

During the first decades of the nineteenth century, Cincinnati's productive sector was dominated by artisans and artisanal traditions. Although town boosters boasted of the rise of new industry, manufacturing was still in an embryonic stage of development and affected only a small percentage of workers. There were few establishments that united large numbers of workers under a single roof, employed elaborate divisions of labor, or utilized new forms of steam power. Even after the city's first major spurt of industrial growth in 1817, only the city's "woolen manufactory, steam grist mill and glass house," reported one traveler, operated "on a tolerably large scale."[13] As late as 1826, there were but five manufactories that employed more than 20 workers and none more than 50.[14]

The vast majority of Cincinnati's skilled workers labored in small, unmechanized shops, engaged in a custom trade with familiar patrons, and preserved traditional patterns of learning and practicing the mysteries of the craft. Millwrights, coopers, cordwainers, carpenters and joiners, bricklayers, and other master craftsmen regularly met to set prices, review standards of the craft, and tighten control over apprenticeship.[15]

Those willing to venture westward were pleased with the high prices or wages they could command. The desperate need for labor guaranteed better wages and steadier employment than could generally be found in the more labor-glutted eastern cities. Cincinnati was a "fine place for mechanics," wrote Thomas Carter in 1813. "Carpenters and masons can make five to ten dollars a day, bricklaying is about $3.50 a thousand. ... Mechanics here can make their fortunes in four or five years."[16] Although the enthusiastic Carter may well have exaggerated the actual scale of daily wages, artisans who passed through Cincinnati during the first quarter of the century repeatedly spoke of the favorable position and "high price of labour" in the city.[17] Newspapers were constantly filled with advertisements for journeymen and apprentices. The demand for labor so exceeded the local supply that masters and manufacturers, like merchant and iron manufacturer Martin Baum, traveled east to recruit skilled workers.[18]

Unskilled laborers also prospered in Cincinnati. Men with strong arms and backs could always find work at the docks, on building sites, or driving drays. Similarly, apprentices were so scarce that papermaker C. Wadsworth offered the unprecedented bonus of $100 in cash, a suit of clothes worth $25, and nine months in night school for any lad who would serve a full term with him.[19]

Working-class prosperity did, however, have its momentary disruptions. During the Panic of 1819, a "Friend of the Poor" wrote of the spread of unemployment and uncertainty among those "who have hitherto been considered in easy circumstances."[20] Nevertheless, the Panic did not last as long nor were its effects as severe in Cincinnati as elsewhere. Even in the midst of depression, skilled and unskilled workers still found conditions much more favorable than those of eastern cities. "Perhaps there is no town of equal size in the United States," wrote one recently arrived artisan, "where mechanics are better paid for their work, than they are in Cincinnati; or with more promptness. If many of them have experienced losses, and this is not disputed, it is not more than has been felt by other places; and they are not so great, by half, as those of some of the Eastern cities, which contain a like number of mechanics."[21]

Women also found ways of supplementing family income in this labor-starved city. Although a few managed to run their own business, most wives and single girls sewed clothing at home for merchants and tailors who sold their products in southern and western markets. Employment could also be found doing a variety of domestic chores: washing, cleaning, and mending.[22] Labor shortages created additional demands and favorable terms for young girls willing to apprentice themselves in the "household arts" of spinning, sewing, and knitting.[23] Although women and girls did not make their ways into any of the traditional crafts until the late 1820s, when some chair- and cabinetmakers began producing for regional markets, labor demand was so great that they occasionally found employment in the city's paper mills.[24]

Working-class families also marveled at the low cost of food and housing in Cincinnati. The area's plentiful supply of livestock and agricultural products meant that foodstuffs could be secured at a minimal cost. One could buy "every kind of provision very cheap," boasted Thomas

Carter; a quarter of a bear could be obtained for 27¢, while a similar amount of deer went for a mere 25¢.[25] For those with less exotic tastes, the abundant supply of pork guaranteed a high-protein diet for little money. Even the poorest of souls, observed one English resident, was accustomed to eating meat six times a week.[26] Indeed, the city's rising status as a leading hog-packing center soon earned it the dubious sobriquet "Porkopolis."

While the rapid expansion of population frequently caused periods of crowding and displacement, Cincinnati workers generally lived in better and cheaper housing than their eastern brethren. "House rent for a mechanic," Henry Melish reported in 1811, "is about sixty dollars, but most of them soon get houses of their own."[27] No other city, boasted local residents in 1820, had a higher percentage of working-class homeowners than Cincinnati; some 32.3 percent owned their own homes.[28]

The paucity of wage data makes any pronouncement concerning changing standards of living somewhat suspect. Nevertheless, from a purely economic point of view, Cincinnati's skilled and unskilled workers, *as a class*, appeared to have maintained a higher standard of living before 1825 than afterward. Men were able to earn more and spend less on the basic necessities than at any time before the Civil War. In 1806, room and board in a good boardinghouse cost an artisan about $104 a year; eleven years later it had risen to $150. By 1860, room and board in a cheap boardinghouse averaged about $175. Those wishing to live in nicer quarters, particularly families renting homes, usually paid between $240 and $300 a year in rent in 1860 — an increase of 300 percent over home rentals for 1810.[29] Food costs were no less affected by increases in prices. The cost of the eight most basic food items rose 59.4 percent between 1825 and 1860.[30] Wages, although also rising, did not rise as fast as food or housing costs. Daily wages for skilled workers in 1860 ranged between $2.00 and $2.50, while unskilled laborers earned between $1.10 and $1.30.[31] Thus, even if we were to factor for inflationary and deflationary trends, the cost of basic necessities clearly outstripped the growth of real income after 1825.

Although most economists have argued that real per capita income rose between 1825 and 1860, their tendency to average the tremendous gains made by merchants, manufacturers, and real-estate speculators with the modest accumulations of workers tends to distort the true economic picture of the period. While individual workers in particular trades may well have increased their standard of living, the working class, when taken as a whole — at least in Cincinnati — never regained its widespread prosperity of the early nineteenth century. As native- and foreign-born labor poured into the city after 1826, forcing a general decline in the artificially high wage rates, Cincinnati workers gradually lost the vaunted position which they once held over their eastern counterparts.[32]

Creating A Cooperative Economy

This early economic prosperity contributed to more than just the material wellbeing of the working class; it helped to lay the foundation for a common civic language, ideology, and mythology which would come to be shared, at least in part, by all classes. Working-class belief in an ideology that saw the world in terms of the harmony of the producing classes rather than of class conflict was substantiated by the economic and social interactions of the first quarter century. In later years, particularly after the opening of the Erie and Miami canals inaugurated a new era of commercial and industrial capitalism, the interests of artisans, farmers, merchants, and manufacturers would head in different and often antagonistic directions. However, during the initial decades of settlement, Cincinnatians appeared to work and live in the midst of a cooperative economy and society.

Jeffersonian fears that commercial and industrial development would pit class against class, thereby destroying the fabric of the republic, appeared less a problem in Cincinnati than in other cities. Unlike New York, Philadelphia, or Baltimore, where more developed market economies fostered greater divisions between and within classes, in Cincinnati the limited resources and markets of its frontier economy created a situation in which artisans, farmers, and merchants could easily work together.[33] Although economic cooperation and mutuality were born out of necessity rather than virtue, they nevertheless generated a world in which republicanism and producer ideology appeared to work in tandem.

When Timothy Flint arrived in Cincinnati in January 1816, he attributed its prosperous condition to the close interactions between town and countryside. "The wonderful improvement of the town," he noted in his journal, "only keeps pace with the advancement and cultivation of the country."[34] Indeed, the growth of agriculture did contribute to the prosperity of merchants and, to a lesser extent, artisans. The surplus crops and livestock that farmers of the Miami Valley brought to town on market days not only provided local residents with their necessary foodstuffs but also gave merchants their chief object of trade for southern and eastern markets: 90 percent of the city's downriver trade in 1819 was in agricultural items grown or processed outside the city. Farmers also aided artisans, not only through cheap foodstuffs but also by purchasing household and agricultural implements from local craftsmen and by spurring the development of a number of trades dependent upon hog byproducts: candle and soap makers, glue makers, bristle and comb makers, and so forth.[35]

While farmers helped to feed the city, merchants were responsible for generating much of its early wealth and economic growth. Though certainly benefiting from farmers, merchants also furthered agrarian prosperity by encouraging them to produce for the market and providing them with the supplies and long term credit often needed until a new farm turned a profit. Merchants also contributed to broadening the scope of the city's export trade. Although Cincinnati was the major trading center of the Northwest Territories by 1805, the limited number of productive farms and the hazards and expense of transporting goods to distant markets restricted trade to the surrounding hinterlands. Under the enterprising and ambitious efforts of a small cadre of merchants such as Martin Baum, James Riddle, William Noble, and James Findlay, men who traveled throughout the South Midwest creating new markets, expanding old ones and devising more efficient ways of transporting goods, Cincinnati soon developed into the "Great Emporium of the West."[36]

The fortunes of merchants, farmers, and artisans took a dramatic leap forward as a result of two events: the War of 1812 and the development of the steamboat. Before steamboats appeared on western waters in 1811, Cincinnati's trade patterns, although profitable, had been confined to a slow downriver export trade with the South and an expensive transmontaine import trade with eastern merchants. As imports continued to outpace exports, capital drained steadily eastward to Philadelphia and Baltimore.[37]

The exigencies of war, the expansion of eastern commercial capitalism, and the technological perfection of the steamboat, particularly after 1817 when the vessels began to travel up as well as downstream, wrought a permanent alteration in market relations. Waterway shipping costs were so greatly reduced that it became cheaper and quicker to ship goods — as well as settlers — across the Atlantic to New Orleans and then upstream to points along the Mississippi and Ohio Rivers, than to transport freight across the Alleghenies.[38] Cincinnati's leading merchants, anxious to exploit new commercial possibilities, quickly established offices and sent agents to New Orleans and eastern cities. These efforts soon paid off as local exports between 1815 and 1817 rose from $545,680 to $1,619,000. The rapid growth of trade and population during the second decade of the century propelled Cincinnati far ahead of its western rivals and established it as the Queen City of the West.[39]

The expansion of population and commerce brought increased work and prosperity for its skilled and unskilled workers. Building tradesmen were particularly heartened and enriched by the constant demand for the construction of new homes and shops. Workers also benefited from the fluctuations of the market, as excess farm products which could not be sold in distant cities were often unloaded in local markets for a pittance.

Unlike eastern mechanics, who found themselves increasingly plagued by the intrusions of the market and growth of manufactories, Cincinnati's artisans found that they could enjoy the benefits of an expanding economy without, at least for a time, finding their crafts or lives adversely affected by it. Although a number of craftsmen did sell goods to farmers in the surrounding valleys, and were thus at least minimally involved in a market economy, few produced specially for distant markets. Of the city's traditional crafts, only tanners, and to a lesser extent clockmakers, furniture makers, chandlers, and hat and clothing makers were engaged in any substantial export production by 1826.[40]

The city's manufactories, not its artisan shops, supplied merchants with their small percentage of manufactured goods for trade. The first manufactories, built and owned largely by merchants, were intended to supplement rather than to compete with traditional crafts. Until the late 1820s, the city's manufactories generally served the expanding commercial-agrarian sector — sawmills, gristmills, and flourmills — or developed entirely "new" industries such as machine building and foundries.[41]

The persistence of artisanal modes of production and the slow growth of manufactories in Cincinnati, though the result of a number of interacting factors, was largely a consequence of the flow of local investment into commerce and real estate. The relative newness of the city meant that fledging merchant-capitalists, as well as masters, had less time to accumulate fortunes than their eastern counterparts and consequently had less capital available for speculation. While merchants such as Martin Baum, Jacob Burnet, and James Findlay channeled money into new manufacturing ventures, most of their peers found that real-estate speculation and commercial expansion offered higher profits and lower risks. Land speculation, in particular, seemed an almost certain path to fortune. Real estate values on the city outskirts rose dramatically from less than $1 an acre in 1789 to $6.50 in 1805, and $50 – 100 an acre in 1817. Shrewd speculators, Thomas Carter observed in 1813, could make a profit of 100 percent within twelve months. Even as late as 1826, the most cautious land investors could expect a return of 10 – 18 percent per annum.[42] Speculators could also make considerable profits by lending money, procuring 36 percent per annum on small loans and 10–20 percent on large ones.[43] When compared to these options, manufacturing appeared a poor investment indeed. Rather than tying up money in risky industrial ventures, merchants preferred simply to import whatever goods local artisans could not produce — a decision made easier by the favorable credit terms offered by eastern merchants.[44]

Republican ideology was another, though more subtle, factor inhibiting the growth of manufacturing. With memories of the Revolution still fresh in their minds, most Cincinnatians remembered Jefferson's advice that the "happiness and permanence of government" resided in preserving a society of "independent and virtuous husbandmen."[45] While Cincinnati's citizens were part of a growing national effort to redefine classical republicanism so as to include merchants and artisans among the ranks of the virtuous, they feared that manufacturing would undermine the health of the republic by creating a dependent class of laborers with little independent will. "We are told," remarked one concerned citizen, "that the inhabitants of the great manufacturing establishments abroad are generally depraved . . . . We fear that the same result will take place here."[46] A factory worker, as even staunch Federalist Daniel Webster agreed, could not be a good citizen because he was "necessarily at the mercy of the capitalist for the support of himself and his family."[47] Even those favorable to industrial expansion were careful to admit its subservient position to agriculture. "Factories may be built," cautioned one local newspaper editor in 1818, "steam boats may be built, but if our agriculture is suffered to languish, they must fail to their own supply, and will eventually decay and bring ruin upon their proprietors."[48]

The effects of war and the rapid development of the steamboat acted to mitigate republican suspicions and foster the expansion of the manufacturing sector in ways favorable to merchants, artisans, and farmers alike. The government's desire to purchase western manufactures in place of boycotted British wares combined with high prices, constant shortages of eastern and European goods, and the sudden availability of new sources of capital to prompt a number of Cincinnati businessmen to invest funds in the previously undeveloped manufacturing sector.[49] The fervid lobbying for domestic manufacturing that gripped the city at the end of the war was cloaked in appeals to patriotism and profit. In addition to expanding the interests of agriculture, commerce, and the crafts, new manufactories would also serve as bulwarks of independence. They would end the nation's dependence upon England and the city's dependence upon eastern markets and capitalists, a dependence that had turned Cincinnati into a debtor economy.[50]

The "new" manufacturers who responded to the twin lures of patriotism and profit were not "old" artisans but "old" merchants such as James Findlay, John Piatt, and William Greene. Although these men financed the construction of several new manufactories, the Panic of 1819 soon brought a halt to any large-scale expansion of the city's industrial sector. Credit dried up and outstanding bank loans were called in, and the flow of investment capital into manufacturing ground to a halt. When prosperity finally returned in 1822, investors once again put their money and hopes back into commerce and land.[51]

While the overall expansion of the manufacturing sector after 1819 was not, as some city boosters lamented, "so great as could be wished," it nevertheless developed in a way that served the mutual interests and prosperity of merchants, artisans, and farmers and provided the material basis for later efforts to recast republican ideology. Merchant-capitalists, though generally leery of investing in manufacturing, welcomed the rise of the steamboat industry. Its facility for rapid transportation of goods and quick turnover of cargo and travelers made the steamboat a desirable object for investors. Boats that cost no more than $35,000 to $50,000 to build could, on occasion, turn profits as high as $25,000 per voyage.[52] Attracted by this new opportunity for wealth, local capitalists, led predominantly by the city's larger merchants, commissioned the building of Cincinnati's first steamboat in 1816. The venture proved so successful that by 1819 one quarter of all western steamboats were being built in Cincinnati.[53]

The rise of a local steamship industry would eventually cause conflict. Initially, however, it benefited manufacturers and artisans alike. Iron foundries, boiler and machine manufactories, and metalworking shops were quickly erected to meet the growing needs of the industry. By 1826, just nine years after the opening of the city's first major foundry, Cincinnati boasted four foundries employing 54 men, five steam engine and finishing establishments employing 126 men, and three boatyards employing over

200 men.[54] Steamship production also created more work and new opportunities for artisans without undermining traditional craft structures. With the exception of foundries, machine shops, and boatyards, steamship construction remained a largely decentralized industry. Production needs were farmed out to cabinet- and chairmakers, upholsterers, tinsmiths, and blacksmiths who continued to work in small independent shops. Although the output of the manufacturing sector grew from $1,059,049 in 1819 to $1,850,000 in 1826, only 15 percent of the workforce in 1826 labored in crafts or industries employing an average of more than ten persons per shop.[55]

The intersection of interests and complementary nature of early economic growth also served to reinforce the artisans' faith in the producer ideology. While artisans in more economically advanced eastern cities frequently viewed merchants as nonproducers, in Cincinnati the artisans saw them as allies, if not part of the producing class, whose work added to the common wealth of the entire community. Moreover, the merchants of this tightly knit community also subscribed, at least publicly, to many of the tenets of producer ideology. During the Panic of 1819, for example, they joined with farmers, artisans, and laborers in condemning the "Monster" banks — the bastion of nonproducers — for robbing the producing classes of their hard-earned wealth, homes, and businesses. When local banks were forced to call in loans in 1818–1819, overextended merchants and manufacturers, as well as artisans, had their property seized in lieu of payment. Of course, few merchants publicly confessed that it was *their* nonproductive speculation in real estate that had contributed to their eventual distress. Nevertheless, despite their complicity as nonproducers, merchants avoided the wrath of artisans and farmers, who saw them as fellow sufferers of misfortune. It was the banks, the sole institution which profited from distress and emerged as one of the city's major property owners, that became the objects of public villification.[56]

The overt harmony that characterized relationships between the producing classes also prevailed among artisans. The favorable position of skilled labor and the preponderance of traditional craft production served to minimize tensions between labor and capital. Journeymen worked in a world as yet unplagued by the labor difficulties and conflicts which were emerging in the manufacturing centers of the East. Masters were not yet seen as enemies or capitalists, but more often than not as the journeymen's allies in the struggle for independence and respectability. Masters — not journeymen — organized Cincinnati's first labor associations: tailors (1818) and carpenters and joiners (1819). Their purpose was to set and regulate prices and maintain the integrity of craft standards against recent influxes of "dishonorable" tradesmen who tried to sell poorly made goods at prices below customary scale. Certainly, the appearance of journeymen's societies in the wake of the Panic of 1819 indicated that workers did not always regard their interests as identical with those of their masters. However, these early organizations — the Mutual Relief Society of Journeymen Hatters (1819), the Union Benevolent Society of Journeymen Tailors (1819), the Journeymen Cabinet Makers Society (1819) — served more as benevolent associations than as protectors against capital and the market. Journeymen's unions, as well as strikes, were few and far between before the 1830s.[57]

Traditional expectations of mobility through the trade, from apprentice to journeymen to master, persisted into the 1820s. Earnings were sufficiently high and the costs of starting a new business sufficiently low that ambitious journeymen frequently found themselves able to save enough money to set up a small shop in Cincinnati or some neighboring community. In 1815, after serving his apprenticeship in Baltimore, journeymen cabinetmaker John Mason migrated to Cincinnati; by 1819 he had done well enough to open a shop on the corner of Sycamore and Fourth Street. Similarly, cabinetmakers Moses Clark and Andrew McAlpin found that it took but two years of hard labor to become their own masters.[58] Of course not all journeymen attained the status of master, nor did all masters lead lives of continual prosperity. After working twenty years as his own master, chairmaker Jacob Roll, much to his distress, was forced to leave his shop in 1839 and go to work as an employee of the Ross and Geyer Chair Manufacturing Company.[59]

Despite the fluctuations of individual fortune, Cincinnati workers during the first quarter century — the critical period in laying the foundation of local republican ideology — lived in a more egalitarian and less stratified society than at any other time in the nineteenth century. Classical republicanism warned against the excessive accumulation of wealth and held that the preservation of the republic was dependent upon the ability of its people to maintain a rough equality of wealth. Although property and wealth in Cincinnati were always disproportionately concentrated among the top 10 percent of the taxpayers, they were more evenly distributed during the first decades of settlement than at any subsequent time. In 1799, the top 10 percent of the city's property holders held 34.9 percent of the assessed wealth, while the bottom 50 percent possessed 12.1

percent. The distance between the top and bottom of society grew increasingly skewed during the ensuing years.[60]

Property ownership, as might be expected, suffered a similar decline. Although the constant increase in the absolute number of property owners lent an air of increased wealth and mobility to daily life, the relative percentage of adult white males owning land fell from over 32 percent in 1817 to less than 20 percent in 1832.[61] Thus, even if these standard-of-living figures underestimate the extent of wage increases in the 1840s and 1850s, the mass of workingmen found it increasingly difficult to purchase a home — a key symbol of independence and success — after the first quarter century.

Even the nature of inequality seemed more republican during this early era. Unlike elites of later years, Cincinnati's early men of wealth had all *earned* their fortunes by working in the city; none were born into the lap of luxury. Furthermore, wealth and inequality assumed a more discrete quality in this new society. Passing through Cincinnati in the winter of 1831, Alexis de Tocqueville observed that, although a great deal of wealth had been accumulated, it was scrupulously kept out of public sight. "Inequality both of wealth and education is certainly found in private life," he observed. "But for the outsider these inequalities are not noticeable."[62]

When Cincinnati workers of the 1830s, 1840s, and 1850s bemoaned the passing of better times, they were not simply indulging in wistful reminiscences. Rather, they were recalling a period when labor shortages and communal necessities helped to elevate the standing of the average worker far above his eastern counterparts.

A Republican Society

Economic life was only one part of the artisan's world, only one element in the shaping of working-class consciousness. Spatial development, social life, and politics also helped to promote closer interconnections among the classes and contribute toward building a local mythology of mutualism and egalitarianism.

The mingling and close interactions between the classes were not always a matter of choice. Regional geography prompted the creation of a small, compact city which simply lacked the physical space to achieve the impersonality of larger eastern cities. Cincinnati lay in the midst of a terraced basin which was surrounded by a steeply rising chain of ridges. The first terrace, the Bottoms, extended from the river to Third Street, reaching a maximum elevation of sixty feet above the Ohio River. The second level, the Basin, rose sharply from Fifth Street and extended five miles up the Mill Creek Valley, rising to an eventual height of 110 feet. The final level, the Hilltops, consisted of a series of steep hills that rose some 400 – 500 feet above the river.[63]

The difficulties in clearing forest lands, the general dependence upon the river, and the impregnability of the surrounding hills led people to settle within a one-half-mile radius of the Ohio. There were no vacant blocks in this compactly settled city, nor were there any sharp distinctions, as would be the case in later years, between residential and business areas. The vast majority of the city's early commercial, manufacturing, residential, and leisure structures were all clustered within a tightly integrated square mile near the public landing.[64]

To call this early settlement a "walking city" would be an exaggeration. People did not journey to work so much as saunter a few hundred yards from home to shop. As late as the mid 1820s, journeymen and apprentices frequently lived with masters in the rooms above their shops — rooms which doubled as school houses for young apprentices. The constraints of space also precluded the development of class-dominated or ethnically dominated neighborhoods. Although the wealthy lived in larger and better constructed homes, the surrounding alleys and back streets were inhabited by the city's poor and middling classes.[65] By living and working so close to one another, early residents were forced to achieve a mutual awareness and understanding of the conditions of daily life among various classes.

The absence of a formal or extensive sphere of leisure was another important characteristic of the period. "We have as yet," boasted Daniel Drake in 1815, "no epidemic of amusement among us."[66] Even those relentless city boosters, Mansfield and Drake, were forced to admit in 1826 that the city's new museum and theater were greatly lacking in public patronage.[67] With the prospect of wealth ever at hand, men seemingly preferred to devote their time and energy to work rather than to useless amusements. "Every bee in the hive," wrote the ever sarcastic Frances Trollope in the late 1820s, was "actively engaged in the search for that honey of Hybla, vulgarly called money; neither art, science, learning,

Figure 1 Cincinnati in 1800.
Courtesy of the Cincinnati Historical Society

nor pleasure can seduce them from its pursuit."[68] Undoubtedly, men of all classes made frequent trips to local taverns or partook in furtive evening visits to illegal gambling dens. Even so, the little free time that existed outside these activities was generally spent at home with family and friends or in church- or civic-related activities.

This lack of an extensively developed leisure sphere and the heavy public emphasis upon the importance of work enhanced popular beliefs in republican equality and the producer ideology. All male members of society, rich and poor alike, were actively engaged in some form of labor, for men of leisure were openly disdained as effete aristocrats. De Tocqueville observed in 1831 that the absence of a distinct leisure class led Cincinnatians to boast that work joined all men as equals. "In Boston, in New York, in Philadelphia, in all great towns of the coast," reflected the French traveler, "there is already a class which has acquired property and which had adopted sedentary habits and wants to enjoy wealth not to make it. In Ohio everyone has come to make money." In Cincinnati, he insisted, there was

> not a single, absolutely not a single man of leisure. . . . Everyone has his work, to which he devotes himself ardently. As yet people don't know what

upper classes are; the pell mell is complete. The whole society is an industry
. . . . Work is honored and leads to all else.[69]

      Cincinnati's volunteer fire companies, more than any other
organization, acted to perpetuate the links between civic virtue, amusement,
and republican sentiment. Participation in fire companies aided in breaking
down distinctions between economic, social, and political life and in creating a greater sense of egalitarianism and community service. Organized
in 1808, the members of these volunteer fire companies came from all
economic, religious, and ethnic groups. Every male between sixteen and
fifty, regardless of his position in society, was required to perform this
public duty. Manufacturers, merchants, masters, journeymen, apprentices,
foreign-born, native-born, rich, and poor all belonged to one of these early
companies.[70] Upon the outbreak of a fire, company members abandoned
their workshops and rushed to the scene of the conflagration. It was "no
uncommon thing," reminisced one old fire fighter, "to see the old solid
citizens in their broadcloth and gold-rimmed spectacles," actively fighting
the fire with their employees.[71]
      Fire companies also served as the breeding grounds for many
of the city's political leaders. A number of men who later became public
officeholders either served or had served as officers in one of the various
fire companies. Although many of them came from the ranks of merchants
and manufacturers, they had mingled with journeymen and laborers as
equals in the performance of public duty and had been chosen by them to
hold office in the company; this may well have dissipated potential class
hostilities or alienation from local government.[72]
      Taverns and saloons, though less venerated than fire compa-
nies, provided another forum for the mingling of the classes. Before the
growth of fashionable hotels and restaurants in the 1840s made them less
respectable, taverns served as gathering spots for men of all backgrounds.
Masters and journeymen, merchants and clerks would frequently assemble
at Ernst's, Yeatman's, McHenry's or Wingate's to drink, argue about politics, or read the local and eastern newspapers which innkeepers kept on
hand for their customers. Taverns also played an important civic function
by playing host to town meetings and frequently serving as the seat of local
government until well into the middle of the second decade.[73]
      Women's associations also served as an important integrative
force for Cincinnati's population. Traditional roles as housekeepers and
home producers — roles played by well-to-do women as well as poor, for

there were few servants in this early society — tended to limit the time women could devote to socializing outside the home. Nevertheless, women formed a number of their own organizations: the Female Society for Charitable Purposes, the Female Auxiliary Bible Society, the Female Auxiliary for the Benefit of Africans, and the Union Sabbath School. Although most of these associational activities revolved around church and charitable functions, they still served to unite a wide range of women in bonds of sorority and social service.[74]

While the world outside the home was generally viewed as male terrain, some aspects of urban life joined the sexes as well as the classes. Nowhere in this small but ambitious world of laboring men and women was economic, social, and political life more fully integrated — literally and figuratively — than in the market place. The market place held special meaning in this early society, for it served as the arena of public interaction where men and women met as equals in the pursuit of business and pleasure. In an embryonic city which lacked extensive grocery and retail stores, the city's markets emerged as the central gathering places for farmers, merchants, workers, housewives, and daughters eager to purchase, sell, or exchange goods and opinions. It was quite common, noted one visitor, to wander down to the market just after dawn and find it crowded with several hundred wagons, their tailbacks turned down to form a counter and owners ready for business. Heated negotiations over prices were interspersed with exchanges concerning the social and political problems of the day. Like the city's taverns, the market place also played its role as the gathering place for public ceremonies, political speeches, rallies, and parades.[75]

Long after changes in economic and leisure life had produced greater inequalities and divisions among the city's inhabitants, politics persisted as the one activity in which all white males over twenty-one could participate as equals. Property qualifications set by the state legislature in 1808 were soon abandoned in favor of enfranchising all adult males who had resided in Cincinnati for more than a year.[76] In terms of the sheer quantity of community participation, party politics was by far the city's most important associational activity. Familiarity with local parties and politicians was so widespread that until the 1830s campaign advertisements simply listed a slate of names, without mentioning the party affiliations or offices being sought.

Constitutional promises of equality were probably more fully realized in politics than in any other sphere of urban life. Men who may have deferred to one another in economic dealings met as equals in the political sphere to discuss and fulfill the duties and obligations of citizenship. Unlike the prerevolutionary cities of the East and South, there were no entrenched elites in Cincinnati to control or dominate local politics. Political leadership was drawn largely from the active members of the working community — merchants, manufacturers, artisans, and innkeepers — and not from the more suspect ranks of the professions or from an elite propertied class. Although artisans and laborers never achieved a dominant role in the political system, they were elected or appointed to more offices than any group except the city's merchants. Between 1819 and 1834, merchants held 56 percent of the city council seats (the most powerful position in city government). Artisans held 22 percent, professionals 14 percent, and various other persons held 8 percent. The dominance of city government by merchants, however, was as much a result of the reluctance of artisans to run for offices that paid no salary as it was a manifestation of the political power of commercial elites.[77]

The seeming egalitarian and mutualistic tendencies of political and social life were informed by and unified within the larger and more powerful concept of citizenship. In a city, as well as a nation, struggling to forge a distinct identity, republican theories of citizenship served to unite Cincinnatians in a common identity and sense of purpose. Citizenship, as it developed in late-eighteenth-century America and early-nineteenth-century Cincinnati, was a theory of political behavior which emphasized collective loyalty and dedication to the public good over personal or class interests. Local obituaries, for example, reserved their greatest praise for those citizens who had contributed to the virtue, not the wealth, of the city. When printer John Carpenter met an untimely end serving his country during the War of 1812, he was eulogized as a "true American and zealous advocate of our excellent republican institutions." More importantly, however, Carpenter had exhibited the highest form of virtue: he placed political duty to the commonwealth above personal beliefs and immediate economic interests. Carpenter, noted his eulogizers, had been against the war. Nevertheless, he understood that in a republican society,

when called upon by the proper authority it was the duty of every citizen to obey. In compliance with this truly patriotic principle, at the call of his country he willingly relinquished the prosecution of a lucrative business and the society and endearments of an amiable family, to encounter the perils and hardships of a winter campaign in our Indian frontier.[78]

Early settlers devoted little attention to working out any systematic statement of republican ideology; it simply developed as a series of local rituals and seemingly shared understandings. Nevertheless, throughout the course of the nineteenth century, Cincinnati's residents used the concept of citizenship along with republican rhetoric and rituals as a binding force which cut through socioeconomic differences to unite all men in the shared and egalitarian identity of American citizen. Cincinnatians took pride in exhibiting what they considered proper forms of "republican" behavior. After sending for a tailor to take his measurments for a coat, Captain Frederick Marryat was taken aback when the artisan "returned for answer that such a proceeding was not *republican,* and that I must go to him."[79] Women were no less concerned with presenting themselves as daughters of the republic. "Hundreds of half-naked girls," remarked a bewildered Frances Trollope in 1828, preferred to work in paper mills "for less than half the wages they would receive in service" because they deemed the latter a demeaning and unrepublican position.[80]

The egalitarianism and civic virtues that republican ideology professed to represent were most prominently reaffirmed at the annual Fourth of July celebrations. Independence Day was an occasion of great festivity and ceremony in Cincinnati, the one day which consistently joined men and women of all walks of life in paying tribute to their patriotic spirit and revolutionary traditions. The entire community would gather in a familiar ritual of parades, orations, readings of the Declaration of Independence, and evening dinners which praised republican virtues. These yearly rituals, while celebrating the unity of all citizens, were particularly important in strengthening the bonds of working-class harmony and unity. The hierarchies and divisions which may have plagued various crafts and craftsmen during the year were laid aside as masters and journeymen marched together not as employer and employee, but as fellow citizens and purveyors of the mysteries of the crafts.[81]

While all classes cooperated in the growth of the city, artisans laid special claim to republican virtue. Addressing a crowd of 800 mechanics in July 1819, cabinetmaker John Smith boldly told his fellow craftsmen that without them

society would sink into savage barbarism. It was justly said, by the orator on the last anniversary, that 'mechanics are the bone and sinew of the nation.' To you we are indebted for the comforts and conveniences of our habitations; for our clothing to secure us from the inclemency of the season; for accelerating our commerce on the grand waters of the Ohio and Mississippi, and for the weapons of war to defend our country in times of necessity.[82]

Indeed, concluded Smith, this was a world which the artisans had made!

In 1826, with Cincinnati's pioneer days long over, Edward Mansfield and Daniel Drake took time to reflect upon the city's past, present, and future. Cincinnati, they insisted, had fulfilled the promises of the Revolution. "There is, perhaps, no place in the United States more favorable for observing the influence of our republican system upon society at large, than in Cincinnati." Its social, economic, and political system created a harmonious and egalitarian world which, rather than generating class conflict, fostered the "assimilation of all classes to each other." Citizens recognized and acted on behalf of the "true interests of the state." It was also a world which honored the producer's ideology, a world "where labor receives its reward, and enjoys it in security."[83]

Yet, at the same moment that Drake and Mansfield celebrated the accomplishments of their frontier-turned-urban republican society, numerous cracks and fissures which had been barely perceptible in earlier years began to widen and to threaten the very foundations of Cincinnati's self-professed republican world. As the spread of commercial and industrial capitalism created greater divisions within and between economic, social, and political life, Cincinnati workers commenced their long struggle to return justice and equality to a republican world gone awry.

CHAPTER TWO

Cracks in the
Republican World

Arriving in Cincinnati in the Spring of 1833, German traveler Carl Arfwedson, like Thomas Carter, was pleasantly surprised by his new surroundings. "Cincinnati is in every respect an extraordinary city," he wrote in his diary, "the only one, perhaps, on record, which has, in the course of twenty five years, sprung up from nothing to be a place of great consequence."[1] Indeed, in the decades following the opening of the Erie, Miami, and Ohio canals, Cincinnati was the fastest growing city in the West. As cheap land, easy travel, and hoped for opportunites continued to lure settlers westward, the Queen City's population mushroomed from 16,230 in 1826, to 40,382 in 1840 and 70,409 in 1844. Similarly, as new technologies were developed and craft production was reorganized to meet increased regional demands, the commercial center of the West also emerged as its manufacturing capital. With a population in 1840 only twice that of Pittsburgh or Louisville, Cincinnati nevertheless employed 10,287 people in its shops and manufactories, compared with 2,345 for Pittsburgh and 1,606 for Louisville, and 2,044 in its commercial sector compared with 589 and 641, respectively. Little wonder, then, that one local editor was moved to predict that the "future destiny of Cincinnati cannot be less than the *LONDON* of the western country."[2]

Not all Cincinnatians, however, shared this boomtown optimism. While the growth of the city's economy and the expansion of local enterprises brought greater wealth to many citizens, they also precipitated more frequent outbreaks of discontent and protest among journeymen. So long as the workers' economic position had remained relatively prosperous and the integrity of the crafts intact, there had been minimal cause for dispute between masters and journeymen. Mutual prosperity had been the greatest guarantor of harmony between and within the classes. Yet, as commercial capitalism increasingly impinged upon the crafts, altering the nature and material rewards of productive life and widening the gap between individual and collective prosperity, earlier sensibilities of harmony, mutuality, and cooperation were replaced by a growing sense of inequality, injustice, and declining commonwealth. By the mid-1830's, class conflicts emerged with increasingly greater force and bitterness.

Although the voices of discontent were confined initially to the trades most radically affected by new market relations, the disastrous effects of the Panic of 1837 led a wide array of workers to question and protest what they viewed as the growth of inequality and dependency. The economic depression that began on the morning of May 17, 1837, ate away at the saving and independence of thousands of men and women. Certainly, the initial cracks in the republican world did not begin on that May morning. However, it was in the aftermath of the Panic that earlier republican promises of egalitarianism and the disappointments of daily life clashed with increasing intensity. As discontent and conflict tore away at the foundations of their republican society, merchants, manufacturers, masters, and their allies endeavored to use ideology to minimize growing class tensions and to reaffirm traditional beliefs in harmony, mutuality, and commonwealth.

Commercial Capitalism
and the Division of Interests

By the late 1830's, the frontier world of Thomas Carter had changed dramatically. Wholesale commerce, new manufactories, and participation by masters in regional and national markets now rivaled small commercial and locally oriented craft ventures as the best paths to success. As the city's economy expanded and grew more varied, so too did the responses to economic development. For some citizens, like cabinetmaker Charles James, new forms of trade and production meant new prosperity and opportunity, while for others, like shoemaker Augustus Roundy, they were causes of regret and despair.

James typified a new generation of artisans who welcomed the expansion of markets as opening new opportunities for independence — and for wealth. After working as a journeyman in Philadelphia, James came to Cincinnati in 1824 and within four years had saved enough money to open a small chairmaking shop. Encouraged by the expansion of transportation networks, the soaring costs of eastern imports, and the increased regional demand for furniture, James shifted the focus of production from custom-made quality furniture to inexpensive ready-made furniture for steamship companies, hotels, and homeowners throughout the Midwest.

James' entrepreneurial instincts led him to alter traditional modes of production by expanding and consolidating his operations. He began hiring a number of chair painters and fancy ornamentors — craftsmen who usually worked independently of chairmakers — and later he opened a warehouse on the public landing, from which point he could better "supply the persons in other cities and towns." By the mid 1830's, James had fully realized his ambition to become one of the city's largest and most prosperous chairmakers.[3]

While James represented the new entrepreneurial part of the producing classes, shoemaker August Roundy typified a more traditional element who greeted recent economic developments with ambivalent and often hostile reactions. Like Thomas Carter, Roundy, who was thirty-one, left his home in Beverly, Massachusetts, and set out for Cincinnati in the the hope of achieving independence — that is, sufficient money to buy a shop and home. "I shall never be happy," he wrote his father, "until I am a free man."[4]

In June 1838, after fourteen days of travel by railroad and steamboat, Roundy arrived to find Cincinnati "an exceedingly pleasant city," where people from all over the country came "in hopes of an opening" and a new chance in life. Optimism soon turned to disappointment, however, as he discovered that the lure of fortune had dramatically changed the character and values of his craft. Wholesale shoe stores, which imported cheap ready-to-wear shoes from eastern manufacturers, had begun to rival the custom shop as the backbone of the trade. Lacking the capital to set up his own small operation and finding demand for journeymen dulled by the depression, Roundy was forced to take a low-paying job as a shoe dealer in John Westcott's wholesale store. Although considering his employer "a *very shrewd* man," Roundy was contemptuous of Westcott's insatiable thirst for money. Working Saturday to Saturday, Westcott, once a craftsman himself, was "contented with nothing but a continual stream of *money* flowing into his pockets." Although he owned four stores in Cincinnati and several in Dayton, Westcott repeatedly cheated his employees out of their rightful earnings.[5]

In the spring of 1839, Roundy quit Westcott's employ and opened a small shop with fellow New Englander A. G. Cheever. Unable to compete with the more established custom shops and refusing to engage in what he viewed as the degraded ready-to-wear shoe business, Roundy soon abandoned his traditional calling and ventured in to the lard oil business. Roundy did not make a good manufacturer, however, for he found himself both confused and reluctant to be ruled by the continuous fluctuations of the market. In the summer of 1845, having been literally and figuratively burned at his new business, Roundy decided to return to Beverly. "I find," he wrote to his father, "that it will take all the time to get a living here and I feel persuaded I can have a living by working all the time [in the] East."[6] Despondent at his ill fortune, Roundy found that the world of independence and opportunity which Thomas Carter had so vividly portrayed several decades earlier no longer seemed to include those who simply wished to secure a living by plying their crafts in the traditional and time-honored ways.

The new era of commercial capitalism that James welcomed and Roundy lamented was symbolically inaugurated on the morning of March 17, 1828, when several hundred citizens, their lusty cheering augmented by the repeated booming of militia cannons, lined the banks of the Miami Canal to greet the first canal boats to enter the city. After a series of laudatory speeches, the revelers adjourned to McFarland's tavern to celebrate what they hope was the dawning of a new age of prosperity.

Like much of the nation, Cincinnati residents were swept up in the tide of optimism generated by the transportation revolution. Although Cincinnatians had long participated in a market economy, the extent of their participation had been limited by poor transportation networks and frequent shortages of investment capital. These obstacles were rapidly removed in the mid-1820s and 1830s as the Ohio legislature embarked upon an ambitious program of canal and road building projects aimed at joining the state and its western, eastern, and southern neighbors in a national market network. By 1834, the state's two principal canals, the Ohio and Miami, provided an extensive transportation system which linked the entire Ohio Valley to the Great Lakes in the North and subsequently, via Lake Erie and the Erie Canal, to eastern markets. Several smaller but no less important regional canals provided new routes, especially for Cincinnatians, into the expanding western frontier.[7]

Market possibilities were also expanded by the construction of numerous state roads and private turnpikes throughout the region. By 1833, the National Road extended to the state capital at Columbus, while numerous turnpikes provided cities like Cincinnati with direct access to previously inaccessible hinterland markets. Moreover, the reliability and cost of road transportation was significantly improved after 1831, as paved highways replaced the old dirt roads which often proved impassable in winter months. Although the railroad mania would not sweep the state until the late 1840's, by 1844 the Little Miami Railroad provided Cincinnati merchants and manufacturers with access to their previously isolated northeastern neighbor, Xenia, some 65 miles away.[8]

The expansion of transportation networks and markets was enthusiastically portrayed by the proponents of internal improvements as furthering the growth of the city's cooperative economy and republican society. New trade routes, reasoned Benjamin Drake and Edward Mansfield, provided greater opportunities for prosperity and independence, thereby creating a stronger economy and more virtuous citizenry. Ohio's "moral powers," they insisted, had advanced "in a corresponding ratio with her physical resources." Increased trade, the state's Canal Commission said, would benefit all citizens by diffusing "wealth, activity, and vigor to the whole of the state." Linking the expansion of markets to the expansion of democracy, French traveler Michel Chevalier observed in 1835 that transportation innovations served to "reduce the distance not only between different places, but between different classes."[9]

Mutual prosperity did indeed appear to persist in the era of expanded market capitalism. Farmers, merchants, and artisans all shared, at least initially, in the new wealth created by a burgeoning regional trade. Commercialized farming, previously limited to areas near cities, rivers, or other waterways, skyrocketed in the 1820s and 1830s as new transportation networks provided farmers with cheap and easy access to major market centers. As the number of new farms and cash crops continued to rise, so too did the amount of corn, hogs, flour, wheat, and whiskey that poured into Cincinnati.[10]

Merchants found themselves sharing in the wealth generated by the new agrarian prosperity. As Cincinnati became the regional depot for the buying, selling, and processing of agricultural goods, local exports rose from $1 million in 1826 to $4 million in 1832 and to $6 million in 1835. Rising farm incomes and rapidly expanding regional population also created greater demand for drygoods — demands which Cincinnati merchants were only too happy to service. By the late 1830s, over one third of the city's imports were reexported to villages and towns throughout the West.[11]

Artisans and manufacturers also profited from the growing regional trade. Increased demands for agricultural implements, stoves, machinery, and various household goods helped to create more work and jobs for a wide range of craftsmen. Expanded transportation networks also aided masters and manufacturers by providing them with easier and cheaper access to raw materials (wood and iron) and new forms of power (water power along the Miami Canal). Despite the deleterious effects of the depression, the value of craft and manufactured goods rose from $1.85 million in 1826 to $17.4 million in 1841.[12]

Internal improvement projects also provided new opportunities for the city's unskilled laborers. As competition for canal and road workers increased, both within and between states, Ohio contractors were forced to raise wages from $5 a month plus board in 1825 to $13 plus board in 1828 and to $20 in 1838. Similarly, increased canal and steamboat traffic also created greater demand and higher wages for dockworkers and rivermen. As the demand for labor grew, unskilled workers discontented with their lot in Cincinnati could now seek their fortunes in other parts of the state and region.[13]

Internal improvement projects also aided farmers, merchants, artisans, and especially manufacturers by attracting vast amounts of new capital into the city and state. By 1844, as domestic and foreign capital flowed into high yielding canal bonds, Ohio had deposited nearly $10 million of its new funds into selected state banks. Cincinnati proved one of the main beneficiaries; its banks increased in number from three in 1815 to twelve in 1841, and its banking capital from $750,000 to over $5.8 million.[14]

While the broadening of transportation networks and markets brought greater wealth to large numbers of citizens, the expansion of commercial capitalism within commerce, manufacturing, and the crafts gradually undermined earlier working-class sensibilities of a mutualistic and cooperative economy. Despite the optimistic portrayals of city boosters of a continuing and enriched interdependent republican economy, the city's various economic sectors appeared to grow more distinctive, highly specialized, and independent of one another. While the transportation revolution may well have reduced the distance between the cities, it also seemed to widen the distances between and within the classes.

Although manufacturing and craft production were viewed as growing sources of prosperity, commerce remained the city's dominant economic sector. Yet, as trade expanded and the range of mercantile activities increased, divisions of wealth and power among merchants grew more pronounced. By the early 1830s, the commercial sector divided into three distinct groups: wholesale merchants, commission agents, and retail shopkeepers.

Mansfield and Drake in 1826 described how the modest merchants of earlier years had given way to "large mercantile firms . . . which have transacted business on an extended scale: two of these import directly from Europe."[15] By the 1830s, the frontier entrepreneur who ventured into the countryside in search of cheaper supplies and new markets was supplanted by a generation of merchant princes who dared to compete with eastern wholesalers for control of the entire western trade. Numbering approximately 100 in 1840, these men made their fortunes by traveling to New York, Philadelphia, Baltimore, and Europe to buy vast quantities of dry goods which they then brought back to Cincinnati, stored in their own warehouses, and, when the price was right, sold to commission agents and retailers throughout the West. Shifting their visions and ambitions well beyond the modest dreams of earlier merchants, the most daring wholesalers inaugurated an international trade, mostly in Cincinnati pork and machinery, with merchants in Europe, the West Indies, and South America.[16]

As the goods shipped in and out of the city by wholesale merchants continued to increase in the 1830s and 1840s, so too did the number of commission agents. Although less prosperous than wholesalers, these commercial entrepreneurs made a good living as middlemen between local retailers, eastern manufacturers, and regional farmers. In addition to handling the shipment of crops and drygoods in and out of Cincinnati, more aggressive agents also made purchases for hinterland farmers, arranged to store their produce in local warehouses during the winter, and bought stock for country storekeepers. Although commission agents and wholesalers accounted for only 4 percent of the working population in

1840, they controlled 28.7 percent of all monies invested in commercial enterprises.[17]

Rounding out the commercial sector was the "backbone" of the mercantile class, the local retailer who traded in drygoods, groceries, and hardware. Retail operations were valued at $12.9 million in 1840, compared with a combined total of $5.2 million for wholesalers and commission agents. Yet, even ordinary retailers underwent a major transformation in the 1840s as the general store of Thomas Carter's day gave way to shops which specialized in the sale of one or two commodities such as hats, shoes, clothing, or books.[18]

The growing divisions within the commercial community were partially reflected by the establishment of a Chamber of Commerce in 1839. Whereas in earlier years merchants had allowed matters of common concern to be settled by the city council or at informal meetings in local taverns, by the late 1820s and 1830s more prosperous merchants spearheaded a drive to create a distinct self-governing organization. Although ostensibly formed "for the purpose of establishing uniform regulations and unison of action" in promoting the city's mercantile interests, the Chamber's very existence proclaimed the emergence of an important special-interest group. Similarly, its control and domination by more prosperous mercantile firms also emphasized the growing distance between the city's large merchants and small shopkeepers.[19]

The expansion of commercial capitalism also wrought important changes within Cincinnati's productive sector. As greater numbers of manufacturers and masters produced for expanded markets, they precipitated a sharp increase in the size and diversity of the city's productive pursuits: the number of workers engaged in shops and manufactories leapt

Table 2.1 Distribution of Occupations, 1819–1840

Occupation	1819	1826	1840
Commerce	248	800	2,044
Manufacturing	1,238	3,000	10,287
Transportation and Navigation	—	500	1,756
Professions	77	97	377
Total	1,563	4,397	14,464

SOURCE: Maurice F. Neufeld, "Three Aspects of the Economic Life of Cincinnati From 1815 to 1840," *OAHQ* (January 1935) 44:71; Benjamin Drake and Edward D. Mansfield, *Cincinnati in 1826* (Cincinnati, 1827), p. 57; *Compendium of Abstracts of Statistics of the United States. 6th Census, 1840* (Washington, 1841), p. 307.

by 242.9 percent between 1826 and 1840, while the total range of mechanical pursuits rose by 58 percent.[20] The increased quest for greater
profits in the new market economy, while contributing to the city's overall
growth and prosperity, also caused sharper divisions between and within
its manufactories and artisan shops. By the mid-1840s, production had
assumed three distinct identities: "new" industries, which lacked any extensive artisanal tradition; "old" crafts, which continued to produce in
customary ways; and "market" crafts, which engaged in new capitalistic
ventures.

　　Although commerce and craft production dominated the city's
economic landscape through the mid 1840s, manufacturing, the once feared
agency of dependence, quietly but steadily emerged as the agent of future
prosperity. "Few, even of our own citizens," reported census taker Charles
Cist in 1841, "are aware of the extent and importance of the manufacturing
interest in Cincinnati. Its operations have grown up so silently and gradually, extending, in the course of twenty years, the workshop of the
mechanic with his two or three apprentices, to a factory with from thirty
to fifty hands; and adding constantly, without parade, some new branch of
industry to those already existing, that we do not appreciate or notice their
progress."[21]

　　The upsurge of manufacturing activities in the late 1820s and
1830s initially expanded the range of the city's "new" industries without
intruding upon the traditional crafts. Indeed, manufactories did not make
their way into the "older" crafts until the mid 1840s. As in earlier years,
the growth of the manufacturing sector was linked to the growing needs
of the steamship industry. With increased trade and passenger travel along
western waterways sparking an upsurge in local steamboat production —
from 14 vessels in 1825 to 33 in 1840 — the total number of machine and
boiler shops, foundries, iron works, and rolling mills increased from 11
establishments employing 109 hands and producing $213,000 worth of
goods in 1826 to 109 establishments employing 1,250 hands and turning
out an annual product worth $1.7 million.[22]

　　Although Cincinnati's machinists and founders had their
origins in the steamship industry, by the late 1820s they had branched out
into new and distinct areas of production. Perfecting the technologies which
they had first used on steamboats, engine builders began to manufacture
cotton gins and sugar mills for southern markets and grain mills for the
Middle West. By 1841 the city's 21 engine and foundry shops, the largest
single element in the new industrial sector, employed 678 men and pro-

Figure 2 Cincinnati Steel Works (c. 1840).
Early factories were modest enterprises which rarely employed more than 50 workers.
Courtesy of the Cincinnati Historical Society

duced $885,257 worth of goods.[23] The growing demands of steamship
producers and engine builders also spurred the growth of a number of
other "new" industries. By 1841, Cincinnati boasted two rolling mills, three
type foundries, five sheet-iron works, and a variety of other metal-producing
establishments.[24]

The increased efficiency of the steamboat, as well as improved
transportation networks also contributed to the phenomenal expansion of
the city's meatpacking industry. The number of hogs processed in Cincinnati increased from 25,000 in the early 1820s to 199,00 in 1839, and the
Queen City, or Porkopolis as some called it, emerged as the nation's largest
pork supplier, sending its products throughout the United States, and to
South America and Europe. By 1841 the meatpacking industry employed
more men and turned out more goods for export than any other trade or
industry. The largest 48 packing houses required the services of 1,220 men
and turned out an annual product of $3.1 million[25]

While city boosters praised the expansion of manufacturing and commercial capitalism as consistent with the demands of a modern republic, masters and journeymen found themselves more divided in their opinions of these capitalistic endeavors. Many traditional craftsmen continued to regard manufactories as symbols of dependency. Yet younger journeymen and laborers often welcomed them as agencies of opportunity and upward mobility. Carpenter Robert Moore was one such man. Raised on an Indiana farm, Moore came to Cincinnati in 1824 and apprenticed himself in the "useful calling of carpentry and joinery." His choice of trades, he later reminisced, had been dictated by his father, a former carpenter, who praised his fellow craftsmen as "producers of the permanent values of the country," and warned his son against entering manufactories—bastions of dependence and subservience. Moore never completed his term, however, for a year later he left his master to work as a pattern maker in Anthony Harkness' engine-building manufactory. Although Moore, like his father, held independence, not the accumulation of great wealth, as his ultimate goal, he saw that the future lay with the new manufactories rather than with the old crafts. Working in Harkness' shop, he insisted, "suited me better than my former employment, and I made great progress therein, as draughtsmen, foremen, and as assistant superintendent." Indeed, after a number of years, Moore achieved his life's modest ambition: a partnership in Harkness' business.[26]

Like Moore, many other craftsmen found that the growth of manufacturing did not impinge upon the traditional crafts so much as it created new opportunities for artisans and laborers. Early engine shops, foundries, and hardware manufactories, for example, expanded the range of production by turning out goods not previously made in smaller shops. Similarly, the growth of pork-packing operations, although bringing with it forms of labor organization more in line with regimented factory than craft production, nevertheless contributed to the prosperity of artisanal trades which either served the industry or utilized its byproducts: coopers, shoemakers, tanners and curriers, and so forth. Moreover, new industries also provided alternative job opportunites for men who labored in increasingly crowded trades. Carpenters, cabinetmakers, joiners, upholsterers, metal workers, and laborers found ready employment with steamship makers, engine builders, or founders, while building tradesmen, farmers, and laborers frequently spent their previously unemployed winter months working in the city's meatpacking establishments.

Although most manufactories relied heavily upon hand production — there were only 15 steam engines in use in 1826 and 50 in 1836 — and kept division of labor to a minimum, manufacturers nevertheless inaugurated radical changes in the way work was conducted. Cincinnati's new industrial capitalists, moving to centralize the ownership and control of production, gradually abandoned the traditional practice of subcontracting work to independent artisans. Previously diversified and mutually independent shipbuilding operations, reflected ship carpenter E. W. Vanduzen, were centralized in the 1830s as a handful of ambitious cabin builders and machine makers "combined their capital and formed one company, thereby building a boat complete with all her equipment ready to raise steam and make the trial trip."[27] Similarly, men such as hardware manufacturer Miles Greenwood endeavored to increase efficiency and productivity by gathering greater numbers of workers under a single roof. Between 1826 and 1841, the average number of workers in the city's foundry and engine shops rose from 25.2 to 43.3, while that of its rolling mills increased from 13.5 to 74.[28]

While Cincinnati remained a city dominated by artisans, the expansion of market capitalism wrought a broad and uneven panorama of change among the crafts. Although many artisans continued to work in customary ways, several trades underwent alterations in the locus of their markets, the organization of work, and the relationship between master

Table 2.2 Approximate Number of Workers
in Selected Trades and Industries, 1826 – 1841

	1826	1841
Machine Shops & Foundries	180	678
Traditional Metal Works[a]	60	306
Blacksmiths	92	294
Meatpacking Houses	—	1,220
Building Trades	640	1,501
Boot & Shoe Shops	257	652
Cabinet & Chair Shops	142	512
Printers	58	362
Tailor & Clothing Shops[b]	132 men	1,008 men
	467 women	4,000 women
Total	2,028	10,533

SOURCE: Drake and Mansfield, *Cincinnati in 1826*, pp. 64 – 66; Charles Cist, *Cincinnati in 1841* (Cincinnati, 1841), pp. 54–58; Charles Cist, *Sketches and Statistics of Cincinnati in 1851* (Cincinnati, 1851), pp. 258 – 61.

[a] Includes brass-, copper-, tin-, and silversmiths.

[b] Totals include outworkers.

and journeymen which began to separate their experiences, concerns, and needs from those in other crafts.

It was the changing nature and role of masters and markets, not technology, that precipitated the initial transformation of the artisan's world. Before 1826, the vast majority of Cincinnati artisans produced small quantities of custom-made goods for city and local countryside markets. By the late 1820s, however, a number of more ambitious craftsmen joined the city's manufacturers in seeking out and producing greater quantities of goods for new regional markets. As the potential scope of their business increased, a new generation of master-capitalists altered the focus of traditional production and assumed a number of responsibilities they had previously entrusted to merchants: they purchased their own raw materials and supplies, merchandised their own wares, solicited distant business by advertising in newspapers, opened their own warehouses, and speculated in wholesale ventures by consigning ready-made goods to commission agents around the country.

The most dramatic foray into market production occurred within the city's furniture trade. Hoping to fill the greater regional demand for furniture, artisan entrepreneurs such as Charles James, John Saxon, and Andrew McAlpin dramatically altered craft traditions. They shifted the thrust of production from well-made custom work to inexpensive ready-made furniture, hired greater numbers of journeymen to meet new production needs, and opened larger shops and new warehouses along the public landing. Masters who had previously relied upon word-of-mouth business, or had advertised "made to order" goods for customers in the immediate vicinity, now encouraged individuals, merchants, and businessmen throughout the West to come to their newly opened warehouses, where a vast array of furniture was "kept on hand." Not all masters, however, welcomed this change of affairs. Chairmaker John Denison, though reluctantly conceding the necessity to advertise, railed against poorly made wholesale work and pledged that his aim was "to get custom [work] and merit a continuance of support." Although custom work continued to dominate the trade in terms of the sheer number of its employees, by the early 1830s well over 50 percent of the furniture built in Cincinnati was sold to areas outside the city.[29]

The form and effects of market capitalism varied from trade to trade. Although boot- and shoemakers did not embark upon wholesale production until the 1850s, journeymen like Augustus Roundy nevertheless found themselves and their craft affected by the marketing ventures of master-capitalists. Merging the role of master and merchant, boot- and shoemakers such as Timothy Whiting, Henry Castles, and Roundy's employer, John Westcott, found it increasingly profitable to buy ready-to-wear shoes from eastern manufacturers which they then resold to store-keepers throughout the South and West. Whiting, for example, after returning from his semi-annual trip to New England with several hundred pairs of shoes, promptly dispatched them to agents in Pittsburgh, Nashville, Freiburgh, Virginia, and Plattsburgh, New York.[30] However, since most Cincinnatians expressed a distinct prejudice against the eastern work "because so much of it was poor," Whiting and others, hesitant to pass up an opportunity for more business, continued to employ custom workers to meet local demands. By 1844, 25 wholesale operations had joined the city's 168 custom shops in supplying shoes for local and regional customers.[31]

Clothing production also underwent important changes in the 1830s and 1840s. Well before the introduction of the sewing machine in the late 1840s, greater regional demand for inexpensive clothing led increased numbers of master tailors to abandon or curtail their custom operations in favor of turning out ready-to-wear clothing and "slop" work —cheap attire for farmers, sailors, and slaves—which they sold throughout the South and West. The ensuing rise of subcontracting — often run by men with little or no trade background—and the expansion of the putting-out system altered both the traditional setting of work and the sexual composition of the work force. Whereas in 1826 the city's clothing trade consisted of 35 custom shops which employed 132 men and 467 women, by 1841 813 men and nearly 4,000 women — "who sew at their own homes" — were employed by ready-to-wear clothing bosses, while only 195 men continued to work amid the city's 60 custom shops.[32]

The growing demand for printed materials also prompted the gradual expansion, specialization, and reorganization of the printing trades — developments which contributed to making Cincinnati the publishing center of the West. During the first decades of the century, there was little specialization among printing establishments; as late as 1825, virtually all printing was done in one of the city's nine newspaper shops. In 1828, however, Ephraim Morgan, a former apprentice, journeyman, and part-owner of the Cincinnati *Western Spy*, and John Sanxay, seizing upon the possibilities for greater profits in an expanded market, broke with tradition and opened the first shop to specialize solely in book and job printing. As others soon followed Morgan and Sanxay, the once all-encompassing printing trade was slowly divided into three specialized areas: newspaper and magazine shops, book publishers, and small, independent job shops.[33]

The increased specialization of business was frequently accompanied by the reorganization of production and introduction of new technologies. As in the furniture and boot and shoe trades, master printers who, as one old journeyman reflected, had previously discharged the "manifold duties of foremen, compositors, pressmen, clerk, mail-men, and carriers," were superseded by new master-capitalists, publishers concerned with the business aspects of the trade. Although printing operations within most newspaper and book publishing houses continued to rely upon highly skilled hand operations, publishers such as Stephen L'Hommedieu and Charles Starbuck moved to increase the efficiency and productivity of their work force by having their journeymen specialize in composing (typesetting) or presswork and by assigning greater numbers of apprentices to perform the unskilled tasks of the trade. When these changes still proved insufficient to meet the growing demand for his newspaper, the *Gazette*, L'Hommedieu, over the protests of his journeymen and even some of his partners, replaced the newspaper's old hand press in 1835 with the city's first steam-powered press.[34]

While changes in the trades often created more jobs and opportunities for men and women, they also wrought what many workers regarded as detrimental changes in the organization and values of craft production. As opportunities for obtaining greater profits in a market economy grew more widespread, masters abandoned older customs in favor of new capitalistic modes of operation. Whereas in earlier years the price of goods had been set according to a notion of a "fair" return on labor, by the 1830s prices were increasingly determined by prevailing market conditions. In order to compete effectively against producers in other cities, masters were forced to drive their operating expenses as low as possible. As certain costs, such as transportation, were beyond their direct control, many accomplished this end by lowering the prices or wages paid to journeymen and by increasing the length of the work day. Masters also attempted, although with little initial success, to replace traditional methods of payment based upon completed tasks — as delineated in journeymen price books — with a daily wage based upon laboring time.[35]

The drive to lower costs and increase production precipitated further assaults upon traditional craft production. Finding earlier reliance upon allied craft production costly and inefficient, wholesale cabinetmakers such as Charles James, John Ward, and John Mullen expanded and consolidated their operations by hiring their own fancy ornamentors, gilders, and upholsterers—craftsmen who traditionally operated independently of the cabinet shops. Journeymen's control over all aspects of production was also eroded as masters in the furniture, printing, and clothing trades discovered that they could further reduce costs by hiring poorly paid women, children, and excess apprentices to perform the relatively simple and unskilled operations of the trade.[36] Not surprisingly, the average size of the city's chair shops rose from 6.3 workers in 1826 to 11.6 workers in 1841, while the number of workers in printing establishments increased from 6.4 to 14.5 men and boys. [37] Although most trades remained unmechanized, by the early 1840s a growing number of the city's larger publishers followed the lead of the *Gazette* and purchased steam-powered presses for their newspapers and publishing concerns.[38]

Capitalistic modes of organization even affected trades exclusively engaged in local rather than regional production. Relations within the building trades underwent major changes as the constant demand for housing gave rise to a new generation of contractors. These new builders, complained journeymen, cared little for craft traditions and attempted "to realize as much profit as possible" by overstocking their jobs with apprentices and lengthening the traditional work day.[39]

Far from creating widespread harmony and contentment, these forays into expanded market production generated increased conflict within the community of artisans. Journeymen's unions and strikes, both relatively infrequent before 1825, grew widespread as angry artisans protested against the diminution of wages, the increased exploitation of labor, and the perversion of the crafts. Journeymen printers, cabinetmakers, and tailors, who no longer saw their employers as paternalistic allies in the upward movement toward independence, dropped the honorific term "master" in favor of the more pejorative and market-oriented term "employer" —a term which also indicated a growing sense of class division within the trade. Changes in production also created bitter internal divisions within the artisanal community. Well before ethnic hostilities tore at the fabric of working-class unity, journeymen of the 1830s saw their world increasingly divided between those who steadfastly upheld the virtues and mysteries of the craft and those who abandoned tradition by venturing into new manufactories or working for degraded wholesale craft employers. Printers, for example, refused to accept "inferior" workers into their unions, while tailors, going one step further, refused to work for masters who gave "any work to females, except such as they [journeymen] dictate."[40]

The growth of manufactories and market production in the

crafts created greater prosperity for many citizens in the 1830s and early 1840s, but it did so at the cost of undermining the sense of harmony and mutuality of interests which had seemingly prevailed during earlier decades. New commercial and productive endeavors increased the wealth of many merchants and masters, but they also sharpened the divisions between and within the city's economic sectors — between wholesale merchants, commission agents, and retailers, and between manufacturers and masters, masters and journeymen, and custom workers and wholesale workers.

CHAPTER THREE

The Decline of Commonwealth
and the Rise
of Working-Class Protest

Celebrating the dawning of Cincinnati's new economic age, the editor of the city directory of 1840 was moved to include a poem dedicated to the "Mechanics of the Queen City."

> Ye merry mechanics come join my song and
> let the brisk chorus go bounding along
> Tho' some may be poor, and some rich may be
> Yet all are contented, happy, and free.
> Ye smiths who forge tools for all trades here below
> You've nothing to fear while you hammer and blow
> All things you may conquer, so happy's your lot
> But be careful to strike *while your iron is hot.*
> Ye builders of steamboats, and foundrymen all
> Time and tide wait for none, keep rolling the ball
> And tho' business is dull, and times they are hard
> Remember Ben Franklin and Stephen Girard.
> Tall oaks from little acorns grow
> May each *Trade* and *Profession* join heart and hand
> To cherish the *arts* and keep *Peace* through the land

Each *Apprentice* and *Journeyman* join in the song
And let the brisk chorus go bounding along.[1]

Despite the poet's professions, not all Cincinnati workers found their lives "contented, happy, and free." The uneven growth and development of the trades was greeted by a wide variety of responses within the working-class community. While some journeymen, masters, and manufacturers continued to realize their dreams of independence, increased grumblings were heard from those who suffered reversals of circumstance, or found their traditional expectations of upward mobility thwarted. In the decades after the opening of the Miami and Ohio canals, increasing numbers of workers bitterly complained about their failure to receive a fair share of the common wealth generated by new market relations.[2]

While wealth and property had always been unevenly distributed in Cincinnati, so long as journeymen received what they considered a fair return on the fruits of their labor, it seemed to matter less that those at the top received more than those at the bottom. Unlike earlier years, however, the boomtown economy of the 1820s and 1830s, journeymen argued, did not bring widespread prosperity to all classes. Despite the "progress of our country from poverty and simplicity to wealth and grandeur," complained the members of the General Trades Union [GTU] — a coalition of the city's trade unions — in 1836, there had been a "gradual sinking" in the relative condition and status of the working man.[3] Indeed, in the years following the appearance of the steamboat, the percentage of wealth held by the bottom 50 percent of Cincinnati's population fell from 9.8 percent in 1817 to 8.1 percent in 1838.[4]

As the GTU's statement indicates, artisan discontent focused upon what journeymen viewed as their declining standard of living in the wake of rising general prosperity. As the influx of workers in the late 1820s and 1830s brought the artificially high wages of the labor-scarce frontier city more into line with lower eastern wage levels, journeymen complained of a considerable worsening in the economic condition of the producing classes. Wages, they argued, did not even keep pace with the rising costs of life's basic necessities. Indeed, although the prices of food and housing continued to advance between 1830 and 1840 — the former increasing by 24.2 percent — the wages of skilled and unskilled labor remained the same or declined. Moreover, real earnings were further diminished by the necessity of accepting depreciated shinplasters in lieu of hard coin.[5]

Whether the workers' standard of living was in fact declining

as severely as they claimed — an issue still debated by economic historians
— is less important than the workers' conviction that such was the case.
In times of severe depression, when all classes suffer misfortunes, such a
situation might be understandable. It was intolerable, however, in the midst
of rising urban prosperity. Beginning in the late 1820s, a small but steadily
growing number of artisans and masters shattered the harmony of the
productive sector by joining together to protest against what they viewed
as the gradual deterioration of their standard of living, their crafts, and
their independence.

Working-class protests, like the expansion of market capitalism, assumed a number of different forms in the late 1820s and 1830s.
Some workers, like the city's tailors, formed producer cooperatives, shops
owned and operated by journeymen, to combat the growing dependencies
of the trades. Others, like Josiah Warren, a follower of Robert Owen and
founder of Cincinnati's Labor for Labor Store, fought the inequities of
capitalism by designing a more equitable system of exchange wherein
the value of all goods was based upon the time required to produce them
rather than considerations of profits. Others, seeking to distance themselves physically and spiritually from a world they held in contempt,
traveled into the surrounding countryside and organized associationalist
communities.[6]

Worker protests followed a number of different paths during
this era, but labor unions and strikes were by far the most common vehicles
for remedying what many artisans viewed as the iniquitous effects of
economic growth. "Quite a new era seems to be dawning upon this class
of society," remarked one editor in 1830. "The members of the various
mechanical professions are manifesting a disposition to unite and act in
concert."[7] Not surprisingly, the initial forays toward unionization occurred
within the trades most affected by new forms of market capitalism. By
1836, Cincinnati's cabinetmakers, printers, tailors, building carpenters, and
workers in at least ten other crafts had organized new trade unions.[8]

In the period between 1826 and the Civil War, union organization and protest in Cincinnati, like production, underwent two major
stages of development: a local phase, in which the distribution system was
seen as the major cause of distress, and an emerging national phase, in
which the production process slowly moved to the forefront of worker
concern. That Cincinnati artisans of the 1830s and 1840s should focus
their grievances against distribution while their eastern counterparts
launched their most critical attacks against changes in production was not

surprising. Despite the growing incursions of market capitalism upon the crafts, Cincinnati was not as yet an industrial city. Division of labor, mechanization, and reorganization of production — three of the hallmarks of an industrial economy — remained much less developed in Cincinnati during this period than in Lynn, Philadelphia, or New York.[9] Indeed, until the late 1840s, when manufactories slowly made their way into the traditional crafts, most journeymen continued to work in small, unmechanized shops. Although Cincinnati's unions were critical of changes in the organization of work, decent wages was their initial goal and equality and independence their rallying cries.

In fashioning their critiques of society, the unions of the 1830s and early 1840s developed a language and mode of analysis that merged traditional tenets of the producer ideology and labor theory of value with the vaunted principles of republican ideology. Proclaiming themselves republicans as well as workers, union leaders insisted that the main battle in society was not between labor and capital, but between the forces of independence and dependence.

Masters were not yet seen to constitute a permanent, self-conscious class allied against labor; they acted as individuals in the pursuit of individual interests. Indeed, unions often included among their members masters who, like their journeymen, opposed the growing degradation of craft traditions. Even those masters who welcomed new market relationships occasionally joined with journeymen, in meetings and organizations, to oppose the use of convict labor in city shops and to lobby on behalf of higher tariffs which would protect their prices.[10]

Despite these frequent professions of common interest, journeymen printers, cabinetmakers, tailors, and building tradesmen mounted a series of strikes between 1829 and 1836 aimed at upholding their independence, securing an honorable standard of living, and protecting the "dignity of the profession."[11] Although critical of changes in production, the most fervid protests revolved around the isssue of distribution — specifically, the failure of masters to distribute their newly gained wealth, the commonwealth of the trade, in a fair and honorable manner. Journeymen's demands for "fair" and "just" wages contained the seeds of radical challenges against the effects of capitalism. The issue of what constituted a fair and reasonable standard of living involved more than simply earning enough money to sustain daily life. Objecting to extremes of wealth or poverty, artisans such as Augustus Roundy and carpenter Joel Brown set independence — freedom from dependence upon the whims of employers or fluctuations of the market — respectability, and comfort as their main goals.

If working in the hopes of securing independence and respectability was deemed a just and fair ambition, then striking in pursuit of those goals was equally just. Journeymen printers went on strike in 1834 in order to secure their rightful claim to a "comfortable living for themselves and their families."[12] Comfort, as striking shoemakers explained several years later, meant securing a "sum not only sufficient for the support of ourselves and our families, but, with appropriate economy, such as will enable us to procure for ourselves, within a reasonable time, permanent homes, which some of us have already accomplished."[13]

Seeing their economic interests as consistent with republican obligations, striking journeymen frequently argued that they were attempting to defend the republic, as well as their trades, by restoring the commonwealth which had prevailed in earlier years. A republic, as city and national leaders had so often insisted, could not exist amid great disparities of wealth and an increasingly dependent citizenry. Rallying workers in defense of their trade and republic, journeymen carpenters called upon "all mechanics to shake off the feelings of submission to the subservience of their rights" and join them in battling for independence, equality, and better working conditions. Similarly, in defending strikers against clergymen, editors, and bosses who denounced them as godless agents of class conflict, the editors of the *Working Man's Friend* argued in May 1836 that artisans were merely asserting their Christian and republican right "to obtain the enjoyment of a fair share of those blessings which the Maker of All has bountifully spread for the benefit of all."[14]

Material conditions, however, constituted only one part of the journeymen's critique of their rapidly changing world. Printers, tailors, and building tradesmen also rallied to defend the integrity and independence of their crafts. Tailors organized their first union in December 1835 to resist employer efforts to dictate prices, a practice which journeymen had "for many years regulated," and to halt the unilateral introduction of women and children into their shops. Reacting equally strongly to masters' efforts to impose new discipline in the workplace, they also demanded the right to continue their traditional practice of using their shops on Sundays for drinking and playing cards.[15] Printers, also concerned with resisting the "recent attempts at encroachments on the rights of journeymen, and to prevent such in the future," went on strike in 1836 to protest against wage cuts and the growing practice of replacing regular journeymen with apprentices and "two-thirders" — journeymen who had not served their full apprenticeship.[16] Similarly, journeymen cabinetmakers responded to the reorganization of production and "introduction of new jobs" by issuing and enforcing new price books in 1830 and 1836 which endeavored to reinstitute their control over prices and "all work made by journeymen."[17]

Like their Eastern counterparts, Cincinnati workers also launched an offensive on behalf of a ten-hour work day. In June 1831, 250 journeymen carpenters and joiners went on strike to protest against the efforts of building contractors to lower costs by extending the length of the work day. The strikers called upon all Cincinnati mechanics to "adopt measures to obtain with us a proper and right adjustment of laboring time."[18] The city's ship carpenters responded by striking for a ten-hour day. They won their demand and to enforce their victory purchased a large bell to ring "so the workmen would know when to commence and when to quit work."[19]

Journeymen's demands for a ten-hour day were framed within the context of republican obligation. The attempt by masters and manufacturers to extend the work day not only proved injurious to the workers' economic and physical well-being, but also undermined the very concept of citizenship. A worker could not fulfill his obligations as a citizen and familiarize himself with the issues of the day and participate in political decision-making if he was working twelve or fourteen hours a day. Extending the work day beyond ten hours, argued the city's carpenters, placed the independent artisan/citizen "nearly on a level with the slave." It also deprived him "of an opportunity to cultivate his mind and not only makes life a burden to him, but injures his health through excess of labour, and must ultimately shorten his days."[20]

As markets expanded and prosperity appeared to grow during the 1830s, so, too, did the number of journeymen unions. Following the lead of workers in Philadelphia, Baltimore, New York, Washington, and Boston, fourteen trade unions representing over 700 journeymen founded the city's first General Trades Union [GTU] in 1836. Declaiming "In Union There is Strength" and "Let Trade Regulate Itself," the GTU pledged to struggle as loyal "citizen[s] of the republic" to restore the artisan to his rightful position and to prevent the "murderous course that has been pursued toward the working classes in other countries" from happening in the United States. To that end, they organized a city-wide strike fund whereby honorable artisans attempting to resist the incursions of corrupt masters would receive $2.50 per week while on strike, plus an additional

$1 for their wives and 25 cents per child. The GTU hoped to establish closer ties with workers in other cities and sent two officers, David Snellbaker and Mark Taylor, to the third National Trades Union Convention in Philadelphia in 1836.[21]

The growth of the GTU, as well as the entire trade union movement, was brought to an abrupt halt by the onset of economic depression in May 1837. The Panic of 1837 led to an unprecedented curtailment in activity and employment across a wide range of commercial and manufacturing endeavors. Even the "oldest inhabitants," Augustus Roundy wrote to his father in 1840, could not "tell of any time that will compare with it."[22] For workingmen and workingwomen, the prosperity of earlier decades was a golden memory. As the weekly wages of artisans and laborers were slashed to a miserable $7 to $10 and $4.50 to $6, respectively, complaints of inadequate standards of living were superseded by the more pressing necessity of simply making ends meet. "Our prices were so curtailed by our employers," complained one tailor in 1840, "that we found it impossible to gain a livelihood."[23] When asked if he had been paid regularly, another embittered tailor responded that he had worked the past two months solely for his board." Even the relatively well off Roundy maintained that he and his wife were able to survive only by taking up to seven boarders into their small home.[24]

Laborers, women, and children were particularly hard hit by the depression. The freezing of rivers and roads during the winters of 1841 and 1842 reduced many dockworkers and rivermen to a state of destitution and forced them to rely upon the beneficence of the Bethel Society for subsistence. Women wage-workers fared equally poorly during the hard times. The earnings of laundresses and seamstresses, which various editors had declared "very inadequate" even in better times, soon fell to a level which, even with considerable frugality, provided a "very precarious living."[25] Women fortunate enough to secure employment in local manufactories such as the Fulton Bagging Factory labored from 6 A.M. to 8 P.M. and for a pittance.[26]

Traditional patterns of family economy were also altered by the impact of depression. Artisan families that had once relied solely or primarily upon the earnings of fathers and older sons were forced to send wives, daughters, and younger sons out to work in order to make ends meet. Young girls who previously would have been at home or in school, noted one resident, were now sent to work cultivating gardens on the outskirts of town for 37½ cents a day.[27] Financially pressed recent arrivals,

like the Schmitt family, were likewise forced to send their young children
to work in the city's dangerous tobacco stripping factories. One formerly
well-to-do Hanoverian migrant, unable to find employment, tearfully lamented the need to send his two young boys out to perform backbreaking
work harvesting crops for six dollars a month.[28]

Men and women of the producing classes soon realized their
worst fears: poverty and dependency. "A mechanick," reflected carpenter
Joel Brown, "is now nothing more or less than a beggar in our business, he
must beg first for work and when his work is done he must beg for pay: a
carpenter is nothing more or less than a slave in this city and slavery I
despise." Yet, those with jobs, no matter how poorly paid, were among the
city's more fortunate citizens. As economic activity ground to a halt,
reported Brown, thousands of mechanics were "throughnout [sic] of employment. . . . [and] obliged to beg."[29] Once-prosperous workers were
forced to line up at relief kitchens; others swallowed their pride and accepted
aid from various charitable organizations, aid often granted only after
humiliating visits by relief committees. Abject poverty also assumed new
dimensions as the number of paupers admitted to the Commercial Hospital
rose from a few hundred before 1837 to 1,035 in 1841 and 1,309 in 1844.[30]

In seeking to redress their rapidly deteriorating economic
situation, Cincinnati workers faced the problems of identifying the specific
sources of distress and plotting a remedial course of action acceptable to
more than a handful of men and women. While many workers could agree
that the times were out of joint, they had greater difficulty in reaching a
common understanding as to why they were. Some workers, clinging to
the vaunted producer ideology, blamed the "great system of speculation,
by which they who produce nothing receive nearly all the products of the
labor of those that produce." Others blamed the "paralyzing influence of a
deranged currency." Still others blamed masters and manufacturers, while
yet others said that the employer was not the "oppressor, for he, like the
journeymen, suffered grievously during the depressed time."[31]

The propensity to dwell upon symbols and the inability of
the majority of workers to integrate their grievances into a systematic
critique of society were not caused by ignorance, but by the growing
complexities and uneven development of economic life. As trade unionism
collapsed under the weight of depressed times, workers were forced to find
new paths of action to remedy the problems of economic distress.

It was in the midst of the depression that a number of more
radical artisans and masters turned to politics as a means to restore eco-

nomic and social justice. During the severe winter months of 1840 and 1841, masters, journeymen, and laborers organized numerous rallies to protest against the "embarrassed condition of the mechanics of this city."[32] When Whigs and Democrats turned a blind eye to their plight, workers, previously content to entrust their interests to the mainstream parties, began to challenge their ability to represent all interests of society. Merging the themes utilized by unions of the 1830s — equity, justice, independence — with longstanding political concepts of citizenship and civic virtue, the newly organized Working Man's Association [WMA] proclaimed in the fall of 1841: "Our [political] institutions, excellent as they are, have hitherto produced but a small proportion of the beneficial results they are calculated to bestow upon mankind; chief of these benefits is equality." The failure to deliver these results, they argued, lay not in the inherent nature of the American political system, but in the seizure and corruption of the legislature by nonproducers and corrupt politicians:

> Our rights are standing upon an apex of wealth instead of its base, supported and upheld in this unnatural way by bad legislation, which not only creates capital as its agency, thereby rendering the family of industry tributary to, and dependent on the family of idleness; gives preference to law over equity, thereby organizing a bodyguard for the protection of rogues; makes justice an article of merchandise and institutes lawyers as its auctioneer.[33]

The WMA announced that its organization marked the beginning of a "new era in the political history of the working classes, who have hitherto been divided and paralyzed in their efforts to attain their true position." It also set out to transform the political world and reinstitute justice by creating a party which would unite the roles and needs of producer and citizen. Echoing the political rhetoric frequently heard between 1788 and 1825, the WMA announced its goal to be that of "carrying out the benign principle of the greatest good of the greatest number." Only such a "dignified and republican course" could assure control of the government by the rightful majority.[34]

Workers' disenchantment with traditional parties grew more pronounced with the eruption of the so-called Bank Riots of January 1842. The pent-up anger and frustrations occasioned by several years of economic depression were unleashed on the morning of January 11, 1842, when several hundred citizens attacked the longstanding symbol of corruption and thievery: the Monster Banks. Reacting to the closing of the Miami

Export Company Bank the previous evening and the failure of other banks to open their doors the next morning, outraged persons, convinced that they had lost their life's savings, moved from bank to bank, smashing windows, breaking doors, and destroying any books, papers, or furniture they could find. The mayor quickly summoned the local militia, but few responded to his call. "The greater part of them," observed one woolspinner, "had not time, for they were busy, in the mob, helping to wind up the affairs of the banks."[35]

The mob refused to honor the sheriff's request to disperse and greeted the dozen or so militiamen who did show up with brickbats and assorted flying missiles. They continued their destruction until all banks were dealt with. Although the names of rioters were never published, the little evidence that does exist indicates that the protestors came largely from the city's artisans and laborers. After repelling an onslaught by the depleted militia, the crowd paused to allow time for several self-congratulatory speeches. Justifying the measures they had taken that morning as acts of popular justice and not, as the mayor claimed, the actions of a lawless mob, one mechanic explained:

We are peaceable, hardworking, law-abiding citizens — the officers appointed to execute our laws have shamefully neglected the trust reposed in them; as a consequence, we, the mechanics of this city, have been swindled out of our hard earnings — we have now assembled to demand our dues or satisfaction, and woe to the officer who will order the military to fire upon us! We have been robbed by their negligence, and now they would shoot us to rid themselves of the responsibility of this neglect. Let them dare to do it — they will learn what it is to beard the working community when roused to a sense of their wrongs.[36]

As the economic crisis deepened and criticism of party politics and government corruption grew more widespread in the following months, increasing numbers of men turned to the WMA and its political organ, the Working Man's Party, to restore law and justice and the producing classes to their rightful position in society. The party would do so not, as one blacksmith cautioned, "by pulling *others down,* but by *elevating themselves* through political action." Calling upon all Cincinnati producers to abandon their old party connections and join together to "feel and know the power they might posses," the WMP began to organize in the shops and wards throughout Cincinnati and in neighboring Fulton, Cheviot, Covington and Newport, Kentucky, and Madison, Indiana.[37]

(a)

(b)

Figure 3 Cincinnati's Working-Class Mayors.
(a) Mark P. Taylor, a former president of the Coopers' and General Trades Unions and a Working Man's Party activist, was the first Democrat elected mayor in Cincinnati (1851 – 1853). (b) David T. Snellbaker, another prominent working-class leader, succeeded Taylor as mayor (1853 – 1855).
Courtesy of the Cincinnati Historical Society

The party held a nominating convention in late March to choose a slate for the municipal elections in April. Acting upon its pledge to be the party of the producing classes, the delegates chose ten candidates from the ranks of the city's journeymen, three from the ranks of masters and small manufacturers, and five from the ranks of small shopkeepers. Hoping to attract naturalized citizens to their cause, the party also nominated at least four foreign-born workers for major city posts.[38] Numerous rallies, parades, and speeches revived the memories of the winter of discontent, and with signal success. The fledging Working Man's party, much to the consternation of established politicos, elected over a dozen of its candidates to offices ranging from city council to school visitor.[39]

Ironically, the party's success was also the cause of its demise. Setting a pattern that would haunt third-party efforts for the rest of the century, Democrats and Whigs quickly moved to co-opt the WMP's more moderate leaders and programs into their own organizations. Following the election, victorious WMP's candidates such as Mark Taylor and David Snellbaker, both former officers in the defunct Coopers' Union and the General Trades Union, were quickly enticed into leaving the workers' party and the union movement in favor of political careers with one of the major parties. Whigs and Democrats, playing upon the rhetoric workers had used to defend their party and earlier unions, insisted that no further permanent political action need be taken by workers. The producing classes had received their measure of justice; any further actions by the WMP would inflame rather than ameliorate conflict. By the spring of 1843, as flush economic times returned and other party leaders followed the path of Snellbaker and Taylor — both of whom went on to become mayors in the 1850s — the WMP was but a memory.[40]

The collapse of the WMP and the return of prosperity did not, however, bring the peace and harmony that politicians and capitalists had promised. By the autumn, the journeymen woodturners complained that despite the sharp upturn in business and prices, the present standard of wages was "less than one half what it was several years ago."[41] Similarly, shoemakers complained that they were reduced to "a state of starvation in consequence of their extreme low wages."[42] "Day laborers," observed one visitor, "were the severest sufferers, for wages declined more than the prices of the articles which they needed for their support and the support of their families."[43]

More discontented than ever because they were not sharing in the benefits of renewed prosperity, journeymen and laborers formed

new unions and once again launched a series of strikes aimed at restoring
their independence and securing, as the shoemakers pledged, the "means
of making ourselves and families comfortable."[44] As economic conflicts
grew increasingly bitter and impasses more frequent, journeymen took their
grievances directly into the public arena and appealed to citizens to serve
as the final arbiters of justice. Playing upon republican sensibilities, unions
posted flyers throughout the city, placed advertisements in local newspapers, and held mass demonstrations aimed at soliciting community support.
Citizens were urged to aid workers by boycotting the shops of unfair
employers. "In accordance with time-honored custom," proclaimed one
shoemakers' flyer in September 1843, and believing that "no workingman
or honorable citizen will countenance these 'underminer' scabs upon the
community, we herewith, without further ado, present their names ["scabs"
and unfair employers] that they may be held up to the scorn and contempt
of all honorable men."[45]

Workers also bolstered the righteousness and legitimacy of
their cause by utilizing many of the symbols and rituals of citizenship.
Imitating the forms of the annual July Fourth parades, hundreds of striking
workers marched through the city streets waving American flags, carrying
banners emblazoned with their demands, and moving steadily behind the
beat of a makeshift fife and drum corps. Though the substance was altered,
the spirit and appearances of 1776 were kept alive by striking men and
women.[46]

It is doubtful that an earlier generation would have recognized
the so-called modern age. The world of 1815 would have likely seemed
wealthier and poorer than their own. Markets and population had expanded, merchants, manufacturers, and masters had grown richer, streets
were paved and lighted, and houses were more numerous and grandiose.
Yet earlier self-professed traditions of harmony, mutuality, and commonwealth had been replaced by conflict, divisions of interest, and acquisitive
individualism. The bonds which had united men and women of an earlier
era seemed to have disintegrated under the impact of market capitalism.

Ideology and the Reconstitution
of the Republic

As economic and political life grew increasingly contentious, numerous
Cincinnatians attempted to alter the role and uses of republican ideology
in order to defuse growing class tensions and to reassert traditional beliefs

in an inherently mutualistic and egalitarian society. Republican virtues had long been praised by city residents, but it was not until the 1830s and 1840s, when the growth of market capitalism appeared to widen the gap between republican promises and daily realities, that republican ideology was feverishly stressed and systematized by a wide range of newspaper editors, civic leaders, businessmen, politicians, and workers. It was almost as if ideology alone could restore the venerated republican community that no longer existed, if indeed it ever had.

The movement to recast republican ideology in an era of increasing commercial complexity did not begin in Cincinnati nor even in the United States. Politicans in the economically advanced European nations of the seventeenth and eighteenth centuries, as J. G. A. Pocock, Caroline Robbins, Joyce Appleby, and others have shown, were actively engaged in efforts to adapt traditional notions of commonwealth in the face of their rapidly expanding commercial societies.[47] Adapting the European debates to the American situation, Federalist and Whig politicians of the late eighteenth and early nineteenth centuries endeavored to forge a new ideological synthesis which merged traditional agrarian republican thought with the new commercial relationships. "During the half century between the Revolution and the age of Jacksonian democracy," observes Rowland Berthoff, "the old categories of republicanism were stretched to explain away—indeed, to justify—the practical economic and social contradictions in which hardheaded, pragmatic Americans, then and since, have perpetually found themselves."[48]

Traditional republicanism, argued numerous Whig, Democratic, and working-class leaders of the period, no longer seemed appropriate in an era when growing numbers of landless citizens sought their independence in the nation's shops, stores, and manufactories. Refuting Jefferson's contention that the virtue and independence of a nation could rest only upon a sound agrarian base, they moved to fashion a more dynamic ideology which viewed commerce and manufacturing as consistent with, not antithetical to, the growth of a virtuous republic. Just as farming could nurture independence, so, too, could trade and industry teach the "manly virtues of the republican citizen" by instilling the habits of "hard work, savings, and reinvestment that were supposed to be the best means for individual success and for the economic progress of the country."[49]

Cincinnati's politicians, newspaper editors, lawyers, and commercial elites were particularly active in reshaping local understandings of republican ideology. Using the prosperous and interdependent economic experiences of earlier years as their model of a well-functioning republican society, these men skillfully combined liberal capitalism, the producer ideology, and local republican rhetoric to create a new republican synthesis which stressed the cooperation of producers, eschewed class conflict, and held that the inequalities which plagued society were merely temporary.

Cincinnati's new republicanism saw men as playing two roles in society: producers in the economic sphere, and citizens in the political sphere. The economic sphere was not divided into classes *per se,* but into larger categories of producer and nonproducer: those who performed productive toil and those, who in the words of one artisan, "do not labor, or produce something useful, [and] must be supported by those who do labor."[50] Yet, while using producer ideology as their starting point, civic leaders, editors, and mainstream politicans redefined and expanded its traditional membership to include merchants, clerks, clergymen, physicians, and lawyers, along with farmers and artisans. Anyone who was gainfully employed, they argued, was a part of the producing class. "One of the most senseless and stupid distinctions that they [journeymen] make," argued one Whig editor, "is that of regarding working men — artizans, mechanics, and laborers — as a separate and distinct class of people, between whom and all others a broad line of demarcation is drawn, and whose interests are different from those of merchants and traders, and generally conflicting." "We are in truth," vowed one clergyman, "all working men and working women too, and have but one great interest — the peace and prosperity of the whole."[51]

Presenting recent economic developments in a more positive light, these civic elites argued that this all-encompassing producing class was made up of three interdependent interest groups—farmers, merchants, and artisans — who, when working in proper harmony, created prosperity for all members of society. "All classes of learning, skill, and industry," argued one new republican, "are but parts of the body politic necessary to make a complete whole, mutually dependent upon each other for their respective foundations."[52] While their specific interests might not coincide at all moments, the overall interaction of these three groups served to secure and protect the ongoing prosperity of the community. "It seldom happens," noted local historian James Hall, "that all these interests are paralyzed at the same time, and when one of them is depressed, there is usually a sustaining power remaining in the others."[53]

The expansion of these various economic sectors, it was argued, ultimately promoted greater opportunities and equality for the whole of society. Although some men garnered greater riches than others, there were no permanent distinctions in this economically fluid world between the rich and the poor, masters and journeymen, or employers and employees. Such were the "fluctuations of fortune and circumstance," explained one editor, that the "rich man of to-day is the working man of tomorrow; and the working man of to-day is the merchant of tomorrow."[54] More important was the belief that in a rapidly expanding economy the success of one man did not necessarily come at the expense of another. There was no irreconcilable conflict between the "masses" and the "men of talent," explained lawyer Timothy Walker, for possible class distinctions were ultimately alleviated by the fact that the leveling disposition of society worked upward rather than downward: "The many may strive to elevate themselves rather than to pull down the few who happen to be above them: in a free and generous competition, the whole will press onward and upward."[55]

Responding to working-class complaints regarding the decline of commonwealth, Cincinnati's new republicanism held that the problems which beset society were caused by corrupt individuals and were not a consequence of an inherently unjust system of production, distribution, or exchange. Republicanism and the market were not inherently antagonistic. If the economy was left alone, free from corrupting influences, it would ultimately reach a natural equilibrium. Whig attorney Bellamy Storer argued, for example, that economic inequality was rooted in the failure of overly acquisitive individuals to distribute their gains in a fair and honorable manner. Instead of being content with a reasonable return on their labors, too many citizens were "desirous of engrossing too much of the wealth of the country, which should be distributed for the common good."[56]

Cincinnati's new republicanism was not simply an ideology imposed from above. Journeymen, through their own newspapers, pamphlets, and meetings, were also active participants in the creation of the city's new republican synthesis. Artisans, although they did not necessarily endorse all aspects of the economic views advanced by mainstream politicians and editors, nevertheless found many of their tenets consistent with their own visions and traditions. Like city elites, artisans appeared to accept the merger of liberal capitalism, the producer ideology, and republican rhetoric. Yet, while elites placed their emphasis on liberal capitalism, journeymen continued to see the producer ideology as the foundation of any new ideological reformulations. Although hesitant to accept lawyers and clergymen, not to mention speculators and financiers, as part of their ranks, artisans seemed willing to include merchants within the producing

class. Defending the division of producers into three interdependent interest
groups, the editors of the labor newspaper *Elevator* explained that "positive
wealth" was initially created by the industry of farmers and mechanics.
Commerce then entered the scene by furnishing "conveyance to a market
for the surplus wealth," where it was "sold or exchanged at fair prices, or
for other descriptions of wealth, which the laborer wants but cannot
produce."[57]

Indeed, masters, manufacturers, and journeymen who participated in market production often saw no contradictions between the
producer ideology and entrepreneurial capitalism. The two worked in
tandem to enrich the individual and the community. Although their faith
in this partnership would be weakened by the rapid expansion of industrial
capitalism and wage labor in the 1850s, journeymen did not yet see the
market as an intrinsic enemy of the producing classes. "If labor were left
free and untrammeled by maladministration of government, or the combinations of wealth," avowed the editors of the *Elevator*, "it would always
command its proper value."[58] Even those craftsmen adversely affected by
new market relations were reluctant to see the world in terms of class
conflict. Like Whigs and Democrats, they spoke in terms of corruption of
essentially sound institutions by nonproducers, avaricious individuals, and
pernicious monopolies. The crises which swept society, insisted GTU
president David Snellbaker, although partially created by selfish masters,
were more deeply rooted in the vicious action of speculators and stock
jobbers who robbed producers of "nearly all the products of labor."[59]
Similarly, the *Elevator* and the *People's Paper*, while not entirely comfortable
with including clergymen and lawyers among the producing classes, directed their most vitriolic attacks against banks — "the deadliest enemy to
popular rights, industry, and republican institutions" — and monopolies —
"fore-runners of monarchies."[60]

As proponents of producer and republican ideology, Cincinnati workers, like the rest of the society, preferred to see their world in
terms of harmony and cooperation rather than of conflict and individualism.
Yet clearly the world of the 1830s and 1840s was far from harmonious.
While economic life might ultimately be restored to a just equilibrium,
what immediate actions could men and women take to combat the present
state of selfishness, inequality, and conflict? What could honest producers
do to set their world right? Were unions and strikes the only solutions?
The answers lay in the second half of the republican constellation: the role
and obligations of citizenship.

Although disparities of wealth and social condition did exist, the political sphere, the higher and classless sphere, counteracted the divisive tendencies of economic life by joining men as equal citizens in the selfless pursuit of the general interests of society as a whole. The political sphere, the source of justice and equality, was the foundation upon which society stood. Unlike economic life, it acknowledged no differences in wealth or status. Breaking with traditional republican formulations, workers and elites argued that a virtuous citizenry was possible even if people were not economically independent. "Every citizen, with or without property," proclaimed the editors of the *Elevator*, was "an integral part of the whole."[61] The obligations of citizenship, not the possession of property, formed the core of virtue. To be sure, men often pursued particularistic interests in their economic endeavors. However, when acting as citizens, "all who live by toil, employers and employed, have one common interest: and that is to forget past differences, and unite as brethren for the purpose of promoting common views, and concerted political and social action upon all subjects concerning their general welfare."[62]

Unlike their European counterparts, or even some of their more radical eastern counterparts, Cincinnati workers did not view the state as an instrument of oppression. The American government, they argued, was the democratic creation of ordinary men and was not a repressive agency imposed upon them by kings or aristocrats. "Our admirable system of government," boasted the constitution of the GTU, "knows no difference between individuals."[63] It was their equal access to political power, insisted one artisan, that prevented American workers from degenerating into a permanent and revolutionary class such as plagued Europe. As he put it:

> In America, the claims of labor are more fully recognized — the workman is not so badly hemmed in by feudal legislation, and however much there may yet remain to be done for the elevation of the laboring classes, this fact stands confessed by all, that in no other nation than this, is Labor represented — in no other is the workman — sovereign. Hence we have no revolutions.[64]

The state legislature, the penultimate arbiter of justice, was perceived by workers and capitalists alike as — in theory at least—a neutral, classless body which pursued the most good for the most people. So long as it remained free from corruption and men honored the obligations of citizenship, the legislature would act to correct the imbalances and inequities of economic life fairly and justly. "When things go right in this department," observed one worker, "then all is well; but when aristocracy and corruption find their ways into the halls of legislation, then are the rights of labor cloven down and trampled upon."[65] When such occasions did occur, it was incumbent upon the people, the ultimate sovereign power, to kick out corruptionists and thereby restore justice to the political arena. Although political parties were the usual vehicles for achieving such ends, the political sphere transcended the narrow confines of partisanship. "True patriotism," argued the founders of the Working Man's Association, "knows no party but country."[66] If parties became corrupt, then citizens had to take direct action and fulfill their republican duties.

These reformulations of republican ideology attracted a wide range of support within Cincinnati. They were not, as one might expect, simply viewed as the self-serving beliefs of elites and politicians. Rather, republican ideology was sufficiently ambiguous so that labor and capital, while often using it for different ends, each pledged an unwavering commitment to its own interpretation of its visions and ideals. Capitalists, for example, saw market capitalism as fully consistent with republicanism, while workers remained equally convinced that the producer ideology remained at the core of a just republican economy. Similarly, workers and mainstream politicans alike could point to the municipal elections of 1842 as proof that the state was not controlled by corporations, speculators, or nonproducers. While artisans in eastern cities were often suspicious of their legislatures, in Cincinnati, the election of WMP candidates reinforced workers' faith that in times of economic distress honest producers could enter the political arena, be elected by fellow citizens, and proceed to right the imbalances of economic life.

Yet, while republicanism and producer ideology were frequently used by workers to defend and justify their economic grievances, they also acted to limit the nature and scope of working-class radicalism. The workers' faith in the producer ideology led them to misread the roots of modern economic crises. Cincinnati's workers tended to see distribution, not production, as the primary cause of their distress. Similarly, their belief in the fundamental harmony of the producing classes led many workers to overlook the growing class divisions and competing interests which characterized market capitalism.

Moreover, capitalists and politicians were successful in using *their* understanding of republican obligations to defuse potentially radical movements. The longevity and militancy of Cincinnati's early labor unions were limited not only by internal problems, but also by the ability of employers, editors, clergymen, and politicians to portray these organizations as purveyors of class conflict. Journeymen, seeing themselves as loyal republicans as well as workers, were particularly sensitive to such accusations. Defending themselves against those who labeled their unions as unrepublican "conspiracies against society" and "antimonopoly monopolization," printers, cabinetmakers, and others insisted that their organizations were merely *temporary* bodies aimed at remedying specific economic imbalances and injustices. Indeed, lamented one radical labor editor, once demands for "fair wages and good pay" were met, the union dissolved and did not reconstitute itself until the next crisis.[67] Even the Working Man's Association cautioned its members in 1841 that permanent "combinations of Journeymen against employers, or of employers against Journeymen," were "alike injurious to both."[68] Journeymen apparently took this advice to heart, for not one Cincinnati union pursued an uninterrupted course of existence between 1828 and the Civil War.

Republican concepts of citizenship and political obligations also cut two ways: while they sparked independent political actions, they also discouraged it. If workers had united and voted along class lines in local elections, they *could* have dramatically altered the character of Cincinnati's development. But they did not do so. Although workingmen occasionally brought their economic concerns directly into the political sphere, their parties, like their unions, were seen as temporary agencies of justice. While such transitory forays might well be needed to rid the legislature of corruptionists, permanent class-based parties, as elites and politicians so often insisted and workers concurred, were not consistent with classless republican obligations. Moreover, mainstream parties, as was the case in 1842, were particularly effective in co-opting working-class leaders and demands. Though they undermined the party's very foundations, they nevertheless left working-class voters with a sense that they had succeeded in forcing Whigs and Democrats to respond to their grievances.

During the ensuing years of strife and conflict, republican ideology served as a constant reminder of a more prosperous past and the promise of a better, more egalitarian future. Although that ideology continued to be redefined by various classes throughout the century, Cincinnati workers utilized their understandings of republicanism to provide them with a metaphor and image of a more perfect world which they could use to fashion their critiques of contemporary life and legitimize their crusades for social and economic justice. Yet, while ideology would serve them at particular moments, it was also used by elites to create deep tensions concerning the worker's main obligations in society. Although more often than not artisans perceived the struggles of worker and citizen as complementary, there were times when their interests as producers and their obligations as citizens appeared to clash. When such crises occurred, ought men to act as citizens or as workers? Which was the higher obligation? These dual roles and the tensions they often produced were crucial in shaping the nature of working-class consciousness and informing their responses to the growth of industrialization.

PART II

The Age of Manufacturing
(1843 – 1873)

CHAPTER FOUR

The New City:
The Capitalists' View
of Growth and Progress

In the decades between the return of prosperity in 1843 and the onset of a major national depression in 1873, Cincinnati underwent a dramatic period of growth and development which altered virtually all aspects of urban life. The rapid, and what appeared to many citizens as the almost magical, expansion of population and business during this era soon transformed the Queen City from a relatively small homogeneous city of native-born Protestants to a diverse metropolis containing thousands of foreign settlers; from a city dominated by commerce and the crafts to one in which manufacturing emerged as the central element of economic life. Indeed, by 1860, less than three decades after manufacturing had begun in earnest, masters, manufacturers, and capitalists had transformed Cincinnati from a modest regional producer of goods to the nation's third largest industrial center, surpassed only by New York and Philadelphia.

Between 1843 and 1873, Cincinnati, like many of the nation's other leading producing centers, entered a new stage of industrialization: the era of manufacturing. Although this new era was accompanied by important changes in social and political life, its most immediate and profound impact was felt within the city's economic sector. While an earlier generation of historians frequently equated industrialization with mechanization and the rise of behemoth factories, in Cincinnati, and elsewhere, the transition from the artisan's world to the world of manufacturing was not rooted in or characterized by technological innovations, but by the decision of capitalistically oriented masters and manufacturers to increase the volume, efficiency, and profits of production by restructuring the way work was conducted. Describing the rise of manufacturing and industrial capitalism in Philadelphia, one group of historians conclude that "significant changes in the organization of work, authority relations, and production techniques transformed the role of craftsmen long before mechanization was introduced."[1]

In Cincinnati, as well as Philadelphia, artisans found their work world dramatically altered well before machines and massive factories came to rule the day. A midpoint between the era of traditional craft production and the more mechanized and routinized workings of modern industry, the era of manufacturing was marked by important changes in the centralization of labor, the organization of production, the nature of work, the composition of the working class, and eventually the nature of working-class consciousness. The new era of manufacturing did not, however, signal the destruction of the artisan's world; the latter was enveloped, not replaced, by the former. Yet, while manufacturers continued to rely heavily upon the skills of their craftsmen those skills were plied in new and what many persons viewed as alienating settings of production.

The onset of this new era of industrial life produced a wide array of responses from local citizens. Workers, although they found that the number of job opportunities greatly increased, nevertheless protested against what they viewed as the gradual degradation of their crafts and exploitation of their labor. Similarly, native-born Protestants ranted against the growing number of foreign-born Catholics, atheists, and radicals. Yet, amid this growing turmoil, various manufacturers, capitalists, and civic elites endeavored to minimize the significance of these conflicts by forging a new republican vision which depicted industrialization as an integral part of an expanding world of opportunity, prosperity, and independence. Envisioning themselves as men deeply concerned with advancing the interests of the republic, not merely of one class, they drew upon traditional republican beliefs, values, and symbols to legitimize the tremendous changes in economic life and to portray their new world as one which aided the material and moral well-being of all citizens. Later chapters will take us inside the workers' world. We begin here with a description of the capitalists' vision of growth and progress — the new city as seen from above.

Between 1843 and 1873, as Cincinnati established itself as a major industrial center, traditional artisanal production was increasingly superseded by the rapid expansion of new industries and the dramatic reorganization of the crafts. Whereas earlier residents like Thomas Carter and Augustus Roundy would have been appalled by the steady decline of craft traditions and the rise of manufactories, by the early 1840s a new generation of more capitalistic oriented producers welcomed manufacturing as a source of new wealth, new opportunities, and greater independence. Men like hardware manufacturer Miles Greenwood typified this new breed of capitalists who envisioned the new forces of production as fully consistent with traditional republican values.

Born in Salem, Massachusetts in 1807, Greenwood accompanied his parents on their westward odyssey as they journeyed to Blysdell's Mills, Indiana, and later to Cincinnati in search of new opportunities and modest prosperity. In 1825, frustrated by his inability to make a decent living as a farmer or tavernkeeper, and disillusioned by what he viewed as an increasingly selfish and competitive world, Greenwood's father moved his family to Robert Owen's utopian community at New Harmony, Indiana. In New Harmony young Miles obtained many of the skills and values that would shape his later career and attitudes as a manufacturer. Although the members of New Harmony rejected the acquisitive values of market capitalism, they nevertheless believed that, in order to place their community on a more secure economic foundation, traditional craft production had to be supplemented by more modern forms of manufacturing. Consequently, young Greenwood was sent to Pittsburgh to master the art of engine and metal manufacturing. Returning many months later to assume control of New Harmony's foundry, Greenwood soon met with disappointment as economic hardships led to the dissolution of the utopian experiment. Determined to utilize his new skills, Greenwood bid adieu to his family and friends and journeyed to Cincinnati in 1829, where he took a job as finisher in T. J. Bevan's foundry.

Greenwood's experiences at Pittsburgh convinced him that manufacturing, not small craft production, would provide the most secure path toward economic stability and independence. A large, well-run factory, he reasoned, one which produced a variety of goods for a wide range of regional and national customers, would be better equipped to withstand depressions and market fluctuations than the traditional artisan's shop. In 1831, Greenwood and his friend, engine-maker Joseph Webb, pooled their life savings, borrowed $500 from a local bank, hired ten hands, and opened a modest manufactory which produced stoves, engines, and various metal goods for the rapidly expanding steamship industry. Whereas most metal working operations of the era tended to be conducted in a series of separate and moderately small establishments, Greenwood gradually reorganized this seemingly inefficient and costly arrangement by consolidating these previously independent operations into a single manufactory. Instead of subcontracting work to others, Greenwood used his growing profits to expand and regularize his control over production by hiring upwards of 400 men and building his own foundry, machine, blacksmith, and finishing shops on the land adjacent to his original hardware manufactory. By the 1850s, Greenwood's Eagle Iron Works, which produced more than 1,500 distinct articles, was heralded by a Parliamentary delegation from England as the "most extensive, and certainly the best conducted and most sytematically arranged establishment for the production of miscellaneous hardware in the United States."[2]

Greenwood brought to Cincinnati not merely a new vision of reorganizing production, but also a firm belief in the collective benefits of manufacturing. Never fully abandoning the idealism of his New Harmony years, Greenwood envisioned the expanding world of manufacturing as an

Figure 4 Miles Greenwood and the Employees of the Eagle Iron Works (c. 1871).
Courtesy of the Cincinnati Historical Society

integral part of a new, more modern republican society. Far from being the source of immiseration and dependency, the manufactory, at least in Greenwood's eyes, provided the greatest promise for the prosperity of the individual and the entire community. Large manufactories like the Eagle Iron Works created numerous jobs, steady work, and greater opportunities for the hard-working laborers who, like Greenwood's father, came West in search of a better and more secure life. Indeed, Greenwood was extremely proud that during forty years of business he never once closed his operations or missed a weekly payroll — an accomplishment that few masters had equaled. Moreover, Greenwood attempted to be a good republican citizen, not merely a selfish manufacturer, by hiring a teacher to instruct his young employees for two hours each morning, and by participating in a wide range of community activities.

Sharing the same goals as men like Thomas Carter and Augustus Roundy, Miles Greenwood believed that it was the new manufactories, and not the traditional crafts, which would ultimately provide citizens with the security and independence that had so long eluded his family and the families of countless other working men.

The Industrializing City: An Overview

Few of its early settlers would have recognized the Queen City of the middle decades. The first and most obvious change was the transformation of the city's physical landscape. As politicians annexed neighboring communities to accommodate the rapid swelling of population and business, the compact city of earlier years had expanded from one to seven square miles by 1870. The poorly lit and frequently impassable dirt roads of earlier years gradually gave way to wide, paved, gas-lit streets which were elegantly lined with beautiful trees. The modest ramshackle wooden frame buildings of the first decades were replaced by more impressive stone and brick structures. Similarly, the city's growing wealth was evinced by a proliferation of handsome churches, lavish hotels, ornate homes, new theaters, museums, libraries, and a wide array of elegant retail shops. Cincinnati was a wonderfully modern city, gushed one traveler in 1854, a city that presented a welcome change from the "frightful fashionable extremes" of

New York and the "dullness, methodical simplicity and Quaker rigidity" of Philadelphia.[3]

Between the early 1840s and 1870s, Cincinnati underwent a dramatic period of urban, social and economic growth. As internal and foreign migration swelled, particularly after the European depressions and political upheavals of the late 1840s and 1850s, the Queen City's population mushroomed from 46,388 in 1840, to 115,435 in 1850, 161,044 in 1860, and 216,239 in 1870 — an increase of 366 percent in thirty years. The percentage of foreign-born residents rose, from 21.9 percent in 1825 to 47.2 percent in 1850. Bringing with them what many established residents viewed as strange new languages, customs, and religions, German settlers soon supplanted British migrants as the city's main ethnic group. Similarly, the skilled Protestant Scotch-Irish of earlier years were supplanted by a steady stream of unskilled Irish Catholic laborers who fled from the famines which gripped their homeland. Although the number of new arrivals declined after the Civil War, from 1850 onward immigrants and their native-born children nevertheless constituted well over 50 percent of the city's population.[4] Only the city's black population failed to increase its relative size during this era. Although increasing in absolute number, the percentage of black residents steadily declined as racism and frequent race riots deterred blacks from migrating to the Queen City.

The influx of immigrants also changed the character and compositon of the city's working class. Between 1840 and 1860, the peak years of migration, foreign-born men and women increased their percentage of the total labor force from 35.3 to 68.7. First-generation Germans, who tended to enter the city's crafts and manufactories, saw their representation in the job sector grow from 19.5 percent in 1840, to 43.2 percent in 1850, and 41.6 percent in 1860. Similarly, Irish workers, who found numerous opportunities in unskilled labor, rose from 7.5 percent in 1840 to 15 percent in 1850, and to 18 percent in 1860. The percentage of English, Scottish, and Welsh workers, once the dominant source of foreign-born labor, declined from 8.3 in 1840 to 5.3 in 1850, and 3.2 in 1870. Although the percentage of foreign-born workers declined after midcentury, as late as 1890 first- and second-generation immigrants constituted 73.8 percent of the city's prime working-age populace (18 to 44 years).[5]

This rapid increase in population was paralleled by an equally dramatic period of economic expansion. At midcentury, Cincinnati's shops and factories employed nearly as many workers (29,401) as the combined total for St. Louis, Pittsburgh, Louisville, and Chicago (30,147). Indeed,

(a)

(b)

Figure 5 Views of Cincinnati.
(a) Cincinnati in 1846; (b) Cincinnati in 1865.
Courtesy of the Cincinnati Historical Society

Table 4.1 Native- and Foreign-Born Population, 1825 – 1870

Year	Total	Native-Born		Foreign-Born		Unknown	
		n	%	n	%	n	%
1825	15,540[a]	1,815[b]	78.1	509[b]	21.9		
1840	46,338	6,594[b]	53.6	5,698[b]	46.4		
1850	115,435	60,558	52.5	54,541	47.2	336	0.3
1860	161,044	87,430	54.3	73,614	45.7		
1870	216,239	136,627	63.2	79,612	36.8		

SOURCE: Walter Glazer, "Cincinnati in 1840: A Community Profile," Ph.D. diss., University of Michigan, 1968, p. 102; Charles Cist, Cincinnati in 1841 (Cincinnati, 1841), p. 39; Census Office, Statistical View of the United States: 1850 (Washington, 1854), p. 399; Census Office, Ninth Census: Statistics of the Population of the United States (Washington, 1872), pp. 231 – 32.
[a] 1826 Population
[b] Adult White Males

Table 4.2 Foreign-Born and Black Residents as a Percentage
of the Total Population, 1826 – 1870

Year	Germans	Irish	British	Blacks
1825	2.5[a]	7.0[a]	10.5[a]	4.2
1840	28.0[a]	6.0[a]	10.0[a]	4.5
1850	28.9	12.5	4.2	2.8
1860	30.4	12.0	3.3	2.3
1870	22.9	8.6	2.2	2.7

SOURCE: See sources in Table 4.1.
[a] Adult White Males

until the late 1860s, when Cincinnati was surpassed by Chicago, no Western city employed a greater number or higher percentage of workers in its industrial sector. Those seeking employment in the city's commercial sector also found plenty of opportunities. The total number of wholesale merchants, shopkeepers, clerks, and the like, rose from 7,450 in 1850 to more than 12,000 by 1870. The most rapidly expanding sphere of employment, although by no means its most lucrative, was the city's personal services sector. Increases in wealth and disposable income, as well as the number of unskilled and semiskilled men and women, prompted a veritable explosion in the number of servants, laundresses, barbers, saloon and restaurant employees, and the like: from 2,620 in 1850 to more than 13,000 by 1870.[6]

The city's rapidly expanding economy, civic boosters said, also created more avenues of employment for women. Throughout the first several decades of the century, women had to support themselves or help supplement the family income largely by working at home — either in their own homes as seamstresses or in the homes of others as domestics. Although these remained the dominant areas of employment, after 1843 women found work in a number of new areas, most notably as teachers, sales clerks, and in many of the city's new manufactories. By 1870, 9,927 (58.1 percent) of all employed women labored in the personal services sector, 5,967 (34.9 percent) in the manufacturing sector, 598 (3.5 percent) in the professions, 526 (3.1 percent) in commercial endeavors, and 63 (0.4 percent) in farming, transportation, and other miscellaneous jobs.[7]

This bourgeois vision of an era of progress and prosperity, was not shared by all working-class families. Certainly, some found increased employment opportunities, particularly for women and boys, a welcome means of securing the additional savings that would allow them to buy a home or a business. Peter Schmitt, the son of a relatively well-to-do German blacksmith, recounted how he was sent to work in a tobacco factory specifically to help to pay for the family's new home. Yet, for many other families, the increased employment of women and children was a reflection of hard times. Families like the Rattermans and Auternichs, having spent all their savings journeying to Cincinnati, were forced to send their sons, daughters, and, occasionally, wives, to work in order to make ends meet. Among many of the city's Jewish families, a working mother was seen as a sign of shame and poverty, not happiness and prosperity.[8]

Moreover, despite capitalists' claims of shared prosperity for all producers, the distribution of wealth in Cincinnati grew increasingly skewed. Whereas between 1817 and 1838 the amount of wealth held by the top 10 percent of the city's taxpayers remained fairly constant, changing from 54.2 to 55.4 percent, by 1860 they had increased their holdings to 67.1 percent. Conversely, the wealth of the bottom 50 percent of the taxpayers declined from 8.1 percent in 1838 to 2.4 percent in 1860. While the recently arrived foreign worker might well, as one observer argued, "secure to himself an independence which he could not hope to attain in Europe," the working class as a whole saw its share of the new prosperity steadily decline.[9]

Whatever their ultimate impact upon the city's workers, these years brought a period of unprecedented wealth for the city's commercial and manufacturing elites. The rapid growth of Midwestern and Western towns and the continued expansion of roads, canals, and railroads created ever-greater demand and more accessible means for the production, sale, and distribution of surplus goods to distant markets. While pork, whiskey, machinery, hardware, clothing, and furniture remained the mainstay of the city's southern trade, in the 1840s, and particularly after the Civil War, wholesale merchants and commission agents used agricultural goods, pork, pork byproducts (soap, candles, etc.), and various manufactured products to form the basis of an increasingly prosperous trade with eastern and international merchants. Indeed, by the early 1850s, farmers, slaughterers, and merchants combined their talents to make Cincinnati the world's leading pork market. As the city's wholesale houses expanded in number from 25 to 50, merchant princes increased their sales from a modest $4 million in 1840 to over $25 million by midcentury. Small shopkeepers also prospered as the total volume of the city's commercial trade rose from $74.3 million in 1841/42 to $463.6 million in 1870.[10]

Although continuing to grow and prosper in absolute terms, Cincinnati's reign as the commercial center of the West had come to an end by midcentury as new railroad lines leading out of the Atlantic Coast bypassed the Queen City in favor of northwestern depots in Chicago and Cleveland. Having failed to embrace the railroad as rapidly as they had the steamboat, the city's merchants and capitalists could only moan as the bulk of the East-West trade of the 1850s and 1860s shifted from rivers to rails and consequently away from Cincinnati. The western grocery, grain, flour, and pork trade, once the exclusive claim of Cincinnati, slowly moved toward Indianapolis and Chicago, while Cincinnati's virtual monopoly on the southern trade was undermined in 1859 as St. Louis and Louisville established direct rail links to New Orleans and Nashville. It was not until the opening of the municipally owned Southern Railway in 1877 — a rail line which provided direct access to burgeoning southern cities such as Atlanta, Charleston, Birmingham, and Knoxville — that Cincinnati significantly reversed its relative commercial decline.[11]

Unseated as the Queen of Commerce, Cincinnati assumed a new crown: the Queen City of Manufacturing. Although the steamboat eventually lost out to the railroad, the technology and entrepreneurial skills it helped foster, as well as the ensuing labor supply, markets, and capital which it brought west, were critical factors in reorienting Cincinnati's economy from commerce to manufacturing. Whereas visitors of earlier years had generally addressed their observations to the city's physical beauty and its wide array of commercial endeavors, travelers of the middle decades marveled at the astounding breadth and importance of Cincinnati's manufacturing interests. It was the "character of these manufacturing districts," English visitor William Chambers remarked in 1853, that was "making Cincinnati one of the wonders of the New World."[12] Indeed, between 1840 and 1870 the value of the city's annual production leapt by an astounding 677 percent — from $16.4 million to $127.5 million — while the number of people laboring in the city's shops and factories rose by 230 percent — from 10,287 to 33,972. Similarly, the amount of capital invested in manufacturing increased by 194 percent — from $14.5 million in 1840 to $42.6 million in 1870.[13]

Table 4.3 Value of the Annual Product of the City's Leading Ten Trades, 1841 – 1870 (in '000s)

1841		1851	
1. Meatpacking	$3,074	Meatpacking	$5,760
2. Clothing (ready-to-wear)	1,223	Soap & Candles	4,490
3. Butchers	1,098	Foundry Castings	3,676
4. Feed & Flour	816	Whiskey	2,857
5. Furniture	676	Butchers	2,850
6. Foundry Castings	668	House Carpentry	2,116
7. Steamboats	592	Clothing (ready-to-wear)	1,947
8. Printing & Publishing	518	Feed & Flour	1,690
9. Boots & Shoes	488	Furniture	1,660
10. House Carpentry	418	Printing & Publishing	1,276
Total Top Ten	$9,571	Total Top Ten	$28,322
Total All Industries	$17,780	Total All Industries	$54,550
1860		**1870**	
1. Clothing	$6,516	Meatpacking	$9,344
2. Meatpacking	4,525	Clothing	9,080
3. Whiskey	3,656	Furniture	4,017
4. Soap & Candles	3,207	Breweries	3,299
5. Furniture	2,560	Machinery	3,294
6. Machinery	2,081	Printing & Publishing	2,761
7. Flour & Meal	1,773	Whiskey	2,714
8. Printing & Publishing	1,503	Soap & Candles	2,502
9. Boots & Shoes	1,392	Leather	2,071
10. Leather	1,093	Iron (Forged, Rolled)	1,844
Total Top Ten	$28,306	Total Top Ten	$40,926
Total All Industries	$46,995	Total All Industries	$78,905

SOURCE: Cist, *Cincinnati in 1841*, pp. 54 – 58; Charles Cist, *Sketches and Statistics of Cincinnati in 1851* (Cincinnati, 1851), pp. 258 – 61; *Manufactures of the United States in 1860; Compiled from the Original Returns of the Eighth Census* (Washington, 1865), pp. 453 – 56; *Ninth Census — Volume III. The Statistics of the Wealth and Industry of the United States* (Washington, 1872), pp. 714 – 5.

Note: Figures for 1860 and 1870 underestimate the actual value of production. Manufacturing statistics during this era often varied depending upon who was conducting the census. Federal enumerators, for example, tended to underestimate the actual size and value of production, while local Chamber of Commerce reports bolstered figures by including neighboring Newport and Covington, Kentucky in their statistics. Consequently, if the reader notices different figures being used for the same years at various points in the book, it is because of a shift in sources.

Vast diversity, not simply absolute size, characterized the city's productive sector in the new era of manufacturing. Unlike one-industry towns such as Cohoes, New York, or Lynn and Waltham, Massachusetts, Cincinnati's path of industrialization was never associated with nor dependent upon the fate of one particular product. This was a city, remarked local statistician William Smith in 1855, which exhibited "not the growth of some one great fabric of cotton, wool, or glass, such as may be found in Lowell, Lawrence, or Pittsburgh, but a variety of kinds and branches of the Arts and Manufactures from the coarsest to the finest."[14] Nor was the process of industrialization dominated only by newer industries such as machinemaking, hardware, or iron and steel. As masters in various crafts abandoned tradition in favor of modernizing production, they helped to transform many of the city's relatively small trades into major industrial producers. By midcentury, Cincinnati ranked among the five leading national producers of pork, machinery, furniture, ready-made clothes, soap and candles, boots and shoes, whisky, ale, and books. Three decades later, though slipping to seventh in overall manufacturing, Cincinnati was the nation's leading producer of carriages, furniture, glycerine, coffins, plug tobacco, wine, and whiskey; the second largest producer of clothing, boots and shoes; and among the top seven national producers of saddles, harnesses, sawed lumber, tanned and curried leather, printed goods, foundry products, blacksmithing, and marble and stone goods.[15]

The expansion of manufacturing in Cincinnati in the 1840s and 1850s was led largely by men who had worked their way up through the crafts — men who, like Miles Greenwood, used the profits of small shops to expand the size and scope of their operations. Although newspapers like the *Gazette* undoubtedly exaggerated when they claimed that "nine-tenths of the rich men among us . . . [had] commenced life as poor men, and laid the foundation of their fortunes by saving a part of the scanty proceedings of their daily toil," there was much truth in their claims of upward mobility in the new world of manufacturing.[16] Engine-makers David Griffey, Amos Holabird and Jabez Reynolds, coppersmiths William Robson and Jeremiah Kiersted, furniture manufacturers Henry Boyd, Robert Mitchell, and Frederick Rammelsberg, clothing manufacturers Jacob Kornblueth and Sebastien Myer, soap- and candlemakers William Proctor and James Gamble, the leading producers in their particular endeavors, had all begun as journeymen before embarking upon their careers as manufacturers.

While these men achieved greater financial success than most,

Table 4.4 Career Patterns and Place of Birth of the Leading 10 Percent
of the Manufacturers of 1850

Prior Occupation	Number	Percentage
Journeyman in Same Trade	67	60.9
Journeyman in Different Trade	10	9.1
Teamster or Carter	2	1.8
Merchant or Shopkeeper	17	15.5
Clerk or Bookkeeper	6	5.4
Farmer	1	1.0
Take Over From Father:		
journeyman in manufactory	5	4.5
clerk in manufactory	2	1.8
Totals	110	100.0
Native Born	67	60.9
Foreign Born	37	33.6
Unknown	6	5.5
Totals	110	100.0

SOURCE: The career patterns of these men were gleaned by tracing their histories through a number of local biographies and industrial histories. The following sources were particularly useful: M. Joblin, *Cincinnati Past and Present* (Cincinnati, 1872); A. N. Marquis, ed., *The Industries of Cincinnati* (Cincinnati, 1883); Andrew Morrison, *The Industries of Cincinnati: Manufacturing Establishments and Business Houses* (Cincinnati, 1886); [International Publishing Company], *Leading Manufacturers and Merchants of Cincinnati and Environs* (Cincinnati, 1886); [J. W. Leonard], *The Centennial Review of Cincinnati: One Hundred Years* (Cincinnati, 1888); Cincinnati *Times Star*, *The City of Cincinnati and Its Resources* (Cincinnati, 1891); Rev. Frederic Goss, *Cincinnati the Queen City, 1788–1912*, 4 vols. (Cincinnati, 1912), vol. 4; Charles Greve, *Centennial History of Cincinnati and its Representative Citizens*, 2 vols. (Chicago, 1904), vol. 2.

the path they took was one followed by many of the leading manufacturers of 1850. Indeed, an analysis of the career patterns of the men who made up the top 10 percent of the manufacturers in Cincinnati in 1850 (339 men) indicates that of those whose backgrounds could be traced, 74.5 percent had worked their way up through the ranks, either in the same or in different crafts. Only seven men had traveled the seemingly easy path of taking over their father's business. Yet, even in these cases, five of the seven had worked as journeymen before becoming employers. Moreover, these were men who had often lived and labored in Cincinnati for a considerable number of years. At least 44.5 percent of the elite of 1850 had lived in Cincinnati since 1840.[17]

Little wonder then that these former artisans were so optimistic about the benefits of manufacturing. Like their less numerous predecessors of the 1820s and 1830s, ambitious manufacturers of the 1840s and 1850s saw tremendous opportunites awaiting those willing to abandon tradition in favor of more capitalistic modes of production. Taking advantage of expanded markets and transportation networks, the vast increase in the available labor pool, and the increased accessibility of investment capital, these men moved to expand the scale and reduce the cost of production by restructuring the ways in which work was conducted. They centralized formerly separate operations into a single workplace and under the control of a single boss. They restructured daily work responsibilities by initiating greater specialization and division of labor among skilled and unskilled workers. They paid their employees a weekly wage rather than a customary price for completed work. They introduced new machinery designed to reduce the time and cost of production. And they altered the traditional social relationships of production by hiring larger numbers of women and children.

As manufacturers in new and old industries alike centralized and expanded their operations, an increasing number of workers found themselves moving from small shops to moderately sized and large manufactories. Whereas in 1850, approximately 67.4 percent of the workforce labored in shops of one to 49 people, by 1870 nearly half the men and women, 49.4 percent, worked in manufactories employing 50 or more. As table 4.5 indicates, the most striking expansion of the era occurred among those workplaces employing more than 100 people. Although vastly outnumbered by small shops, these large manufactories increased their hold on the labor force from 20.4 percent in 1850 to 33.2 percent in 1870.

This new era of manufacturing was not characterized, however, by a sudden shift from small handicraft shops to large, highly mechanized factories. On the contrary, the rise of manufacturing and spread of industrial capitalism was a gradual and uneven process which affected

Table 4.5 Distribution of Workforce By Size of Establishment, 1850–1870

Size of Workplace	1850		1870	
	Shops	Employees	Shops	Employees
1–49	1,207	11,210	2,312	18,880
50–74	20	1,140	68	4,210
75–99	11	885	22	1,856
100+	21	3,395	67	12,398
Totals	1,259	16,630	2,469	37,344

SOURCE: Statistics were compiled from data in the U.S. Census Office, "Census of the United States, Manufacturing Schedule, Hamilton County, Ohio," 1850 and 1870; and printed census statistics.

different industries at different times, and to varying extents. In some endeavors, such as machinemaking, hardware, and furniture, manufacturers embraced change with rapid enthusiasm, while in other trades, such as tobacco and carriage making, they proceeded more slowly. Moreover, the rate of industrial development was often uneven within as well as between industries. While some furniture makers, boot- and shoemakers, and book-makers were quick to reorganize production, erect large buildings, and employ hundreds of workers, others rejected new capitalistic modes of production and continued to produce their goods in time-honored ways.

The new era of manufacturing did not signal the demise of the artisan or of small-shop production. The growth of manufactories often contributed to the growth and development of many old and new small shop endeavors. The astounding expansion of the city's pork and brewery industries served as a boon to the small independent cooper shops which supplied factories with barrels. Increased iron production often resulted in work overflows which were in turn subcontracted to local blacksmith shops. The expansion of sugar refineries provided greater quantities of cheap sugar for local confectioners. Thus, it is only when we compare the *relative* rates of growth and importance that the small artisan shop appears to have suffered so drastic a fate. In terms of absolute numbers, traditional artisanal production continued to lead a healthy existence throughout the century.[18]

The new era of industrialization was also marked by the introduction and utilization of new forms of power. Whereas in earlier decades steam-powered machinery had been confined almost exclusively to the city's heavier metal and machinemaking manufactories, by 1870 it had gradually spread into a wide range of new and old industries. Machinery did not, however, replace the artisan as the primary force in production. Rather, it was generally confined to performing the rough and unskilled work of the trade. Furniture manufacturers, while continuing to rely upon artisans to perform the skilled aspects of production with their traditional hand tools, utilized new steam-powered planing machines to take "from manual labor its severest as well as most unprofitable drudgery; the ripping up and planing out flooring boards."[19]

Yet, while hand power and hand tools continued to dominate the production process in most trades and industries, an increasingly greater perentage of the city's leading manufacturers incorporated some aspect of the new technology into their daily operations. An examination of the firms which constituted the top 10 percent of the manufacturing sector in 1850 and 1870 reveals that the percentage of manufactories relying solely upon hand power dropped from 40.5 percent in 1850 to 28.4 percent in 1870, while those employing steam-power in one or more of their operations rose from 47.6 percent to 69.3 percent.[20]

The new era of manufacturing also brought important changes in the social composition of the workforce and the workplace. While social interactions on the job were initially altered by the influx of foreign-born and often foreign-speaking workers, the virtually exclusive male domain of the workplace was permanently shattered by the entry of large numbers of women and children. Although the vast majority of women employed in the productive sector continued to labor as seamstresses, either in their homes or in sweatshops, by midcentury traditional forms of family economy were dramatically altered as increasingly greater numbers found new, and often better paying, jobs working in the same factories as their fathers, husbands, and brothers.

Not surprisingly, women and children found their greatest chances for employment inside the city's new manufactories. By hiring these relatively low-paid workers to perform unskilled tasks, manufacturers were able to maximize the labor of their skilled craftsmen. Furniture manufacturers, as one contemporary observed, employed women and children to carry out much of the lighter kinds of work, such as painting and varnishing and preparing cane seats.[21] Printers and publishers relied upon this cheap labor force to execute the relatively easy but tedious folding, sewing, and binding operations. Textile manufacturers employed women and children to run the looms, spindles, and frames. The city's larger boot- and shoemakers, like Filey and Chapin and E. G. Webster, employed them to perform stitching, bindings, and rough work.[22]

Table 4.6 Distribution of Women and Children in Manufactories Employing Fifty or More Workers, 1850–1870

| | 1850 | | 1870 | | | |
| | Women | | Women | | Children | |
Shop Size	n	% in shop	n	% in shop	n	% in shop
50–74	30	2.6	811	19.3	247	5.9
75–99	195	22.0	309	16.6	44	2.4
100+	800	23.6	3,592	29.0	665	5.4
Total (50–100+)	1,025	18.9	4,712	25.5	956	5.2

SOURCE: U.S. Census Office, "Manufacturing Schedule, Hamilton County, Ohio," 1850 and 1870.

As manufacturers increased the scope and organization of production, so too did they come to increase their reliance upon women and children. Indeed, by 1870, 79.0 percent of all women employed in the manufacturing sector worked for manufacturers or clothing contractors who employed fifty or more people. If we break these statistics down by industry, we find that in 1850 women made up 60.2 percent of the city's clothing workers, 52.3 percent of its textile operatives, and 16.2 percent of all boot and shoe factory workers. By 1870, as more manufacturers altered traditional forms of production, the range of factory work for women and children expanded to include clothing (60.2 percent), tobacco (50.6 percent), textiles (40.6 percent), boots and shoes (35.5 percent), and printing and publishing (21.4 percent).[23]

Manufacturers lauded the increased employment of women as a sign of greater opportunity for families, but those entering the factories often perceived it as a mixed blessing. While factory work frequently brought in more money than working at home — women could earn $8–11 a week in 1850 in a furniture or textile factory as opposed to $7 a week laboring at home as seamstresses — these new settings of production were fraught with considerable dangers to health and safety. Hundreds of workers were frequently packed into factories which provided little ventilation, few sanitary facilities or fire escapes, and inadequate protection from dangerous machinery. Moreover, many viewed work outside the home as a threat to the nature of family life. The need to supplement family earnings often forced young boys and girls out of the home earlier than many parents would have liked and prevented them from completing their schooling. With daughters and sons in the factories and unable to help them with the housework, the lot of mothers often grew burdensome and lonely. Families may very well have grown more prosperous, but prosperity had its costs.[24]

The Language, Imagery, and Ideology of Manufacturing

Had Thomas Carter and Augustus Roundy lived in Cincinnati at midcentury, they would have been both impressed and horrified by their new urban world. Never before had there been so much wealth, so many avenues of opportunity, and so many promises of prosperity. Yet at the center of

this new wealth loomed a force which had been feared by faithful republicans of earlier decades — manufacturing. While most citizens would have
undoubtedly agreed with Edward Mansfield that theirs was a world "in a
rapid revolution, a peaceful revolution, in which it is visible to all eyes, and
felt by all persons," there was less certainty concerning the consequences
of this revolution.[25] Could virtue, democracy, and independence survive in
an economy dominated by manufacturing? Could a city, let alone a nation,
enjoy true progress in a world whose direction was increasingly being
determined by large manufacturers rather than by artisans? Expressing the
fears shared by many citizens throughout the country, one local resident
asked in 1829:

> Is this country then, to have entailed upon it that lamentable state of things,
> which has been ascribed to the manufacturing districts of Europe? Are
> thousands and tens of thousands of human beings to be doomed to misery
> and wretchedness, from soon after leaving the cradle, till they descend to
> the grave? And pass through life with minds so little expanded, as scarcely
> to exhibit any symptoms of rationality, beyond the routine of their daily
> employment?[26]

The initial answer to these questions came from the city's
bourgeoisie. Between the late 1830s and the early 1870s, manufacturers,
market-oriented masters, capitalists, newspaper editors, clergymen, and
various civic leaders responded to the concerns and fears of the citizenry
by forging a new vision of the role and future of manufacturing. Building
upon ongoing local and national efforts to redefine traditional ideology in
a dynamic capitalistic age, which we have discussed earlier, these men
endeavored to create a new republican constellation which regarded manufactories not as Satan's strongholds, but as an integral part of a modern
expanding republic. Through their use of words, public exhibitions, institutions, and architecture, they set out to revise previous images of manufacturing and to portray it and its ensuing technologies, not as agencies of
dependency and immiseration, but as republican forces which advanced
the interests of the individual, the community, and the nation.[27]

That capitalists had to struggle so hard in defense of manufacturing indicates that not all citizens shared their belief in the complementary unity of industrialization and republicanism. Although these men
were by no means a closely united class, being internally split by many of
the same issues which divided workers — slavery, ethnicity, politics, and

economic policies — Cincinnati elites, in the decades before the Civil War, gradually, and often haphazardly, endeavored to alter the thoughts and attitudes of citizens by focusing their praise and defense of manufacturing around two key themes: manufacturing as a process which aided the material and moral well-being of the citizenry, and manufacturing as a process which was clearly under human control.

Unlike European industrial cities, where manufacturing had allegedly brought great wealth to a few individuals and misery to the masses, in Cincinnati, it was argued, its benefits were dispersed to a wide array of people. By creating thousands of new jobs, opening thousands of new paths of opportunity and independence, and providing thousands of working-class families with more goods at lower prices, manufacturing, insisted the directors of the Ohio Mechanics' Institute, had proved to be of great "importance and useful to the community." The introduction of manufacturing in New England, reasoned the editors of the *Gazette,* had brought greater "comfort" and "independence" to all classes, and, "while the man of wealth has not been reduced in means, the great body of the people have advanced rapidly in the possession of the real comforts of life."[28]

Manufacturing also strengthened the independence and virtue of the nation. "No nation," declared Dr. John Craig, "can be truly independent, unless it can furnish from its own resources, all the necessaries and substantial comforts and conveniences of life."[29] Moreover, by prompting the expansion of the entire economic sector, manufacturing had also contributed to the preservation of true citizenship, for an independent and virtuous citizenry could not survive in a city where large masses of people were unemployed.

The proponents of manufacturing also portrayed it as a force which furthered the moral and spiritual conditions of men and women. While many of Cincinnati's capitalists may have privately equated progress with increased wealth and luxury, their public pronouncements held that *true* progress had to be measured by moral and intellectual as well as material standards. Holding forth as republicans concerned with the continued virtue of their city and nation, these men praised manufacturing, not for its profitability, but because its practical application helped to improve the human condition. The new forces of production, Edward Mansfield told one audience, represented more than mere pecuniary gain; they were "an essential element in the continued happiness and progressive elevation of the human mind."[30] By instructing mechanics in the values of hard work, temperance, and perseverance, explained civic leader Charles

Cist, manufacturing had played a vital role in improving the moral character of the city's youth: the "trustees of the future destinies of our great republic."[31] Indeed, the ability of manufacturing to combat vice and idleness, avowed the Reverend G. T. Flanders, had helped to create a new, more moral "Age of Enterprise," wherein spiritual and material progress joined together to produce an enlightened Christian public spirit.[32]

Manufacturing also improved the physical and intellectual nature of work by transforming and easing the burdens of daily toil. Just as citizenship had raised men from a debased political condition, so, too, did manufacturing elevate labor to a higher plane by removing, as one association of manufacturers noted, "the incubus of servile toil, the doom of unremitting labor."[33] Pre-industrial labor, explained Edward Mansfield, had relied upon brutal physical exertions which left men "neither happier, wiser, nor richer." The new era of manufacturing, with its elaborate "division of labor," had altered that lamentable situation: it "economises time, creates values, and enables a portion of society to pursue knowledge, and make a business of instruction."[34] Never before, avowed one minister, was labor "so honorable, dignified and revered. Labor and respectability are more closely allied."[35]

Unlike the degraded English textile mills, which often allegedly reduced men, women, and children to mindless idiots, manufacturing in Cincinnati augured the onset of a new and higher era of production wherein the "labor of the body [is] directed by the labor of the intellect." The mechanic arts, as manufacturing was frequently referred to, required the merging of man's physical and intellectual capacities with the principles of art and science. It encouraged, even demanded, men "to think, to enquire, to learn, to instruct."[36] By emphasizing the "union of correct scientific thought with skillful bodily labor," explained the board of directors of the Ohio Mechanics' Institute, the city's manufacturers, unlike their European counterparts, had successfully converted the "comparatively unformed and dark" minds of "many unfortunate youths" into "instruments of much good . . . [which] contribute largely to the peace and harmony of society."[37]

The city's bourgeoisie also attempted to demystify technology and to humanize their new economic world by placing man at its center. Breaking the often mysterious workings of manufacturing into its constituent elements, they presented citizens with a new trinity of production which portrayed steam power, technology, and the mechanic as the source, the agent, and the controlling force of all recent progress and prosperity. Unlike Manchester, Birmingham, or Sheffield, where manufacturing often appeared, at least to fearful Americans, as a process in which machines seemed to rule mercilessly over men and women, in Cincinnati manufacturing was portrayed as the triumph of human power over the forces of nature. Steam and machinery, the public was frequently reminded, were but manifestations and extensions of human power. All machines, all manufactured goods, Cist noted, were "works of the hand," and therefore works of man. The "greatest achievement of modern times," he argued was not the "evolvement of artificial motive power," but its subjugation to the human will.[38] Technology was not an independent force, but a dependent tool. It was the servant, not the master of mankind; a force which was clearly controlled by and for citizens. Human effort had built the city's factories; human effort had given life to machines. As one contemporary poet wrote:

> Work sows the seed;
> Even the rock may yield its flower,
> No lot so hard, but human power,
> Exert to one end and aim,
> May conquer fate and time
> Press on.[39]

Although manufacturers and capitalists were largely responsible for the changes in productive life, their public pronouncements proclaimed that the central hero of the age was the person who had harnessed nature, mastered scientific principles, and effectively controlled the new forces and powers being unleashed upon the world — the mechanic. He was portrayed as the protean character, the transcendental hero of his age. He was the POWER behind the power; the man who, of all men, most nearly approached the "perfection of nature."[40] While contemporaries also lavished praise upon the city's merchants and clerks, it was the mechanic who emerged as the chief object of popular adulation. He was exalted as the "only source of wealth," the "life-blood of the community," the "salt of the land," and a "minister in this great and glorious priesthood as a co-operator with the Almighty Architect."[41] It was only through the efforts of the mechanic and the mechanic arts that the city would continue to prosper. Short stories, poems, articles, and editorials of the era urged prospective brides not to forsake the virtuous mechanic for the lesser man of greater wealth. They also implored parents not to inflate themselves with false pride by encouraging their children to enter the already crowded ranks of the often parasitic professions.[42]

It was a short rhetorical leap from the paragon of progress to the cornerstone of the republic. Public speakers and editorialists repeatedly compared the mechanic to the heroes of classical antiquity. He was the Greek warrior who fought to preserve democracy and saved the *polis* from physical and moral destruction. He was both the redeemer of traditional democratic values and the agent of future progress. Such praise, however, also entailed certain obligations. As men on "a heaven appointed mission," mechanics were not expected to debase themselves by participating in strikes or wage disputes. "Let them not in the spirit of complaint and fault finding lament their hard lot," U. T. Howe advised the members of the Ohio Mechanics' Institute, "or complain that they were trodden down . . . but let them put their hand earnestly to the work of education and self-improvement."[43]

In order to ensure the continued development of democracy and human progress, masters and manufacturers spearheaded a drive to create new institutions which would train men in all aspects of the modern mechanical arts and educate young apprentices in the values and behavior which capitalists believed appropriate to the new era of production and progress. The most notable of these was the Ohio Mechanics' Institute (OMI). Founded in 1828 by the city's leading masters and manufacturers with the dual purpose of moral and material improvement, the OMI sought to advance the "true interests of that portion of the community whose name its so distinctively bears" and to "facilitate the diffusion of useful knowledge and to promote improvements in manufactures and the mechanical arts."[44] The OMI offered special classes in the arts and sciences, numerous lectures and "rational entertainments," and a well-stocked library as a means of awakening "a proper interest in the pursuit of knowledge" and ensuring the "good moral character" of journeymen and apprentices.[45]

The veneration of the mechanic and of human enterprise and power reached a peak on May 30, 1838, when the private world of the workplace formally entered the arena of popular culture. On that day, the OMI sponsored the first in a series of annual Mechanic's Exhibitions intended "to exalt, to a higher degree, the dignity of labor."[46] Works produced in the shops and manufactories by artisans and at home by housewives and daughters were put on display to compete for prizes — $50 for the winners — and public admiration. Men, women, and children were encouraged to come and spend their leisure time browsing through the various exhibits. Pragmatic as well as laudatory, the exhibitions were intended to publicize Cincinnati's emergence as a major manufacturing center and to attract new business to the city. Advertisements were placed in the newspapers throughout the Midwest urging merchants and consumers to come and "view the variety and quality of our manufactures."[47] These efforts at boosterism proved successful, for by midcentury the fairs attracted over 1,200 visitors a day.

The categories and manner in which the various exhibits were displayed, while reflecting the growing importance of manufacturing and machinery, also served to reaffirm the continued hegemony of human power. Of the five general exhibition categories — Machinery, Raw Materials, Manufactures, Fine Arts, and Household Crafts (embroidery, jellies, baked goods, etc.) — the last three constituted the most numerous and prominently displayed items of the exhibitions. Despite its increased significance in the work world, machinery was greatly underplayed in comparison with handicrafts and the fine arts. The few machines that were exhibited were generally placed in the far corners of the hall and exhibited as static objects, as symbols of potential power which relied upon the greater activating powers of man. Indeed, facilities for the operation of steam machinery were not installed until 1852. By isolating machines and keeping them powerless, the board of directors presented citizens with a visual statement that may well have allayed fears that new industrial forces would somehow overpower society. Clearly, mechanics were still the dominant force and machines merely the dependent agents of their will.[48]

This belief in human power as the dominating force behind the growth and transformation of the city and the belief that manufacturing and democracy went hand in hand was also reflected in the form and style of the city's buildings. While buildings are primarily erected for functional purposes, their size, use of space, and particular modes of design often implicitly reveal underlying values and concerns. Lacking any master plan for urban development, Cincinnati's architecture was free to reflect the immediate images, moods, desires, and symbols of its dominant ideology.

The classical imagery — the power of the *demos* — so frequently employed in the public rhetoric of the era, also emerged as the city's predominant architectural motif. The classical revival, which swept over much of the eastern United States between 1810 and 1815, reached Cincinnati shortly after its rise to western commercial supremacy in the 1820s. Unlike the South, where classical architecture, used predominantly in designing plantation homes, often emerged as a symbol of ostentation and a glorification of the planter elite, in Cincinnati it was employed mainly in the design of churches, public, and commercial buildings, not private homes, and stood forth as the symbol of democratic promise and progress. Indeed, stalwart republicans like Thomas Jefferson had long embraced classical architecture as an important way of inspiring citizens with visual symbols of democratic virtues and ideals.[49]

For men of business, classical architecture also served as a means, whether intentional or not, of obscuring the growing inequalities of the age. Rather than employing ornate styles of architecture which would distinguish and glorify the edifices of business, capitalists chose a more popular style of design that would visibly link the spatial expansion of capital to the image of Greek liberty. Although business edifices were rapidly displacing men and women from their downtown homes, classical architecture helped to humanize the aesthetic appearances of the physical plants of capital — to portray business as the symbolic if not the actual extension of the power of the people, not of elites, and to associate its spatial growth with the expansion of democratizing forces rather than of selfish and particularistic interest groups.

Classicism was most heavily adopted by the city's older capitalistic interests — commerce and finance. Manufacturing, the actual and symbolic home of the city's sources of modern power, received relatively little architectural attention. Few factories or artisans' shops exhibited the intricate and elaborate masonry fronts which adorned many of Cincinnati's commercial buildings. Rather, the art and power of industry were confined to the inside of the workshop and not its external façade. The mechanic's workplace, like the mechanic, was modest but powerful. Simple exteriors belied greater internal strength. Touring the downtown central manufacturing district in 1848, the future Secretary of the Treasury, Hugh McCulloch, described the area as "filled with buildings of plain exterior, which upon entering, we found to be alive with running wheels and active skilled hands, turning out all kinds of articles."[50]

Traditional republican fears regarding manufacturing, particularly the dangers of turning Cincinnati into an American version of the dreaded English industrial city, were abated in part by the modest size of the city's new manufactories. The feelings of dwarfishness and personal insignificance which one often experiences amid the towering skyscrapers and enormous factories of today and the sense that buildings, not people, are the center of public attention, were minimal during the first half of the nineteenth century. The modest size and style of the city's manufactories were not, however, necessarily dictated by ideological considerations but by the limits of building technology and capital. The primitive state of iron-column construction confined the size of most buildings in Cincinnati to less than four stories. The city's first five-story building did not appear until 1847; and, in the years before the Civil War, only an occasional factory or warehouse rose to the then dramatic height of six stories. Moreover, during this period of capital accumulation, manufacturers, even had they wanted, lacked the funds to build massive factories. Instead, they gradually expanded their operations by using growing profits to construct a series of smaller buildings adjacent to one another. Expecting to find another Sheffield, Hugh McCulloch was struck by the modest size of Cincinnati's factories. A city "without large factories, and yet a manufacturing city," he noted with surprise, "was an anomaly."[51]

The physical appearance of the Queen City also contributed to fostering a more positive image of manufacturing. Charles Cist took great pride in comparing the relative aesthetics of production in Cincinnati and its chief rival, Pittsburgh. In the latter, the factory completely dominated the appearance of the city. Upon nearing the outskirts of Pittsburgh, the visitor was greeted by a "dense cloud of darkness and smoke"; upon entering, the "hissing of steam, the clanking of chains, the jarring and grinding of wheels and other machinery, the glow of melted glass and iron, and burning coal beneath, burst upon his eyes and ears in concentrated force." The "whole city . . . was under the influence of steam and smoke," with coal and steam engines reigning as the "pervading influence of the place."[52]

Industry assumed a totally different guise in Cincinnati. Here manufacturing was clean and unobstrusive. The "productive industry of our mechanics," Cist boasted, was kept "to a great extent out of sight." While marveling that Cincinnati was "one great beehive of activity — exhibiting more activity than New York," and producing everything that "ever was manufactured," recent arrivals such as William Sherwood were amazed to discover the absence of behemoth factories and industrial pollution. The easy accessibility and cheapness of water and wood led to their widespread adoption as the main source of fuel in the Queen City. Thus, unlike Pittsburgh, where coal was generally employed, Cincinnati's skies were left remarkably uncontaminated by dirt and soot. Industrial progress was not only human but clean.[53]

While buildings served in part to enhance the image of democracy and to promote the symbolic power and glory of the people, they nevertheless belied a growing competition over which groups or interests were to secure permanent space in the city. The external aesthetics of buildings reveal one aspect of urban imagery and ideology. However, the choice of construction materials provides a significantly different insight. In the Age of the Artisan, a high percentage of Cincinnati's buildings were constructed of wood, regardless of an individual's or company's wealth. As the steamboat trade and manufacturing added to the prosperity of the city and its residents, they also precipitated a change in the choice of construction materials — from cheap wood to more expensive and ornate brick and stone. Whereas in July 1816, 74.8 percent of the city's buildings were made of wood, 23.4 percent of brick, and 1.8 percent of stone, by 1850 57.5 percent of all edifices were constructed of brick.[54]

This shift from wood to brick had several important political implications which served to undercut elite claims of democracy and progress for all during the era of manufacturing. In the first decades of the century, all interests and classes were relatively impermanent and subject to the vicissitudes of nature. The shift from wood to brick was not simply a revelation of changing popular tastes, but also an expression of growing wealth and inequality; only wealthy citizens and well-to-do businesses could afford brick's high construction costs. The less affluent members of society — artisans, mechanics, and shopkeepers — continued to build with wood. This was particularly true after 1833, when the introduction of balloon framing dramatically lowered the cost of building with wood.[55]

People and their wooden homes were but transient urban phantoms compared with the brick buildings of the downtown area that endured for decades. By 1850, virtually all the new buildings in the central and business parts of the city were built of brick. Conversely, 414 (89.2 percent) of the 464 frame buildings erected that year were constructed in areas populated by working-class families.[56] By midcentury, although mechanics still dominated the imagery and public rhetoric of the Age of Manufacturing, it was the physical structures of capital which were becoming permanently entrenched on its soil. Thus, while the city's buildings served to enhance popular images of democracy and liberty, they also stood forth as symbols of the growing power and authority of the capitalistic class.

Moreover, the praise of the mechanic did not accurately reflect the changing and frequently deleterious conditions of working-class life in the new age of manufacturing. The image of the independent creative mechanic was sharply contradicted by daily realities and struggles. Although workers shared a number of common beliefs with manufacturers (the importance of education, mobility, and republicanism), they often found themselves disagreeing with their employers' definitions of "progress" and how industrialization affected their lives. Indeed, the new bourgeois ideology of industry could not explain the continued growth of working-class resistance, the many strikes, struggles, and drives for unionization which also characterized the era, or the reasons why workers sought to create a very different world than that envisioned by capitalists.

Consequently, in order to understand the growing divergence between ideology and daily life, we must look beneath the rhetoric of the city's elites and the sweeping portraits of a happy, prosperous, and independent world, and see how manufacturing transformed the nature of work and the role of the worker.

CHAPTER FIVE

Inside the Workplace: The Transformation of Work and the Working Class

For many Cincinnatians, the transition from handicraft production to manufacturing, and eventually to modern industry, appeared to bring new job opportunities, new avenues for wealth, and an ever-increasing supply of inexpensive goods. Yet, while manufacturers, capitalists, and civic elites heralded these changes as harbingers of progress and prosperity, Cincinnati's workers did not always share their optimism. Far from seeing their position in the workplace and in society strengthened by industrialization, many artisans found their customs, skills, and expectations of independence gradually undermined.

While the lives of the city's residents were shaped by a number of different influences — race, gender, ethnicity, religion, culture, and politics — the activity which consumed most of their time was work. In transforming an endeavor which demanded eight, ten, or twelve hours a day, six days a week, and spanned twenty, thirty, or forty years of a lifetime, industrialization not only affected the economic development of the city, but also the ways in which people thought about themselves and the world at large. Yet, despite the enormous amount of time spent in the workshop, there were few moments before the 1880s when the role of *worker* held the same meaning and indicated the same interests for all workers, few moments when men and women acted in concert as a united, self-perceived working class. Industrialization, although impinging upon the lives of all workers and their families, did not produce a single working-class experience. Rather, in a multi-industry city like Cincinnati, it bred a wide variety of working-class experiences and responses. As various trades and industries passed through increasingly developed stages of production, and as the technological and organizational innovations introduced by manufacturers grew more varied and complex, work assumed new forms and workers new identities.

During the course of the nineteenth century, industrialization acted to divide Cincinnati's manufacturing workforce into four general categories: small-shop artisans, factory artisans, factory laborers, and outworkers. Because historians have generally assigned occupational categories

Table 5.1 Changing Status of the Majority of Workers Within Cincinnati's Leading Fourteen Industries, 1840–1890

	1840	*1890*
SMALL-SHOP ARTISANS	Building Trades Tobacco Boots & Shoes Printing & Publishing Furniture Carriage & Wagons Metal Working Machinery Hardware Brewing	Building Trades
FACTORY ARTISANS	Iron & Steel	Iron & Steel Tobacco Boots & Shoes Printing & Publishing Furniture Carriage & Wagons Metal Working Machinery Hardware Brewing
FACTORY LABORERS	Meat Processing Pressing/Cooking (Oils, Candles, etc.)	Meat Processing Pressing/Cooking
OUTWORKERS	Clothing	Clothing

SOURCE: See chapter 5 note 1.

with an eye toward simplifying the measurements of social mobility, workers have been classified solely on the basis of skill: as skilled, semi-skilled, or unskilled. The categories of artisan, factory artisan, factory laborer, and outworker represent an attempt both to incorporate and to move beyond these more traditional occupational schemas by considering the *total* work experience of wage earners — by taking into account not only the level of individual skills, but also the settings and conditions under which work was performed. Given the uneven rate of development within and among various industries, a worker's status, wage, activity, needs, and consciousness were determined not so much by his or her absolute level of skill, but by the relative scope of expertise he or she was required to apply during production. Assuming that the skills of two furniture workers were equally high, it seems reasonable to expect that, despite their similar knowledge of the craft, the person performing a wide array of operations in a handicraft shop of five or six people was likely to experience a very different work world from that of his equally skilled counterpart who performed a limited number of tasks — often aided by machinery and helpers — in a factory of 100 workers.

　　Although the artisan dominated the productive world of the ante-bellum city, he was eventually superseded by an important transitional figure: the factory artisan. American working-class history has generally centered around the cultural, economic, and political world of the artisan. However, factory workers were the most numerous element of Cincinnati's working-class population in the late nineteenth century. Far from being apathetic or apolitical, it was the factory artisans, and not the more established small-shop artisans, who were at the forefront of the most radical working-class action in nineteenth-century Cincinnati: the May Day Strikes of 1886.[1]

　　By reconstructing the uneven development of these new forms and arenas of work, we can begin to understand how changes in production affected the development of working-class life, consciousness, and politics. More specifically, we can begin to understand why some workers launched vociferous protests in the 1840s and 1850s, while others remained silent until the 1860s, 1870s, or even longer. In order to obtain a more complete portrait of industrial development, we shall briefly explore some of the important changes which occurred in the era of modern industry after 1873, as well as those which occurred during the era of manufacturing.

The Rise of the Factory Artisan

At the center of the handicraft stage of production stood the traditional artisan. Masters and journeymen, as we have seen, were highly skilled, relatively well-paid hand craftsmen who, having served a period of apprenticeship, possessed and utilized a knowledge and expertise in the entire workings of their craft. Work was usually conducted in a small shop, and the only children present were boys seeking to learn the mysteries of the male-dominated trade. Although artisans relied upon a variety of tools — most of which they owned themselves — they were simple tools directed and powered by the force and feel of the hand and the knowledge of a trained mind. Custom, rather than the demands of the market or the master, usually determined the setting, pace, wages, and quality of production.

Industrialization so altered the general nature of production among the city's fourteen leading industries that by 1890, in only one industry, the building trades (carpenters, masons, plumbers, etc.), did artisanal modes of production and organization remain relatively unaltered.[2] As more and more masters and manufacturers abandoned their small shops and endeavored to increase the output and profits of their new factories by reorganizing traditional forms of production, the artisan was gradually transformed into a new type of worker: the factory artisan.

Caught in the transition between the worlds of handicraft production and modern industry, the factory artisan was the peculiar product of an industrializing world: a worker neither as skilled as his artisan predecessors nor as semi- or unskilled as the emerging factory proletariat. The shift from small shop to factory did not eliminate the need for the artisan's skills, but it resulted in their greater subdivision and particularization. What distinguished the factory artisan from the artisan was not the level of any one particular skill, but the narrow range of skills actually utilized in daily work procedures. Whereas the traditional artisan was expected to produce a complete product, the factory artisan was required to master only a small number of constituent operations. The artisan shoemaker who worked on one shoe at a time or the protean printer or cabinetmaker who performed a wide array of operations slowly gave way to a new generation of "specialists" — a somewhat ironic term since these men were really "particularists" who worked on only one or two parts of the constructive process. Reviewing the dramatic changes which had altered the character of the shoe industry over the past several decades, one saddened commentator noted in 1877:

> The race of shoemakers is rapidly dying out, and in their place is springing up a number of specialists, such as machine-operators, cutters, lasters, bottomers, trimmers, healers, edge-setters, etc., who while experts at their particular branch, would be utterly at a loss, if called upon without machinery, to make a complete pair of boots and shoes.[3]

The position of the artisan was further weakened after the depression of 1873, when falling prices, led manufacturers to adopt "new systems" of management aimed at "depriving the workingman of his skill and maturing a generation of unskilled men and women."[4] Discovering that they could reduce labor costs by employing fewer skilled workmen, manufacturers sought to abandon artisan-controlled apprenticeship programs in favor of teaching young workers only one or two particular skills. With the gradual dissolution of the apprenticeship system in the 1860s and 1870s, later generations of factory artisans frequently found themselves lacking the range of skills which would enable them to move easily between different departments of the factory, or wherever the best pay and working conditions could be obtained.

Manufacturers also endeavored to increase productivity and to limit the power of their workers by transferring control of production to management-appointed supervisory personnel. While not all tradesmen lost meaningful control over work or apprenticeship, by the early 1880s, the overall governance of daily work life — the hiring, firing, and assigning men to jobs, decisions formerly made by masters and journeymen — was increasingly assumed by new foremen and factory superintendents. Commenting on the present and future dangers posed by these attacks on apprenticeship and worker control, Ohio's Commissioner of Labor Statistics wrote in 1878:

> The fact that there is but little if any thorough teaching of trades at the present time, is demonstrated by the fact that but few machinists can build an engine, few shoemakers who can make a shoe. . . . The machinist may be a first class vice hand, the shoemaker may be a splendid trimmer . . . [but] their future is dependent upon their ability to secure employment at such a speciality. Thus is the so-called apprentice system preliminary to the

total extinction of the class of thorough mechanics that, under the old system, made mechanism a fine art.[5]

As one might expect of such a transitional figure, the factory artisan was forced to accustom himself to the values and work routines of two different worlds. Like the artisan, the factory artisan was generally well-paid, possessed relatively high skills, occasionally, as in the case of the city's machinists, continued to own some of the means of production (i.e. the tools, or "kits," of the trade), and, while often aided by machinery, controlled the manner and pace of his work. He also resembled the artisan, as we shall see in later chapters, in his strong reliance upon trade unionism as a means of protecting personal and craft interests.

Nevertheless, the productive world in which the factory artisan operated grew increasingly dissimilar to the one known by the artisan. Factory artisans were wage laborers who sold their labor time rather than the particular product of their labor. Instead of working alongside master craftsmen who produced a limited number of goods for local markets, they worked as employees of capitalists who sold their goods in regional, national, and international markets and organized their production with an eye toward maximizing profits rather than producing quality goods. Traditions of independence and self-regulation on the job were eroded not only by the particularization of skills and adoption of more sophisticated machinery, but also by the introduction of management-appointed supervisory personnel into the various departments of the factory. In short, the determination of the quality and quantity of production — decisions once shared by masters and journeymen — passed increasingly out of the control of labor and into the hands of management.

The contrast between these two worlds was described by immigrant furniture craftsman Oscar Ameringer. Arriving in Cincinnati in the spring of 1886, Ameringer quickly found a job in one of the city's larger furniture factories. Having served his apprenticeship in his father's small handicraft shop in Germany, Ameringer was struck by the new world of modern industrial production which he found in Cincinnati:

> There was no resemblance between the work in that furniture factory and father's shop. Here everything was done by machine. Our only task was assembling, gluing together, and finishing, at so much a chair or table; the two specialties of the factory. Speed came first, quality of workmanship last. So long as the product passed the inspection of the foreman, well and good. How soon it would fall apart was the least of his and our worries.[6]

The rise of the factory artisan and factory production was by no means a uniform process. Enormous variations in the reorganization of labor, the introduction of new machinery, and changing market structures among the city's leading industries created divergent factory artisan experiences. In some industries, the transition from the age of the artisan to manufacturing and modern industry occurred in a relatively short time, while in other industries it spanned several decades. This pattern of uneven development and differing work experiences can best be understood by exploring the changing nature of work in several of Cincinnati's major industries.

Furniture Workers

In few industries was the transition from handicraft to manufacturing more dramatic than in the city's furniture trade. In little more than three decades, manufacturers transformed Cincinnati's furniture industry from a minor producer of local custom work to one of the nation's leading manufacturing centers. Indeed, by 1846 Cincinnati reigned as the nation's largest furniture producer. Between 1841 and 1890, the value of the industry's annual product skyrocketed from $763,600 to $7.5 million, and the number of its employees from 591 to 5,077.[7]

The nature of work and the role of the worker underwent several stages of change during this rise to industrial prominence. The initial departure from traditional modes of artisanal production began in the 1820s, but it was not until the early 1840s that manufacturers such as Robert Mitchell, Frederick Rammelsberg, Charles Johnson, and George Coddington, men who had worked their way up through the craft, dramatically altered the nature of production by centralizing dozens of workers in large manufactories which specialized in the wholesale production of only one to two quickly made and cheaply produced items such as chairs, bedsteads, or bureaus. By the end of the decade, these entrepreneurs had succeeded in dividing the furniture industry into two distinct sectors: small artisan shops which continued to turn out finely made, relatively expensive custom work for local sale, and a number of larger manufactories which produced inexpensive, ready-made furniture for sale in distant markets. As

Table 5.2 Distribution of Labor in Selected Industries
By Size of Workplace, 1850–1880 (in percent)

	1850		1870		1880	
	50–99	100+	50–99	100+	50–99	100+
Building Trades	0.1	0.0	—	—[a]	2.1	4.2
Furniture	29.0	30.4	14.3	44.5	22.7	52.6
Carriages & Wagons	0.0	0.0	34.0	11.1	22.5	61.8
Printing & Publishing	0.0	11.6	29.2	34.7	26.5	31.1
Boots & Shoes	12.5	8.5	20.4	18.8	10.3	60.0
Cigars & Tobacco	0.0	0.0	12.9	8.7	9.4	58.4
Metal Working	0.0	0.0	15.8	0.0	37.5	0.0
Machinery	12.1[b]	18.1[b]	16.7	42.5	16.4	63.5
Hardware			20.7	50.8	9.6	81.0
Iron & Steel	12.0	41.5	10.8	89.2	32.3	67.7
Meat Processing	0.0	0.0	0.0	0.0	39.3	27.1
Pressing/Cooking	16.6	0.0	24.3	20.5	6.1	38.1
Clothing[c]	4.6	16.4	16.6	59.7	10.8	66.0

SOURCE: Statistics were compiled from data contained in U.S. Census Office, "Census of the United States, Manufacturing Schedule, Hamilton County, Ohio," 1850, 1870, 1880.

[a] Data for 1870 are not sufficient to provide accurate figures.

[b] Figures for 1850 reflect the combined totals of machine and hardware shops.

[c] Figures vary here since some manufacturers included outworkers in their totals while others did not.

early as 1856, over two thirds of the furniture manufactured in Cincinnati was exported to western and southern markets.[8]

These new manufactories were distinguished not only by their size and products, but by their reorganization of traditional methods of production. Artisan generalists were gradually transformed into factory artisan specialists who not only produced a limited number of items, but also worked at a limited number of operations. In the factories of leading wholesale manufacturers such as Johnson and Meader, Mitchell and Rammelsberg, and Clawson and Mudge, artisans now worked exclusively as varnishers, carpenters, and finishers, and were assigned to separate rooms where they devoted their whole energies to completing only one constituent part of the final product.[9]

Touring the three-story Clawson and Mudge factory (which employed 180 workers) in December 1849, local reporters marveled at how bedsteads, in various stages of completion, passed rapidly from department to department, floor to floor, until finished products finally reached the warehouse ready to be stored or shipped. "Each man," they observed, " was engaged in a particular branch of the business, and all operations moved with harmony and regularity." The reporters were also struck by the number of relatively unskilled men, women, and children — a sight not generally seen in the city's artisan shops — engaged in the less demanding aspects of production.[10] Charles Johnson, for example, attempted to maximize the skills of his factory artisans by hiring several dozen poorly paid women and children to work at the relatively unskilled and laborious task of caning seats.[11]

Although machinery was often used in these new ventures, the initial shift toward the mass production of furniture was accomplished largely through the reorganization of traditional handiwork. Mechanization, although it contributed to the growth and expansion of these early factories, appeared to follow rather than initiate the reorganization and transformation of production. Indeed, factories were built, labor centralized and divided, and skills particularized well before the widespread adoption of steam-powered machinery in the 1850s. Only four of the nine largest furniture establishments in 1850 relied upon any form of steam power. Moreover, the first machines used by manufacturers impinged very little upon the skills required for intricate operations such as carving, turning, or assembling. Rather, they were limited to performing the most basic tasks of furniture construction: the rough cutting, boring, and planing of wood. Nor did these early machines reduce their operatives to mere attendants, for the human hand and expert eye were still needed to guide the machine so as to fashion the wood into specific patterns.[12]

The movement toward the greater mechanization, division, and systematization of production was also accompanied by efforts to instill greater discipline and new work habits among factory employees. Since a delay in one department would slow down operations throughout the factory, manufacturers endeavored to replace traditional artisan work rhythms, which were often characterized by alternative bouts of slow and frenzied work and frequent pauses for drink or conversation, with more regular work habits which would allow materials to pass quickly from floor to floor without any unnecessary delay. These efforts to instill steadier and more sober work rhythms among employees—especially those who worked with expensive machinery—as well as the manufacturers' ability to expand the size of their workforce, were greatly aided by the city's growing pool of skilled foreign craftsmen who were often desperate for work. Journeymen who were accustomed to taking a dram or two during the work day often found themselves replaced by more temperate native- and foreign-born

artisans. Chair manufacturers, reported one English visitor, generally preferred to hire American and German craftsmen, "the English and Scotch
being rejected on account of their intemperance."[13]

The new emphasis on discipline and sobriety, the elaborate
division of labor into a series of component tasks, and the attempt to speed
up production were measures undertaken by virtually all of the city's leading
wholesale firms. Initially few in number, these manufactories quickly
emerged as the industry's main centers of employment. By 1850, although
only nine manufactories (6.6 percent of all furniture establishments) employed more than fifty people, they nevertheless accounted for 59.4 percent
of the industry's workforce — a percentage they maintained for the next
twenty years.[14]

The third major stage in the transformation of furniture production — the era of modern industry — began shortly after the Panic of
1873. As the city's economy grew increasingly depressed and money scarce,
local and regional demand for furniture shifted away from the more expensive products of the small artisan shops toward the less refined, but
cheaper goods of the factory. Moving to reduce the risks of bankruptcy,
which were, as the Chamber of Commerce noted, particularly high among
the industry's "small producers," manufacturers and other capitalists pooled
considerable sums of money and applied them to the construction of a
"number of large manufacturing establishments."[15] These mammoth factories, often chartered as corporations, struggled to survive the vicissitudes
of depression by further increasing the scale and quantity of production
and reorganizing the "business end" of the industry. By 1880, although
small shops still vastly outnumbered large factories, the latter employed
75.3 percent of the workforce. Moreover, 52.6 percent of all furniture
workers labored in factories employing more than 100 people (as compared
with 44.5 percent in 1870 and 30.4 percent in 1850).[16]

For many furniture workers, the ensuing growth of these
larger, more highly mechanized and routinized factories, led to a further
diminution in the breadth and range of skills required for production. The
rapid and widespread adoption of new machinery, noted one observer in
1877, had "to a very great extent done away with the skills and experience
so absolutely necessary a few years ago to the making of furniture."[17] Work
assumed a more highly specialized and systematized form in these new
corporate factories. At the Sextro Furniture Company, established in the
midst of the depression, the manufacturing process was so "systematically
arranged" that a simple table or rack wound up passing through 20 or 25

hands before it reached the warehouse.[18] Operations at the Mitchell and Rammelsberg factory grew so large that by 1880 its 600 workers were spread out among five buildings, each devoted to a particular phase of the production process. Indeed, a survey in 1878 of 139 of the state's leading furniture establishments revealed that operations had been so intricately divided that only 60 percent of the industry's workforce were categorized as skilled laborers.[19]

The new emphasis on the more intricate division of labor and increased mechanization of production can be partially seen from the following table, taken from the *Thirteenth Annual Report of the Commissioner of Labor,* which compares the number of operations, workers, time, and labor costs of production at different stages of industrial development.

Whatever the product, the general results were the same: division of labor, particularization of skills, and mechanization of production allowed factory artisans to produce the same quantity of goods in a shorter amount of time and at a substantial reduction in labor costs. "Confined to a speciality" and working exclusively "by the piece," a factory employee, concluded a state report in 1877, could "turn out an immense quantity of work." Yet despite his high productivity, the worker's wage bore "no proportion to the work done."[20]

This new era of industrialization did not eliminate the need for skilled craftsmen. Carvers, turners, sawyers, and other skilled furniture men found "constant employment" throughout the 1880s.[21] Although assisted in part by new machines, these men continued to hew and shape wood largely through the guidance of the hand and the traditional knowledge of the craft. The factory artisan, observed one census official, was "always the master of the machine, and never the machine the master of the opertive."[22] Nevertheless, by the last two decades of the century it was clear that the furniture artisan had given way to the factory artisan. By 1890, 86.8 percent of those engaged in general furniture production (exclusive of coffins, billiard tables, and chairs) labored in one of the city's 62 factories, while only 13.2 percent (476 men) continued to ply their craft in time-honored ways amid the city's 106 custom shops.[23]

Carriage and Wagon Workers

In no industry was the transition from handicraft shops to large-scale factory production accomplished more rapidly than in the city's carriage and wagon industry. Unlike the furniture trade, where the transition took

Table 5.3 Comparison of Furniture Production By Hand and By Machine Methods in Individual Factories, 1850–1897

Type of Article	Quantity	Year of Production		Different Operations Performed		Different Workmen Employed		Time Worked				Labor Cost	
		Hand	Machine	Hand	Machine	Hand	Machine	Hand Hours	Hand Minutes	Machine Hours	Machine Minutes	Hand	Machine
Bureaus	12	1850	1897	9	15	3	15	120	—	60	6.0	$21.15	9.19
Bureaus	12	1866	1896	18	21	1	36	443	—	108	40.8	110.75	21.72
Bedsteads	12	1866	1897	15	35	5	52	571	—	41	6.4	141.90	6.07
Bedsteads	12	1860	1895	14	43	2	55	246	—	43	18.0	49.20	5.95
Chairs	12	1845	1897	24	58	7	51	92	—	13	21.9	9.50	2.01
Chairs	12	1856	1895	15	28	10	36	181	—	47	55.8	18.76	8.84
Desks	12	1852	1897	10	111	1	82	792	—	266	1.1	108.00	46.53
Desks	12	1850	1897	10	80	1	67	396	—	257	39.2	54.00	49.75
Tables	12	1860	1894	13	27	3	20	564	—	83	16.8	87.60	12.84
Tables	12	1867	1896	17	21	1	10	354	30.0	134	24.4	88.63	25.39

SOURCE: U.S. Commissioner of Labor, Thirteenth Annual Report of the Commissioner of Labor, 1898 Hand and Machine Labor, 2 vols. (Washington, 1899), 1, 46–49.

place over the course of several decades, virtually the entire carriage industry was altered within a single decade. As late as 1870, carriage making, although growing in importance, was still a minor handicraft industry in Cincinnati; it produced $1.4 million worth of goods and employed 1,081 workers. Ten years later, the Queen City manufactured more carriages and wagons than any other city in the nation. The value of goods produced exceeded $5.9 million a year and the number of employees more than tripled, to 3,707. By 1891, Cincinnati manufacturers so dominated the national market that the value of Cincinnati's annual product was twice that of its nearest competitor, New York.[24]

While a number of factors contributed to the meteoric rise of this industry, the onset of its productive transformation can be traced to Lowe Emerson and J. W. Fisher, who in 1872 pioneered the use of interchangeable parts in carriage production, an innovation which enabled them to manufacture vast numbers of ready-made carriages. "Prior to 1872," one manufacturers' report observed, "there was no wholesale trade in carriages; there were custom shops but nothing was made for the trade."[25] Carriages were produced in small shops, with masters often relying upon the services of a number of independent and allied craftsmen — wheel-wrights, blacksmiths, upholsterers — to help them produce a finished product. In 1870 only one manufacturer employed more than 100 workers. However, as numerous masters and manufacturers followed the lead of Emerson and Fisher, an industry previously geared toward turning out a small number of quality carriages was transformed into one oriented toward the manufacture of inexpensive, mass-produced vehicles which were sold throughout the United States, Europe, Latin America, and even Australia. The conversion from small shops to large factories occurred so quickly that by 1880 the value of production in the two leading carriage firms exceeded the entire city output of 1870.[26] Indeed, by 1880 small artisan shops employed less than 15.7 percent of the workforce, while large manufactories employed 84.3 percent — 61.8 percent of whom worked in factories of 100 or more employees.[27]

Emerson and Fisher reorganized work routines by placing greater emphasis on the specialization of work assignments and the syste-matization of the production flow within the factory. Several hundred workers and vast quantities of raw materials were brought into the factory with the aim of building more carriages in less time and for less money than ever before. Carriage work, like the inaugural stages of wholesale furniture production, was divided into a series of component operations with artisans assigned to special departments. Each man was expected to apply a particular skill to only one or two phases of the construction process. However, unlike the path taken by the furniture industry, the rise of large carriage factories was immediately accompanied by the introduction of and widespread reliance upon the latest and most highly developed steam-powered machinery.[28]

From the factory artisan's point of view, industrialization, while seemingly bringing greater profits to manufacturers, threatened to diminish his wages in accordance with the diminished use of his skills. Opportunities for opening one's own shop or even securing alternative forms of employment declined in the face of the rapid expansion of more costly and highly specialized factories. Unlike their artisan predecessors, the factory artisans of the 1880s were no longer complete carriagemakers, but specialized bodymakers, wheelmakers, trimmers, painters, woodwork-ers, and engineers.[29] Although perhaps exaggerating the plight of the carriage worker, State Labor Commissioner Alonzo Fassett shared the factory artisan's concern for the allegedly undesirable effects of industrialization:

> In the old days, before machinery supplanted the mechanic, it took a man to drive the jack plane, shape the iron and construct the vehicle; now a delicate child guiding a machine can do most of this work. . . . Invention has centralized the industry, and the effect makes it more difficult to find remunerative employment. It has not only made the productive power of each person intensely greater, but it has brought new productive forces as competitors in the gainful occupations.[30]

Printing and Publishing Workers

During the first decades of the nineteenth century, masters, journeymen, and apprentices, working amid the city's small shops, were able to meet the community's modest needs for printed materials. However, as local and regional demand for newspapers, books and commercial work increased rapidly in the 1830s and 1840s, printing entrepreneurs gradually divided the trade into three separate areas: newspapers, publishing houses, and jobbing shops. For Cincinnati's journeymen printers, these changes brought a steady decline in their range of skills, shop autonomy, and prospects for independence.

The most dramatic changes in the nature of work and in the role of the worker first occurred within the city's newspaper establishments. With Cincinnati's emergence as a major western newspaper center in the 1820s and 1830s, the master artisan who had risen through the ranks of the craft to own and operate his own shop was gradually replaced, as we saw in chapter 2, by a new breed of more capitalistically oriented publishers. Their success in dividing and reorganizing work, employing new steam-powered machinery, and undermining their workers' control over production enabled them to transform their trade from a small craft operation based upon strong traditions of worker autonomy and familial ties into a more highly specialized capitalistic industry.[31]

Finding traditional methods of production inadequate to meet the growing demand for newspapers, men such as Stephen L'Hommedieu, publisher of the Cincinnati Gazette, moved to increase the speed and output of their operations in the early 1840s by replacing their slow hand presses with much swifter and more productive steam-powered machines. Having already limited the tasks of his journeymen to composing and presswork (reporting and editing having been assigned to other "specialists"), L'Hommedieu further reduced the range of skills exercised by his artisans by assigning many of them only to the task of mastering his new equipment. Although a first-rate artisan was capable of running off 200 to 300 sheets per hour on the newspaper's old Stanhope hand press — a machine that required the knowledge of thirteen distinct operations, L'Hommedieu found that his new steam-powered press allowed a slightly less proficient man to turn out over 800 pages in the same time. L'Hommedieu's success soon prompted other publishers to adopt his methods.[32]

The publishers' joy over these new arrangements was not shared by their journeymen, for printers saw the adoption of steam-powered presses and the accompanying division of labor as threats to their skills and job security. New presses were developed which required even less skill to operate, and journeymen bitterly complained that publishers were able to expand their workforce and reduce costs by hiring "stupid half-breed workmen" rather than "real genuine artisans — men of taste and genius, who understand the business in all its branches."[33] These new machines, one printer lamented in 1870, could "be managed, more or less, by partially skilled workmen and learners."[34] While many pressmen remained skilled workers throughout the century, they were no longer trained or used as all-round printers; they became press "specialists," often working on and gaining a knowledge of only one particular type of machine.

Although press work was affected by mechanization relatively early in the century, typesetting — or composing — persisted as a strictly handicraft operation until the last quarter of the century. While many printers bemoaned the decline of presswork into a mere "mechanical exercise," composing was still generally thought of as the "more intellectual portion of typographic handicraft."[35] The compositor, the most skilled and autonomous of all newspaper workers, was responsible for selecting the proper type face, setting the type, justifying the lines, laying out the page, proofreading, and locking type into a case ready for the printing press. Moreover, compositors had to perform their tasks with great speed as well as accuracy.

The introduction of automatic composing machines in the 1880s gradually undercut the skills and authority of the city's compositors. The first piano-like composing machine divided the compositors' work among three men: one to operate the keyboard, another to justify the lines, and a third to redistribute the type. Although these machines still required a high degree of skill and dexterity, the new linotype machines of the early 1890s reduced the number of necessary workers to one or two skilled men. Whereas a good hand compositor might set 2,000 ems an hour, a team of less-skilled men trained at these machines could type out 4,000 to 6,000 ems in the same time.[36]

Further innovations in the printing process — stereotyping, electrotyping, and photoengraving — although opening up new avenues of employment, led to an even greater specialization and fragmentation of the printer's trade. As the work, skills, and needs of printers grew more divergent, pressmen, stereotypers, and others left the all-encompassing ranks of the Cincinnati Typographical Union and established their own separate organizations. By the early 1880s, the varying interests of the industry's workforce were protected by seven distinct unions.[37]

These changes in the division and specialization of labor were also accompanied by attacks upon traditions of self-regulation and worker-controlled apprenticeship programs. During the first decades of the century, the internal workings of the printing shop were governed and supervised by the journeymen's "chapel." These "chapels," explained the members of Cincinnati Typographical Union No. 3, were responsible for drawing "up the rules for the government of the room" and regulating "whatever pertains to the quality and amount of work done, conduct of the men, and the needs of the paper.[38] Although union shops were often able to maintain chapel traditions, those laboring in nonunion establishments — roughly half of the city's shops in the latter part of the century — found their assignments, as well as the pace and regulation of work, increasingly dictated by publisher-appointed foremen. Moreover, publishers in union and nonunion shops alike were frequently successful in limiting the present and future power of their workers by ignoring traditional training programs, which limited the tasks and numbers of apprentices in any one establishment and by hiring large numbers of men whom they trained to perform only a small number of operations. "Many of the evils that attend the prosecution of type- and press-work," one angry journeyman objected in 1870, "arise from the want of a good system of apprenticeship, now almost totally ignored throughout our country." This dismal state of affairs, he continued, had resulted in a rising number of "pseudo-printers . . . [men] with a want of proper appreciation of the typographic art," who were used by publishers "to degrade and cheapen" the status of the artisan.[39]

The increased demand for printed matter in the first half of the century also spawned the development of a new kind of capitalistic enterprise — the publishing house. Until the mid-1830s, all publishing and commercial work was done by a single, all-purpose shop. However, in 1835, Ephraim Morgan abandoned his newspaper concern and opened the city's first establishment exclusively devoted to publishing books and magazines. Morgan's rapid success soon encouraged other printers and businessmen to specialize. Indeed, publishing houses expanded so rapidly that by 1856 Cincinnati reigned as the leading publishing center in the West and the fourth largest in the nation — a position it maintained into the 1880s.[40]

The specialization of labor and diminution of skills which slowly altered the nature of newspaper work were even more pronounced inside the city's larger publishing concerns. By 1859, William Smith, the nation's leading publisher of school books (a success due in large part to Smith's ability to finagle William McGuffey, author of the country's most popular textbook, out of his copyright), had separated his 120 workers into three contiguous buildings, each performing a different phase of the production process: printing, binding, and shipping. Smith's firm was able to speed up and economize the cost of manufacture and employ more "efficient means of carrying on every department of their business to the best advantage." He purchased the latest machinery, had its operatives specialize in particular tasks, and employed steam elevators and a steam railway system to carry materials within and between their various buildings. "Order, system, and perfect execution of duty," remarked one duly impressed visitor, prevailed throughout the company's operations.[41]

Journeymen printers in these estalishments also found their working conditions significantly altered by the growing use of stereotyping and the "petticoat invasion" of the 1850s — the hiring of women as compositors and pressworkers. The perfection of stereotyping — the manufacture of a molded duplicate of the initial type face of a book — undermined the job security of compositors by frequently eliminating the need to reset subsequent editions. Furthermore, since books and periodicals were printed under less severe time constraints than daily newspapers, publishers were able to reduce their costs by employing less proficient printers (who received lower wages than their newspaper brethren), as well as large numbers of semi- and unskilled laborers. As women were often forced to work for less money than journeymen or "two-thirders," they proved particularly attractive to cost-conscious publishers. Touring one of the city's larger publishing houses in 1854, printer-turned-author William Coggeshall was struck by the presence of some fifty women busily engaged in setting type. "And we have no doubt type-setting is to become a regular employment for a large number of females." Women, Coggeshall continued, were also making dramatic forays into the pressrooms of the city's publishing concerns. Charles Morgan, he noted, was able to reduce his expenses, as well as to rid himself of the troublesome presence of union printers, by employing thirteen women to work alongside his twelve regular pressmen.[42]

Smith and other book publishers also radically altered the nature of their bookbinding operations. Journeymen who once performed these chores as part of the process of completing a book now found themselves replaced, or their labors limited, by the increased use of women and girls. Assigned to work at one of many subdivided tasks, "neatly-dressed, intelligent females," observed the ever-present Charles Cist, were "engaged in folding the sheets, arranging them in proper order, and . . . stitching and sewing them, with the aid of machinery."[43] Unlike journeymen printers, who still exercised a modest degree of control over their work, management-hired supervisors assumed greater control over the setting of the work routines, wages, and pace of production in publishing houses. Although males continued to dominate the trade, by 1880 women and children constituted 33 percent of the workforce in the city's eight largest publishing firms.[44]

By the latter part of the century, only the city's jobbing establishments — small shops which usually handled modest commercial jobs such as printing posters, sheet music, business forms and cards, and so on — continued to operate along traditional lines. Unable to afford expensive steam-powered presses, jobbers relied heavily upon the traditional skills and work routines of compositors and pressmen. Yet even these unmechanized shops experienced changes which many journeymen viewed with grave concern. The higher costs entailed by the labor intensive nature of these small shops, as well as the severe competition among the city's numerous jobbers, forced many masters to overstock their establishments with low-paid boys and, occasionally, women.[45]

The attractiveness of job work was also offset by the consistently lower wages paid to regular journeymen. Compositors and pressmen working in these shops in the late 1870s earned anywhere from 10 to 30 percent less than those employed in newspaper establishments.[46] Consequently, many printers were faced with the choice of continuing artisanal traditions in the poorly paying job shops or forsaking the small-shop setting in favor of the higher wages offered by newspapers and some publishing houses. Yet, while many journeymen might aspire toward higher wages, few could expect to become their own masters. The vastly increased costs of machinery and other equipment needed to start up a shop, and the stiff competition which they faced from other jobbers and newspapers — which also maintained job shops — meant that most printers, like their counterparts in other trades, would remain wage laborers. In any event, by 1890 capitalists had so transformed the industry as to leave its 4,194 workers more divided than almost any other group of craftsmen.

Boot and Shoeworkers

The transformation of the shoe industry from handicraft to modern industry stretched out over several decades. Unlike the furniture or printing industry, where mechanization initially played a small but important role in altering traditional forms of production, the initial changes in boot and shoemaking were brought about as a consequence of changing market structures, the increased centralization of labor, the more extensive division of labor, and the development of new hand tools. As late as 1841, said Charles Cist, "the entire consumption of leather here, was by custom-work boot and shoemakers." Surplus leather not used by local artisans was sent eastward where it was made into ready-to-wear shoes.[47] However, by the mid-1840s, a number of ambitious masters, such as M. A. Westcott, C. W. Williams, L. L. Filey and L. Chapin, hoping to displace eastern manufacturers as the main suppliers of ready-to-wear shoes for the burgeoning western market, abandoned their small shops and entered the field as wholesale boot and shoe manufacturers.[48] Shoemaking, like the furniture industry, soon divided into two distinct sectors: traditional custom shops and wholesale manufactories, each operating in different ways and each supplying different markets. By 1860, the industry's 1,795 workers labored either in one of the city's 31 manufactories, its 314 shops, or, in some instances, at home as outworkers.

The new forms of labor organization initiated by wholesale manufacturers altered the nature of production and the composition of the workforce well before steam-powered machinery made its way into their shops. Moving their operations from a small shop to a large warehouse, the Filey and Chapin Company, the "greatest shoe factory in the world" exclaimed one visitor in 1851, divided their 150 employees into eight separate rooms, each devoted to one particular aspect of production.[49] Instead of having their journeymen work on one shoe at a time, Filey and Chapin, like their eastern counterparts, "carved up their crafts into a range of repetitive tasks distinguished by quick and easy mastery of simple techniques."[50] In addition to restructuring customary work patterns, wholesale manufacturers also endeavored to lower their costs by "grinding the wages of the operatives to the lowest point of subsistence."[51] While journeymen continued to perform the most highly skilled operations of the trade, such as cutting, lasting and bottoming, large numbers of boys were hired to do the rough work involved in preparing the leather and women and girls to perform the relatively simple stitching and binding operations. Machinery did not make its way into these factories until the adaptation of sewing machines to the making of uppers in the early 1850s — an innovation which did not appreciably affect artisans since the sewing of uppers had already been assigned to women.[52]

Despite these early efforts to reorient traditional forms of production, large manufactories did not readily replace small artisan shops. Unlike the furniture industry, where wholesale operations proved an immediate success, attempts to produce shoes upon "an extensive scale," the Chamber of Commerce reported in 1860, frequently "proved unprofitable"

— or at least less profitable than custom work.[53] Journeymen continued to work in relatively small shops longer than in most other major trades: 79 percent of the workforce in 1850 and 60.8 percent in 1870 labored in shops employing less than fifty people.[54] "Every ante-bellum shoemaker," explained one observer, "was or could be his own employer, and boots and shoes passed directly from the producer to the customer."[55] Indeed, as late as the mid-1860s, masters like German immigrant Lorenz Puchta still found it most profitable to increase their production by employing greater numbers of outworkers who completed their tasks at home, often aided by their wives and children.[56]

Despite the persistence of traditional methods of production, by the late 1860s and 1870s the reign of the artisan came under siege. "Until quite recently," the state's labor commissioner noted in 1875, "boots and shoes, both for men and women's wear, were made entirely by hand, and generally by individual workmen, who worked independently of one another."[57] The successful adoption of a vast array of new machinery by their eastern counterparts — leveling machines, heel burnishing machines, sandpaper machines, and more sophisticated sewing machines which could both stitch shoe uppers and attach them to soles — led Cincinnati manufacturers to buy new machines, hire greater numbers of workers, and initiate even greater specialization and divisions of labor. "In no manufacturing business," reported the Bureau of Labor Statistics in 1878, "has machinery made such rapid changes as that of making boots and shoes."[58]

As more shoe manufacturers began to produce for regional and national markets, and small shops gave way to larger factories, skills and production techniques were severely altered. By 1880, 70.3 percent of all shoemakers worked in factories employing more than 50 people, with 60 percent laboring in establishments of more than 100 employees.[59] Journeymen entering these large edifices of production found their skills steadily eroded by the increased particularization of work assignments. Instead of one artisan working on one pair of shoes until it was completed, the new generation of factory artisans were divided into highly systematized "teams" of four men: the *heeler,* who took the shoe from the sewing machine (usually operated by women), placed lasts on them, leveled the bottoms, and put on the heel; the *trimmer,* who trimmed the heel and shaped the shoe; the *burnisher,* who set the edge, stoned the heel, and applied the initial layer of polish; and, the *finisher,* who buffed the shoe, made the shank, and prepared the final product for shipping. Teams were further divided into first, second, and third class production units, with each receiving a decreasingly lower piece rate for their work. Whereas in 1851 an accomplished journeyman working in one of the early wholesale manufactories could be expected to complete six pairs of shoes in a day, the four-person team of the 1870s could produce upward of thirty to forty pairs a day.[60]

With the gradual disappearance of artisan-controlled apprenticeship from the factory, the expertise and breadth of skills possessed by older craftsmen were slowly lost to newer generations of young workers. Boys entering shoe factories in the 1870s were rarely taught the complexities of the craft, for they were hired, "not that they might learn a trade, but that their cheap labor might be utilized." The "pretense of teaching them a trade," noted another critic of the new system, was "not even kept up."[61]

Unions made vigorous efforts to prolong the power and importance of the artisanal shoemaker, but like so many of their counterparts in other trades, in the decades after 1873 their world was transformed by industrialization. Although the number of custom shops rose from 340 in 1871 to 606 in 1890, the number of masters and journeymen laboring in those establishments declined from 1,500 to 1,224 — the latter representing only 23.5 percent of the industry's workers. Factory artisans also found the composition and cultural traditions of the once male-dominated trade dramatically altered by the employment of large numbers of women. The intricate division of labor into a series of semi-skilled operations allowed manufacturers to lower costs by hiring women to perform shoe-fitting operations. By 1890, over 1,400 women (36.4 percent of the industry's factory operatives) were employed on a regular basis — a number and percentage surpassed only by the clothing industry. The growth and success of these wholesale operations was such that by 1890 Cincinnati ranked second only to Massachusetts in the production of boots and shoes.[62]

Metalworkers

"For years," remarked one iron molder in 1877, "the city of Cincinnati has been looked upon as the leading foundry city of the west."[63] Indeed, in the decades following the rise of the steamboat, manufacturers succeeded in transforming the various metal trades into one of the nation's largest and most important industrial centers. During the second half of the century,

Cincinnati reigned as the country's leading manufacturer of machine tools and safes and one of the largest producers of foundry and machine goods, stoves, mantels, grates, and hardware. The number of workers employed in these various endeavors rose from 1,507 in 1841 to 4,656 in 1860 and to over 7,000 by 1880.[64]

Since the rise of these "new" industries has been elaborately detailed in a series of recent works, we shall only explore some of their key changes.[65] During the early decades of the nineteenth century, when masters directed most of their energies toward meeting the needs of the steamship industry, metalworking was divided among a number of independent establishments. Raw material produced in the foundry, often with the aid of outside patternmakers, would pass to a hardware or machine shop and finally to a separate metal-finishing establishment. By the late 1830s, however, as metal and machine manufacturers moved into new areas of production — stoves, sugar mills, cotton gins, etc. — they endeavored to increase their volume and efficiency, while lowering costs by consolidating these previously independent operations into a single enterprise under the control of a single boss. Rather than relying upon others to provide him with goods and services, manufacturers like Miles Greenwood moved to regularize and cheapen operations by building their own foundries, blacksmith, machine, and finishing shops on a single lot.[66]

These early changes, then, were primarily directed at centralizing production. They did not, as in other crafts, severely alter the nature of traditional skills. Although new machines and production techniques introduced in subsequent decades permitted the handling and fabricating of bigger products, the continued reliance upon highly skilled hand labor to transform raw materials into finished products enabled puddlers, molders, machinists, patternmakers, and the like, to preserve their skills and control over production longer than most other artisans. Describing a situation which held true for most of the city's metalworkers, one iron molder noted in 1873 that "unlike other branches of mechanism, the introduction of machinery has in no manner assisted at increased production; the entire increase of individual production comes from the muscle and sweat of the molder."[67] Thus the persistent labor-intensive nature of their industry and their superior knowledge of their craft allowed journeymen metalworkers to preserve the right to hire, fire, and supervise their assistants and helpers and to govern daily operations far longer and more effectively than most other factory artisans.[68]

While mechanization did not intrude deeply upon the skills

of these "labor aristocrats," as historian Eric Hobsbawm has called them, by midcentury, and most especially in the last quarter of the century, metalworkers often found their skills and autonomy eroded by the reorganization and increased specialization of their labor. Iron molders, previously accustomed to performing all the operations of their craft, soon found their work assignments divided among three "specialists": the floor molder, who continued to prepare the largest and most complex molds; the bench molder, who prepared smaller molds which required less strength, skill, and dexterity; and the core molder, an even less skilled man, who prepared dry-sand cores.[69] Similarly, stove molders also found their skills and customs radically altered in the late 1860s by the introduction of the "cutting up" system. Instead of having journeymen build an entire stove, as had been their tradition, manufacturers sought to speed up production by dividing, or "cutting up," the work among three men: one made the stove top, another the bottom, and another the side. Moreover, complained one unhappy stovemaker, instead of allowing journeymen to decide who would perform each operation, manufacturers instructed their foremen to work a man at all three jobs until he "gets to know what is his 'best hold,' and he is usually retained on that class of work" forever.[70]

The increased specialization of labor, declining control over apprenticeship, and rise of the machine-tool industry wrought equal havoc among the city's machinists. Until the late 1870s, machinists generally worked either as bench hands — men who shaped the raw metal with hand tools — or as floor hands — workers who took the bench hands' product and assembled it into a finished engine. In either instance, these men "still 'guided the tool rather than the other way around,' which left considerable latitude for judgment and need for a trained hand."[71] However, the rise of the machine-tool industry and the ensuing specialization of labor during the last quarter century gradually revolutionized the character of the trade by producing "powerful machine tools, which do the work faster and with greater accuracy than was possible under the old conditions."[72] As new machine tools were perfected and work assignments were further specialized, there gradually arose, as one historian has noted, an "important distinction, which was formally unknown, between the all-around machinist, who can interpret a blue-print and execute any part of the work required by it with any tool or machine, and the specialist (e.g., the planer hand or the slotting-machine hand), who can only do work of a particular kind on a particular machine."[73] Moreover, lamented one former machinist, the manufacturers' success in eliminating "any system in our workshops whereby our boys can be educated in the arts, sciences and mysteries of mechanical industries" condemned future generations of workers to "technical ignorance" and greater insecurity.[74]

Factory Laborers

Industrialization also fostered the creation of a new kind of worker — the factory laborer. These were the men, women, and children who worked at the tedious and unskilled tasks created by greater divisions of labor and reorganizations of production in the factory system. They were the assistants of iron molders, the press feeders who aided pressmen, the shippers and helpers in tobacco factories, the page folders in publishing houses, the caners in chair establishments — in short, an unskilled labor force which helped to maximize production within essentially skilled industries.

There were two distinct paths from which factory laborers emerged. Many factory jobs were created as a consequence of the reorganization of traditional crafts as they passed from handicraft to manufacturing to modern industry. Other workers were utilized in the city's "new" industries, which lacked traditions of artisanal organization and which early in the nineteenth century adopted many of the characteristics of modern industry. Production in these industries was so systematically organized and skills were so limited that factory laborers made up the dominant part of their workforce.

It was the method and control of production, and not simply the size of the workplace and the presence of large numbers of men or machines, which most distinguished these factory laborer-dominated industries from factory-artisanal industries. At its most advanced level of production, modern industry, explains political economist Harry Braverman, was characterized by the "progressive elimination of the control functions of the worker, insofar as possible, and their transfer to a device which is controlled, again insofar as possible, by management from outside the direct [work] process."[75] Although no nineteenth-century Cincinnati industry completely reached this highly advanced stage of industrial development, in the city's meat-processing and pressing/cooking industries the nature of the product, the early division and specialization of labor, the introduction of assembly-line production techniques, and the heavy reliance upon steam-powered machinery resulted in the creation of a labor force which required only a minimal level of necessary skills. In contrast to factory artisans, factory laborers served as attendants to rather than as controllers of machines, as workers who accustomed themselves to, rather than determined, the workflow.

The factory laborer was certainly the most economically vulnerable of all workers. Since the extent of necessary skills tended to be quite limited, new laborers could be trained and put to work in a relatively short time. Consequently, demands for higher wages or protests against poor working conditions and seasonal employment often prompted manufacturers to fire striking workers and replace them with the seemingly ever-present hordes of unskilled and transient laborers.

While the general trend of Cincinnati's major industries was away from labor-intensive production and toward a greater reliance upon capital and machinery, nowhere was this more evident than in the factory-laborer dominated industries. Not surprisingly, the ratio of capital investment to labor costs as a percentage of the annual value of production was significantly higher among factory laborer industries than factory artisanal industries, which in turn were higher than artisanal industries. When looking at the following table, one should bear in mind that the higher the ratio, the more capital-intensive was the industry, and that the lower the ratio, the more labor-intensive it was.[76]

Table 5.4 Ratio of Capital Investment to Labor Costs as a Percentage of the Annual Value of Production Among Cincinnati Industries, 1860–1890

	1860	1870	1880	1890
Construction	1.8	2.0	1.3	1.1
Blacksmithing	− 0.9	—	− 0.7	1.5
Boots & Shoes	− 0.8	− 0.7	− 1.0	1.7
Printing & Publishing	2.0	1.8	2.0	3.0
Furniture	1.9	2.3	2.0	3.0
Carriages & Wagons	1.2	1.6	1.1	2.3
Machinery	1.9	2.6	2.5	2.6
Hardware	1.6	2.2	2.3	2.1
Brewing	7.4	6.3	7.7	8.4
Iron & Steel	1.8	2.5	3.4	2.4
Meat Processing	13.7	12.6	16.7	4.5
Pressing/Cooking	6.8	6.5	6.9	6.5
Clothing	1.3	1.9	2.6	3.1
All City Ratio	2.2	2.7	2.6	2.9

Notes: See chapter 5 note 76 for discussion of methodology.

Once again, we see that the path of industrialization was not the same for all industries. The rise of Cincinnati's factory labor industries can best be explored by examining the development of the meat-processing and pressing/cooking industries.

Meat-Processing Workers

The introduction of assembly-line organization and mass-production techniques did not begin, as is sometimes thought, in the automobile factories of Henry Ford, but in the biscuit manufactories of eighteenth-century England. The first widespread use of this technique in the United States occurred in the early slaughtering and packing houses in Cincinnati. Ford's inspiration for continuous line production came, as he himself noted, "from the overhead trolley that the Chicago packers" used in dressing beef, an innovation which they in turn had adopted from their Cincinnati predecessors.[77]

Although other ante-bellum industries may have employed more workers or utilized greater numbers of machines, none surpassed the meat-processing industry in its rationalization of production and diminution of all necessary skills to their lowest possible level. The development of this industry, and its particular emphasis on and concern about the relationship between time and production, was shaped by a number of critical influences: the brief seasonal character of meat processing, which restricted it to cold-weather months and helped to promote large-scale production; the availability of a vast pool of seasonal laborers; the easy access to outside markets which hog raisers enjoyed from the 1830s onward; and the expansion of national and international markets.[78]

Cincinnati always furnished neighboring areas of the Ohio Valley with their necessary supply of processed pork, but it was not until the early 1830s that local packers sold their products in national and international markets. Production expanded from 25,000 to 35,000 packed hogs a year in the 1820s to 350,000 to 400,000 hogs by the 1850s. One rather imaginative visitor to the "city of pigs" calculated that, if all these hogs were turned into sausages, they "would make a girdle long enough to encompass the whole globe along the line of the equator."[79] By 1851,

Cincinnati had established itself, not only as the "principal pork market in the United States," but as the "largest in the world."[80]

By the 1830s, mass production and intricate particularization of labor tasks were standard procedures among the city's larger packing establishments. "The division of labor," reported one English visitor in 1834, was "brought to as much perfection in these slaughterhouses as in the pin manufactories of Birmingham."[81] Having made the obligatory tour of the city's larger meathouses, western traveler and commentator Charles Fenno Hoffman was similarly impressed by the highly systematized nature of the work process. "The minute division of labor and the fearful celerity of execution in these swinish workshops," he wrote in 1834, "would equally delight a pasha and political economist; for it is the mode in which business is conducted, rather than its extent, which gives dignity to hog killing in Cincinnati."[82]

Slaughtering and packing operations, initially conducted under separate roofs, were so well organized as to create a continuous flow of production which required a minimum amount of time and skill from each worker. In this early "Disassembly Line" process, each worker, rather than moving around the workshop completing a number of different operations, was assigned a particular spot beside a long table, where he awaited the arrival of the soon-to-be dispatched hog. As the carcass passed down the table, each man would perform only one particular operation: cleaning the ears, removing the bristles, scraping the hide, and so forth.[83]

In order to obtain a clearer picture of the early workings of Cincinnati's "pig system," we might follow the fortunes of a typical ill-fated hog as it entered the slaughterhouse of a Mr. Clearwater, and then proceeded, somewhat worse for the visit, to the packing house of Samuel Findlay. Having been unceremoniously driven through the streets of Cincinnati, the country hog entered the rear pens of Clearwater's slaughterhouse, whereupon it was led up a ramp and knocked unconscious by a blow on the head. A worker pushed the hog down a long incline and on to the slaughtering table. Upon the animal's arrival, the worker manning the first station cut its throat. The carcass then passed down to two scalders who placed it into a boiling tub. After a short time, the body was removed and passed to four scrapers, who, after removing the hair and bristles, passed it to six shavers. Having subjected the carcass to a final cleaning, the shavers pushed it down the table to the off-bearers, who hung it up and gave it over to the washers. The slaughtered animal was removed to the dry house and allowed to hang for several days. In addition to these various operations, the hog's entrails and excess fat were removed by a gutter and given to the gut cleaner, who readied them for delivery to one of the city's many soap, candle, and oil manufacturers.[84]

Once the carcass was completely dried, it was taken to a packing house like that of Samuel Findlay's, where a similarly elaborate assembly-line process was employed. The hog was hoisted to the top story of the building and passed downward through a number of different rooms, where specialists waited to complete their one particular asignment. After the packers had completely disassembled the carcass and placed the meat into separate barrels containing bacon, ribs, steaks, mess pork, and the like, the final product was moved to nearby docks and loaded on to waiting boats.[85]

Although no machinery was used in these ante-bellum establishments, the work rhythms of these meat men assumed a machine-like precision. Dazzled by the activities which he observed in one Cincinnati slaughterhouse, Frederick Law Olmstead wrote the following account of his visit:

> Walking down to the vanishing point we found there a sort of human chopping machine where the hogs were converted into commercial pork. A plank table, two men to lift and turn, two to wield the cleavers, were its component parts. No iron cog-wheels could work with more regular motion. Plump falls the hog upon the table, chop, chop, chop, chop, chop, chop, fall the cleavers. All is over. . . . Amazed beyond all expectations at the celerity, we took out our watches and counted thirty-five seconds from the moment one hog touched the table until the next occupied its place.[86]

The efficiency of production was further increased by the integration of slaughtering and packing operations, the adoption of the horizontal wheel and loop in the 1850s, and the introduction of the overhead railway track in the early 1860s. The former mechanism enabled manufacturers to eliminate much of the unnecessary space and motion required of table work. After killing, scalding, and scraping operations had been completed, gambrel sticks were affixed between the hog's legs and the carcass was hoisted on to one of eight large hooks surrounding the outer edge of an overhead wheel six feet high and ten feet wide. The hog was then easily swung from worker to worker, who each performed his assignment in close proximity to the next. After the animal was completely dressed, the carcass was lifted from the hook and brought to a nearby cooling room.[87]

The overhead railway track further reduced production time. It was an extensive overhead pulley system, which allowed carcasses to be quickly sent to all parts of the factory by the mere push of the hand. Inspecting one "model pork house" in the winter of 1862, a local reporter concluded that, while this new machinery was "very simple" in nature, by moving carcasses past workers in rapid succession it reduced the amount of time required for killing, cutting, and rendering to one half that of smaller non-assemby-line establishments. Furthermore, by eliminating the need for any manual conveyance and maximizing the regularity of production, the overhead railway track enabled two or three men to do the work previously performed by ten or twelve.[88]

During the following decades, the continued introduction of new machinery increased the speed at which animals moved from pig pen to barrel and further minimized the already low skills of Cincinnati's meat workers. Whereas in 1850 none of the industry's leading producers relied upon steam-powered machinery, by 1870, 13.3 percent of the large wholesale establishments utilized some kind of steam power. Ten years later, all 20 of the 39 leading meat houses that reported their sources of motive power indicated that they used steam machines. By 1890, the meat-processing industry ranked sixth in the value of machinery per operative, placing it ahead of machine making, metalworking, and textiles.[89]

While mechanization seemingly jeopardized the job security of meat workers, one invention, refrigeration, benefited both employer and employee. The introduction and perfection of refrigeration equipment in the late 1860s and early 1870s turned slaughtering and packing into year-round activities. Not only did refrigeration add to the wealth of manufacturers, but it also helped to make meatpacking a permanent trade for many workers. The previous seasonal nature of meatpacking meant that few men could afford to earn their livings solely as meat workers. Owners generally drew their employees from the vast number of eager job-seeking transient workers who flooded the city in winter months, or from the ranks of Cincinnati's construction workers, who frequently found themselves in need of employment during slack winter months.[90]

For these workers, often desperate for employment at any pay, the low skill requirements of the industry worked to their benefit. With the coming of refrigeration and the inauguration of a summer packing season, this transient element of the working class took on a more stable and permanent form. Wage demands and organizational efforts, which in winter months could easily be ignored by employers, assumed new dimensions during the summer months—a time of labor shortages in Cincinnati. Here then, was one of the many contradictory tendencies of industrialization. It generally acted to fragment and reduce the power of workers. Yet, as Cincinnati's meat-processing industry shows, it could also create new, more secure opportunities for employment.

Pressing/Cooking Workers

Another industry, or rather industries, in which the factory laborer played a dominant role early in the century was the pressing/cooking industry. As the production of soap, oil, candles, paints, chemicals, medicines, and drugs all involved similar combinations of pressing, grinding, mixing, cooking, and cooling, and as many of these products — although listed as separate endeavors in census returns—were manufactured within the same plant, these technologically related operations are herein grouped together.

At the beginning of the nineteenth century, the manufacture of these various products required little proficiency on the part of the general work force. Some skills were needed, but production generally relied more upon human strength than expertise. The manufacture of soap, the most important of these constituent pursuits in Cincinnati, involved four basic stages of production in the 1820s and 1830s: boiling, mixing, drying, and cutting. The prime ingredient, lard, was placed in a large cauldron and boiled together with assorted salts and chemicals until the mixture separated into two basic substances: soap and lye. Using a long-handled dipper, workmen removed the liquid soap and placed it into smaller buckets, which were carried into the framing house and poured into wooden frames. After drying for four or five days, the soap was separated from the frame and cut into slabs by workers using a hand wire tool. The finished product was then packed and sent off to market.[91]

By the early 1840s, a relatively minor local kettle trade was rapidly expanding into a mechanized, steam-aided, international industry. Steam rendering — the process of separating fats and oils from animal tissue — made it possible to obtain fat, not only from kidneys and bowels, as had hitherto been the case, but from the entire carcass. Hence, manufacturers were able to achieve vast increases in the quantity of lard extracted from each animal at no extra cost. In the following decades, as new

machinery helped to cheapen and maximize soap production, annual output rose from 2,708 boxes of soap in 1845–1846, to 42,182 boxes in 1855
– 1856, to 271,636 in 1875 – 1876, and to 1,011,831 boxes in 1890.
Throughout the second half of the century, Cincinnati consistently ranked
as one of the world's leading centers of soap manufacturing.[92]

    While it often helped to increase the profits of manufacturers,
mechanization adversely affected the already low status of soap workers,
either by reducing their primary function to that of machine attendants or
by eliminating their jobs altogether. Hand mixers and soap cutters were
forced to search for new jobs as their unskilled tasks were taken over by
steam-powered blending and cutting machines. Those men whose sole
obligation was to oversee the boiling of liquids found the already slight
discretionary judgment that they used being steadily eliminated. Manufacturers were able to regulate and control necessary boiling time by using
steam coils to heat huge cauldrons. As early as 1859, new labor-saving
machinery allowed the Procter and Gamble Company, the nation's largest
manufacturer of soap and candles that year, to operate its two-factory,
multi-million-dollar business with but eighty employees.[93]

    Given the relatively advanced nature of Cincinnati's soap
industry, it is no surprise that the first extensive survey of Ohio soap and
candle employees, taken in 1878, classified 61.9 percent of the workforce
as unskilled. A survey of one Cincinnati factory, taken a year earlier,
indicated an even higher percentage of factory laborers: 75 of the company's
100 operatives were categorized as unskilled laborers.[94] Although no such
breakdown was recorded for later years, it seems likely that, since many
manufacturers followed the lead of Procter and Gamble, the economic
security of workers grew increasingly tenuous.[95]

    The productive histories of other pressing/cooking operations,
such as the manufacture of candles, oils, chemicals, drugs, and paints,
followed much the same course as that of the soap trade. Charles Cist
observed that by 1859 Cincinnati already contained 24 manufactories —
"mostly on a large scale" — which produced star, adamantine, opal, tallow,
lard oil, red and tallow oil, soap, and glycerine.[96] As in the city's soap
factories, mechanization not only lessened the dependence upon human
control, but also made human presence entirely superfluous in certain
operations. In candle factories, molding machines gradually replaced hand
molders. In oil, paint, medicine, and chemical establishments, hydraulic
presses displaced millstones and other hand-operated crushing devices. In
several factories, like that of chemical manufacturer William Gordon,

mechanization and the regularization of production grew so advanced that only a handful of workers were needed to attend to the machines. In such factories, work requirements were reduced to one or two simple tasks: starting and stopping machines, watching over boiling cauldrons, or simply carrying finished products to various parts of the factory.[97]

Despite its adverse effects upon many workers, mechanization did not always mean an absolute displacement of labor. As more successful manufacturers enlarged their operations and diversified into related areas of manufacture, new workers were hired to fill expanded needs. The development and perfection of new machinery often opened entirely new fields of production. The invention of William Fee's cotton-seed huller in 1857 and its subsequent improvement in later years fostered the inauguration and expansion of the cotton-seed-oil business. The proliferation of mixing and grinding machinery precipitated the growth of a number of firms specializing in the production of ready-made, premixed paints. While only a few men were needed in the basic manufacturing process, large numbers of manual laborers were hired to carry, label, store, and deliver cans of paint. Nevertheless, while industrialization often meant the creation of new jobs as well as the loss of old ones, they were new jobs which, more often than not, reduced workers to the lowest position in the laboring hierarchy — unskilled factory laborers.[98]

Outworkers

Amid the growth of Cincinnati's manufacturing sector, there emerged yet another type of worker — the outworker. This was a mode of labor not so much distinguished by levels of skill — for they varied greatly among outworkers — as by the setting in which work was performed. The "putting out" system, as it was commonly known, was utilized by artisans, manufacturers, and merchant capitalists. Instead of maintaining large numbers of workers in their shops, master shoemakers, such as Timothy Whiting, Henry Castles, and Lorenz Puchta, would take the shoe measurements of their customers, cut out stock and fit up the lasts, and then send the work out to journeymen who, after completing the work at home — where "entire families often worked together or shared responsibilities through an informal division of labor" — would return it to the master's shop.[99] Similarly,

(a)

Figure 6 Inside the Workplace.

(a) Otto Zimmerman's Print Shop (c. 1870s – 1880s). Although compositors (foreground) continued to set type by hand for most of the century, pressworkers (background) found their handicraft status eroded by the introduction of steam-powered presses after the 1830s. (b) L. Schreiber and Sons Iron Works (c. 1889). During the early stages of an industry's development, skilled workers often used machines to assist them in their tasks. (c) The Disassembly Line (c. 1860). Early techniques of assembly-line production were pioneered in Cincinnati's ante-bellum slaughterhouses. (d) Procter and Gamble Soap Packing Operations (c. 1892). The increased division of labor and mechanization of production allowed manufacturers to hire women and children to perform the unskilled aspects of production. (e) Procter and Gamble Heating Ovens (c. 1892). The need for human skills and expertise were dramatically eroded during the latter stages of industrialization. (f) and (g) Cincinnati Artisans (c. 1880s). Industrialization did not signal the complete demise of artisanal production. A number of craftsmen continued to ply their trades in traditional ways.

Courtesy of the Cincinnati Historical Society

(b)

From *Harper's Weekly* (Feb. 4, 1860)

(c)

(d)

(e)

(f)

(g)

manufacturers and merchant-capitalists, particularly those in the clothing trade, attempted to minimize their costs by assigning work to contractors who, in turn, hired people to work on the particular products within the confines of small shops or homes. At the end of the week, the contractor would pick up all the completed goods, pay the workers — usually by the piece — and bring the material to the warehouses or the factories of the manufacturer.[100]

Although outwork persisted as a common practice in many eastern cities through the 1860s, most especially among handloom weavers, shoemakers, tailors, hatters, and cigarmakers, it had become much less common among most Cincinnati trades by the 1850s. A small number of shoemakers and cigarmakers continued to rely upon outworkers, but only clothing manufacturers employed them in significant numbers. Unlike other industries where outwork was merely a supplement to shop or factory production, in clothing production it remained at the heart of the industry and gave work to a majority of its workforce.

Clothing Workers

The rapid growth of the ante-bellum clothing industry in Cincinnati — probably "unprecedented in the United States," insisted one state official — was generally attributed to the interaction of four major factors: increased demand for crude and fine clothing for farmers, sailors, slaves, and city residents; the migration of large numbers of German Jews, who often possessed tailoring skills and modest amounts of capital; the invention of the sewing machine; and the presence of vast numbers of women willing to work for Cincinnati clothing manufacturers.[101] By midcentury, Cincinnati was not only the dominant clothing center of the West; it was also the nation's leading producer of ready-to-wear garments. Thirty years later, only New York produced more clothing than the Queen City.[102]

During the early part of the century, the production of clothing was characterized by a "rough division of labor between the household and the artisan shop."[103] Since women were generally expected to sew their own clothing, journeymen tailors, working either in small custom shops or at home, usually concentrated on making better grades of men's garments. After cutting the fabric in their shops, tailors would often bring unfinished garments home, where their wives and daughters would assist them in simpler sewing operations. The tailor would then take the semifinished product to the shop, where a final fitting and inspection would be made. In addition to a custom trade, the clothing industry also employed several hundred women who worked at home making "slop" goods — inexpensive clothing for farmers, sailors, and slaves — or sewing dresses for wealthier families.[104]

Although custom tailoring remained the purview of skilled journeymen, the influx of large numbers of immigrants in the 1830s and 1840s and the subsequent expansion of "slop" work to include cheaper grades of men's and boy's clothing gave rise to a substantial ready-to-wear clothing trade. Ambitious tailors, particularly recently arrived German Jews such as Jacob Kornblueth and Sebastien Myer, and merchants such as Jacob Elsas, Philip Heidelbach, and Lazarus Bloch — men who had accumulated modest savings while working as peddlers — seized upon this new line of endeavor as an opportunity to obtain greater wealth and independence. Instead of gathering large numbers of workers in a central shop, a move which would have necessitated considerable expenditure for rent, fuel, and equipment, these ready-to-wear clothing entrepreneurs relied upon a contracting system which utilized the services of thousands of female outworkers. Under this early contract system, manufacturers or merchants would buy large lots of cloth which would be cut into a series of basic patterns by the small number of tailors they employed and then given to contractors. The contractors, middlemen with little or no background in the craft, would in turn subcontract the work to individual tailors and large numbers of women who worked at home. After a week or two, the subcontractor would pick up the work, pay his outworkers the agreed-upon piece rate, and then deliver the completed goods to the contractor, who in turn would take it to the manufacturer.[105] Although early census figures did not distinguish between custom and outwork operations, by 1841 the industry's 86 establishments employed 813 men, who worked largely inside the shops, and over 4,000 women, who sewed at home either in Cincinnati or in neighboring areas. Ready-to-wear clothing proved so profitable that by midcentury over 1,500 men and 10,000 women worked for one of the city's 48 wholesale, 86 retail, or 160 merchant tailoring shops.[106]

No group of workers in ante-bellum Cincinnati was so poorly paid or more severely exploited than these outwork women. "If ever a class of individuals were entitled to the special legislation of the country," insisted one workingmen's newspaper in 1844, "it is the . . . [seamstresses who] comprise a large portion of the community, earn a very precarious living, and many of them, in situations anything but comfortable."[107] An investigation into the working conditions of seamstresses, conducted in 1853, revealed that, while an outworker might earn between three and six dollars a week, there were many women who earned only one dollar. Even if they were employed every working day of the week for an entire year, the committee reported, seamstresses, after paying for room and board or contributing to their family's expenses, were frequently left with as little as thirteen dollars a year.[108]

The invention of the sewing machine in the mid-1840s provided a tremendous stimulus to the growth of the ready-to-wear clothing trade and vastly increased the need for outworkers. Early entrepreneurs were frequently frustrated by the slow pace of hand labor and their discovery that garments were often sewn too differently from one another to be sold as part of a ready-to-wear lot. The sewing machine solved these problems by allowing for a standardized stitch which produced a more uniform product in a shorter time. "A person skilled in the use of the machines in operation here," remarked one manufacturer in 1854, "would do as much work as ten ordinary needleworkers."[109] Productivity was further increased by the greater division and specialization of labor. Instead of having women make an entire garment, as had been done in the early period of outwork, employers began subdividing tasks among several women. "As many as seventeen hands," Cist noted in 1859, were often "employed upon a single pair of pants."[110] As the price of machines fell to $35 to $40 by the mid-1850s — $75 to $100 for better models — manufacturers and contractors often purchased large numbers which they lent, rented, or sold to women to use in their homes. Moreover, the adoption of the sewing machine, which required relatively little skill to operate, also expanded the available labor pool by opening up employment to women who had not "properly learned the art" of hand stitching.[111]

During the last half of the century, Cincinnati's ready-to-wear clothing industry, already the largest in the nation, was further altered by two developments: the dramatic upsurge in demand for such clothing during and after the Civil War, and the subsequent proliferation of the "sweating" system. The intense competition for lucrative government contracts to produce thousands of sundry garments for Union soldiers helped to revolutionize the city's ready-to-wear clothing industry by prompting manufacturers to adopt increasingly uniform standards and measurements for the rapid production of vast amounts of clothing. As demand continued to rise in the postwar years, merchants and manufacturers such as Philip Heidelbach, Jacob Elsas, May Fechheimer, Jacob Seasongood, and Jonathan Shillito — all of whom also owned department stores — used the profits accumulated during the war to open large clothing factories which produced goods for their stores as well as retail establishments in other cities. Although they relied upon outworkers to supplement production, they also strove to increase the speed and efficiency of their operations by employing dozens of skilled tailors and women in their new factories. The introduction of new hand tools (the long knife and sword knife) and rotary cutting machines in the 1870s and 1880s, and the increased demand for ready-to-wear women's cloaks and millinery, prompted the further expansion of centralized production.[112] Lured by the prospects of higher pay and more steady work, many of the city's custom tailors abandoned their small shops to work as cutters and inspectors in the new factories. By 1890, although male outworkers continued to outnumber those directly employed in shops and factories (6,213 to 2,248), only 637 tailors labored in more traditional settings, while 1,611 earned their living in the growing number of ready-to-wear clothing factories.[113]

While outwork remained the dominant setting of production in the last quarter century, it, too, assumed new forms. As large numbers of Russian and Polish Jews as well as Italians poured into the city in the 1880s and 1890s, the contracting system of earlier years was gradually superseded by the "sweating" system. Instead of relying upon middlemen to subcontract work to various tailors and seamstresses, manufacturers found that they could lower costs by giving work directly to the growing number of ambitious "sweaters." These "sweaters" were usually immigrant tailors who worked at lower prices than those charged by previous contractors and conducted their operations in abysmal and unsanitary tenement flats — "dark little dens of rooms, with insufficient light, and air, amid surroundings of unutterable filth or squalor." Instead of relying solely upon the labors of their family, sweaters also employed "from six to a dozen 'hired hands'" who traveled from their homes to work inside tenement sweatshops.[114]

Although sweating developed at a slower rate in Cincinnati than in many of the eastern cities where eastern Europeans first migrated, by the early 1890s it served as the central mode of operation within the clothing industry. A committee sent by the state Bureau of Labor Statistics to assess the conditions of the industry in 1894 reported that 83.2 percent of the operations they visited were conducted in family apartments or tenement flats; only 16.8 percent of the 214 workshops they inspected were run out of regular shops or factories.[115] Although sweating did not draw women and children out of the home, as factory labor did, the committee noted that it tended to convert workers' homes into workshops far worse than most outside establishments. In addition to maintaining their traditional family roles and responsibilities, women and children were also converted, often by their husbands and fathers, into exploited wage laborers. Reporting on the squalid condition of work and the increased exploitation of household members and hired hands, the committee described the setting of several "sweatshops" on Central Avenue:

> C-G, a cloak maker, and two helpers, operating three machines, work in a small room fifteen feet square, which is also used as a sleeping room. Bundles of clothing lying about the floor and bed. C-G is making coats at 25 cents each. He pays man helper $5 a week and girl 75 cents a week.
>
> A-S, a Polish Jew, was found making cloaks in the third floor rear of a Central Avenue tenement. The man and his wife cook, eat, and sleep in the same room where the man was working two machines, assisted by a boy of 14, who made sleeves and did the binding, receiving $1.50 a week. The wife was lying sick on the bed and there was dirt and disorder on all sides, the room close and stuffy and the cloaks littering the floor and bed. The house is one of the vilest four-story back tenements in town; bad ventillation and sewerage, decaying swill and rubbish fill the air with fetid odors. A scarlet fever card tacked on rooms on the floor below, and half-naked children were running back and forth freely. Man receives 30 cents a cloak, but does not do the pressing. Only four months employed since July 1893, and average earnings $5 a week in that time.[116]

By 1890, some 24,593 men, women, and children worked in the city's clothing industry, thereby making it the largest employer in Cincinnati. Of the 21,472 people who toiled as operatives and pieceworkers, rather than as sales or office personnel, only 8,145 (37.9 percent) were fortunate enough to secure full-time positions; the remaining 13,327 (62.1 percent) struggled to survive as outworkers.[117]

Work and a Working Class?

In Cincinnati, as elsewhere, industrialization produced a myriad of experiences among workers which acted both to unite and to divide men and women. The factory system on the one hand centralized hundreds of men, women, and children into single buildings, where they often encountered similar challenges to their skills, health, and future economic security — problems which seemed likely to enhance the possibilities of greater mutual understanding and cooperation among workers. Yet industrialization also brought with it a tendency toward the greater separation of workers along lines of skill, sex, ethnicity, age, and wage — changes which often seemed to divide Cincinnati's working class into a number of working classes, the members of which experienced different working conditions, needs and expectations.

The frequent divisions and tensions that plagued working-class life in the years between the 1840s and 1880s were not caused entirely by the rise of the factory system or the actions of capitalists. The vast influx of immigrants during this period served to transform the composition, expectations, and traditions of the city's working class. Tradesmen often found themselves divided not only along lines of skill, but ethnicity as well. Whereas in 1840 native-born workers dominated virtually all major trades and industries, by 1870 they formed a majority in only four and a plurality in just eight more.

Yet, while ethnic hostilities often divided artisans, there were

Table 5.5 Occupational Distribution of the Manufacturing
Workforce By Place of Birth, 1840 – 1870

	1840				1870			
	N-B	Ger	Ire	ESW	N-B	Ger	Ire	ESW[a]
Construction	81.4	4.6	4.6	9.4	39.6	47.0	8.8	5.2
Tailors[b]					51.8	34.8	8.3	2.2
Shoemakers[b]	38.1	38.1	9.5	14.3	30.4	47.2	12.1	5.1
Hatters[b]					45.8	29.2	12.5	8.3
Printers	68.2	22.8	4.5	4.5	69.7	15.9	6.9	4.1
Machinists[c]					49.7	28.3	7.5	8.1
Blacksmiths[c]	52.2	21.7	8.7	17.4	27.0	47.4	18.2	4.1
Iron Molders	88.9	11.0	0.0	0.0	44.0	33.0	10.3	7.5
Tanners & Curriers	50.0	30.0	20.0	0.0	25.6	64.4	4.0	1.5
Laborers	22.2	55.6	18.5	3.7	22.2	37.3	35.6	2.1

SOURCE: Walter Stix Glazer, "Cincinnati in 1840: A Community Profile," Ph.D. diss., University of Michigan, 1968, pp. 261 – 73; Ninth Census: Volume I. The Statistics of the Population of the United States (Washington, 1872), p. 783. These figures do not include the children of foreign-born workers who also constituted a considerable percentage of the trades by 1870.

[a] Abbreviations stand for Native-Born, German, Irish, and English-Scotch-Welsh.
[b] 1840 figures for tailors, shoemakers, and hatters are grouped together.
[c] 1840 figures for machinists and blacksmiths are grouped together.

also issues which drew the common support of the wide range of workers. For many native- and foreign-born artisans, the rise of the factory system "threatened to transform 'the Great Republic of the West' into a 'European' country"; to destroy not only their present way of life, but also their visions of future independence as masters in their own shops.[118] For these men, factories, contrary to the optimistic predictions of capitalists and civic leaders, loomed as visible symbols of impending doom — loathsome institutions which threatened to convert the artisan into a mere proletarian, a dependent member of the industrial rabble.

Despite the protestations of these men, it was not always clear that the factory system was deleterious to the immediate economic well-being of *all* workers. Early generations of Cincinnati factory workers were not oppressed proletarians living on the constant edge of starvation. In terms of their immediate interests, the vast number of new jobs created by the expansion of factory production was often seen as a blessing, particularly by recently arrived immigrant families desperate for work. Indeed, many immigrants found that factory work provided better wages and more opportunities than could be obtained in Europe.

While the long-run tendency of industrialization, and particularly factory work, was toward the diminution of skills, in the short run, the risks to the future independence, job security, health, and life itself were frequently offset by the lure of higher wages for those willing to labor in the city's new factories. Boot- and shoemakers, both male and female, engaged in factory production in 1890 earned 15.3 and 81.9 percent higher wages, respectively, than their custom shop counterparts. Printers who sacrificed small-shop environments and went to work on the city's newspapers averaged higher annual incomes than those who chose to labor in smaller book and job shops. Women entering the city's furniture factories were generally guaranteed better wages than those employed in custom shop work.[119]

Although many workers benefited from the factory system, the paths of industrialization were so varied and complex that there was no hard and fast rule — either within or between industries — as to which setting of work offered the better rate of pay. Male furniture workers, unlike females, earned more by working in custom shops than factories; yet both could obtain even higher wages if they were willing to work in one of the city's massive coffin factories. In no industry were the comparative economic advantages and disadvantages of factory and small-shop work more confused than in the clothing industry, where Cincinnati's male tailors discovered that wages often varied according to the specific product line and productive setting. If they worked in the men's clothing line, higher wages could be earned in custom shops; if they worked in women's clothing, wholesale factories were the most lucrative settings of employement.[120]

Those employed in industries dominated by factory laborers often viewed their lot as a mixed blessing: surprisingly high wages for unskilled work, but little job security. Pressing/cooking workers, according to the census returns of 1880 and 1890, received relatively good wages, but at the cost of a constant fear of displacement by new machinery and the knowledge that any protest against low wages or working conditions was likely to prompt manufacturers to fire them and hire new workers in their stead. Meat-packing workers, although well paid during busy winter months, were often forced, even after the introduction of refrigeration, to find other areas of employment during slack summer months. For some men, such a seasonal arrangment proved to be no problem, for it coincided with their return to other jobs, such as construction work or farming. For others, however, it meant long months of unemployment and tramping from city to city in search of a job.

Many artisans remained resolute in their hatred of factory life, but others who entered these new workplaces discovered that they offered many advantages over small-shop working conditions. The use of factory laborers to perform the more menial aspects of production often freed artisans from tedious work and permitted them to concentrate on more enjoyable skilled tasks. Although finding much to criticize about industrialization, few Cincinnati floor molders — the most highly skilled members of the trade — complained of relinquishing less interesting bench or core molding work to the new breed of factory molder specialists.[121] Nor was it always clear, as some artisans argued, that small-shop production promised a more secure form of employment than factory work. Since large factories were often less affected by market fluctuations or minor depressions than small shops, they were frequently able to offer their workers more stable and longer periods of employment. Addressing the issues of job security and factory working conditions, one machinist explained:

> Large firms can hire help to better advantage than small ones. The mass of workingmen like to feel that their situations are as permanent as possible, and this they cannot do when employed in a small shop. For one of limited means to secure the services of an expert and really valuable assistant, extra considerations must be offered, and even these will not retain such labor if

the work seems likely to fail. The highly paid assistant hired in this small way, must be frequently employed upon a class of work which in a large shop would be done by the most unskilled, inexperienced, and, of course, poorly paid laborer.[122]

    Mechanization was another area in which the immediate experiences and interests of workers did not always coincide. Although the introduction of increasingly sophisticated machinery eventually led to a diminution of skills and displacement of factory workers, its immediate integration into daily production was seldom accompanied by a drastic drop in wages. On the contrary, *those industries with the highest average investment in machinery per operative often tended to be the industries which paid the highest annual wages.* This may have happened because of the continued necessity of maintaining a large work force in which the factory artisan still controlled rather than served the machine. It may well have been due to management's offers of immediate incentives to keep and pacify workers not yet replaced by machines. Or it may have simply been the result of greatly increased productivity, which permitted high wages while it increased profits. Whatever the cause, efforts by workers in one industry at one particular time to resist the onslaught of mechanization might well be ignored by highly paid workers in other already mechanized industries.[123]
    These varied divisions of interests existed not only between industries but also within individual factories. Rather than create a single industrial union which would represent the interests and needs of all factory workers, factory artisans organized themselves along distinct craft lines. Furniture men, for example, formed an array of mutually exclusive trade unions. Within any single factory, one might find a dozen separate organizations made up of cabinetmakers, carpenters, parlor frame-workers, upholsterers, varnishers, wood carvers, and wood turners. Similar craft divisions also occurred in virtually every other major industry. The fragmentation of factory workers was further accentuated as many union men, motivated by ethnocultural hostilities, formed separate unions to represent native- and foreign-born workers in a single trade or even a single factory.[124]
    While industrialization *ultimately* created similar problems, conditions, and needs for many workers, the formation of a common and simultaneous set of working-class responses to industrialization was hindered by circumstances in which not all industries, not all factories, and not all workers faced the same problems at the same time, to the same degree,

or with the same effect. One might argue theoretically that all people who did not own the means of production and labored for wages constituted a single working class. Yet, how could one expect the formation of a single working-class consciousness when the nature of work and the experiences of workers varied so dramatically among the city's major industries? Furthermore, if the interrelationship of production, interest, and consciousness appears so extraordinarily varied among the major industries we have briefly examined, consider how much greater the complexities of working-class life and identity would seem if we were to add to our considerations the city's trade, transportation, and service workers, as well as the rest of the manufacturing sector.

Work, then, bred a myriad of working-class experiences and a multitude of identities. It was an activity which contained endless contradictions; an activity which served as both a barrier and unifying force; an activity which produced shared experiences and dissimilar experiences; an activity and role around which thousands of men, women, and children could sound a common rallying cry, and around which thousands of men, women, and children could just as easily fragment.

CHAPTER SIX

A World Grown Apart: The Economic Struggles of Cincinnati Workers, 1843 – 1861

After 1843, as the local and national economy once again entered a period of prosperity, earlier prophecies that manufacturing would lead the way to new wealth appeared to come true. Despite economic recessions in 1854 and 1857, masters and manufacturers succeeded in raising the value of their annual output from $17.8 million to 1841 to $47 million in 1860. As manufacturing and commercial activities prospered, the value of real and personal property rose from $6.5 million in 1838 to $42.9 million in 1850 and to $93 million in 1860.[1] Yet, despite this increase in urban wealth, Cincinnati workers, the people praised by elites as the engines of progress, grew increasingly embittered by what they perceived as a growing and unjust gap between individual and collective prosperity.

Rejecting the dominant elite visions of progress and prosperity, journeymen, laborers, and outworkers initiated a new era of working-class protest aimed at restoring and protecting their status as producers, consumers, and citizens. Despite their common quest for justice, ante-bellum workers did not unite as a single, self-conscious class to resist the growing power of capitalists. Rather, they generally operated as isolated groups of craftsmen, each pursuing the particular interests of its trade. Given the widespread discontent with the alleged inequities of industrial capitalism, one is led to wonder why workers did not unite as a single class and use their economic and political power to try to redirect the course of daily life. Was it only the uneven development of trades and the different needs of tradesmen that prevented such a common class alliance?

While economic experiences constituted a vital part of daily activity, the nature of working-class consciousness and of opposition and accommodation to the new age of manufacturing was also shaped by factors outside the workplace. The workplace provided only one perspective from which men and women viewed the world. Social and political loyalties, as we shall see, at times united workers; but they also served to divide them and turn their attention away from the immediate concerns of economic life. Indeed, the most protracted political battles of the 1840s and 1850s were not fought over economic questions, but over issues emanating from the social sphere: temperance, Sunday closing laws, and the spread of immigrant culture. Despite the growth of unions and strikes, common class struggles against capitalists were frequently undermined as native-born wage earners, holding their obligations as citizens paramount to their roles as workers, joined with masters and manufacturers to battle their foreign counterparts over the social and political issues which appeared to threaten the stability of the republic.

Workers and the Economic Sphere

Manufacturers, merchants, politicians, and various civic elites welcomed the city's new economic era, but many of Cincinnati's workers complained bitterly that the earlier "Golden Age" of commonwealth and shared prosperity had come to an end. Despite the expansion of manufacturing operations and the dramatic increase of urban wealth during the 1840s and 1850s, journeymen and laborers found their standard of living and prospects for independence severely diminished. Although wages gradually rose after 1842, they generally failed to keep pace with the rapidly rising costs of living. "Provisions, clothing, rents, and fuel," grumbled journeymen coopers in 1847, had "to be purchased at an increased price; that is to say, two dollars for what you could have bought last year for one." Nevertheless, while everything they consumed appreciated in cost, coopers' wages remained relatively unchanged.[2] "Sorry indeed," added the city's iron molders, "will be the condition of the operative if compelled to pay higher prices with reduced means, or submit to the deprivation of necessary comforts."[3]

Many workers exaggerated the extent of inflation, but food and housing costs did outstrip the general increase in wages. Between 1842 and 1850 the average wages of journeymen and laborers rose by 40 percent and 25 percent respectively. Food costs, however, increased by 57 percent, while room and board in even the most modest accommodations rose by 80 percent.[4] Even rabid civic boosters like Charles Cist were struck by the declining economic position of the city's producing class. "The great problem of the age," he observed in 1849, "is, and for some years past has been, what is the proper means of securing to labor its adequate remuneration, and its just social position in the community — at present, the one being far short of its proper earnings and the other a libel and satire on our republican institutions, which proclaim all men free and equal."[5]

Workers found their relative economic position equally dismal throughout most of the 1850s. Addressing a gathering of 2,000 members of the newly reorganized General Trades' Union in 1853, one speaker complained that there had been "no advance in wages for twenty years past, while the expenses of living to the laboring man has increased by 50 percent."[6] Moreover, the modest economic gains won by many workers during a prolonged series of strikes in 1853 were gradually eroded by recessions in 1854 and 1857. Indeed, when looking at the decade as a whole, we find that while the wages of journeymen and laborers increased by an average of 30 percent, the costs of food and housing rose 60 percent and 28 percent respectively.[7]

Whether in fact the workers' standard of living was declining as severely as many claimed was less important than their widespread conviction that such was the case. Although their earnings were generally comparable to those received by journeymen and laborers in eastern cities during the 1840s and 1850s, Cincinnati workers, having grown accustomed to higher wages than their eastern counterparts, resented what they perceived an an unjustifiable decline in their previously well-to-do economic position. Indeed, wage grievances were but one aspect of growing working-class discontent. Rising land prices and the introduction of new and costly machinery into various branches of manufacturing made the prospects for independence — purchasing a home or starting a business — even more difficult. "Business and capital," complained one workingmen's newspaper in 1852, "were rapidly centering into a few hands, and consequently the condition of the toiler" and the prospects for upward mobility were becoming "more and more unfortunate."[8] Moreover, the dreaded specter of dependence was given a new visual dimension by the rapid growth of slums and the rising number of destitute beggars who roamed the city's streets.

These complaints of growing inequality and declining prospects for independence were of considerable merit. Although a number of individuals managed to work their way up the proverbial ladder of success, the relative wealth of the working class, when taken as a whole, continued to decline in the decades before the civil war. While the top 20 percent of the city's taxpayers increased their share of the total urban wealth from 71.1 percent in 1838 to 82.3 percent in 1860, the bottom 50 percent saw their relative holdings fall from 8.1 percent to 2.4 percent. Similarly, the proportion of homeowners dropped from 6.0 percent in 1838 to 4.6 percent in 1850.[9]

The bitter resentment over disparities in wealth and living conditions was also fueled by the increasingly visible contrast between the modest homes of the working class and the ostentatious accommodations of the elite. Disdaining the simple wood and stone abodes of earlier years, successful manufacturers, merchants, and professionals began to erect lavish Georgian mansions on the nearby hilltops and grandiose brick buildings in the fashionable downtown areas. "The contrast in living quarters," observed one German visitor, "is amazing. There are expensive houses, occupied by wealthy Yankees, and wretched houses where foreigners live in miserable poverty."[10]

Embittered by what they viewed as an unfair decline in their standard of living during an age of expanding prosperity, artisans, factory workers, and day laborers adopted a number of strategies to restore some semblance of justice and equality. The nature of these struggles, however, like the changing nature of the city's industries, was greatly varied. For some workers, like grocery clerk Charles Reemelin, the path to independence lay in individual initiative. Men who joined organizations which sought to secure "more wages than they merit," he contended, "accumulate ill-will against themselves, while those who get less than they deserve, accumulate credit for merit" and were thus more likely to succeed.[11] For others, like journeymen printer Henry Ogden, collective action, in the form of trade unionism, promised the most effective means to promote the rights of labor. Coming to Cincinnati in 1847, after having worked a number of years in Lexington, Kentucky, Ogden happily discovered that the members of the Cincinnati Typographical Union, unlike their unorganized southern brethren, were able to protect the wages and security of regular journeymen by limiting the spread of "two-thirders"—journeymen who had not served their full term as apprentices — in the city's shops.[12] For others still, like seamstress Mary Smith, producers' cooperatives owned and run entirely by workers promised the only true path to justice and independence. Believing unions to be of limited utility in combating the evils of the wage system, Smith, a widow forced to support her children on the miserly sum paid to her by clothing contractors, joined with several dozen seamstresses in May 1853 to set up a producer cooperative whose members would share equally in the profits of their labor.[13]

Although there are no statistics to indicate what percentage of workers followed each of these paths, labor unions were by far the most important instrumentality which workers used to remedy what they viewed as the detrimental effects of the new era of manufacturing. Between 1843 and 1861, unions, like the production process itself, passed through two stages of development. During most of the 1840s, trade unions, generally organized as local and temporary bodies, focused their activities upon securing a fair share of industry's new wealth. By the early 1850s, however, as industrialization intruded more deeply into the traditional sectors of the city's crafts, unions slowly became more permanent and national in nature and broadened their focus to include demands for greater control over the course of production.

In the autumn of 1843, as the city's shops and factories resumed their productive endeavors, Cincinnati workers moved to revive the unions which had dissolved in the wake of the Panic of 1837. Although changes in markets and production gradually altered the nature of the trades, the new unions of the 1840s, like those of the 1830s, directed their challenges not at industrialization *per se,* but at the failure of the employers to distribute its material rewards in what workers thought was an equitable fashion. Generally accepting the basic characteristics of industrial capital- ism — factory wage labor and the private ownership of the means of production — these ante-bellum unions tended to organize around three basic issues: the pursuit of "fair" wages, the protection of craft integrity, and financial aid to needy members. These efforts to protect their crafts and to secure a fair distribution of profits were seen as essential to the immediate and future needs of working-class families. Before the institution of federal social security or union retirement programs, workers' wages had to be sufficient to support their families and generate enough savings to provide for them in their old age. Moreover, in the absence of unemployment insurance or workman's compensation, the small weekly allowance that unions granted their members during periods of distress was a critical bulwark against absolute destitution.[14]

Despite their frequent denunciations by employers, newspaper editors, and clergymen, union members did not perceive their organizations as agents of radicalism. Combining the tenets of the producers' ethic with the promises of the new industrial ideology, workers argued that, if labor and capital were truly partners, as civic leaders said, then the former was certainly entitled to a "fair" share of the city's new industrial wealth. Yet workers insisted that such was not the case. Despite repeated public professions of commonwealth, journeymen coopers protested in 1847, "labor is not rewarded as well as capital; an unfair division of their mutual profits is made."[15] Although "harmony and a mutual reciprocity of benefit," had once existed between employers and employees, added the city's iron molders, the former, not content with their recent increases in wealth, were "endeavoring by unrighteous and iniquitous exactions, to force from the latter that to which they are entitled by every law, human or divine — a just remuneration for their labor."[16]

Demanding "fair" prices and "just" wages, workingmen and workingwomen launched a series of strikes and protests to secure what they asserted, and capitalistic ideology had promised, to be their rightful claim to a fair and honorable standard of living. Although unionization and strikes were most pronounced in the trades and industries undergoing the most dramatic changes in production — those of the printers, shoemakers, cabinetmakers, tailors, and building tradesmen (who railed against the rising number of contractors) — workers' grievances were nevertheless directed against what they perceived as the more pressing problem of an inequitable system of distribution. Distinguishing their actions from those of European malcontents, journeymen shoemakers, sounding a theme that would become the leitmotiv of the decade, insisted that their strike was not an instrument of radicalism but of justice. "We deem we ask for nothing but what is right," they said in 1843, "and submit to nothing wrong." Journeymen did not demand "an extravagant price," but only a just compensation which would allow them "to secure the means of making ourselves and our families comfortable."[17]

It was this seemingly republican quest for equality and justice that served as the organizing theme for the protests of the 1840s. Of the fourteen strikes which occurred between October 1843 and December 1849, all but one were fought for better wages and hours.[18] Journeymen bakers, denying the selfish motives ascribed to them by employers, simply requested that they be paid "an honest and fair remuneration for their labor."[19] Striking oak coopers, having adopted a bill of prices which they deemed "just and equitable, affording no more than a just price for their labor," pledged themselves, "as men of honor, to assist one another in obtaining their just rights."[20] Swept up by similar desires for justice, female factory operatives at one cotton manufactory went out on strike in June 1849 — the first such strike by the city's factory laborers — to protest against a further cut in their already low wages.[21]

While fourteen strikes may seem small in number, all, except that of the cotton workers, were trade-wide actions. That is, union demands were issued on behalf of all workers in a trade and not, as became the strategy after midcentury, merely for those in one or two shops or factories. Consequently, an ante-bellum strike was a dramatic and serious event since it usually brought a complete, or nearly so, shutdown of business within the trade. Only when demands were successfully negotiated, or when employers recruited sufficient numbers of strikebreakers, did business recommence.

As in the 1820s and 1830s, strike demands were often supplemented by direct appeals to the community. Flyers were posted around town and advertisements placed in newspapers by striking workers explaining the causes of their actions and appealing to citizens to support them in their just cause by boycotting the shops of unrepublican employers. Drawing upon the rituals which had proved so effective in the 1820s and 1830s, workers also endeavored to legitimize their strikes and link their demands as producers to their rights as citizens by re-creating the revolutionary spirit of 1776. Marching to the beat of fife and drum corps, carrying American flags and union banners, striking workers paraded through the city streets calling for justice, equality, and an end to tyranny.[22]

Even though workers used the same language and shared the same grievances, working-class unity during the 1840s rarely extended beyond the immediate interests of individual trades. While their perceived rights as producers and needs as consumers helped to spark particular union struggles, the latter often acted to undercut broader forms of mutual support. Looking for the "cheapest" goods they could find, regardless of "whether the seller pays his journeymen the regular prices," printers, coopers, and building tradesmen were chastised by one workingmen's daily

in December 1843 for patronizing the scab shops being struck by journeymen shoemakers. Ignoring what the editors insisted was the "self-obligation"
of every artisan "to uphold his brother workmen, without distinction of
branches," these men had weakened the overall strength of the labor
movement by placing their needs as consumers over the common interests
of all producers.[23]

By the early 1850s, however, isolation among the trades and
traditional forms of working-class protest were gradually altered by the
changing nature of production and the changing composition of the producing class. As greater numbers of journeymen found their wages, skills,
and job security eroded, the lines between employers and employees began
to broaden and harden. Masters and manufacturers, many of whom seemed
to spend more time attending to "business" needs than to working on the
shop floor, were increasingly viewed by journeymen as capitalists — as
opponents, not allies, of the producing class. These new perceptions did
not occur at once, however, but tended to arise shortly after a trade or
industry had experienced changes in its traditional patterns of ownership
or production. Striking journeymen hatters, for example, drew a sharp
distinction in August 1852 between old-time "Practical Hatters" who had
"served an apprenticeship to the business" and a new breed of wholesale
manufacturers who had merely bought their way to the top. The former,
who treated their journeymen "as skillful artists," had "come up to the mark
like men" and granted the wage demands. More mercenary manufacturers,
however, men who viewed their employees as mere commodities, had
refused to accede to the journeymen's just request.[24]

As various unions found their trades similarly degraded by
the rise of "dishonorable" capitalists, they began to restrict their membership
to include only those "practical" men who worked in their shops on a full-
time basis. Yet, these alliances between journeymen and small shop masters
often proved short-lived. When master printers refused to support journeymen in their actions against newpaper publishers, the journeymen left
the all-encompassing ranks of the Franklin Typographical Society in 1849
and organized a new union made up entirely of journeymen.[25] Finding
themselves in similar straits, journeymen tanners, bricklayers, seamstresses,
and others joined the printers in adopting resolutions which prohibited any
master or manufacturer from joining their organization.[26]

Divisions and mistrust between journeymen and employers
were further widened as masters and manufacturers, recognizing that their
interests and needs had changed, began to organize their own trade asso-

ciations. Traditional beliefs in the unity of the producing class continued to erode as brewers, butchers, building trades masters, linseed oil manufacturers, and newspaper publishers initiated new employers' associations in the late 1840s and 1850s. The growing divisions between labor and capital assumed a new public dimension in March 1859, when masters and manufacturers from all industries joined together to form the Mechanics' and Manufacturers' Exchange. Organized for the express purpose of promoting and developing the "resources of our Industrial Community," the Exchange also assumed the tasks of collecting manufacturing statistics, arbitrating disputes between local manufacturers, and enforcing basic rules of conduct among its members. Although technically open to all persons "engaged in mechanical and manufacturing pursuits," the Exchange's considerable annual dues of ten dollars prevented all but the city's well-to-do masters and manufacturers from joining.[27]

It was amidst this growing atmosphere of mutual suspicion, wage stagnation, and the continual rise of new manufactories that greater numbers of Cincinnati workers turned to unions as a means to improve their material conditions. Meeting in August 1850 to discuss the "present disorganized state of society," journeymen and laborers in the city's eighth ward insisted that "the increasing degradation of labor, which is now taking place throughout the city, under the wages system," could be remedied only by "a united and determined effort" on the part of the city's working class.[28] During the following eleven years, over 67 different groups of workers heeded this advice and organized new unions. As in earlier years, the greatest thrust for unionization came from the ranks of the city's artisans and its new emerging factory artisans. Printers, furniture workers, shoemakers, tailors, building tradesmen, tanners, iron molders, machinists, and other artisans organized nearly 75 percent of the decade's new labor associations.[29]

Factory laborers, outworkers, and various day laborers initiated at least seventeen (25 percent) of the decade's new unions. In December 1853, several dozen seamstresses in the ready-to-wear clothing industry, angered by manufacturers and contractors who paid them only three-fifths as much as male outworkers, and frustrated by the reluctance of the tailor's union to come to their aid, organized the Cincinnati Sewing Society #1 —a union composed entirely of female outworkers.[30] Several months later, the city's porkpacking employees, equally dissatisfied with the low wages, long hours, and poor working conditions, formed Cincinnati's first factory laborer union.[31] During the following years, building trades' laborers, draymen, hackmen, longshoremen, rivermen, gardeners, milkmen, waiters, and other unskilled workers organized their own unions.

Despite this upsurge in unionization, Cincinnati workers often remained divided by craft, skill, gender, race, and ethnicity. Artisanal unions, although often speaking of the common interests of the producing class, nevertheless excluded unskilled laborers, women, and blacks from their associations. Moreover, as production in various industries grew more specialized, so too did the focus of organizational activity. Instead of forming one union to represent all skilled members of their trade, journeymen often organized along increasingly narrower craft or even product lines. As furniture and shoe manufacturers concentrated on producing one particular product — cabinets or chairs in the first instance, ladies' or men's shoes in the second — their journeymen responded by forming two distinct unions, one to represent each branch of the trade. Similarly, as iron molding grew more specialized in the late 1850s, machine molders, insisting that the parent stove and holloware union did not adequately represent their interest, organized their own association.[32]

The character of the city's unions was also shaped by the influx of thousands of foreign-born workers in the 1840s and 1850s. Germans, at times displacing native-born craftsmen, moved into all aspects of woodcrafting; Englishmen quickly assumed important positions in metal and machine foundries; Irish workers found jobs in the city's building trades and various unskilled pursuits. The barriers separating native- and foreign-born workers were increased, not only by their frequent competition for jobs, but also by the latter's tendency to isolate themselves into distinct ethnic labor organizations. While a number of German journeymen joined existing native-dominated unions, German coopers, tailors, cabinetmakers, tanners, machine shoemakers, carpenters, butchers, brewers, printers, and unskilled building-trades workers organized separate trade bodies.[33]

Immigrants also helped to steer the city's labor movement in more radical directions. English and German craftsmen, having left their native lands in part to escape what they thought were the deleterious effects of industrial capitalism, urged their new laboring brethren to resist the spread of proletarianization in the United States. Germans exhorted American workers to see production, not simply distribution, as the source of their problems; to see the forces of organized capital, not individual employers, as their true opponents. Irish workers, although generally coming from agrarian backgrounds, were nonetheless schooled in a long tradition of resistance to oppression. Journeyman shoemaker James Doran, insisting that the tyranny in America was often "as bad as that in Ireland," urged his countrymen to fight their new bosses in the same way they had fought their old landlords. "If we are to be run over in this way [by manufacturers]," he told a gathering of striking shoemakers in April 1858, "we might have staid [sic] in Ireland where we had to work to sustain the English government."[34]

Despite their frequent antipathy for these new foreign competitors, a number of unions listened to and acted upon these pleas. Engineers and machinists at the Cincinnati, Hamilton and Dayton Railroad urged the city's workers to join them in resisting the rise of a "new system of management in direct opposition to our feelings as men, our pride as mechanics, and our rights as citizens."[35] While the vast majority of strikes and protest continued to revolve around wages and hours, traditional demands for justice were slowly infused with new attacks upon the production process. Of the 35 strikes initiated between January 1850 and April 1861, 29 were fought entirely over demands for better wages and/or hours.[36] Six others were either partially or completely caused by efforts to secure greater control over the inner workings of the city's shops and factories: control over the regulation of work and apprenticeship, over union recognition, or to protest the introduction of nonunion foremen and employees.[37]

The two most protracted strikes of the decade, ones which foreshadowed the direction which labor radicalism would take in the latter part of the century, occurred in those very industries — printing and furniture — where the reorganization and division of labor affected the work and status of artisans most dramatically. These changes generated a new attitude among the city's printers: their present and future wellbeing lay not simply in the quest for higher wages but also in the need to reestablish control over the practical workings of their craft.

In February 1851, the members of the Cincinnati Typographical Union (CTU), already involved in a widespread movement to establish a national union which would resist the arbitrary power of publishers, adopted a constitution which, in addition to proclaiming their right to set prices, announced their intention to regulate "all things appertaining to the management of the printing business under its jurisdiction."[38] Moving to protect themselves from the growing tide of cheaply paid "two-thirders," the CTU also issued a new "Plan of Apprenticeship" which detailed the wages, work responsibilities, and length of time that all apprentices had to serve. Moreover, in order to protect apprentices from being locked into a narrow, specialized skill, the union insisted that boys be trained and allowed to work on all aspects of the trade.[39]

Although the plan was initially accepted by the city's publish-

(a)

Figure 7 The Ethnic Working Class.
(a) Jackson Brewery Workers (c. 1870). Germans dominated the city's brewing, clothing, leather, and woodworking trades. (b) Teamsters (c. 1890s). Irish workers found employment as teamsters, draymen, longshoremen, and unskilled laborers. (c) James Morton & Co. Planing Mill Employees (c. 1870s). Germans, Irish, and native-born workers all competed for jobs in the city's construction trades.
Courtesy of the Cincinnati Historical Society

(b)

(c)

ers, a bitter battle erupted in November 1853 when a number of employers attempted to circumvent the agreement by hiring large numbers of apprentices to replace regular journeymen. Led by Henry Ogden and Hiram Young, journeymen who had come to Cincinnati to avoid such practices, the union quickly passed a resolution limiting the number of apprentices to three in large shops and to one in small shops. Spurred on by a new spirit of militancy which followed the organization of a National Typographical Union in May 1852, the union also informed publishers that henceforth all printers had to join the CTU or relinquish their jobs. Any violations of these provisions, they promised, would lead to a shutdown of all newspapers.[40]

Refusing to accept what they termed the "arbitrary rules dictated by the printers to their employers for the government of their office," all but three newspapers joined the *Daily Columbian* in preferring a strike rather than acceding to such "unwarranted" demands.[41] Unlike earlier confrontations, insisted the owners of the *Gazette,* this was more than a simple controversy over wages. Union terms were "infringements upon the rights of proprietors" and blatant attempts "to carry their assumption of control over the mechanical part of our business."[42] Although willing to grant their journeymen higher wages, publishers pledged that their newspapers would continue to be "entirely run within our own control — to be conducted according to our own rules and arrangements, without reference to any combination or society."[43] They placed advertisements in newspapers around the country offering good wages and steady work to nonunion compositors and pressworkers — male or female — willing to come to Cincinnati.[44]

The CTU sought to legitimize and win popular support for its markedly more radical struggles by combining traditional concepts of justice and rights with explicit references to prevailing market conditions. If employers could use the excuse of "poor market conditions" to justify their need to lower wages or alter production, then workers could point to improved market conditions to justify their demands. In requesting local merchants and mechanics not to patronize struck newpapers, printers explained that, while publishers presently reaped profits equal to four or five times the cost of labor and materials, they perisisted in hiring cheap "half-breeds." Consequently, the honest republican printer had been *forced* to battle for greater control of the workplace in order to preserve his "inalienable right to control of his own labor, and prices thereof."[45]

The bitter and prolonged battle between printers and publishers generated a sense of cross-trade unity and mutual support unseen since the days of the General Trades Union of 1836. Various journeymen, perceiving the "present struggle as involving principles of vital importance to . . . every other branch of mechanics," quickly rallied behind the striking printers.[46] In a rare display of ante-bellum working-class solidarity, several hundred workers from a number of different trades joined with striking printers on the morning of November 29 and paraded up and down every major street in Cincinnati. The demonstrators ended their march at the Fifth Street Market, where they proceeded to adopt several resolutions supporting the printers and vowing not to purchase any struck newspaper. Their boycott proved effective. By March 1854, all but three of the city's newspapers had acceded to the union's demands.[47]

The strike marked a significant victory for the CTU, and its impact extended well beyond the printing community. The feelings of mutualism engendered by the strike prompted several thousand foreign- and native-born workers to suspend their mutual hostilities and join the ranks of the recently reorganized General Trades Union, organized in March 1853 to protect "the interests of the working portion of the community." It was not until the printers' strike, however, that the GTU began to attract the support of a wide range of trades.[48] In a city where working-class unity was frequently undermined by craft, skill, and ethnic divisions, as well as by the differing needs of those laboring in small shops and large factories, the GTU provided an important central body to foster greater mutual understanding and support among all workers. Meeting in December 1853, the GTU, suddenly sixty unions strong, adopted a series of resolutions supporting the printers and proclaiming that "all trades have an equal and identical interest, and . . . if united, we could better resist the encroachments of capital and secure to ourselves a more just compensation for our labor." Endeavoring to counteract the dominant tendency toward narrow craft interests, the GTU also called upon its members to subordinate their "personal interests to the good of the whole."[49]

In addition to drawing more workers into the GTU, the printers' strike also helped redirect the focus of working-class grievances. The union's struggle to control the practical workings of the trade, announced the GTU's leadership, was a clear signal that workers would no longer accept their employers' unilateral right to control the course of industrialization. "We believe the time has come," the Journeymen Tinners' Union announced in late November, "when labor must take its stand upon a just and equal ground with capital."[50] The sense of mutuality which had characterized earlier relations between journeymen and masters, the city's bookbinders agreed, had been replaced by a new ethos in which capitalists used their power "for the oppression of the laboring masses." Consequently, in order to preserve their rights and protect the dignity of their professions, unions were obliged to follow the path of the printers and "adopt such rules and regulations as will serve to protect their own interests against encroachments of the employer and capitalist."[51] By the time the strike had drawn to an end, dozens of other unions had issued similar resolutions announcing their right and intention to assert *their* vision of how the new era of manufacturing ought to proceed.

The growing labor militancy of the late 1840s and 1850s led manufacturers and their allies to launch a fervent anti-union campaign. Appeals to republican sensibilities and the obligations of citizenship, frequently used by workers to defend their actions, were also employed by unsympathetic newspaper editors to challenge the legitimacy of labor unions. Denouncing "all such Trades Unions or Associations . . . [as] odious in the extreme," the *Herald* declared that their attempt "to overawe employers, or compel journeymen to unite with them" was an "infringement of Liberty" and a violation of the basic principles of a republican society.[52] The editors of the *Christian Advocate and Journal,* the organ of the Methodist Episcopal Church, condemned the unions' "spirit of anti-aristocracy and monopoly" as unchristian, "absurd, and blasphemous."[53]

Manufacturers also employed the forces of the state to undermine the strength of organized labor. Following a walkout by union machinists in March 1852, engine manufacturer Anthony Harkness, one of the city's wealthiest and most influential employers, persuaded the chief of police to post his men outside his factory. When union leaders attempted to enter the building the next day to persuade nonstrikers to stop working, they were promptly arrested for attempted riot.[54] Similar scenarios were repeated throughout the decade as striking tailors, furniture workers, and railroad laborers were arrested and brought to court on charges ranging from conspiracy to attempted murder.[55] These capitalistic manipulations of the courts and police, argued the outraged editors of the *Nonpareil,* made it perfectly clear that governments "will do nothing for Labor — they make laws for Capital."[56]

As conflicts between employers and employees grew more pronounced, the image of a harmonious world of producers drawn by Alexis de Tocqueville in the 1830s had virtually disappeared by the early 1850s. "We are divided into castes," printer and author L. A. Hine bitterly observed in 1856, "the rich, the poor, and the competent livers." The city's vast hordes of nonproducers, "lawyers, physicians, clergymen, teachers, merchants, and those who live on their revenues"—men who were "exempt from the dangers to which other classes are exposed" — had come to constitute a new "aristocracy — those who abstain from physical labor."[57] Yet, despite increased perceptions of economic stratification and class conflict, the excitement and sense of fraternalism generated in the winter of 1853 – 1854 soon died down as Cincinnati was gripped by economic recessions late in 1854 and again in 1857. "Winter," observed one editor in 1855, "found our mechanics out of work, our manufactories silent, our coal yards empty, hungry and nakedness among the poor . . . and distressing embarrassments among businessmen."[58] The revival of trade in 1856 was short-lived as the city and nation entered an even more severe period of depression in the autumn of 1857. When the collapse of trade and credit forced manufacturers to shut down or curtail their operations, thousands of men and women found themselves out of jobs. "Morning, noon and night," reported the *Times*, "at the landing may be seen scores of idle men."[59] With the exception of the printers, carpenters, and shoemakers, the city's trades unions all dissolved as journeymen desperately took whatever jobs they could get, regardless of pay or working conditions.

With the return of prosperity in 1859, tradesmen once again moved to revive the labor movement. Earlier struggles for control of the workplace, however, faded into the background as battles for higher wages occupied the center stage of labor actions. Of the nine strikes initiated between 1859 and April 1861, only three — two by printers and one by furniture workers — involved broad questions such as union recognition and greater control over the workplace. While most struggles of this period focused on bread and butter issues, not surprising in the wake of several years of hard times, the strike of the furniture workers is worth brief mention since it was the first major industry-wide strike directed at the city's new factories and factory owners.

While furniture manufacturers boasted of the health and prosperity of their industry, their employees argued that they saw little in the way of significant material advancement for themselves. In March 1859, German and American journeymen, who had previously operated within separate ethnic unions, joined together to protest against low wages and the increased degradation of their labor by forming the Cincinnati Cabinetmakers' Union. Led by men from the "larger manufactories of the city," the union soon attracted 500 men — approximately 86 percent of the trade's journeymen.[60] The new union adopted a form of organization successfully employed by the city's printers and appointed a series of shop committees to govern and represent the interests of skilled workers in each major furniture factory.

Within a matter of days, the union presented factory owners with two major demands: restoration of wages to prerecession levels and formal recognition of the union and its shop committees. In order to ensure that these committees would have the full support of all workers, native- and foreign-born, the union also insisted that "each cabinet-maker working in Cincinnati, without reference to the language he speaks, is obliged to join the Union."[61] Large manufacturers, such as Mitchell and Rammelsberg, George Henshaw, Frederick Knoblaugh, and H. B. Mudge, quickly responded by organizing an employers' association to resist the "arbitrary and unreasonable" demands of their employees. Had the union confined itself solely to the issue of wages, they declared in a joint statement, "there would be little difficulty in arriving at a speedy and amicable adjustment." Yet wages were not the main issue. Workers were endeavoring to dictate rules and regulations which properly belonged to employers. Lashing out against demands for shop committees and forced unionization, they pledged themselves to oppose "any interference in the control or management" of their factories.[62]

Union members, equally determined to oppose further encroachments on their independence, went out on strike. By the end of March, as newly organized factory carpenters joined them on strike, the cabinetmakers succeeded in bringing furniture production to a halt. Only the three smaller factories which acceded to union demands were allowed to continue their operations. Moving to break down the impersonal relations of factory life and to promote more fraternal feelings between German and native-born craftsmen, strike leaders held daily meetings at Workingmen's Hall to report the progress of their negotiations. Demonstrations and rallies attracting upwards of 700 men and women were also organized to publicize the workers' demands throughout the community.[63]

By early April, virtually all manufacturers had expressed their willingness to grant the desired wage increase. However, they refused to budge on the questions of shop committees and the closed shop. Despite the initial enthusiasm shown by cabinetmakers and carpenters, the desire for higher wages eventually won out over the commitment to union control. On the afternoon of April 8, the union's executive committe voted to end the strike by dropping all but its wage demands. Within a week, factories were reopened and business proceeded as usual. The organization and control of factory production remained in the hands of manufacturers.[64]

Although labor unions served as the most popular vehicles of working-class protest, they were essentially reformist bodies which sought to ameliorate rather than to change the fundamental structures of the industrial system. The progression from wage demands to struggles over the control of work certainly indicated a greater awareness of the complexities of industrialization. However, it did not challenge the basic principles of industrial capitalism: wage labor and the private ownership of the means of production. Higher wages or greater shop control did not alter the fact that wage laborers, like the products they turned out, were commodities to be bought at a given price by any manufacturer.

Rejecting what they viewed as the narrow confines of trade unionism, a number of workers advocated the formation of producer cooperatives as the only means of effecting long-term solutions to the problems of industrial inequality. "Strikes, and societies, and orders," observed the editors of the Nonpareil, "have sometimes afforded temporary relief, but they all come very short of that permanency, which is indispensable to the happiness and comfort, and even necessities of nine-tenths of our laboring population."[65] Only producer cooperatives, enterprises owned and operated entirely by workers, insisted one group of journeymen, would free men and women from industrial oppression and enable them to "receive the profit and benefit of their own toil."[66] Meaningful independence, explained one tailor, would not be obtained until workers abandoned wage strikes in favor of the "true doctrine of renouncing all together the wage system."[67]

The cooperative movement, although begun in the 1820s, achieved its most dramatic and widespread success in Cincinnati during the late 1840s and 1850s. The movement found its greatest support in those industries where productive life was being subjected to the greatest change. A number of German tailors, disgusted with the constant decline in wages and the increased power of greedy contractors, abandoned their shops in August 1850 and organized the Journeymen's Tailor Cooperative Store. By obtaining a large number of small contributions from journeymen, the tailors insisted that their venture would "enable the members to obtain the advantages of large capital," while simultaneously "securing [to them] the profits of their united labor."[68] Similarily, in May 1853 a group of seamstresses in the city's ready-to-wear clothing industry left their employers and set up their own cooperative enterprise.[69] Groups of stove molders, foundrymen, cabinetmakers, and printers also turned to worker cooperatives as an alternative to wage labor.[70]

These various cooperatives, although often influenced by strong elements of idealism, were not backward looking efforts which sought to ignore or escape from an industrializing world. Rather, they were attempts to provide an alternative path of industrialization, one which rejected what workers saw as the undesirable social relations of industrial capitalism without rejecting industrialization itself. In virtually all instances, these cooperatives were designed to compete in a market economy with the express purpose of securing profits for their members. Capital was raised by selling stock to workers; those who could paid in one lump sum, while others agreed to make modest weekly payments until their obligations were met.

This merger of idealism and economic realism was most clearly reflected in the organization of the iron molders' cooperative. Embittered by the failure of their wage strike in February 1847, twenty Cincinnati molders quit their jobs and organized a cooperative venture known as the Journeymen Molders' Union Foundry. By August 1850, the initial capital stock had expanded from $2,100 to over $5,000, while membership had risen to 52 active journeymen. In addition to operating a factory on the outskirts of town, the molders opened a retail store in downtown Cincinnati and hired a full-time business agent from among their ranks to solicit business from nearby areas. The cooperative prospered for more than three years and drew the attention and praise of eastern visitors like Horace Greeley. The venture's early success, however, soon led to its downfall. Fearful of the impact which the cooperative would have upon their future operations, the city's stove manufacturers, willing to take a short-term loss to protect their long-term interests, launched a bitter price war which eventually drove the molders out of business.[71]

The most ambitious cooperative venture of the period was the Home City project. Not content with establishing one or two factories, the founders of Home City sought to create an entire cooperative city. Fifty ambitious journeymen and a number of sympathetic well-to-do local residents mapped out plans in the summer of 1849 to buy a tract of land sufficiently large to house a community of 5,000 people. As envisioned by its founders, Home City would be an egalitarian community in which each citizen would be his or her own employer. Male residents, drawn exclusively from the region's practical mechanics, would run the city's manufactories on a completely cooperative basis. Homes would be purchased from the common land, and families would remain "secure forever without payment of a rental to a landlord."[72]

Visiting Home City in the spring of 1850, a Cincinnati reporter described how its initial settlers had "struggled for about a year almost against hope." But "self-denial, perseverance and heroism" had won the victory. The city was a beehive of activity as resident carpenters built houses for new families, while others busily worked in the city's foundry and shoe shops producing goods for market.[73]

Unfortunately, local newspapers provide no information about the ultimate fate of the project. What little we do know indicates that Home City, like the local associationalist experiments of the mid-1840s, was an attempt to restructure, not merely reform, the economic, social, and political life of the community. Going a step beyond most ordinary producer cooperatives, Home City's residents believed that industrialization and the preservation of community life could go hand and hand. Unlike some of the region's earlier communitarian movements, the Home City experiment was not based upon religious fervor but grew out of the conviction that any lasting egalitarian community had to be built upon a solid economic foundation. Once this was achieved, an intergration of social, political, and economic activity would follow. An associationalist tract of the period summed up what appeared to be the main goals of the Home City project — goals which reflected the community's attempt to preserve republican ideals in a new economic age:

> Establishing a concert for action and unity of interests (not a community of property) . . . of dignifying Labor and rendering it honorable and AT-TRACTIVE — of dividing equitably the product of their labor, every individual receiving a fair share according to the part taken in producing it, and giving Labor, Skill, and Capital, each a just proportion or dividend — of realizing collective economies—of introducing every facility and the most efficient means of education, moral, mental and physical, which will be extended to all children without exception — of living together in friendly union and concord, and enjoying the varied pleasures of extended and congenial social relations, and the pursuits of useful industry, and exalting art and science and of directing their energies and talents so as to conduct the greatest happiness of the Whole.[74]

Despite the varying forms of discontent and protest expressed by numerous workers, Cincinnati's ante-bellum laboring community operated more as a series of largely unconnected interest groups than as a self-perceived working class. Neither unions nor producer's cooperatives united Cincinnati workers on a sustained basis. The drama, intensity, and apparent solidarity which so often occured during strikes soon disappeared after immediate demands were met. Given the central role of work and frequent discontent over the course of industrial development, one wonders why overt forms of class conflict remained so limited: Why did Cincinnati's workers not unite as a self-conscious class to fight what many saw as the detrimental effects of economic change?

The answers are complex. The amorphous and seemingly incomprehensible nature of industrialization provides us with one partial explanation; the different rates of industrial development and the different experiences and needs of various tradesmen offers another. The frequent movement of workers in and out of Cincinnati was yet another factor which influenced the nature of protest. One study of geographical mobility between 1840 and 1861 shows that only 72 (21.9 percent) of a sample group of 329 people remained in the city during these two decades.[75] While the influx of laborers who had experienced hardships in other cities may well have enhanced the radical direction of labor protest, the rapid turnover of population undoubtedly made it more difficult for any union to sustain its leadership or membership over long periods.

In searching for more satisfactory answers to these questions, one must venture beyond the workplace and the economic sphere, for working-class mentality was not simply a reflection of changes in production. While work may well have consumed the greatest portion of an individual's day, it was only one part of a broader life experience; other roles and considerations were critical in forging a sense of self-identity. Commitments and problems raised by immigration, religion, morality, leisure, and politics were often seen as more important than those originating in the workshop. The sense of mutualism generated by common economic struggles was often eroded as workers battled one another over the pressing social and political issues of the day. Consequently, the nature of protest and passivity during the era of manufacturing can be understood only by examining the social and politicial lives and loyalties of the city's working class.

CHAPTER SEVEN

A World Grown Apart: The Social and Political Lives of Cincinnati Workers, 1843 – 1861

L ike so many other aspects of working-class life, leisure and political activities were replete with contradictions. While the experiences gained in saloons, voluntary associations, ethnic societies, churches, and party politics often strength ened the bonds of mutuality and camaraderie forged in the workplace, they also acted to divide workers and turn their attention away from their immediate economic concerns. As the number of social and political activities expanded in the 1840s and 1850s, the primacy of the role of *worker* was gradually eroded as it vied among a number of new and often competing identities: Masons, Turners, volunteer firemen, Catholics, Prot- estants, Jews, Democrats, Whigs, Know-Nothings, Republicans, and so forth. Indeed, these social and political associations, organized around ethnic and religious loyalties, often bound men and women more securely than relations at the point of production. Possibilities for working-class unity based upon common economic exploitation were repeatedly under- mined, particularly after the influx of foreigners in the late 1840s, as workers squared off against one another and joined various capitalists and elites to battle over the contentious social, moral, and political questions of the day.

Workers and the Leisure Sphere

As the rigors of economic life grew more arduous, Cincinnatians organized an unprecedented number and variety of activities to provide themselves with fun, relaxation, and, occasionally, knowledge. By 1854, the city housed over 800 saloons and beer halls, 450 card parlors, 30 pool halls, 30 bowling alleys, and more than half a dozen theaters and museums.[1] In addition, local residents also organized dozens of voluntary associations with such intriguing names as the Grand Order of Planets, the United Ancient Order of Druids, and the Improved Order of Red Men. As men and women sought new outlets to combat their frequent dissatisfaction with work, the number of these associations expanded more rapidly than the general population: while the latter increased by 248 percent between 1840 and 1860 the former rose by 368 percent.

Unlike earlier years, when the limited availability of social activities acted to join people of all backgrounds as seeming equals in the quest for pleasure and relaxation, the rapid expansion of leisure pursuits tended to splinter local residents along more pronounced class, ethnic, and religious lines. Well-to-do merchants, manufacturers, and professionals, growing more conscious of their status and wealth, abandoned plebian saloons to drink at the city's more respectable taverns. They also joined exclusive organizations, such as the Philomatian, Erophebic, and Semi-

Table 7.1 Voluntary Associations Incorporated in Cincinnati, 1803–1860

	1803–1820	1821–1830	1831–1840	1841–1850	1851–1860	1803–1860
Unions	—	2	4	4	22	32
Church & Religious Societies	1	8	18	25	51	103
Secular & Benevolent Societies	—	10	16	17	78	121
Social, Educational, & Cultural Societies	—	2	9	6	26	43
Totals	1	22	47	52	177	299

SOURCE: Incorporation statistics were drawn from two main sources: Hamilton County Incorporation Records, 1, County Recorder's Office, HCC, and the Annual Report of the Secretary of State, to the Governor of Ohio. For the Year 1885 (Columbus, 1885), pp. 147–205.

Notes: Secular and benevolent societies include those organizations that provided mutual aid for their members; social, educational, and cultural societies that did not offer such benefits were listed under a separate category.

Colon clubs. Workers spent their free time at the city's more inexpensive saloons, gambling parlors, racetracks, and other popular haunts, such as Shire's Theater, which provided them with an endless series of minstrel shows, bawdy farces, and burlesque performances. Similarly, native-born and foreign-born residents, Protestants, Catholics, and Jews, also organized a number of ethnic and religious associations to serve their particular needs.[2]

During the 1840s and 1850s, these varied social pursuits emerged as a source of bitter class, ethnic, and religious conflict. Just as various native-born elites attempted to set the course of the city's economy and ideology, so too did they try to create a social culture which would reflect the values and practices of the new industrial world. Social activities which were generally accepted as part of the dominant social mores of the late eighteenth and early nineteenth centuries — drinking, gaming, Sunday amusement — were now viewed by elites as unacceptable manifestations of an outdated era. Indeed, these activities stood in opposition to the new bourgeois culture that valued sobriety, thrift, Sabbath observance, self-discipline, and adherence to vaguely defined "American" principles. The city's former New England residents, remarked one traveler, were particularly active in setting this new moral tone: "The New England influence prevailed to such an extent, that Cincinnati seemed like a second Boston."[3]

Insisting that the "popular amusements of a place indicate the character of their civilization, and especially do they manifest the moral condition," newspaper editors, civic elites, clergymen, manufacturers, merchants, and professionals began to distinguish between two types of social activities: productive and nonproductive leisure.[4] The former included those activities which were directed toward benefiting the material, moral, social, and intellectual life of the individual. Classes and lectures offered by the Ohio Mechanics' Institute, literary societies, debating clubs, churches, and the "better" class of voluntary associations were praised as useful investments in self betterment.

The discipline and knowledge gained in these productive activities, it was claimed, would help to alleviate the tensions generated in economic life and increase an individual's prospects for mobility and independence. Common social intercourse, avowed the Odd Fellows, would lead employers and employees to regard each other "as equals, as brethren, all working in different paths . . . . The rich will cease to be arrogant — the poor will forget to be servile, for each will equally feel a man."[5] Although they perceived themselves as classless organizations, voluntary associations such as the Odd Fellows, Masons, and Red Men, which were invariably dominated by their well-to-do members, nevertheless served as social mechanisms for inculcating men with the dominant ideals of hierarchy, deference, temperance, and self-discipline. Members of the Improved Order of Red Men, who moved up within the associations' elaborate hierarchy only by exhibiting "good moral character [and] industrious habits," were instructed to refrain from drink, idleness, and "profane, vulgar, or indecent language."[6] Similarly, the Masons, in addition to praising the values of regular attendance, both at meetings and on the job, also informed recent inductees that all true Masons were expected to "meekly receive their wages without murmuring or mutiny."[7]

Religious activities were also praised by various elites as a proper arena of productive social activity and a means of solving many of life's daily problems. Churches, and such various religious associations as the Catholic Aid Society, the American Protestant Association, and the B'nai B'rith, provided their congregants with moral solace, instructions on the Sabbath, and material aid in times of economic distress. While religious principles, as a number of scholars have shown, were occasionally used by radical workers to legitimize class struggles, ministers more frequently acted to undermine class loyalties by arguing that an individual's role and obligation as a Protestant, Catholic, or Jew took precedence over any narrow occupational identity.[8] The problems of the modern world, a number of clergymen asserted, would be better solved by trusting in God than by engaging in political or economic struggles. Denouncing the efforts of labor unions "to mend the existing state of human society," Methodist ministers urged their parishoners to abandon these sacrilegious crusades and "live and get along as God has ordained."[9] Similarly, Catholics were told that any secular organization or doctrine of progress which taught people to look for happiness in this world was "false and to be rejected even without examination."[10] Although not always adhering to this advice in prosperous times, thousands of workingmen and women consistently flocked to the city's churches and revival tents to pray for God's help during periods of economic recession.[11]

The proponents of the city's new social ideals also directed vituperative attacks against the nonproductive leisure activities that workers found so appealing. "Many of our so-called recreations," the editors of the *Enquirer* lamented in 1859, "are becoming so popular, particularly with our workingmen, as to excite much anxiety in regard to the character of their effects upon the public morals and prosperity." Rather than elevating men, as leisure activity ought to do, these frivolous entertainments tended "to consume the earnings and deprave the morals of the producing classes among us."[12] The "many diversions in the way of balls, etc.," engine manufacturer A. B. Latta agreed, "gradually drew their [workers] interest in another direction," thereby impeding their chances for success.[13] Equally disturbed by the "wordly and soul-corrupting amusements of the day," the city's Presbyterian, Methodist, and Baptist ministers demanded a complete shutdown of all saloons, beer halls, and other "improper amusements."[14]

A number of prominent manufacturers, such as Miles Greenwood, A. B. Latta, and shoe manufacturer C. W. Thorpe, poured considerable sums of money into the Ohio Mechanics' Institute (OMI). Instead of wasting time in saloons, gambling dens, or disruptive labor protests, the OMI's board of directors said, men should better their "moral character" and position in life by taking evening courses in geometry, bookkeeping, grammar, chemistry, or algebra. Although drawn to the organization during the late 1820s and 1830s, when it was run largely by small shop masters and journeymen, workers proceeded to abandon the OMI once its leadership and direction passed into the hands of large manufacturers in the mid-1840s. Incensed by the efforts of capitalists to control *their* organization, C. W. Thorpe reported to his fellow board members in January 1847, journeymen demanded that OMI directors should "all be *mechanics,* and that the *President* should be chosen from among the *active* young mechanics."[15]

Thorpe's report, however, fell upon deaf ears. Three years later an "oldtime member" complained that the "affairs of the institute are *not* now controlled by mechanics . . . [but by] aristocrats." The OMI, another journeymen concurred in August 1850, was "a *mechanics'* institute only in name."[16]

As various elites attempted to use moral, religious, economic, and political pressure to enforce their ideas of a proper social order, leisure activities became a sphere of frequent conflict and contention. Throughout the 1840s and 1850s, struggles over the control of work were frequently accompanied by struggles over the control of leisure. These assaults on working-class culture, however, produced a mixed set of responses. In some instances, workers combined to oppose these bourgeois intrusions; at other times, workers were bitterly divided by competing social beliefs. The crusades to abolish volunteer fire companies and to close the city's saloons provide two major examples of the social complexities of working-class life.

The city's volunteer fire companies, we have noted, were perceived as the proud symbols of community interaction and cooperation.

In an era of growing class and ethnic tensions, these companies were among the few organizations that joined men of all classes and backgrounds in the pursuit of public service and camaraderie. Cincinnati's firemen, exulted the editors of the *Gazette* in 1844, treated each other as "associates — friends — brothers; and when out in the performance of their duties, suffer no jealousies to bring them into collision."[17] The "warm-hearted and impulsive Irishman, the steady German, and the enthusiastic American," the editors continued, "have worked peacefully together."[18]

By the late 1840s, as the increased demands of business forced manufacturers, merchants, and professionals to withdraw from the organizations, fire companies became overwhelmingly working-class in composition and character. "The volunteer companies," reflected Donn Piatt, a critic of these developments, "gradually passed under the control of the worst classes gathered about town. The costly structures, built to protect the engines became club houses for organized ruffianism."[19]

An examination of the membership lists of the early 1850s indicates that Piatt's "ruffians" were journeymen and laborers — the same volunteers who had been so lavishly praised only a decade before.[20] Although part of the criticism of the fire companies arose out of their inability to protect property adequately, civic leaders seemed equally concerned with the growing social and political power of these working-class organizations. Fire companies were perhaps the only major voluntary association which united German, Irish, and native-born workers in a common cross-ethnic alliance. Although unions actively pursued the economic rights of their members, they generally did little to promote an ongoing sense of unity and mutuality outside the workplace or union hall. It was not until the early 1850s that a handful of unions endeavored to bridge the gap between the economic and social lives of their members. Typographers organized a union cricket club and began to hold annual balls; a number of German trades unions organized workingmen's singing and literary societies; engineers, machinists, draymen, and others sponsored day-long picnics and river excursions during hot summer months. However, union social events were few and far between.[21]

Fire companies, then, served as the city's most important multiethnic working-class social organizations and they frequently rejected elitist notions of proper behavior and decorum. Despite the pressure to outlaw all drinking in the firehouse, the Independent Fire Engine and Hose Company #2 merely agreed in August 1850 to encourage members not to "partake of any liquor while on duty at a fire."[22] Similarly, distrusting what they viewed as the increased capitalistic manipulation of the courts, the same company also defeated a motion which proposed the expulsion of any member "who shall be arraigned before any civil tribunal for any misdemeanor, and . . . found guilty."[23] Manufacturers were especially frightened by the occasional attempts by company members to link their roles as workers to their activities as firemen. In September 1848, several months after a bitter strike was lost by the city's iron molders, one company introduced a motion, which the company captain subsequently vetoed, to prohibit members from putting out any fire which might occur at the Yeatman and Shields' foundry.[24]

Fire companies also emerged as an important political force able to mobilize considerable numbers of votes on behalf of their proven friends. Firemen frequently used their power at the polls to obtain higher appropriations from their ambitious allies on the city council. Recounting the fate of several councilmen who refused to accede to company demands, one observer described how "a parade [organized by the companies] led by a dray bearing a coffin advertised the fact that the two councilmen held responsible for defeating an appropriation had signed their political death warrant."[25]

In 1852, angered and worried by the growing power of their firefighters, manufacturers, merchants, insurance company executives, and a number of political leaders mounted a campaign to abolish the companies and replace them with more easily controllable paid firemen. On March 9, 1853, despite the vigorous protests of Irish, German, and native-born workers, the opposition forces, led by Miles Greenwood, succeeded in establishing the nation's second paid fire department. (Baltimore's was the first.) Flushed with its success, Greenwood's committee boasted that it had finally shut down the lamentable engine houses "where innocence and virtue and the hopes of fond parents are bartered for idleness, profanity, and intemperance, and the other consequences sure of following, viz. rioting, debauchery, and bloodshed."[26] Yet, by so doing, Greenwood and his group had also ended the reign of the city's most important multiethnic worker-dominated leisure association — an association which apparently posed too many threats to the city's reigning capitalists to be tolerated.

While workers frequently united to oppose control by capitalists over fire companies and the OMI, debates over sociopolitical issues, most particularly temperance, wrought deep internal division within the working-class community. Temperance, argued various politicians, manufacturers, and clergymen, promised the best solution to the ills that beset society — poverty, crime, disease, and stagnating social mobility. The problem of dependency, which workers so often addressed, was rooted not in the economic relations between employers and employees but in the latter's fondness for drink. Alcohol, argued one temperance newspaper, held journeymen in "a more degrading and damning servitude than that which the poor Negro is subjected to."[27] Those who swore off this social evil, they promised, would find it easier to move up the ladder of success, for their sober and industrious habits would earn them the good will of employers and lead to steady raises and promotions.

As the campaign to limit, and later to prohibit, the sale of alcohol swept the city, a number of workers and unions joined with local reformers in endorsing the temperance cause. The reasons for this support, however, varied greatly. For the thousands of journeymen who joined organizations such as the Templars of Honor and Sons of Temperance (SOT), abstinence did seem to promise a better path to individual success. Indeed, more than half the building tradesmen — the most prominent group within the organization — who joined the SOT between 1844 and 1850 had succeeded in becoming independent contractors or lumberyard owners by 1856.[28] These organizations were also supported by various working-class women who argued that saloon life drained the pockets of the family breadwinner and prevented men from fulfilling their obligations as husbands and fathers. Meeting at Foster Hall in August 1851, one group of concerned women pledged themselves to use their influence "with fathers, husbands and brothers, against everyone, who, alike recreant to every feeling of self-respect and principle of republicanism," opposed the closing of the city's saloons and beer halls.[29]

The temperance campaign also attracted the support of a number of radical working-class newspapers and leaders, such as printer H. T. Ogden, who believed that sober and disciplined men were needed to do battle against the organized forces of capital. "The only mode of reforming the world," advised the editors of the Nonpareil, "is to prepare the mind for higher manifestations; to increase its power, to preserve its equilibrium." Alcohol only degraded minds and made the struggle for justice more difficult to organize and sustain.[30] Similarly, a number of unions, like the German United Tanners, though critical of the city's seemingly elite-dominated temperance societies, nevertheless embraced the cause as a means of rescuing workers "from the mire of vice, penury, and distress." Their constitution, adopted in February 1854, required total abstinence by members, both inside and outside the workplace.[31]

Not all workers found the temperance crusade alluring. The bonds of unity forged during economic struggles were often torn asunder by bitter clashes over such highly politicized social issues. Despite their common commitment to economic radicalism, the members of the iron molders' cooperative foundry suffered a devastating blow when disgruntled anti-temperance men withdrew from the enterprise after the passage of a series of temperance resolutions.[32] Similarly, various German and Irish workers, who viewed the temperance campaign "as an infringement of the rights and liberties of individuals," joined with manufacturers to lobby against any political candidate "who favors the temperance humbug."[33]

The campaign to shut down the city's saloons was also viewed by some journeymen and laborers as an effort to eliminate the locales of many union meetings. Unions such as the stonemasons lacked permanent meeting halls and were perpetually short of funds. Often, they gathered in the rooms provided free by local saloon- and beer-hall keepers. Saloons also provided workers with an inexpensive source of food. For the mere cost of three cents per glass of beer (or five cents for two), a man could feast to his heart's content upon the free hot and cold snacks set along the bar. For workers desperately trying to make ends meet, these low-cost meals were an absolute necessity, not a vice.[34]

Figure 8 Wielert's Saloon (c. 1875).
Saloons served as a place of amusement for some and a source of contention for others.
Courtesy of the Cincinnati Historical Society

Although leisure activities continued to remain a point of contention between workers and elites, as well as among workers, the influx of thousands of immigrants in the late 1840s and 1850s gradually shifted the primary focus of social conflict toward seemingly more important ethnic and religious issues. Economic and social divisions between native-born workers and native-born employers were often set aside as the two joined forces, as citizens, to protest against what they viewed as the proliferation of non-English speaking, non-Protestant, beer-guzzling radical European malcontents, whose unwholesome habits were seen as threats to American values and institutions. "The society of Cincinnati," Polish visitors Frances and Theresa Pulszky remarked in 1853, "lacks cohesion." New immigrants, who insisted on retaining their national customs and manners, had caused the city to divide "into coteries — which have little intercourse with one another, — not into classes, as in other places."[35] As social life assumed an increasingly ethnic character, cultural hostilities often superseded class divisions as the main focus of community conflict.

Not all immigrants, however, met with equal suspicion. English-speaking, Protestant Scottish, Welsh, and English immigrants, who generally settled in alongside native-born citizens and appeared to adhere to the city's dominant cultural mores, were praised for their "devotion to liberty and the elevation of man."[36] Their leisure and political activities were seen to reflect a keen understanding and appreciation of the republican values and institutions which governed community life.

Native-born citizens were less accepting of those foreigners who did not or would not conform to "American norms." "When an immigrant casts his anchor amongst us for life," the nativistic editor of the *Times* proclaimed in 1848, "he should forthwith Americanize all under his influence."[37] Germans, Jews, and Irish Catholics, with their seemingly strange and un-American social, political, and religious customs, were the principal targets of local scorn and, quite frequently, violence. "The increase in the number of emigrants, particularly from Germany and Ireland," German-born schoolmaster Frederick Gustorf reported in 1835, "has caused great apprehension among cultivated Americans . . . . [and] is discussed in the newspaper as being very disadvantageous to the institutions of the country."[38]

These apprehensions grew even more pronounced following the massive wave of German migration to Cincinnati in the 1840s and early 1850s. Unlike earlier generations of German immigrants, who had allayed nativistic fears by learning to speak English and by joining native-dominated associations, the recently arrived "Forty-Eighters" — so named for the political revolutions which shook Germany in 1848 — chose to isolate themselves geographically, economically, socially, and politically. They moved into the northern perimeter of the city, popularly referred to as Over-the-Rhine, and quickly established a wide array of German businesses, newspapers, beer gardens, theaters, churches, schools, rifle clubs, musical and literary societies, and mutual aid associations. This Teutonic enclave, with its shop signs all in German and a bustling population who spoke their native tongue and wore "palmetto hats, light blouses, and white trousers," and whose males adorned their upper lips with elegant mustaches — a custom not yet fashionable among American men — stood in sharp contrast to the rest of the city.[39] Upon walking over the Miami Canal bridge, which separated Over-the-Rhine from the rest of the city, "one passes," remarked a local reporter, "from the results of New England Puritanism to the most decided and peculiar phase of German civilization."[40] The overt German character of associational life, concurred another observer, made Cincinnati appear like "the Munich of North America."[41]

For many Germans, the desire for isolation was born not so much of an explicit rejection of American customs as of a desire to preserve their own traditional forms of community life. Although native-born citizens frequently saw Germans as a single ethnic body, the Over-the-Rhine area was, as one historian has noted, more "like a score of villages each overlapping in the same limited area."[42] Indeed, German social life was as diverse and varied as that of their native-born counterparts. Catholics, Jews, and Protestants each organized their own churches and societies.[43] Regional hostilities, which had plagued Germans in their homeland, were also brought to Cincinnati. "The Plattdeutsche," explained Fredericke Huake, editor of the *Volksfreund*, "is against the High German, the Swabian against the Bavarian, the Wurtenburger against the Prussian."[44] German community life was also divided between more conservative longtime residents, known as "Grays," and radical recent arrivals, known as "Greens."

Despite the diversity of German settlers, their efforts to maintain close ties with their native land and the similarity of many of their social values and customs caused many native-born residents to view them as a single and highly suspect body. The Germans' fondness for drink and their tendency to violate the sanctity of the Sabbath were two of the more important causes of nativistic resentment. Temperance leaders, who saw drink as the major reason for the declining economic and moral condition of the city's populace, were appalled by the proliferation of German beer halls and saloons. Between 1854 and 1860, the number of places which served alcohol rose from 800 to 2,000. For Germans, however, drinking among friends was an important social tradition. "When the evening came, and the toilings of the day were over," explained cabinetmaker Heinrich Ratterman, "then the German would seek to meet his friends, and in social company a melodious song and a frugal glass of wine or beer would wipe the cares of life from his eyebrows." Every Thursday night, Ratterman recounted, he and the members of his singing society gathered at the Rising Sun Tavern, located in the heart of the Over-the-Rhine area, where they would sing, discuss politics, and down a quart of beer.[45]

Civic and religious leaders were also disturbed by the German custom of pursuing their social pleasures and business activities on Sundays. The Germans, noted one traveler in 1854, "have succeeded in practically abolishing the Sabbath, as they virtually ignore that divine institution even as a day of rest, keeping their stores open the whole day."[46] Instead of attending church, Mrs. Karl Tafel reminisced, "whenever a Sunday morning promised fair weather," she and her friends, most of whom were all Forty-Eighters, "would set out bright and early with laughter and song and . . . march to woods or to Longworth's Wine Garden."[47] Although Tafel and others viewed Sundays as time for pleasure and recreation, not "the rest of the tomb," they found themselves denounced by "narrow-minded Puritans" and "fanatical Methodists" who railed against any violation of the "Puritan Stabbath."[48]

These hostilities were further intensified by the seemingly radical nature of a number of German social organizations. Unlike most native-dominated associations, which prohibited their members from engaging in any political or religious debates, the *Turnverein* (Turners) and the *Freimänner* (Freeman's) societies, the city's two largest German associations, encouraged social *and* political intercourse. The Turners had been organized after Napoleon's conquest of Germany. They were a semi-militaristic society designed to prepare young Germans for the future struggle for liberation. Led by recently arrived Forty-Eighters such as Gustav, Louis and Adolph Autenrieth, who fled Germany because of the radical activities of their father, a number of young Cincinnati Germans founded the nation's first Turner society in November 1848. The Turners organized social, gymnastic, and paramilitary activities and raised funds to support revolutionaries still fighting in Europe. They also joined compatriots throughout the nation in speaking out for the rights of organized labor and against slavery and its extension into the territories. Their overt involvement in political affairs, their fondness for drink and their tendency to walk the city's streets dressed in military uniforms elicited grave suspicion and hostility from many native-born residents. Turners were so disliked, explained one German, that they frequently "had to take to the side streets" in order to avoid being stoned.[49]

The Freeman's Society, founded in 1852 by the city's "free-thinking" German socialists, was even more radical in its social and political views. Organized to combat "American religious, social, and political prejudices," the society, which had attracted some 600 members by February 1853, spoke out against slavery, temperance, Sunday closing laws, the manipulations of organized religion, and social, political, and economic injustice.[50] Gathering "every Sunday and evenings" at Freeman's Hall, which also served as a frequent site of labor meetings and rallies, the society's members passed their time discussing politics, participating in the organization's singing and dramatic clubs, attending its regular series of lectures and debates, or simply drinking in the hall's bar.[51]

Despite their self-perceived position as the "heirs of the 'Enlightenment,' and the apostles of historic rationalism," and their professed admiration and dedication to republican principles, the Freemen were widely denounced by suspicious native-born citizens and newspaper editors as radical socialists who refused to speak English, adopt American ways, or "become citizens of our republic."[52] Their members, said one conservative critic, did "not believe in the Bible, nor a God in light of the Christian Church."[53] Baptist ministers, angered by the Freeman's proclivity for alcohol and anticlericalism, condemned the organization for being "on the side of intemperance and crime, and against good order and sobriety."[54] Even liberal reformers like Rufus King denounced the Freemen as "a German Infidel gang."[55]

German workers and employers, who were usually not welcomed in many of the city's existing associations, often pursued their leisure activities along ethnic rather than class lines. Organizations like the Turners and Freemen promoted common social bonds. The ranks of the Turners, although consisting mainly of skilled artisans, were also filled with furniture manufacturers, brew masters, merchants, commission agents, clerks, and laborers.[56] Even the more radical Freeman's Society, although it refused to grant membership to the city's leading German capitalists, nevertheless elected a number of small manufacturers and entrepreneurs to its board of directors.[57] Although these organizations did not necessarily stem the tide of class conflict, common efforts by employers and employees to pursue

(a)

Figure 9 German Social Life.

(a) Cincinnati Maennerchor (c. 1857). Germans were particularly active in bringing their social institutions to the United States. (b) Cumminsville Turnverein (c. 1880). The Turners attracted Germans of all economic ranks and united them in the pursuit of common ethnocultural goals. (c) Cincinnati Schuetzenplatz (c. 1860s). The Schuetzenplatz served as a shooting club, beer garden, and picnic grounds for the German community at midcentury.

Courtesy of the Cincinnati Historical Society

(b)

(c)

their right to spend their leisure hours as they saw fit undoubtedly served to deflect class antagonism within the German community.

Cincinnati's Irish residents, like the Germans, also found in social activities a means to preserve their cultural and political ties to the homeland. Although spread out in a number of different wards, Irish migrants who came to Cincinnati during and after the famines of the 1840s quickly established a number of religious and secular associations such as the Catholic Young Men's Society, the St. Patrick's Roman Catholic Benevolent Society, the United Irish Society, the Ancient Order of Hibernians, and the Shield's Guards. In addition to providing their members with spiritual and material support, a number of these organizations also tried to break down growing class conflicts and unite all Irish men and women, regardless of wealth or status, behind the greater cause of Irish nationalism. Lamenting the "cursed and unholy causes of disunion, which presently interfere in preventing a hearty and whole souled, a laudable and permanent combination of Irishmen," the leaders of the Emmet Club, organized in February 1848, urged all Irishmen to place their common ethnic and religious ties above their narrow class interests. If this could be accomplished, McCarthy O'Reidy prophesied in 1848, then "the golden mean will speedily become the great focus to which the daily laborer, the mechanic, the merchant, the lawyer, the physician, the man of wealth, the poor and pennyless will all converge."[58]

Although Irish employers and employees, like their German and native-born counterparts, often found themselves divided at the workplace, social organizations such as the Emmet Club, the United Irishmen, and the Irish Relief Association helped to attenuate class conflict by joining all of Erin's sons and daughters in a common identity and cause. The Committee for Irish Relief, organized in 1847 to raise money to save "thousands of our fellow creatures [in Ireland] from starvation," drew its leadership from a wide range of classes. Journeymen and laborers, such as shoemaker Peter Griffin, tanner J. McCabe, and street paver Thomas Huggins, united with bankers, merchants, and manufacturers, such as Charles Conohan, Henry Emerson, and R. W. Lee, to support their friends and families back home.[59]

Although many of these voluntary associations professed a deep loyalty to American values and praised the United States as the "great Republican theater of human activity and enterprise," Irish social and religious customs, particularly their love of alcohol and commitment to Catholicism, were nevertheless viewed by many nativisits as posing serious threats to community values.[60] "The name of 'Irish,'" observed the editors of the *Catholic Telegraph and Advisor* in 1853, "has become identified in the minds of many, with almost every species of outlawry."[61] Athough all foreigners, as well as blacks, were greeted by older Protestant residents with grave suspicion, Irish and German Catholics were adjudged the most direct threat to a republican society. The growth of the Catholic population from a negligible minority in 1820 to 35 percent of the city's churchgoing populace in 1850 frightened many longtime Protestant residents.[62] In "no other city of the union," reported one visitor in 1851, "have I observed such deep catholicity . . . as in Cincinnati."[63] Protestant citizens, fearing the threat of popery, issued hundreds of anti-Catholic tracts which proclaimed the complete incompatibility between republicanism and Catholicism. American Catholics, explained one tract, could not possibly remain "as free and unshackled in their allegiance to Civil Governments as Protestants," for they were all *"subject to the great Autocrat of all the Roman Catholics, the Pope of Rome."*[64] Even the generally radical workingmen's newspaper, the *Nonpareil*, joined in criticizing the Catholic church. "There are doubtless among us many Catholics by name who are good Republicans," it declared, "but to that extent they are not good Catholics. The two facts are incompatible with each other."[65]

Protracted Irish opposition to the reading of the King James translation of the Bible in public schools and the creation of numerous parochial schools further served to excite nativistic feelings. For Catholics in Cincinnati, and elsewhere in the United States, the issue of the Bible represented a life and death battle for salvation which transcended all other issues. Schooling their children in the Protestant Bible, they believed, would deprive them of "communion with the saints" and prevent them from entering the gates of heaven upon their death.[66] If Protestants would not honor these religious convictions, then good Catholics had to respond by creating their own schools. The city's Protestants, however, viewed these schools not simply as alternative institutions but as direct attacks upon the city's dominant religious and political values. Catholic parochial schools, argued one member of the public school board in 1853, were "discouraging a proper feeling of nationality, and encouraging sectarianism, that must be considered by all reflecting men, as Anti-Republican, and in direct violation of the letter, spirit, and laws of our Republican institutions."[67] One Protestant minister went so far as to claim that the "present plan of Rome is to conquer America, as a portion of Europe was won back from the Reformation — by the teaching of our children; and waiting quietly till a generation has grown up into Romanists."[68]

(a)

(b)

Figure 10 Religious and Ethnocultural Conflict.
(a) and (b) From the 1830s until the end of the century, Catholics and Protestants — as well as
Germans, Irish, Jewish, and native-born citizens — repeatedly clashed over the issue of public aid
to parochial schools as well as a wide array of other religious and cultural questions.
Courtesy of the Cincinnati Historical Society

Workers and the Political Sphere

For city residents long nurtured in republican ideology, politics appeared as the one sphere of activity in which all citizens, regardless of wealth, religion, or place of birth, met as equals. Although capitalists were gaining greater control over economic life, they, like their employees, could cast but one vote at the polls. For radical working-class leaders, politics did indeed appear as an arena where all workingmen could meet to redress injustice and inequality. If local workers united as a class, they argued, they could use their majority position within the electorate to alter the character of public and private life. But they did not do this. The vast majority of workers chose to pursue their concerns within the city's mainstream parties, and they steadfastly endeavored to minimize class conflict.

In the decades before the Civil War, working-class involvement in politics was channeled in two main directions: participation in national mainstream parties and participation in local political struggles. During the state and national elections held each October and November, the Democratic, Whig, Liberty, American (Know-Nothing), Free-Soil, and Republican parties each offered voters solutions to the growing tensions engendered by slavery and its expansion into the territories. The local political scene was crowded with a myriad of minor parties — temperance and anti-temperance, Bible and anti-Bible, and workingmen's parties — which vied for the loyalty and support of Cincinnati's citizens. Although debates over slavery would have the greatest effect upon the ultimate fortunes of national political life, it was the city's local elections, held each April, which consistently attracted the greatest number of voters to the polls. Indeed, for many citizens these local struggles were of far greater consequence to their immediate concerns than the more distant battles fought in Washington or Columbus.

Throughout the 1840s and 1850s, political life, like leisure, tended to divide the city's working class and turn its attention away from economic ills that plagued the lives of working people. Local politicans, successfully playing upon popular republican beliefs in the higher obligations of citizenship, insisted that the social, moral, and religious questions which threatened the stability of the republic were of far greater importance than the minor economic concerns that divided employers and employees. From 1843 until the late 1850s, local elections revolved almost entirely around ethnocultural issues. Political concerns for the detrimental consequences of industrialization and the problems engendered by the growing inequality of citizens were superseded by struggles over temperance, Bible reading in public schools, the spread of Catholicism, Sunday closing laws, prostitution, gambling, and a wide array of nativistic issues — voting restrictions, citizenship requirements, and immigration policies. Not until 1861, when a number of men moved to revitalize the moribund Workingmen's Party, did wage earners once again endeavor to link their roles as workers and citizens in a common political struggle.[69]

With the collapse of the Workingmen's Party following the election of 1842 and the ensuing cooptation of party leaders and platforms by Whigs and Democrats, the contentious social and ethnocultural issues which plagued leisure life moved into the forefront of municipal and county politics. Six of the nine muncipal elections held between 1843 and 1851 revolved primarily around the struggle to limit or prohibit the sale of alcohol. It must have been a strange sight, and for many a bitter one, to see radical workingmen like H. T. Ogden share the same platform and espouse the same cries for temperance as manufacturers like Miles Greenwood.[70]

The temperance crusade was only one of several political issues which divided and weakened the labor movement. In additon to protecting their school system from the onslaught of Catholicism, native-born Protestant workers and manufacturers also united to oppose the formation of separate public schools for German children. Fearful that their children would quickly forget their native tongue, Germans traded their support of Democratic candidates in the late 1830s and 1840s for the state legislature's approval of a bill to create a number of public schools in Cincinnati which would be conducted in German and English. Native-born residents, who viewed public education as a great democratizing force and a vehicle for inculcating American values, were outraged by the political manipulations of the German community. Separate schools for immigrants, it was believed, would ultimately breed disloyalty to the American system by perpetuating undesirable European ideas and values. Public schools, school board president Rufus King argued during a renewed flare-up with immigrants in the early 1850s, were vital in imparting an American "sense of order and discipline, the glow of industry, and emulation."[71] By using their political power to achieve their own schools, Germans had shown themselves to be the enemies of true republican ideas — enemies who had to be stopped at the polls before their influence spread too far.[72]

Anti-foreign and anti-Catholic prejudices grew more intense

during the 1840s and 1850s, and the economic struggle between labor and capital was often dwarfed by the political struggle to save the American republic from the onslaught of popery and infidelity. Nativistic politicians urged workers and employers to suspend their minor quarrels and honor their obligations as citizens to protect the city from the growing number of foreigners who crowded the banks of the Ohio River. The newly organized American Republican Party, the forerunner of the Know-Nothing movement, called upon voters in 1845 to "purify the Ballot-box" by electing only loyal native-born Protestant candidates.[73] Although the party received less than one hundred votes, its principles were adopted and advocated by a number of Protestant ministers and organizations such as the American Protestant Association. Declaring that "genuine American principles" were "identical with those of Protestant Christianity," the Reverend Charles Boynton predicted that the power of the nativistic movement would soon cause the "dissolution of the present great parties of the county" and the rise of a new party "formed upon moral questions" and rallying around the "*Protestant American flag.*"[74]

When the city's mainstream parties entered a period of deep internal turmoil in the early 1850s, it seemed that Boynton's prophecies would come true. With Whigs and Democrats internally divided over the slavery issue, the American Party, popularly known as the Know-Nothings, reemerged to offer voters an alternative. Pledging that they would unite the city and nation on "pure Republican principles," the party vowed to "redeem their country from the curse of Popery and foreign intolerance."[75] Among other things, the Know-Nothing platform called for American rule by Americans, reform of naturalization laws, opposition to papal influence, and the encouragement of American art, industry, and genius. Such measures, it promised, would "bring peace and plenty" to workers and employers alike. "Wages and prices . . . [would] be advanced," and "merchants, manufacturers, mechanics, and laborers — all were to be immediately relieved the moment the *reform* ticket was elected."[76] By the fall of 1854, the party had attracted enough support from workers and capitalists alike to sweep the county elections by a 7,000-vote majority.[77]

In Cincinnati, as well as in cities such as Philadelphia, Boston, St. Louis, and Louisville, working-class support of nativistic campaigns was greatly enhanced by the parallel timing of the mass influx of immigrants with the onset of the new age of manufacturing. For many native-born workers, immigrants, not the dramatic reorganization of production or the rise of new factories, appeared as the most visible and comprehensible cause of labor's declining fortunes. Immigrants not only challenged the accepted social and religious mores of community life; they were also perceived as a serious threat to the economic prosperity of native-born journeymen and laborers. Nativistic claims that immigrants lived off the taxes of the producing classes were not entirely unfounded. Immigrants, who frequently arrived in Cincinnati with little or no money, received a significantly larger proportion of city relief funds than native-born residents. Throughout the 1850s and into the early 1860s, Cincinnati's foreign-born population received between 67.8 and 85 percent of all outdoor relief expenditures. Irish migrants caused the greatest single drain, drawing off 21 to 42 percent of annual relief aid, while Germans received 17 to 29 percent of relief funds.[78]

Resentment against immigrant labor penetrated deep into the core of native working-class life. The growing gap between employers and workers of the late 1840s and 1850s often paled in comparison with the widening rifts between native and foreign-born laborers. Playing upon anti-Catholic working-class prejudices, one newspaper inquired during the early 1850s:

> Are not nine-tenths of the people who are hired in this city Catholics? Have they not been driving out and superseding Protestant laborers and servants? Has not the Catholic power by this means enabled them to increase in 15 years so as to fill ten or fifteen churches instead of one?[79]

Desperate for work, immigrants frequently obtained jobs by consenting to work for less money than their American counterparts. In so doing, they often provoked immediate retribution from displaced wage earners. A delegation of angry native tailors paid a visit in the autumn of 1848 to a German tailor known to sell his products for less than the going rate. Entering the shop, located in the Over-the-Rhine area, the tailors "*basted* the proprietor, sheared his hair, branded him in the seat with a *goose*, and finally *served him up* in a piece of muslin."[80] Similarly, a bitter fight erupted at a construction project near the Miami Canal when Germans attempted to displace Irish laborers by agreeing to work for one dollar a day — twenty-five cents less than the Irish received.[81] Further altercations among native, Irish, German, and the city's few black workers flared up throughout the 1840s and 1850s.[82]

Whatever progress unions may have achieved in tightening the bonds of common interest among workingmen was seriously under-

mined by the formation of nativistic working-class associations like the
Order of United American Mechanics (OUAM). Founded in Philadelphia
following the nativistic riots there of 1844, OUAM councils quickly spread
throughout the East, Midwest, and South. Cincinnati's first council, organized in 1847 and made up solely of the "true born sons of America,"
sought to protect native-born workers from immigrant laborers. The constitution of Washington Council No. 1 declared:

> We, the undersigned, American Mechanics and Workingmen, having for
> years, and more particularly of late, felt the peculiar disadvantages under
> which we labor from foreign competition and foreign combinations, and
> believing, from past experience and present appearances of the future, that
> instead of the evils abating, there is a strong possibility (if not certainty) of
> its increasing; therefore, we feel ourselves bound, by the duty we owe our
> families, ourselves and our country, to provide for our own protection by
> forming ourselves into an association, to advance such objects and carry out
> such principles as shall best promote the interest, elevate the character, and
> secure the happiness of the body of Mechanics and Workingmen of this
> country.[83]

Employing traditional republican rhetoric as their rallying cry,
OUAM members promised to employ only just, "fair and honorable means,
consistent with our duties as citizens, and our social duties to the human
family," to remedy the plight of American labor.[84] Their organization,
vowed printer J. W. Brewer — who found trade conditions worsened by
the proliferation of German printing shops — was designed solely "to
protect the native-born mechanic and laborer from the daily abuse and
degradation brought upon us by the constant influx of . . . . the pauper
labor of Europe."[85]

At the same time that union rhetoric and activities were
attempting to draw sharp distinctions between the interests of labor and
capital, organizations like OUAM were obscuring or attentuating these
differences and reuniting employers and employees in the pursuit of a
seemingly greater republican cause: the preservation of the intergrity and
independence of American labor. Although the organization's constitution
technically excluded "all those who are not native-born Mechanics and
Laboring Men," merchants, clerks, manufacturers, and small shop masters
played an important role in directing the movement. Of the 38 men who
held important council positions between 1847 and 1851, 17 were journeymen, 11 small shop masters, 2 large manufacturers, 4 clerks, 2 mer-

chants, and 2 professionals.[86] Building tradesmen (masters and journey-men), whose productive opportunities were particularly hard hit by foreign competitors, constituted the largest leadership element within the organization. The OUAM also received a good deal of moral and economic support from a number of the city's most prominent manufacturers. Industrial leaders like coppersmith Hezekiah Kierstead, paint manufacturer William Wood, tanner John Ballance, and ready-to-wear clothing manufacturer Samuel Thomas — men who all ranked among the top 10 percent of Cincinnati's manufacturers in 1850 — as well as other major capitalists were among the leading advocates of the OUAM.[87]

Not surprisingly, OUAM leaders urged class cooperation rather than class conflict as the best means to ensure mutual prosperity. Employers, many of whom also supported the Know-Nothing Party, were urged to hire only American-born mechanics. Adhering to these requests, Jesse Timmons, superintendent of construction at the new county court-house, and a loyal friend of the OUAM, instructed his sub-superintendents in August 1854 to hire "none but Americans and Protestants to the exclusion of any and all foreigners and Catholics.[88]

OUAM leaders also attempted to reform the moral character of their members by urging them to abandon the social evils that stood in the way of individual success. "Honesty, Industry, and Sobriety" was the organization's motto. Members who were detected in gambling houses and who frequented saloons were promptly fined or expelled from the organization. Similarly, any member who was "convicted in any court of justice, of any felonies or other criminal offense" — as were a number of striking workers in the early 1850s — would be immediately "expelled, and forfeit all claims [of financial assistance] upon the Council."[89] Although there are no surviving membership lists to indicate the number of men who joined the OUAM, participation had grown large enough by 1850 to require the establishment of four councils, each of which met weekly.[90]

Not all native-born workers perceived immigrants as the main cause of contemporary distress or as the most pressing political issue. During the early 1850s, a number of working-class organizations, such as the Labor and Labor Reform Party (LLRP) and the General Trades' Union, endeavored to bridge the chasm between native- and foreign-born workers and unite two in a common struggle against economic inequities. Struggles over immigration, temperance, and other social and moral issues, proclaimed the LLRP's founders in August 1850, only served to divide workers and obscure the true causes of distress. "The present disorganized state of society, and . . . . the increasing degradation of labor, which is now taking place throughout the city," they explained, were not caused by the influx of immigrants, but by the growing economic and political power of large manufacturers, nonproducers, and monopolists. These men had succeeded in capturing control of the two major parties and guided "them according to their will."[91] Consequently, instead of having a republican government run by "the people," the city's political establishment was "ruled by a moneyed aristocracy."[92]

Echoing the same themes sounded by the Workingmen's Party of 1842, the LLRP urged mechanics and laborers to unite as citizens and correct the "abuses of party politics" by "taking our own votes into our own hands, and sending office-seekers and hangers-on at the public crib to an honest toil for a livelihood."[93] Party leaders such as Irish-born carpenter Samuel Boyce and locksmith James Ireland, and native-born typographer E. B. Reed and millwright Michael Carpenter, urged all workers to abandon religious and ethnic hostilities and form an alliance which would use the producer's ethic and republican principles as the basis for achieving economic and political democracy. "We make no five year distinction between a foreigner and a native," one speaker announced at a party rally, "because a *man* is a man the world over, and wherever he erects the altar of Home there is he, at once, entitled to the equal rights and privileges with every other individual."[94] Its platform pledged the party to enact measures designed to establish labor's independence and secure all its products to those who toiled. The platform also called for the abolition of all laws for the collection of debts, a speedy end to land monopoly, the abolition of capital punishment, and the erection of free schools throughout the nation.[95]

Despite its numerous rallies in native-born, Irish, and German wards, the LLRP failed to redirect the political allegiances of more than a few hundred workers. Democrats, repeating the same strategy which had proven so successful in 1842, coopted the LLRP's more popular leaders into their party with promises of new reforms and more public offices for journeymen. Indeed, Democrats responded to renewed calls for a workingmen's party the following spring by nominating Mark Taylor, a former president of the Cooper's Union and the GTU of 1836, as its candidate for mayor. All hopes for a new workers' party were quickly crushed as journeymen and laborers joined with regular Democrats to elect Taylor to office. When Taylor stepped down in April 1853, he was followed by Democrat David T. Snellbaker, another former president of the Cooper's Union and GTU, who served as mayor until 1855. The election of these two popular working-class leaders put a halt to calls for independent working-class political action.[96]

Whatever success the LLRP and the newly revitalized GTU of 1853 and 1854 had in directing working-class struggles away from internally divisive ethnocultural issues was eventually shattered by the outbreak of three days and nights of rioting in the spring of 1855. On the afternoon of April 2, 1855, a mob of from three to four hundred people, enraged by reports of ballot-box stuffing in German voting districts, descended upon the Over-the-Rhine area and seized and destroyed 1,300 German ballots. News of the alleged German deceit and the "valiant" defense of American voting rights quickly spread throughout the city and precipitated numerous outbreaks of violence against German and Irish residents.

Fearing for their safety, German residents erected makeshift barricades along the entire perimeter of the Over-the-Rhine area. Led by the Turners and Freemen, German men and boys, armed with rifles and a cannon, patrolled the barricades waiting to repel any further attacks. Within a matter of hours, Cincinnati looked like the battle-torn areas of France and Germany. On the evening of April 3, further angered by this unwonted display of German militarism, four hundred nativists, screaming "Kill the Dutch" and "Remember Philadelphia," attempted to storm the barricades. They received the worst of the encounter. The better trained and better armed German riflemen, recounted Rufus King, "were completely an overmatch for the Americans who fled after the first volley leaving two of their party dead on the ground, besides sundry wounded."[97] Scattered incidents of violence, directed at Irish as well as Germans, persisted through the evening and following morning. Not until the evening of April 4 were the police able to restore calm and order.

In the aftermath of the riots, the few efforts to promote working-class political activism and unity were thwarted by the increasingly bitter debate over slavery, the rising fortunes of the Know-Nothings, and the onset of depressions in 1855 and 1857. Between 1854 and 1860, the political arena, in Cincinnati and throughout the nation, was deeply divided over the question of slavery, and most particularly its expansion into the Kansas and Nebraska territories. Indeed, at no time in the city's history were political divisions so deeply felt by mainstream parties as in the half dozen years preceding the Civil War. Democrats found their organization greatly weakened as antislavery German Protestants abandoned the party in favor of the new Republican Party. Cincinnati Republicans, however found themselves equally divided as their antislavery, temperance, and nativistic wings all competed for power and ascendency. Know-Nothings (the American Party) tried to capitalize on these divisions by avoiding the slavery issue altogether. They simply called for the preservation of Union and the rule of America by Americans. Efforts to resurrect the LLRP proved a dismal failure as workers, like the citizenry at large, found themselves caught up in the seemingly greater struggle between the forces of union and disunion.[98]

Working-class political and economic activism was also thwarted by the economic depressions that beset the city between 1854 and 1859. It was not until the renewal of trade activity in the latter year that journeymen and laborers once again began to organize around economic and political issues. The roles of worker and citizen, which had been splintered by the ethnocultural struggles of the past decades, were reunited by a series of dramatic events in 1860. In March, native- and foreign-born workers, outraged by the introduction of a bill in the state legislature which would have made it a felony for any employee to strike against an employer, suspended their mutual hostilities and joined together to oppose the bill's passage. Members of the OUAM, citing the "imperative necessity of combining together to protect our just and legal rights," voted to join with German and Irish workers as a single united "body of mechanics." During the following weeks, several thousand handbills were printed and circulated, and rallies featuring German, Irish, and American speakers attracted upwards of two to three thousand workers.[99]

What had begun as a movement to oppose one particular bill soon developed into a more sweeping effort to integrate and promote the economic, political, and social interests of all Cincinnati workers. Labor leaders, flushed with success in defeating the no-strike bill, revived the dormant General Trades' Union (GTU). GTU leaders, drawn from the OUAM, the German Workingmen's Association, and various native-dominated unions, called upon workers to break down the barriers of mistrust and unite to "oppose the power that has thrown them into an abject position."[100] In addition to setting as its goal the elevation of the mechanic's "rights as a laborer and a man," the GTU also sought the "elevation of the Mechanic in his social relation."[101] Influenced by their German constituency, who viewed social activities as an important means of promoting mutual trust and unity among tradesman, the GTU organized a massive picnic and outing in mid-May 1860 that attracted over 10,000 men, women, and children.[102]

Despite the growing optimism among the ranks of the producing classes, Cincinnati was once again plunged into economic distress by the growing threat of disunion following Lincoln's election. As trade with the southern states steadily declined during the winter of 1860-1861, large numbers of mechanics, seamstresses, and laborers were thrown out of work. Some five hundred workers, meeting at the Sixth Street Market on a blustery January evening, attributed the national crisis to the "acts of designing tricksters, politicians, and demagogues." War, exclaimed machinist Isaac Hedges, would only lead to the mass slaughter of workers, for they, and not the politicians or wealthy manufacturers, would be the ones sent off to fight. Only the organized action of all workingmen, foreign and native, insisted iron molder Frederick Oberkline, could save the republic from dissolution. Endorsing these and similar sentiments, the meeting declared that the prosperity of all workers depended "on the continuance of the Union of the States under the Constitution;" it also adopted a resolution urging the "laboring masses of the country to sever party connections, and unite in Trades' Unions, or similar organizations, and to elect men to office who will look to our interests and execute the laws of the land."[103]

Determined to prevent the outbreak of war, and convinced that mainstream parties could not protect their interests as workers or citizens, hundreds of men, "from the well-to-do mechanic down to the stevedore and other common laborers," joined together early in the winter of 1861 to form a new Workingmen's Party. The party's initial organizing efforts were led by the city's machinists, iron molders, and printers — the three Cincinnati unions which had joined national labor organizations and were particularly active in reasserting their power in the workplace.[104] After bemoaning the depressed economic position of the producing class, the delegates at the party's nominating convention, held on February 16, 1861, adopted a platform which condemned the manipulations of politicians and called for the "maintenance and perpetuation of the States as formed by our fathers and administered under the Constitution."[105] Learning from the mistakes of past years, party leaders attempted to co-opt popular mainstream candidates by endorsing three Democrats and three Republicans who were running for major municipal offices. The remaining eight candidates were selected from among the ranks of the city's "true working men": two machinists, two printers, and one molder, one butcher, one building tradesman, and one flatboat maker.[106]

Prospects for local victory brightened when the Working

Man's Party (WMP) of Newport, Kentucky, won nine of the thirteen city offices contested during the March elections.[107] Yet, despite early optimism, the Cincinnati party met with little success. The Democratic Union Party narrowly defeated the Republicans in a sweep of all major municipal offices. Molder Ansil Robinson, the Working Man's candidate for mayor, received only 589 votes (2.5 percent of the total vote), while the party's most successful candidate, machinist David Smith, won a mere 1,144 votes (4.9 percent). Moreover, the two jointly endorsed Democratic candidates whom the party helped to elect professed no loyalty or obligation to the working-class organization.[108]

The WMP failed because of its inability to persuade workers to forsake traditional party allegiances and its unsuccessful attempt to redefine the rules of the political game. Party leaders were so convinced that their professed support of the Union and republican ideals would attract the support of all reasonable men that they did little by way of perfecting ward organizations or promoting voter turnout—two techniques which were well utilized by Republicans and Democrats. Although party principles were announced in late January, many ward candidates were not selected until two or three days before the election. The elaborate fanfare that was employed to attract attention by mainstream parties was disdained by the WMP. They held few rallies, printed few flyers, and placed few advertisements in local newspapers.

Whereas immediate political success in 1842 had brought long-term defeat to the Working Man's Party, defeat in 1861 prompted a series of actions which augured long term success. Recognizing the need to foster closer links between working-class political economic activities—rather than keeping them apart as had been done in previous years—the leaders of the WMP and GTU effected a close mutual alliance. [109] Indeed, despite the party's eventual defeat, its campaign had succeeded in attracting scores of German, Irish, and native-born workers into WMP and GTU. For one of the few times since the mass migration of the 1840s, there were two central bodies bent upon dissipating ethnic hostilities and internal divisions through a program of common political, economic, and social interaction.[110]

This tenuous alliance between native and foreign workers was soon shattered by the outbreak of the Civil War. Agreeing with Republican politicians that loyalty to the Union was paramount to any immediate economic concerns, a rally of German workers pledged that they would "rise as one man at his [Lincoln's] call, ready to risk their lives in the effort to maintain the victory already won by freedom over slavery.[111] Although a number of workers remained critical of the war effort (the typographers, for example, carried on an active correspondence with southern unions throughout much of the war), as soon as the first shots rang out at Fort Sumter, thousands of Cincinnatians enlisted to defend the Union. Combining the obligation of citizenship with a strong sense of workplace identity, groups of painters, printers, steamboatmen, and other laboring men formed distinct workingmen's companies.[112] Beginning in mid-April and lasting for several years, the battle between labor and capital was overshadowed by the battle to preserve the American nation.

CHAPTER EIGHT

Fighting For Union:
Labor in Opposition,
1861 – 1873

I n April 1865, after four years of bitter war, victorious
Union soldiers returned home amid the tears and thanks
of a grateful nation. In Cincinnati, however, as in many
other industrial cities, the period of widespread jubilation was shortlived.
As numerous manufacturers poured their considerable wartime profits into
expanding and reorganizing factory production, Cincinnati workers increasingly found themselves faced with the specter of a new kind of servitude:
what they called industrial slavery. Beginning in the spring of 1865 and
lasting until the onset of a major national depression in 1873, the men who
had fought to protect the Union against the southern "slaveocracy," embarked upon an economic and political campaign to protect their crafts,
wages, and status as citizens against the seemingly unbridled and, they
thought, iniquitous forces of industrial capitalism.

The battle for the Union begun in 1861 assumed a new
dimension after the surrender at Appomattox as the city's workingmen
endeavored to create new bonds of union among all wage earners. While
workers of the 1840s and 1850s had occasionally joined together in common
class protests, they nevertheless tended to remain divided by differing trade,
ethnic, religious, and political loyalties. Yet, in the years after 1865, Cin-

cinnati workingmen, bolstered by their belief that it was the nation's wage earners, not its capitalists, who had saved the Republic from dissolution, forged an unprecedented series of political and economic alliances which united all types of workers — skilled and unskilled, native-and foreign-born, and even, on occasion, black and white — in a common struggle to obtain justice and preserve the free-labor victories of war. Although these crusades often fell short of their desired goals, the widespread coalitions and networks established by workers during these years laid the groundwork for the more protracted and successful struggles that would sweep the city in the late 1880s.

In the weeks following the outbreak of Civil War, the streets of Cincinnati were filled with constant excitement as local military units readied themselves for what was sure to be a brief and glorious war. "The first sound in the morning is the fife and Drum and and also the last sound at night," George Ware wrote in May 1861, "and all Day men are marching about."[1] When the call to battle finally came, the German Turner Regiment, dressed in the familiar white linen garb of their society, and the Irish Fifth and Sixth Ohio Regiments, equally resplendent in their fine gray and red uniforms, marched out of the city "amid the applauding cheers of vast crowds lining the streets and bidding them God-speed."[2] During the next year and a half, this early joy and optimism turned to bitter sorrow as Union troops suffered repeated bloody defeats on the southern battlefields.

Merchants and manufacturers who remained at home found their anxieties over their kin compounded by a severe economic depression that gripped the city from 1861 to the early months of 1863. The cessation of the city's prosperous southern trade and the Confederacy's repudiation of the considerable debts owed to Cincinnati businessmen, lamented the Chamber of Commerce in August 1861, had caused "the comparative ruin of our commerce and industry."[3] With trade at a standstill, scores of mercantile firms went bankrupt, while hundreds of manufacturers were forced to shut down or severely curtail their operations.[4]

Although many businessmen suffered a precipitate loss of profits, the economic travails of war, remarked one reporter in June 1861, fell most heavily upon the "mechanical and laboring portion of our community," who to a great extent were thrown out of work.[5] By January 1862, over 30,000 men and women roamed the streets looking for work.[6] As the number of unemployed continued to skyrocket, soup kitchens were set up to provide some nourishment for the impoverished families of "worthy mechanics," while thousands of destitute souls flocked to neighborhood police stations to spend the night sleeping on station-house floors.[7] Hard times also prompted scattered outbreaks of violence among desperate wage earners. Screaming "Let's clear out the niggers," Irish dock workers, angered by the attempts of black laborers to underbid them for jobs, initiated a two-day riot in July 1862, which left a trail of destruction that stretched from the city's docks into the black homes along the levee.[8]

Although the human tragedies of war continued until the end of hostilities in April 1865, the city's economic fortunes took a sharp upswing late in 1862 as manufacturers and merchants resumed trade with western and European markets and, more importantly, began filling lucrative government contracts to feed, clothe, and arm the Union's warriors. As federal troops advanced into the western regions of the Confederacy and opened the Mississippi River to trade, Cincinnati soon became the center of supplies for the support of those armies, and "as if by magic, almost every branch of business was stimulated into unexampled activity."[9] During the next two years, reported a jubilant Chamber of Commerce, the city entered a period of prosperity "never excelled, if equalled, since the formation of the government."[10] Manufacturers who produced clothing, shoes, pork, foodstuffs, barrels, soap, candles, hardware, machinery, munitions, and medical supplies for Union troops, they added, "have made profits — beyond previous precedent."[11]

With shops and factories operating at full force, journeymen, laborers, and outworkers once again found steady employment. Yet, while often recovering their old jobs, journeymen — whose unions had collapsed as their members went off to fight in the war — found themselves unable to prevent manufacturers from undermining their economic standing and craft traditions by introducing large numbers of "incapable and uninstructed labor" into every branch of employment.[12] Despite the vast profits made by their employers, mechanics and laborers complained during a joint rally in May 1864, "skilled workmen, who have spent years at low wages — and, in many cases, accumulated hundreds of dollars worth of tools — to become masters of their calling, find their wages not advanced, but decreased, while the novices also obtain no increase of their wages." Such a situation, they exclaimed, was "an insult to labor, degrading the mechanic, and if continued, will destroy the value of trades, and place mechanics upon the basis of European reward [i.e., mere proletarians], and thus, as a consequence, destroy the value of unskilled labor also."[13]

Worse yet, while working men toiled in the factories and on

the fields of battle, farmers, merchants, and manufacturers grew "rich while they slept."[14] Many "who had eked out a bare subsistence" before the war, observed one local writer, "became suddenly immensely wealthy, and in their fine equipages, with liveried servants, rolled in magnificence along the city streets." Channeling their profits into new ostentatious displays of wealth, he added, manufacturers and commercial elites "built princely mansions in the city and on the surrounding heights beyond the city limits."[15] Moreover, the close residential proximity of rich and poor which had characterized ante-bellum community life gradually dissolved as large numbers of wealthy families abandoned the increasingly congested and polluted downtown area for cleaner and more elegant suburban homes.[16]

For the thousands of workers returning home from war, the appearance of such lavish wealth in the midst of declining real wages and craft independence stood as a sharp and bitter contrast to the free-labor struggles of the past four years. Stepping up to the podium in Boston's Faneuil Hall in November 1865, machinist and Civil War veteran Ira Steward, sounding a theme that became the rallying cry of wage-earners in Cincinnati, announced that the men who had crushed the rebel aristocracy in war would now fight to "claim a more equal share in the wealth their industry creates in peace and a more equal participation in the privileges and blessings of those free institutions, defended by their manhood on many a bloody field of battle."[17]

Working-class participation in the Civil War instilled a new sense of legitimacy and righteousness in their postwar demands for justice and equality. Republican beliefs and rhetoric, so pervasive in ante-bellum years, were reaffirmed and heightened by their wartime efforts. It was the nation's workers, espoused one German trade unionist, who had saved "the independence of the republic."[18] The rich had often bought their way out of war.

"Few of the rich," concurred another workingman, "have had anything to do with the war, except as officers, contractors, speculators, and money-lenders to the government. . . . Precious little blood has the war drawn from their veins."[19] As the refrain of one popular working-class song caustically noted: "You gave your son to the war/ The rich man loaned his gold/ And the rich man's son is happy to-day,/ And yours is under the mold."[20]

Cincinnati workers had honored their obligations as citizens by laying down their tools, leaving their families, and risking life and limb to preserve the Union. For them, the Spirit of 1776 was no longer an abstract memory passed down from generation to generation, but a living reality. The nation's workers had refought the struggle for freedom and independence and saved the republic from dissolution.

Common participation in the Civil War also helped dissipate many of the ethnic tensions which had previously divided Cincinnati wage earners. Having fought — and died — alongside their native-born brethren, foreign-born workers had proven themselves to be true republicans, true preservers of the American state. Although a number of postwar unions continued to be dominated by particular ethnic groups, they were now regarded — at least for a time — as *working-class* unions which happened to be made up of ethnic members.

During the summer and autumn of 1865, workers in Cincinnati and throughout the nation, bolstered by their self-perceived role as saviors of the Union, embarked upon a new battle to restore what they viewed as their fallen status as producers and citizens. "For a number of years," argued the returned veterans of the recently reorganized carpenters' union, they had "neglected their individual interest and standing as mechanics" to fight the more pressing battle to save the Republic. Now that the war was over, they called upon all journeymen to join them in a new campaign aimed at "protecting and promoting their own interests and common welfare as mechanics."[21] The leaders of the shipcaulkers' union, noting that their wartime obligations as citizens had made them "forgetful of their own interests," also urged their members to turn their attention toward those issues now "most vital to their existence."[22]

During the following months and years, these memories of self-sacrifice and wartime service served as powerful rallying cries that helped unite workers of all skills, trades, and ethnic groups in a new campaign to restore their fallen unions and obtain what they viewed as a decent standard of living. Heeding the cries of the carpenters and shipcaulkers, journeymen and laborers reestablished at least forty unions by the end of 1865. While decrying the expansion of factory production and the degradation of their crafts, workers nevertheless primarily demanded a fairer share of the profits of their toil. Of the 36 strikes launched between 1864 and 1867 (30 led by journeymen, 6 by unskilled laborers) 34 were fought over demands for higher wages.[23] Working-class struggles for economic justice ran so high during this period that Irish and black stevedores, who had clashed so violently in 1862, joined together in June 1866 and marched en masse to the city's docks to demand better pay for all.[24]

These demands often resembled those of ante-bellum years,

but the nature of the labor organizations making them changed significantly in the postwar era. The Civil War prompted the nation's workers to look beyond the narrow confines of their local trade unions. The struggle for union was continued in a new form after 1865 as Cincinnati's printers, iron molders, blacksmiths, ship carpenters and caulkers, cigarmakers, tailors, shoemakers, coachmakers, and building tradesmen united with fellow craftsmen throughout the country to forge national trade unions which would protect their members against "despotic employers."[25] Cincinnati journeymen also joined a number of national labor organizations which, like the International Industrial Assembly and the National Labor Union, endeavored to break down trade divisions by engaging all skilled, and occasionally unskilled, workers in a common nationwide struggle to defend the rights and interests of all wage-earners.[26]

In Cincinnati, the emergence of a new, more powerful city-wide Trades and Labor Assembly (TLA) signaled the most important local development of the period. Unlike ante-bellum trades assemblies, which were often weakened by the pervasive craft loyalties and ethnic conflicts of their members, the revitalized TLA, organized in the spring of 1864, set out to join and direct all workers in a common struggle "for self protection, and for the promotion of the interests of other labor associations."[27] TLA leaders, drawn largely from the ranks of the city's more militant printers' and iron molders' unions, called upon their fellow journeymen to abandon their traditional disdain for the plight of unskilled workers and help to encourage the "formation of unions among the unskilled laborers of this city."[28]

These efforts were greatly aided by the introduction of a bill in the Ohio legislature in March 1865 which proposed to make it a felony for workers to strike for higher wages. Condemning the measure as a violation of the "fundamental ideals which underlie the superstructure of the Republic," the TLA succeeded in uniting German, Irish, and native-born journeymen and laborers in a successful effort to pressure local and state politicians into defeating the bill.[29] By early autumn, over two dozen unions, heartened by their victory over the "oppression of gormandizing capital," had enlisted in the ranks of the TLA.[30]

Encouraged by their initial success, the TLA moved quickly to join with working-class organizations around the country to lobby for the passage of a measure which they believed would appeal to and unite all wage-earners regardless of trade, skill, ethnicity, religion, sex, or age: the institution of an eight-hour work day. For workers in Cincinnati and throughout the nation, the eight-hour campaign soon emerged as the focal effort to restore a greater measure of equality between labor and capital.

Cincinnati workers of the 1860s did not initially view labor and capital as inherent enemies. Clinging to a vision of work and community rooted in an earlier world dominated by artisans, shopkeepers, and farmers, they still saw labor and capital as essentially equal forces which, under proper conditions, acted in concert to produce individual and collective prosperity. The assertion that labor and capital were "engaged in a life and death struggle, in which one or the other must go down," avowed one printer, was patently false.[31] It was individual capitalists, rather than an intrinsically flawed economic system, that caused misery and distress among the working class. "Adverse relations between capital and labor," one iron molder explained, occurred only when "the *power* that capital gives its possessor" was abused.[32] End the misuse of power by corrupt individuals, and society would resume its natural state of balance.

However, when the postwar growth of industrial capitalism, monopolies, and corporations seemed to threaten this free-labor strain of ante-bellum republican ideology, the cry of "industrial slavery" emerged as a powerful metaphor that rallied workers in the defense of their self-perceived economic and political rights. The eight hour-day campaign, insisted TLA leaders, was less an attack upon what America was than what it was becoming: a nation of dependent, slave-like wage earners who could not fully exercise their rights as workers or citizens. For northern citizens, explained political historian Michael Holt, "the word 'slavery' had long held a definite meaning aside from the institution of black slavery in the South . . . . Slavery implied the subordination to tyranny, the loss of liberty and equality, and the absence of republicanism."[33] Just as many workers had demanded that government intervene to stop the spread of chattel slavery, so too did they now call upon politicians to stem the growth of so-called industrial slavery — a form of servitude which subjected citizens to the arbitrary and autocratic control of manufacturers. It was this desire to *limit*, not necessarily to abolish, the unfettered and unrepublican growth of industrial capitalism which served as the organizing principle behind the eight-hour-day movement.[34]

Arguing that the time was not ripe for the formation of an independent workingmen's party, TLA leaders such as mustard-box man-ufacturer William Haller, blacksmith George Hadley, plasterer John Casey, shoemaker Terrence Mehan, cigarmaker Charles Weibel, printers John Tomlinson and E. F. Bigler, and iron molders Larkin McHugh, Isaac Neal, and Frederick Oberkline — war veterans drawn from the city's German, Irish, and native-born communities — organized an Eight-Hour League to pressure mainstream parties to endorse "this much needed reform."[35] During the dozens of League rallies held that fall and winter, flamboyant orators like Haller, Oberkline, and McHugh repeatedly reminded their listeners that, while civic leaders had often praised labor as the equal of capital and as partners in progress, workers had realized little in the way of real material rewards. "Capital gets the lion's share [of wealth]," McHugh exclaimed at one rally, "denying to its creator its just portion, except when compelled by strikes or competition."[36] Not only were workers robbed of their just earnings, but they also found their very lives endangered by long hours of toil in the city's unhealthy shops and factories. Thousands of men, women, and children, declared one resolution committee, were "hurried to untimely graves from breathing the vitiated atmosphere of the close workshops."[37]

Forced by low wages and dire necessity to labor upward of ten to twelve hours a day, workers often complained that they were mere commodities who, because of the need to feed their families, sold themselves into a day's "bondage." An eight-hour day, argued labor leaders throughout the country, would help remedy this abhorrent situation by drawing, as historian David Montgomery has explained, "a clear distinction between that part of the workman's day which might be purchased for wages and that which remained inalienably his own."[38] Such a measure, insisted local TLA leaders, would ultimately benefit employers and employees alike, for with more "time to improve his mental and moral condition" the laborer would grow "more intelligent, and consequently, more valuable to the employer."[39] With mind and body properly rested, added iron molder Oberkline, "every man would be able to do as much effective labor in eight hours as he now does in ten." Yet, lest manufacturers think that they could continue to exploit their more efficient employees, Oberkline quickly warned that journeymen would reap the profits of their toil by demanding ten hour's pay for eight hour's work![40]

League leaders also portrayed an eight-hour work day as a patriotic measure vital to the continued political well-being of the nation. Various speakers drew upon themes often utilized by elites and politicians and argued that the preservation of a virtuous republic depended upon the willingness and ability of men to fulfill their responsibilities as citizens. To do so, one trade union leader explained in July 1865, a man needed time to "acquaint himself with the political topics of the day, so as to enable him to discharge himself of the duties incumbent upon him as a man and as a citizen."[41] However, by requiring their employees to labor long hours, manufacturers deprived them of the time and energy they needed to fulfill their civic duties. Thereby workers became political as well as economic slaves of capital. Workers had saved the republic from one kind of slavery, said one German journeyman; they now had "not only a right, but a *duty* to take steps" to defend it against the growth of a new kind of servitude.[42]

Underlying these various appeals to citizenship and justice was a more basic desire by workers simply to spend fewer hours at their jobs. As production grew more highly specialized, routinized, and boring, journeymen and laborers sought to have more time for activities outside the workplace. Moreover, an eight-hour day would help to enhance family life by allowing mothers, fathers, and children to spend more time together. It was this desire "to allow the poor workingmen some little recreation during God's sunlight with his family," wrote one mechanic, that led him and his friends to fight for the eight-hour cause.[43]

The TLA rallied the city's workers around the cry of "Eight Hours For Work, Eight Hours For Sleep, and Eight Hours For Mental and Moral Improvements," and soon succeeded in mobilizing a wide range of supporters. Irish building tradesmen, who traditionally remained aloof from independent working-class political struggles, now joined with German and native-born workers to demand the passage of an eight-hour bill. Civic figures such as Judge Edward Woodruff, a prominent leader of the local Irish Fenian movement, the Reverends Nicholas Summberbell and M. P. Gaddis, and the editors of the *Enquirer*, *Volksblatt*, and *Volksfreund* lent further legitimacy to the movement by actively supporting the workers' demands for the eight-hour day. Mainstream politicians were also swept up by the eight-hour fever. With upward of two thousand voters attending League rallies, Democrats and Republicans, observed TLA president McHugh, "being desirous of securing our suffrages," promptly nominated men who vowed to "represent the interests of workingmen in the state legislature." All nine of the Democrats and six of the Republicans running for state office that October, he boasted, had come out on behalf of an eight-hour bill.[44]

Politicians throughout the state eagerly gave similar promises, and Ohio's journeymen and laborers succeeded in electing enough representatives to secure the passage of an eight-hour bill in the lower house in February 1866. The early optimism of autumn and winter, however, soon turned to dismay as senators and representatives, unable to achieve a compromise over several additional amendments, allowed the bill to die in committee.[45] Angered by the broken "pledges made and given before the elections," TLA leaders abandoned their lobbying tactics and called upon workers "to emancipate themselves from their degrading party influences" and to support a "straight-out workingmen's candidate" in a special congressional election in October 1867.[46]

What had begun as a campaign to secure fewer working hours soon evolved into a broader oppositional movement to preserve the very integrity of Ohio's political institutions. Workingmen, explained one journeyman, believed that government was a neutral arbiter of justice for all citizens, and they had "repeatedly appealed to those selected to the legislature [to act] for the general good." Yet, instead of answering these appeals, legislators had corrupted the political arena by acting as the shameless vassals "of capital, the national banks, and the bondholders of the country."[47] Since these men were no longer responsive to the needs of the people, it was incumbent upon honest workingmen to "strike a blow in vindication of the entire purity" of the state by taking political power "into their own hands, to the end that government shall be a government of the people; of the majority, not the minority."[48] Former Civil War General Samuel F. Cary was chosen as the Workingmen's Party nominee that September and ran on a platform which called for an eight-hour work day, more stringent laws to prevent "soulless corporations" from gaining control of public lands, and the restoration of a truly neutral republican government.[49]

Learning from the mistakes of the low-keyed and unsuccessful campaign of 1861, party organizers emulated the rituals of their mainstream rivals and held dozens of rallies, parades, and torchlight processions to create a high pitch of excitement among working-class voters. The TLA leaders, who served as the campaign's architects, also made unprecedented efforts to politicize and recruit the city's foreign-born voters. In a move aimed at luring the support of German voters, who were closely allied with the Republican Party, the TLA moved its party headquarters to Arbeiter (Workingman's) Hall, located in the Over-the-Rhine area. German trade unionists, like molders Oberkline and John Krauth, cigarmaker Augustus Hitzman, and tailor Bernard Tonnies quickly enlisted the aid of their fellow countrymen in organizing ward committees, sponsoring rallies, and delivering speeches — in English and German — throughout the city. Irish workers, who tended to support the Democratic Party, were drawn to the campaign by Cary's outspoken endorsement of Irish land struggles and the ability of party leaders such as Larkin McHugh, iron molder Thomas

Leonard, and printer Frank Rist (men who also served as officers in the city's Hibernian, United Irish, and Fenian societies) to recruit their brethren to the workingmen's cause.[50]

The greatest contribution to party fortunes, however, came from the city's Democrats. Sensing a possible Republican defeat in the making, local Democrats decided to support Cary rather than put up their own candidate. Consequently, when the votes were counted in early October, Cary and his Workingmen's Party defeated the Republican candidate by a vote of 10,390 to 9,431. True to his word, Cary went off to Washington, where he helped to secure passage of the first federal eight-hour law in June 1868, a measure which, however, soon proved ineffective.[51]

Encouraged by their fall victory, the TLA decided to run a full slate of workingmen's candidates in the municipal elections of April 1868. Yet, as had happened in past years, the party's success in October soon led to its demise. Mainstream parties, as they had done before and would continue to do, quickly moved to co-opt the workingmen's most popular candidates by endorsing them on their own tickets. While several of these "coalition candidates" went on to win their campaigns, not a single one of the lesser known men who ran solely on the Workingmen's ticket was elected to office.[52] Working-class efforts at further independent political action soon ground to a halt when the TLA's most influential leaders — McHugh, Oberkline, Neal, and iron molders J. B. Lodge and Ansil Robinson — accepted important positions in the Democratic and Republican organizations. Shortly after being appointed vice-president of the Cincinnati Grant clubs, a repentent Isaac Neal announced that he had "committed a mistake" by involving himself in the workingmen's party. Insisting that it was the Republicans who had done the most for advancing "the interests of the laboring classes . . . and the material interests of the country," he promised "to wipe out that blot by working hard for Grant and [Schuyler] Colfax" in the upcoming presidential election of 1868.[53]

The TLA was decimated by the defection of its leaders and withdrew from direct political action to resume its less ambitious role as a political lobbying group. Although a small number of workers, led largely by the city's socialists and radical trade unionists, continued to run independent workingmen's slates in local and state elections during the next two decades, they rarely succeeded in attracting more than a few hundred votes.[54] Describing how similar scenarios of political cooptation were repeated in countless cities across the nation, historian David Montgomery has astutely remarked that the "capacity of America's polticial structure to absorb talent from the working classes was perhaps the most effective deterrent to the maturing of revolutionary class-consciousness among the nation's workers during the turbulent social conflicts of the late nineteenth century."[55]

It would be a mistake, however, to attribute the decline of independent working-class political action solely to the defection of a few important individuals. Democrats and Republicans, like the TLA, were also able to use appeals to patriotism and the obligations of citizenship to further their own ends. From 1865 through the 1880s questions regarding the guilt for the war and the appropriate course of Reconstruction frequently occupied the center stage of party politics. National, state, and local elections, reflected Andrew Hickenlooper, a prominent Cincinnati Republican, were often dominated by the Republicans' "vigorous waving of the bloody shirt" and the Democrats vituperative attacks against what they insisted were the pro-Negro, anti-white, and anti-labor Reconstruction policies of the Radical Republicans.[56] Workers were repeatedly cautioned by mainstream politicians not to allow their narrow economic and politicial concerns to supersede the more vital issues of the day. "Have you, in your struggle for the eight-hour law," asked one Democrat in 1866, "lost sight of your country and the best interest of the laboring white man?" The importance of the eight-hour law, he argued, paled in comparison to the higher obligations of citizens to voice their "approval or disapproval of the course which the President has taken to restore the Union of the States."[57] The ethnic and occasional racial unity engendered during the early years of the eight-hour campaign was shattered after April 1868 as Germans flocked back to the Republican Party and Irish voters returned to the Democratic organization.[58]

Working-class political unity was also undermined by the efforts of mainstream politicians to resume bitterly divisive ethnocultural struggles over temperance, Sunday closing laws, Bible reading in schools, and the like.[59] Workers were also attracted to mainstream politics by their belief that Democrats and Republicans could offer them more by way of individual and group rewards than any minor workingmen's party. Local and state elections were often decided by no more than 1,000 to 2,000 votes during the late 1860s and 1870s, and Democrats and Republicans gratefully granted their supporters numerous patronage appointments and lucrative public works contracts. This was perhaps the most important reason why the city's considerable number of building tradesmen generally avoided prolonged participation in workingmen's parties. A local Demo-

cratic victory virtually assured Irish building workers more jobs and steady
employment, while a Republican triumph brought the same results for
German contractors, journeymen, and laborers.[60]

With their leadership and potential supporters weakened by
political co-optation, battles over Reconstruction and ethnocultural policies,
and mainstream party promises of immediate material rewards, it is little
wonder that subsequent calls by workingmen's parties to do political battle
against the growing encroachments of capital found little support among
working-class voters. Indeed, it is remarkable that workingmen persisted
in their efforts at independent political mobilization at all.

The eight-hour campaign met with only limited success, but
it nevertheless helped to politicize thousands of local workers and spark
the onset of a new period of economic opposition. Between 1868 and 1873,
working-class struggles in Cincinnati were marked by two important developments: greater cooperation and support among local and national
trade unions and a gradual redirection of strike energies toward combating
the changes occurring in the city's shops and factories. The TLA, by
involving several dozen unions in its political campaign, bolstered its
membership and position of influence within the city's laboring community.
It turned its energies back to the economic arena and once again called
upon all workers to join "in a common effort to ameliorate and elevate their
condition that they may be enabled to protect themselves against the
unrelenting, overreaching grasp of capital."[61]

For the next several years, the TLA fostered greater ties
between foreign- and native-born workers, encouraged further unionization
among skilled and unskilled laborers, and lobbied for various political
reforms that would benefit all producers, regardless of trade, industry, or
skill. By 1870, nearly all of the city's trade unions, responding to the pleas
of TLA and national trade union leaders, had affiliated with one or more
national labor bodies. Swept up by a similar wave of organizational fervor,
unskilled sand haulers, hackmen, gardeners, telegraphers, cooks, sign painters, teamsters, and railroad laborers also formed new local unions.[62]

TLA calls for greater mutual assistance, unlike those issued
by their ante-bellum predecessors, went well beyond mere rhetorical encouragement. The TLA organized a citywide strike fund in 1868 to provide
financial aid to "any union who may find themselves [ready] to resist the
aggression of capital at any time to the extent of their ability."[63] Possibilities
for launching successful oppositional movements against employers were
further increased as national trade unions, as well as the city's militant and

relatively well-to-do molders and printers, provided striking journeymen with additional funds to help support their families during prolonged labor disputes.[64]

While the uneven development of industrialization led different tradesmen to respond in different ways and different times to changing economic conditions, the widespread growth of factory production in the 1860s and 1870s caused a significant shift in the nature and focus of many labor disputes. The greatest threat to postwar workers, exclaimed printer-turned-radical politician L. A. Hine in 1869, was not declining wages, but the rapid centralization of industry and "concentration of the money-power into a few hands."[65] Although a number of war-grown-wealthy manufacturers "sat down in luxurious comfort and independence, their capital and energy lost to business and enterprise," observed one local businessman, more ambitious men, such as Miles Greenwood, chemical manufacturer F. E. Suires, and shoe manufacturer George Stribley, used their wartime profits to buy new machinery, hire greater numbers of workers, and expand the scope of their operations.[66]

Working-class visions and hopes for an industrial world dominated by small independent producers grew ever more faint after the Civil War as wage labor in large factories slowly emerged as the dominant setting of productive life. In 1850, as table 5.2 indicates, in only two industries — furniture and iron and steel — were the majority of workers employed in factories of fifty or more wage-earners. Twenty years later, over half the workers in the hardware, printing, machine, furniture, and iron and steel industries and over 40 percent of the city's carriage, boot and shoe, candle, soap, and chemical workers toiled in large factories. Indeed, by 1870, 49.4 percent of the city's manufacturing workforce labored in factories employing more than fifty workers — 16.2 percent in factories of 50 to 99 and 33.2 percent in factories of more than 100 people.[67] Commenting upon similar developments throughout the nation, the *New York Times* said in 1869 that the rapid expansion of factory wage labor augured the creation of "a system of slavery as absolute if not as degrading as that which lately prevailed in the South. . . . Manufacturing capitalists threaten to become the masters, and it is the white laborers who are to be the slaves."[68]

Working-class fears of unbridled capitalistic expansion were further inflamed by the rapid growth of industrial corporations in the postwar years. In order to raise the large amounts of capital necessary to finance the expansion of their operations, manufacturers often reorganized their family firms or partnerships as corporations and sold stock to the public (usually to merchants, bankers, speculators, and outside investors). This movement toward incorporation, although noticeable during the war years, assumed greater dimensions after 1865. Whereas 22 manufacturing companies, with an average capital stock of $89,000, were incorporated in Cincinnati between 1860 and 1865, 140 new corporations, with an average capital of $144,043, were organized between 1866 and 1872.[69] Several of these firms, such as furniture makers Mitchell and Rammelsberg, soap and candle producers Procter and Gamble, and the Cincinnati Stationary Engine and Hydraulic Works, were capitalized at amounts in excess of the then astounding sum of $800,000.[70]

Labor struggles of the late 1860s assumed two distinct patterns: traditional battles by small-shop artisans and unskilled laborers over wages and more pointed efforts by emerging factory artisans to maintain greater control over the changing nature of production. Since they worked in labor-intensive trades relatively unaffected by the expansion of factory production, ship carpenters, hand coopers, and building tradesmen — artisans who had managed to preserve their strong ante-bellum craft traditions — continued to focus their postwar grievances around wage-and-hour issues. Using the same language and rituals they had employed half a century earlier, these journeymen, who launched three strikes between 1868 and September 1873, marched through the city streets, and called upon citizens to support them in their just attempts to secure wages which would enable them to maintain their families in a fair and republican fashion.[71] Unskilled coalheavers, gas stokers, and telegraph laborers also focused their strikes upon demands for higher wages.[72]

The most protracted battles of the era, however, were launched by the skilled workers who found the setting of their employment shifting from small shops to large factories and their roles as craftsmen changing from artisans to factory artisans. These journeymen not only demanded higher wages; they also expanded the scope of their opposition to include forays against the further erosion of their skills and the proletarianization of their labor. Printers, shoemakers, iron molders, tailors, and cigarmakers, journeymen working in the trades most dramatically affected by the expansion of factory production during this era, initiated three-quarters (17 of 23) of the strikes held in the five and a half years before the Panic of 1873. Twelve of these battles were fought over issues relating to mechanization, the decline of apprenticeship, the influx of women and children into the workplace, and demands for union recognition and greater control over the workplace.[73]

The most militant and successful of these struggles were led by the city's printers and iron molders. While a number of factors contributed to their success, three stand out as particularly important: the relatively labor-intensive nature of their work, their ability to preserve well-established work cultures, and their success in forging close links between their trades' native- and foreign-born craftsmen. Although the percentage of printers laboring in shops employing more than fifty workers rose from 12 percent in 1850 to 64 percent in 1870, and iron molders from 30 percent to 72 percent, these journeymen found their skills less affected by mechanization than most other emerging factory artisans. "Unlike other branches of mechanism," the editors of the *Iron Moulders' Journal* observed in 1873, "the introduction of machinery has in no manner assisted at increased production; the entire increase of individual production comes from the muscle and sweat of the molder."[74] Although they worked in larger surroundings, stove molders, the most important branch of the city's industry, continued to build stoves by hand, often bought their own tools and flasks, hired and paid their apprentices, and occasionally even paid rent for the use of factory floor space (these expenses came out of the piece rate paid by manufacturers for finished goods). Similarly, although the introduction of steam-powered presses limited the range of skills utilized by pressmen, the city's compositors, the most numerous and radical members of Cincinnati Typographical Union No. 3, continued to set type by hand in much the same way as they had half a century earlier.[75]

Yet, printers and molders found their craft undermined by the increased division and specialization of their labor, the flooding of shops with apprentices and non-union men, and the concerted efforts of manufacturers to destroy their unions and wrest from them, as the members of the National Iron Founders' Association vowed in 1866, control over the "government of the workshop and the management of the business."[76] Molders and printers launched a series of militant strikes to preserve the longstanding traditions of their control over the shop. Of the seven strikes carried on by iron molders between 1868 and 1873, two were fought over the employment of non-union men, two over the excessive use of apprentices, two over efforts to protect union wage scales, and one over a general demand for increased wages for all molders. Printers, while able to maintain control over their craft with relatively few strikes, nevertheless launched a battle in 1870 over union recognition at the *Commercial* and a foray in 1873 against the employment of too many apprentices and "two-thirders" in several of the city's printing establishments. With the strong support of their trade's journeymen and their national unions, these two unions won a majority of their strikes.[77]

The relative success of the molders and printers, while attributable in part to their employers' difficulty in replacing them with machines or semi-skilled workers, was also due to their ability to create and enforce elaborate union work rules. While journeymen in other trades often found their overall effectiveness diminished by the formation of separate unions for small-shop and factory workers, molders — despite being represented by three local unions — and typographers forged an organization which sought to protect the interests of all skilled craftsmen regardless of their productive setting.[78]

They infused long-standing traditions of shop organization with a new, almost military-like discipline — perhaps not surprising since many of these men had served in the Union army. The two groups of tradesmen appointed a series of committees in each establishment "for the purpose of controlling prices and enforcing the necessary rules and regulations therein."[79] Any attempt by manufacturers to circumvent these rules was quickly reported to the central union leaders. They in turn dispatched a special committee to meet with the manufacturer in question. If a satisfactory solution was not reached, the union, rather than ordering all members out on strike, simply ordered the individual shop shut down and thereby forced the manufacturer to reach a quick settlement or lose business to competitors. Union leaders were able to maintain strict discipline by paying striking workers a weekly salary (local strike funds were usually supplemented by donations from the national union). They also provided potential strikebreakers with pocket money and train fare out of Cincinnati. Thus, the two unions were generally able to wrest concessions, if not their complete demands, from employers.[80]

These struggles to maintain control over their crafts were also aided by the unions' ability to recruit a majority of the workers in their trades. The molders and printers, who recognized that separate ethnic-based unions made the task of enforcing common trade standards and strikes more difficult, sought to induce German- and Irish-born journeymen — who respectively represented approximately 32 and 16 percent of their workforce in 1870 — to join their organizations. Toward this end, they elected such men as Jonathan Krauth, Joseph Hauck, Patrick Kelly, and James O'Donnell to important union offices; they also held initiation ceremonies in German, endorsed Irish struggles against English landlords, and sponsored a number of social activities aimed at encouraging unity outside as well as inside the workplace.[81] These efforts met with considerable success. Throughout the late 1860s and early 1870s, the molders recruited approximately 67 percent and the printers 60 percent of their trades' skilled craftsmen.[82] Even when German printers decided to organize a separate union in 1873 to govern production in the city's German-language printing establishments, they quickly joined with CTU No. 3 to create a special committee "for the purpose of forming a more perfect bond of fellowship among the two associations, whose aims and objects are in a great measure identical."[83]

Journeymen in other trades affected by postwar reorganizations in production also began to shift their strategy from general calls for fair and just wages to more pointed efforts to preserve greater control over the daily workings of their craft. The previously independent journeymen's men's shoe, women's shoe, and peg-workers' unions of Cincinnati all enlisted in the national ranks of the Knights of St. Crispin in 1868 in order to resist team labor systems and the introduction of McKay pegging (1862) and Goodyear welting machines (1872), which gradually replaced skilled handicraft artisans with semi-skilled male and female machine operatives. Meeting in April 1869 to celebrate their first anniversary, the Crispins announced their intention to "destroy the galling system of slavery that employers . . . have imposed upon our craft."[84] Combining familiar antebellum demands for higher wages that would "elevate ourselves to that respectable position in society that we, as citizens are entitled to," with new intentions "to protect ourselves against the further encroachments of capital," the KOSC launched six strikes between 1868 and 1873 — three over wage grievances, two over demands for union recognition, and one over the introduction of "Greenhands" — apprentices who had not served a full term.[85] Although they carried on fewer struggles than the shoemakers, the city's cigarworkers and tailors (the percentage of these workers laboring for large manufacturers or contractors rose, respectively, from 0 and 21 percent in 1850 to 22 and 76 percent in 1870) also fought a number of strikes against the growth of factory production, the expansion of subcontracting, and the continued degradation of artisanal skills.[86]

Similar conditions of production increasingly led other journeymen to fight for similar demands, but not all of them succeeded. Though the Crispins were able to win a number of strikes and enroll 1,000 men and women by 1871 — some 47 percent of the industry's adult workforce — they were unable to create a common series of work rules and shop committees to permit the organization to govern the workings of the entire industry.[87] Despite the efforts of shoemakers like Emor Davis to coordinate common actions between small-shop and factory workers, the locus of power in the Crispins remained largely decentralized and in the hands of its three constituent unions, and each often worked for its own needs. Struggles against manufacturers were also weakened by the shoemakers' vulnerability to replacement by semi-skilled operatives and by the inability of the native- and Irish-dominated Crispins to recruit the city's German shoemakers — who made up 47 percent of the workforce in 1870 — into their ranks. Although common ethnic bonds were forged during the course of a number of strikes, the most protracted struggle of the period, a bitter battle over demands for higher wages and the Crispin's right to negotiate on behalf of *all* shoemakers, which began in February 1873 and lasted several weeks, was lost when the German cordwainers decided to return to work at their old wages.[88]

Like the shoemakers, cigarworkers also had a checkered history of strength and weakness. Although the trade's German- and native-born craftsmen — each representing 48 percent of the workforce in 1870 — initially organized separate unions, their common desire to maintain high wages and craft standards (cigars were still rolled by hand before 1870) led the two unions to amalgamate during a successful six-month-long strike begun in December 1869. The cigarmakers' victory, however, led several large factory owners to undermine their employees' power by introducing cigar-molding machines that spring. When union men responded by refusing to use the new equipment, they were fired and replaced by a group of workers previously excluded from the craft: women and children. Trade unity was soon weakened as native- and foreign-born artisans, who found themselves sharply divided over the best ways to resist these changes in production and whether or not to organize the industry's new female laborers, once again split into two distinct unions.[89]

Individual journeymen's and unskilled laborers' unions often met with success in their battles against employers. However, broader forms of working-class unity were often undermined not only by the diverging interests of small-shop and factory workers, but also by divisions within the factory itself. Skilled workers, instead of integrating *all* wage earners within one large industrial union, generally clung to more traditional forms of craft organization. As the increased specialization of labor altered their particular interests and earnings, furniture, carriage, shoe, and machine workers organized a myriad of different unions within a single factory. By the late 1860s, for example, chairmakers, cabinetmakers, carvers, woodturners, rubbers, and varnishers working in the city's large furniture factories were each represented by a different trade body. Strikes by one group of workers within a particular establishment were often ignored or only weakly supported by other groups of skilled and unskilled laborers.[90]

Attempts at industrial organization were also made more difficult by white male prejudice against female and black labor. Tailors, although they complained of exploitation by manufacturers, contractors, and subcontractors, made no attempt to help to organize the thousands of female outworkers and operatives who also suffered at the hands of their employers.[91] Even the city's printers exhibited a callous concern for their female counterparts. In the hope of promoting greater trade unity by ending the union's history of gender discrimination, compositor Augusta Lewis implored the members of CTU No. 3 to admit the city's skilled female printers into their organization. "I am sure," she wrote union secretary John Young in November, 1870, "it is much easier for the men to organize women who only ask for justice and protection in the start than it is to fight them when they are doing the men an injustice by taking their places in a strike in the name of doing themselves a right." Union leaders ignored her plea, however, as well as similar requests from black printers. Compositors and pressmen simply regarded these groups as competitors who undermined the wages and jobs of white male printers.[92]

Despite divisions and occasional setbacks experienced by Cincinnati wage earners, the upsurge in union and strike activities during the mid-1860s and early 1870s produced significant economic gains for all sectors of the working class. Unlike the more loosely run unions of antebellum years, the *Enquirer* remarked in 1872, the "comparatively modern growth [of] organization among workingmen, close and efficient organization," had often forced employers to bow to their employees' demands for higher wages.[93] Although deflation brought a general downturn in all prices, the wages of artisans, factory artisans, and unskilled laborers, as table 8.1 indicates, fell less rapidly than food and housing costs — which of course meant an increase in real wages for most workers. Those least affected by mechanization or factory production (for example, the city's building tradesmen) made the greatest strides in advancing their material condition. The city's unskilled day laborers also managed to outpace the cost of living. Indeed, these gains marked the most significant general advance in working-class wages since the early part of the nineteenth century.

Although the expansion of factory wage labor often produced

Table 8.1 Food and Housing Costs and Average Daily Wages of
Journeymen and Unskilled Day Laborers, 1865–1872

	1865	1872	Percentage of Change
FOOD & HOUSING:			
Food (10 staples)	$46.20	$26.39	−43
Housing (monthly rent):			
single room	$10.00	$9.00	−10
modest house	$27.50	$25.00	−9
DAILY WAGES:			
Building Trades			
bricklayers	$4.50	$5.00	+11
plasterers	3.50	4.00	+14
painters	3.50	3.50	0
Stove Molders	$3.60	$4.25	+18
Machinists	$3.00	$3.25	+8
Cabinetmakers	$3.50	$3.50	0
Cigarmakers	$3.50	$3.25	−7
Blacksmiths	$3.25	$3.00	−8
Printers	55¢ per 1,000 ems	50¢ per 1,000 ems	−9
Carriagemakers	$3.75	$3.25	−13
Shoemakers	—	$3.50	
Unskilled Day Laborers	$2.00	$1.75	−14

SOURCE: Ohio Bureau of Labor Statistics, *17th Annual Report of the Bureau of Labor Statistics for the Year 1893* (Norwalk, Ohio, 1894), pp. 808–9; BLS — 1877, pp. 217, 229; BLS — 1878, pp. 252–53; *Gazette*, April 19, 1866; *Enquirer*, August 18, 1868, October 4, 1873; *Commercial*, July 29, 1877.

increasingly similar hardships upon workers, the strength of the city's working class was frequently undermined by divisions between small-shop and factory, skilled and unskilled, male and female, black and white, and native- and foreign-born workers. Consequently, the TLA embarked upon a new campaign in the early 1870s to broaden the scope of mutual support and cooperation both within and among various industries. TLA President and shoemaker Emor Davis explained in February 1871 that the time had come to forge new industrial organizations which would represent the "interests of the working masses, which cannot be acted upon [solely] in special trade organizations." Only by uniting *all* workers within an industry, he insisted, could skilled and unskilled employees hope "to successfully compete with concentrated capital."[94] Two years later, the TLA, led by the city's molders, printers, blacksmiths, and coopers, traveled to Columbus to attend the first meeting of the National Industrial Congress, a "purely

Industrial Association, having for its sole and only object the securing to the producer his full share of all the products" of his toil.[95] Although effective industrial organization would not occur in Cincinnati until later in the century, largely under the aegis of the Knights of Labor, the initial groundwork was laid by the TLA in the early 1870s.

The TLA also urged local unions to use social activities, such as balls, picnics, sports teams, and informal gatherings, as a means of promoting greater camaraderie and unity outside the shop or factory. To that end, the TLA organized a Labor Institute early in 1873 to provide all male workers, regardless of skill, craft, or ethnicity, with an alternative to the manufacturer-dominated Ohio Mechanics' Institute. The Labor Institute held formal weekly meetings and informal daily gatherings where native-born, Irish, and German members listened to lectures and exchanged views on a wide range of contemporary economic, political, and social issues—communism, trade unionism, socialism, land monopoly, monetary reform, temperance, and so forth.[96]

These efforts to use leisure activities as a means to foster greater class bonds and provide workers with an alternative culture to that of the city's elite were most vigorously pursued by the German laboring community. Workingman's (Arbeiter) Hall, constructed by German trade unionists in 1859, was the first building erected in Cincinnati to serve the exclusive needs of the city's wage earners and their families. The top floor of the massive two-story edifice, owned by the Workingmen's League and located in Over-the-Rhine, housed a number of small rooms where various unions (non-German as well as German), benevolent societies, and social clubs could meet for no charge. This floor also contained a large 40-by-60-foot hall which was used as a frequent gathering place for citywide labor rallies and TLA gatherings.

In addition to providing accommodations for these more formal activities, Workingman's Hall also served as a popular center for fun and relaxation. Men interested in drinking in the exclusive company of males could patronize the lager beer hall that occupied most of the first floor. Those who wished to indulge in spirits and also spend time with their families could bring their wives and children to the hall's spacious, tree-lined outdoor beer garden. Here, men, women, and children could sit, drink, talk, and listen to the lively strains of the ever-present German bands. Since Workingman's Hall provided a congenial setting for breaking down the isolating tendencies of daily life, it is probably no coincidence that the most mutually supportive strikes of the period, actions which frequently

(a)

(b)

Figure 11 Baseball in Cincinnati.
(a) Sandlot Game (c. 1850s). Baseball was extremely popular among all classes well before the
Civil War. (b) Sandlot Game (c. 1870s). A number of unions formed baseball teams after the war
as a means of promoting fun and comaraderie outside the workplace.
Courtesy of the Cincinnati Historical Society

saw wives and daughters march alongside or stand in the streets waving banners in support of their fathers, husbands, and brothers, occurred among the city's German-dominated trades.[97]

These varied efforts at concerted social, economic, and political opposition to the growing power of industrial capitalism were brought to an abrupt, if only temporary, halt by the onset of a disastrous national depression in the autumn of 1873. The nationwide downturn left in its wake bankruptcy, unemployment, and misery for millions of merchants, manufacturers, and workers. By October 1, Cincinnati banks were refusing to cash checks, and business was virtually suspended. The city's manufacturers were soon forced to discharge large numbers of their employees. By December, local newspapers estimated that one-third to one-half of the city's manufacturing workforce was without employment. Those fortunate enough to keep their jobs, such as the safemakers at McNeale, Urban, and Company and the furniture workers at Mitchell and Rammelsberg, generally worked only half time and at half their normal pay, and they often received credit slips rather than cash for their labors.[98]

As the question of survival became the paramount concern for many working-class families, earlier struggles for higher wages and greater control over the work process were quickly replaced by the desperate quest for employment. With thousands of men and women looking for jobs, at any pay and under any conditions, scores of unions, as had been the case during the Panics of 1837 and 1854, either suspended their operations or dissolved entirely. Even the militant printers and iron molders, although they continued to operate during the depression, were temporarily forced by pressing economic circumstances to abandon union work rules and wage guidelines.[99]

With their profits plunging to an all-time low and the threat of bankruptcy constant, Cincinnati manufacturers began to seek new methods to combat the deleterious effects of depression. In the belief that the old methods of manufacturing were inadequate to meet the exigencies of the current economic crisis, a number of industrialists embarked upon a new quest to alter traditional forms of factory ownership and production. As small individually owned firms and partnerships slowly gave way to a new wave of corporately controlled businesses during the mid-1870s and 1880s, the world of manufacturing was gradually enveloped and superseded by the new world of modern industry — a world which soon wrought fundamental alterations in the daily economic, social, and political lives of labor and capital.

PART III

The Age
Of Modern Industry
(1873 – 1890)

CHAPTER NINE

The City of Modern Industry: Production and the Changing Images of Progress

Between October 1873 and the return of widespread prosperity in 1885, Cincinnati manufacturers and merchants, although they enjoyed brief periods of flush times, found themselves beset by an unprecedented era of economic depression. For many of the city's smaller merchants, masters and manufacturers, survival, not profits, became a major concern. The prices and demand for goods fell to new lows, and the number of bankruptcies in Cincinnati rose from 167 in 1874, to 322 in 1875, and to 442 for only the first six months of 1876.[1] Prospects for local recovery were further dimmed as the expansion of railroad lines leading to Chicago, Cleveland, St. Louis, and Louisville continued to lure regional trade away from the river-dependent Queen City. Disenchanted with the local conditions, "one after another of our manufacturing establishments and wealthy merchants," the editors of the *Enquirer* lamented in 1874, "are leaving for other points, where facilities are greater [and] taxes lower."[2]

Cincinnati manufacturers, "urged by a necessity as strong as the instincts of self-preservation," embarked upon a determined campaign to develop new methods of production which would permit them to lower costs, increase productivity, and compete more effectively in regional and national markets.[3] As the common crisis of depression prompted leading manufacturers in virtually every major industry in Cincinnati to adopt similar changes within a relatively short span of time, the overall conditions of production grew increasingly more homogeneous. By the middle of the 1880s, the common experiences of Cincinnati workers began to loom larger than their differences as factory life emerged as the dominant setting, and factory artisans and laborers emerged as the dominant members, of the new world of modern industry.

In Cincinnati, as well as in many other industrial centers, the movement toward this new era of modern industry was characterized by the rapid centralization of workers into large factories, the increased mechanization of production, the further subdivision and particularization of skills, the expanded employment of semi-skilled machine operators and unskilled women and children, and the growing separation between the ownership and control of industry. "Provincial methods" of production, the Chamber of Commerce explained, were quickly abandoned as employers applied "their characteriestic energies to the development of cheaper processes and a more economical administration" of business.[4] During the following two decades, as the Ohio Bureau of Labor Statistics (BLS) reported, Cincinnati's industrial landscape was dramatically altered as the "rapid concentration of capital, the massing of machinery in immense workshops . . . [and] the destruction of the possibility of the workman becoming his own employer . . . created a new era in our industrial history."[5]

The small shops and modest manufactories which had employed a majority of the city's manufacturing workforce as late as 1870 were soon superseded by massive, highly centralized factories. By 1880, as table 9.1 indicates, 65.2 percent of the city's manufacturing workforce labored in factories employing over fifty workers. Large factories which employed 100 or more people, although they constituted only 3.5 percent of the city's manufacturing establishments, employed nearly half of all industrial wage earners. Converesely, though the number of artisanal shops and small manufactories rose by 30.2 percent between 1870 and 1880, the number of people working in them fell by 3.3 percent.

The centralization of workers into large establishments represented only one aspect of this new industrial area. The vast amounts of capital required to fund the expansion of their operations led a growing number of manufacturers to abandon their financially limited family firms

Table 9.1 Distribution of the Industrial Workforce By Size
of Establishment, 1870 – 1880

Shop Size	1870			1880		
	Shops	Workers (n)	Workers (%)	Shops	Workers (n)	Workers (%)
1 – 49	2,312	18,880	50.6	3,011	18,263	34.8
50 – 99	90	6,066	16.2	122	8,157	15.6
100 +	67	12,398	33.2	114	25,974	49.6
Total	2,469	37,344	100.0	3,247[a]	52,394[a]	100.0

SOURCE: Statistics compiled from data contained in the U.S. Census Office, "Census of the United States, Manufacturing Schedule, Hamilton County, Ohio," 1870, 1880; *Ninth Census — Volume III. Statistics of the Wealth and Industry of the United States* (Washington, 1872), 714 – 15; *Report of the Manufactures of the United States. June 1, 1880. General Statistics*, 2 vols. (Washington, 1883), 2:393 – 95.

[a] Although the printed census of 1880 lists 54,517 workers in the manufacturing sector, the manuscript census for 1880 did not include figures for the city's whiskey, brewery, and textile establishments. Consequently, the workers in these industries are not included in the 1880 totals.

or small partnerships in favor of organizing highly capitalized corporations. The growth of industrial corporations, begun in earnest after the Civil War, assumed greater dimensions during the depression. Some 256 local manufacturing firms were incorporated between 1873 and 1884 as compared to 162 for the preceding thirteen years.[6] Whereas in 1850, nearly two-thirds of the top ten percent of the city's leading manufactories were owned either by individual families or a small number of partners, by 1880 54.5 percent were organized as corporations or multipartnered (four or more) companies.[7] The value of manufacturing capital in Cincinnati rose from $17.9 million in 1860 to $50.5 million in 1880, and to $104.5 million in 1890.[8]

The growth of corporations and multipartner firms was also paralleled by the rise of a new industrial elite. In contrast to 1850, when 70 percent of the city's leading manufactories were owned and run by mechanics who had worked their way through the craft, by 1880 — as table 9.3 indicates — nearly half of the industrial elite (whose careers could be traced) had simply inherited the business from their fathers.[9] Indeed, the vast amount of capital required to launch a major manufactory during the early 1870s prevented all but a small number of journeymen from rising to the top. Although 58 of the leading manufacturers of 1880 began their careers as journeymen, 42 (72 percent) had opened their factories before 1870 and 26 (45 percent) before 1860. Only 16 (28 percent) of the

(a)

Figure 12 The Factories of Modern Industry.

(a) Lane and Bodley Co. (c. 1886). During the last quarter of the century, capitalists erected mammoth factories which often covered several city blocks and employed several hundred men, women, and children. (b) Procter and Gamble Co. (c. 1875). The expansion of production and growing need for more space during the 1880s led the Procter and Gamble Company to leave downtown and build their Ivorydale plant [(c) c. 1890] on the city's outskirts.

Courtesy of the Cincinnati Historical Society

(b)

(c)

Table 9.2 Distribution of Workforce in Leading Industries
By Size of Establishment, 1870 – 1880

	1870				1880			
	1 – 49	50 – 99	100 +	% in 50 +	1 – 49	50 – 99	100 +	% in 50 +
Iron & Steel	0	90	740	100.0	0	336	705	100.0
Canneries	81	75	0	48.1	6	0	900	99.3
Hardware[a]	945	684	1,682	71.5	331	338	2,844	90.6
Carriages & Wagons	594	367	120	45.1	551	790	2,166	84.3
Machinery	718	294	747	59.2	536	439	1,695	79.9
Clothing	2,038	1,423	5,127	76.3	2,641	1,226	7,508	76.8
Furniture	1,504	524	1,626	58.8	1,120	1,034	2,389	75.3
Boots & Shoes	633	213	196	39.2	966	336	1,948	70.3
Cigars & Tobacco	1,601	263	178	21.6	1,075	316	1,950	67.8
Meat Processing	689	0	0	0	384	449	310	66.4
Printing & Publishing	586	475	563	63.9	1,591	993	1,164	57.6
Saddlery	151	154	0	50.5	270	60	262	54.4
Cooking/ Pressing	554	243	205	44.7	1,307	142	892	44.2
Metal Working	681	128	0	15.8	452	271	0	37.5
Building Trades	—[b]	80	0	—[b]	2,212	50	100	6.3

SOURCE: See sources in table 9.1.
[a] The number of workers listed in several of these industries differs slightly from the totals contained in the printed census. Stove workers, who were included under Foundry and Machine-Shop establishments in the 1880 printed census, are listed here as part of the Hardware industry. A number of minor adjustments were made in several other categories in order to ensure a more accurate representation of an industry's total workforce. See appendix A for a description of the various trades included under each industry.
[b] Data for 1870 were not sufficient to provide accurate figures.

Table 9.3 Partial Profile of the Career Patterns of the Leading
10 Percent of the Manufacturers of 1880

Prior Occupation	n	%
Takes Over From Father	71	43.8
Journeyman to Manufacturer	58	35.8
Merchant to Manufacturer	15	9.3
Clerk to Manufacturer	11	6.8
Professional to Manufacturer	5	3.1
Manufacturers Diversifying into New Businesses	2	1.2
Total	162	100.0

SOURCE: See table 4.4 for sources.

former journeymen who opened factories after 1870 succeeded in entering the ranks of the industrial elite.

The daily operations of these and other major companies were often marked by a growing separation between the ownership and control of production. As corporations became more prominent in the late 1870s and 1880s, factories were no longer exclusively owned by one or two families but also included a number of outside investors, such as bankers A. J. and Louis Seasongood, merchants John Gaff and Albert Gano, and politician Andrew Hickenlooper. Moreover, wealthy manufacturers, such as iron producer Joseph Kinsey, beer magnate Christian Moerlein, and machine maker Issac Greenwald also diversified their capital into a number of new industrial ventures. The Western Glycerine Company, for example, incorporated in 1879, was jointly owned by the Procter and Gamble and Werk families — the city's main soap and candle competitors. Rather than leaving their own firms to attend to this new venture, the Procters, Gambles, and Werks, like many other manufacturers and capitalists, relinquished control of the company's daily operations to an experienced superintendent hired to manage the factory.[10]

The traditional control of daily production was also altered by the changing backgrounds and greater business demands imposed upon the city's new industrial elite. While a number of men, such as stove manufacturer William Resor Jr., machinist Henry Lane, and veneer manufacturer Edwin Albro, trained as journeymen before taking over their father's business, an increasing percentage of the city's major industrialists, as one state report noted, had "no more practical knowledge of the business than the would-be apprentice."[11] Trained in the "business" end of operations and often unequipped to supervise the daily management of the workplace, these men and their "silent partners" generally appointed a factory superintendent and a myriad of department foremen to direct production while they attended to the financial aspects of the company's fortunes. Even though a number of prominent manufacturers like furniture producers J. F. Meader and Joseph Sextro were experienced in the practical workings of their trade, the increased need to oversee other aspects of the business forced them to appoint former journeymen Louis Vogt and T. B. Smith to serve as factory superintendents.[12] Factory owners were often isolated in their business offices: they no longer knew the names of their employees, unlike their fathers, who had prided themselves on knowing them. Inevitably, industrial production, while it often grew more efficient during the last quarter of the century, also seemed to grow ever more impersonal.

Industrial capitalists also turned their energies toward developing new labor processes and managerial innovations that would both decrease their costs and increase their control over the inner workings of their factories. Just as capitalists had come to monopolize the means of production, so, too, did they now endeavor to seize from skilled employees their knowledge and control over the daily aspects of production. The city's carriagemaking manufacturers led the way in restructuring traditional labor processes. Between 1870 and 1880 they quickly abandoned their custom trade in favor of turning out inexpensive mass-produced carriages for sale throughout the world. As a result, the percentage of wage earners laboring in large factories of 100 or more skyrocketed from 11.1 percent to 61.8 percent. Moreover, rather than allowing skilled employees to labor at several different tasks, as was their custom, manufacturers sought to increase the speed and regularity of production by assigning workers to one of several distinct departments where their work was divided into a series of minute repetitive operations. As carriages in their various stages of completion passed rapidly from department to department, each worker, generally aided by new steam-powered machinery, quickly performed only one or two specialized tasks. By utilizing the "best labor saving machinery" and developing the "most economic division of his skilled and ordinary labor," reflected one reporter, a modern carriage manufacturer was able to produce products at "half the price that it costs the 'old fogey' manufacturers to get them up at."[13]

The introduction of new machinery and the elaborate subdivision of operations also permitted manufacturers, such as Louis Cook, Emerson and Fisher, Sayers and Scoville, and the Globe Carriage Company, to reduce their labor costs and dependence upon factory artisans by hiring women and children — 41.1 percent of the workforce in the case of these four factories — to perform many of the unskilled operations previously completed by skilled craftsmen.[14] "In the old days, before machinery supplanted the mechanic," State Labor Commissioner Alonzo Fasset observed in 1887, "it took a man to drive the jack plane, shape the iron and construct the vehicle; now a delicate child guiding a machine can do most of his work."[15] Indeed, daily routines were often so simplified by the mid-1880s that a young employee could be taught all he needed to know in a matter of days or weeks rather than months or years.

As the work process in the city's carriage factories grew more highly divided and particularized in ensuing years, the skilled journeyman was slowly transformed from a complete carriage maker to a less-well-paid "specialist" who labored exclusively as part of a team of bodymakers, wheelmakers, trimmers, painters, or the like. These efforts to reduce the total range of skills utilized by any one worker can best be seen by comparing the manner in which work was performed in an artisan shop in 1865 with that of a highly mechanized factory in 1895. In both instances, the first step in the construction of a carriage began with the cutting of wood for the body, seat, and gears — a process which required 3.7 hours by hand, but only 17.3 minutes by machine. The artisan then spent some 18.8 hours completing various squaring, stocking, and planing operations. The factory artisan, aided by planing machines and assistants, completed the task in a mere twenty minutes. Relying upon a combination of hand tools — saws, chisels, mauls — the artisan spent fours hours preparing the tenons for the body seat. Tenoning machines reduced that time to 11.4 minutes. The tedious and unpleasant process of finishing roughwork by hand files dragged on for 13.5 hours; with sanddrum and belt, the whole operation was completed in 15.1 minutes. Whereas an accomplished artisan could weld, fit, and set axles in approximately four hours, the factory artisan, having mastered the use of the steam-powered trip hammer, finished the job in 57.6 minutes.

The elaborate routinization and division of labor in the modern factory also affected work which continued to be done entirely by hand. Varnishing and painting, usually done by one man in the artisan shop, stretched out over forty hours. By 1895, the work was divided among several men who so perfected their individial tasks as to reduce the entire process to a little over 12.5 hours. Similarly, the making of carriage cushions and backs, a job requiring fifteen hours at midcentury, was subdivided and shortened to two hours by 1895.[16]

Looking back over the contrasting processes involved in carriage making, we find that six artisans in 1865 performed a total of 64 operations in 200.4 hours and at a labor cost of $45.67. Thirty years later, the combined efforts of 116 factory workers performing 72 distinct operations cut the production time to 39.1 hours, and labor costs to $8.10[17]

Carriage manufacturers of the 1870s and 1880s, like their counterparts in other industries, also attempted to increase the speed and regularity of production by exerting greater control and discipline over their workforce. Convinced that the irregular work patterns of small shops were inappropriate to the new era of modern industry, manufacturers sought to hire more disciplined "mechanics who appreciate systematized labor, men willing and able to work in a predetermined way that has been demonstrated to the best and quickest."[18] Those who could not abide by the new system of discipline soon found themselves out of a job. Employers also used more subtle forms of coercion and reward to entice wage earners to adopt more "appropriate" forms of behavior. One manufacturer posted a series of work rules which threatened dismissal for any worker "who smokes Spanish cigars, uses liquor in any form, or frequents pool and public halls." On the other hand, more upstanding employees who "go regularly to church," were promised a slightly reduced work week with no reduction in pay.[19]

    Like the city's carriagemakers, other craftsmen who previously had remained relatively unaffected by industrialization were soon forced to join the growing ranks of the city's factory artisans. Cigarmakers, who for decades had worked in small handicraft shops, found their craft traditions, independence, and control over work undercut by the rapid expansion of factory production. As late as 1870, only 178 cigarworkers (12.3 percent of the craft) labored in factories employing more than 100 people. Ten years later, 1,950 employees (58.4 percent of all cigarworkers) earned their living inside these large edifices.[20] Like their counterparts in so many other industries, cigarmakers were threatened not simply by the growth of large factories, but also by the ensuing efforts of employers to use machinery and cheaply paid female and child laborers to destroy their control over the craft. By 1877, according to the BLS, cigar molding machines had grown so prevalent in Cincinnati that only 15.1 percent of the city's workers continued to roll tobacco completely by hand.[21] Molding machines and automatic bunching machines, which turned out as many cigars in a day as it took a hand laborer a week to produce, diminished the need for highly skilled labor. Thus manufacturers often replaced their higher paid and strike-prone artisans with less costly and less militant women and children. Indeed, by 1880, women and children constituted 35.6 percent of the trade's factory workforce.[22]

    These varied changes in production were adopted by manufacturers in virtually all the city's major industries during the late 1870s and 1880s. "The tendency of the times in the particular character of labor," the *Scientific Artisan* observed in 1878, was "to the specialization of employments, to an extension of the divisions of labor, and to a greater distinctiveness in the lines of these divisions."[23] The "occupations are very few into which machinery has not been introduced," one state official added, "taking the place of brains and muscles, and doing automatically that which in the past required the trained eye and hand to perform."[24] By

(a)

(b)

Figure 13 Industrialization and Cigarworkers.
(a) Hand Rollers (c. 1880s – 1890s). (b) Machine Rollers (c. 1880s – 1890s). Highly skilled male cigarmakers found their artisanal traditions challenged in the 1870s by the introduction of cigar machines and the increased employment of women.
Courtesy of the Cincinnati Historical Society

the middle of the 1880s, coopers, blacksmiths, brewers, tanners, and saddlemakers — artisans who had previously labored in small shops — as well as more established factory artisans toiling in the city's furniture, hardware, machinery, printing, and shoemaking establishments, found their skills, authority, and wages undermined by the further specialization of their labors and the increased mechanization of production.

Manufacturers in the city's brewing, whiskey, candle, soap, chemical, oil, and paint industries also endeavored to strip workers of their ability to set the pace of production. Rather than the machine following the work rhythm of the laborer, the laborer was often forced to follow the rhythm of the machine. "The vast majority of machines" in these industries, the BLS noted in 1878, "are operated by steam; their speed is regulated; [and] their possible production per hour is accurately gauged" and set by employers.[25] The widespread use of more sophisticated machinery, complained one embittered iron molder, "has resulted in massing men and women together in factories and workshops under the control of corporations or individuals, until the mechanic has practically ceased to be a free

Figure 14 Schreiber and Sons Iron Works (c. 1889).
By the 1880s, the factory laborer often served as a mere tender of machines.
Courtesy of the Cincinnati Historical Society

man, and has become the slave of the capital that owns the machinery, or, in other words, he has become part of the machinery."[26]

Factory artisans and factory laborers also found their daily work lives, and occasionally their jobs, further threatened by the increased reliance upon female and child labor. Between 1870 and 1890, the number of women and children employed in the manufacturing sector mushroomed from 8,894 to 22,912. In 1860, women formed a majority of the workforce only in the clothing industry: by 1890 they constituted more than half the laborers in the city's clothing, fur, textile, regalia and society banner, box, bag, and canned foods establishments. Moreover, as industrial production was often simplified "to such an extent that the weaker person can perform what was done of old by strong ones," women and children, as table 9.4 indicates, found new employment opportunities in the city's large factories.[27] With manufacturers able to pay them one-quarter to one-half a man's wages "to do a man's work," it is little wonder that by 1880 women and children represented more than 30 percent of the workforce in Cincinnati's large tobacco factories and more than 20 percent in the furniture, boot and shoe, printing, carriage, coopering, and soap/candle/oil establishments employing more than 50 workers.[28]

Although skilled adult males continued to dominate most of the city's industries, journeymen increasingly found themselves losing control over the training and daily governance of young factory workers — the future leaders of the workforce. Since numerous unions either had dissolved during the depression or were too weak to mount protracted struggles against employers, manufacturers were often able to replace traditional systems of apprenticeship with more limited efforts to teach young employees only one or two particular aspects of their new trade. As one state labor official observed in 1878:

Table 9.4 Distribution of Women and Children in the Manufacturing Workforce By Size of Establishment, 1870 – 1880

Shop Size	1870				1880			
	Women		Children		Women		Children	
	n	%	n	%	n	%	n	%
1 – 49	1,733	26.9	1,493	61.0	2,452	23.4	1,703	33.8
50 – 99	1,120	17.4	291	11.9	1,277	12.2	691	13.7
100 +	3,592	55.7	665	27.1	6,754	64.4	2,647	52.5
Total	6,445	100.0	2,449	100.0	10,483	100.0	5,041	100.0

SOURCE: See sources in table 9.1.

Hundreds and thousands of youth enter our manufacturing establishments in the hope of acquiring a trade, only to find, in a few years, that the life occupation they have chosen is a delusion and a snare. They are perhaps taught to do one particular portion of the work necessary to complete the building of an engine, the making of a shoe, the building of a house, etc., but their proficiency on that one portion seals their fate in that particular establishment.[29]

The "sons and daughters of our laboring classes — and that means more than half our nation," exclaimed one angry German socialist, "have no other choice, than to become factory employees for lifetime at uncertain existence and at decreasing employments and wages, without the least hope for the first ones, to become their own masters."[30]

A partial survey of Ohio factories in 1878 revealed that there were not more than 100 apprentices being trained in all the customary aspects of their trade.[31] While the prospects for individual success certainly remained a possibility, the gradual abolition of apprenticeship meant that young factory workers — as a class — would find the road to prosperity a more difficult one than their fathers. As one cigarmaker explained, young boys working in the city's factories "can earn from $4 to $6 per week, and they being quite young, think that it is extra big money they are making; but when they grow up to be men, then they first see their mistake, for they can not earn any more than when they were boys."[32]

Workers in a vast array of industries railed against the rapid degradation of their crafts and the growing proletarianization of their labor, but in fact the changes which precipitated these complaints also caused a dramatic increase in local production and wealth. Between 1870 and 1890, despite a 30 percent drop in prices between 1873 and 1880, the annual value of industrial production rose from $78.9 million to $196.1 million.[33] The dramatic expansion of low-priced manufactured goods and the completion of the municipally owned Cincinnati Southern Railway (which linked the Queen City to Chattanooga, Knoxville, Atlanta, Charleston, Birmingham, and Meridian) also helped local merchants to increase the volume of their trade from $506.5 million in 1870 to $659 million in 1890.[34] By the beginning of the century's last decade, city boosters proudly boasted of the presence of fifty millionaires in Hamilton County.[35]

Although Cincinnati dropped from the nation's third largest manufacturing city in 1860 to its seventh largest in 1880, it nevertheless emerged from the depression as the most diverse industrial center in the

West. "Nowhere else," remarked one Ohio official in 1887, "are there so many manufacturing establishments, or as many persons employed in industrial pursuits on the same number of contiguous acres."[36] Indeed, by the mid-1880s, Cincinnati ranked as the nation's leading producer of carriages, furniture, glycerine, coffins, plug tobacco, wine, whiskey, and safes; second in clothing, boots and shoes; and among the top seven manufacturers of cigars, saddles, harnesses, beer, sawed lumber, tanned and curried leather, printed materials, foundry products, blacksmithing, and marble and stone goods.[37] Whatever the complaints of their employees, manufacturers could rightfully boast that the 1880s offered more opportunities for employment than at any other time in the city's history.

The emergence of this new era of industrialization was also accompanied by dramatic changes in the visions and images of progress developed by the city's elites. Manufacturing continued to be praised as the foundation of the city's wealth, but moral and material advancement were no longer seen as being generated by the mechanic — the hero of ante-bellum rhetoric. Rather, they were portrayed as the products of the more impersonal and nebulous forces of technology. Civic elites came to speak of progress in terms of cultural and scientific advancement, rather than the growth of a virtuous and independent citizenry. Industry and invention — the principal manifestations of technology — were lauded as the new agencies responsible for the growth and evolution of modern society. Although occasional tribute was paid to the industrial worker, the public image and power of the creator was gradually diminished in favor of honoring his creations. Buildings and machinery, not the men and women who created them, emerged as the primary focus of admiration and adulation in the new world of modern history.

Nowhere was this change in the symbolic role of industry and invention more apparent than at the Cincinnati Industrial Expositions held annually between 1870 and 1888. Organized through the combined efforts of the Chamber of Commerce, Board of Trade, and Ohio Mechanics' Institute, they consistently drew crowds of from 200,000 to 300,000. The expositions were primarily intended to promote greater regional interest in Cincinnati's manufactured goods, but they also served a more subtle purpose: to cloak modern industry and invention in the respectable garb of science, art, and culture and to portray them as the principal powers behind urban progress. The board of directors, drawn largely from the city's leading industrial and commercial magnates, may not have self-consciously conceived of this as an explicit goal of the expositions, but the speeches which they and their guests delivered, and the prominence which they gave to certain exhibitions, gave repeated evidence of such underlying concerns.[38]

With the inauguration of the industrial expositions, machines assumed a new awe-inspiring public role; they were no longer simply private mechanisms of production but forms of art and reflections of cultural and material advancement. There could be "no greater evidence of the cultural and of the social and political advancement of a community," exclaimed Exposition President Alfred Goshorn, "than are illustrated by its mechanical and artistic development."[39] In addition to exposing the public to "various kinds of labor-saving machinery," the board of directors also attempted to promote a "higher art culture" and give their exposition a greater aura of refinement by exhibiting a wide array of paintings, sculptures, photographs, and engravings.[40] Yet, while speakers frequently paid tribute to these varied artistic endeavors, they reserved their greatest praise for the exposition's industrial exhibits. Machinery, keynote speaker George Jones insisted in 1874, unlike the other exhibits, combined beauty with practicality. It was not abstract "artistic refinement which generates in the mind a heightened appreciation of the beautiful, but the practical use and direct appliance of simplified machines."[41] Nowhere, agreed Exposition President Edmund Pendleton, were "Art and her twin sister Industry" — the two forces that "civilize the world" — joined in a more graceful and productive alliance than in the form of modern technology.[42]

The men who had addressed the Ohio Mechanics' Institute Exhibits of the 1840s and 1850s had taken great care to portray machinery as the byproduct of man's ingenuity. Their counterparts of the 1870s and 1880s created a vision which portrayed machinery as independent forms of power devoid of human control. "The breathing engines and the rattling wheels [of machines]" that filled the exposition halls, exulted the Reverend Noah Schenk, "are chanting the poetry of labor."[43] Yet, while the poetry was plainly exhibited for all to see, the poet was conspicuously absent from public view. It was technology, not the human agents who created it, that was being honored at these expositions. Production, as keynote speaker Senator John Sherman avowed, was by far and away the "best test of civilization." And, as "nearly all labor" was presently "performed by machinery," he added, there seemed little doubt about the source of the nation's continued wellbeing.[44]

Despite their claim that the Exposition was intended "to be a museum of human activity," the board of directors managed to choose and arrange their exhibits in such a manner as to separate images of power from their human forms and to display them as the attribute of machinery.[45] Unlike the OMI exhibitions, machines were neither isolated nor kept static. Instead, they were accorded the main place of honor in a massive and grandiose 27,600-square-foot building appropriately named Power Hall. This was Power Hall in the most literal sense, for its several hundred running exhibits produced the power necessary to light and operate the other exhibition halls.

Although the Exposition contained several other buildings, it was Power Hall which consistently attracted the largest crowds and was considered the "most valuable in the Exposition."[46] Daily contests among machines were staged for the edification and amazement of spectators. Winning machines, often the same ones which were undermining the skills or displacing workers from their jobs, were awarded prizes for contributing to the advancement of human progress.

One can only speculate as to the psychic effects produced on workingmen and workingwomen, who, often dressed in their best Sunday clothes, spent their leisure time and the considerable sum of twenty-five cents for the privilege of viewing the same machinery they had built or worked alongside during the week. Yet, once exhibited at the Exposition, these machines assumed a new aura and a new identity; they were the same, and yet not the same, machines of the workshop. In Power Hall they stood isolated from their creators and operators. In the Cincinnati exhibitions, as well as at other industrial fairs around the nation, machines — which workers and sympathetic allies insisted were "superseding man . . . more rapidly than he can be transformed from the manual drudge to the intelligent overseer of machinery" — were presented to the general public as the symbols of the new industrial world: as works of beauty, art, and progress.[47]

This tendency toward honoring the product rather than the producer was also evinced in the changing appearance and architectural motifs of the city's buildings and factories. The classical architecture which had been used in ante-bellum years to link the expansion of capital with the image of democracy was gradually replaced by a melange of Gothic, Victorian, and Renaissance designs which honored the power, presence, and authority of business and industry. In Cincinnati, as well as throughout the nation, the Victorian era was a time of monumental buildings constructed in monumental style. As cast-iron-column construction and general building techniques grew more sophisticated, the modest two- and three-story buildings of previous years gave way to a large number of "massive and imposing" structures.[48] Factories which stretched out over several city blocks or rose to unprecedented heights became increasingly commonplace in the city of modern industry.

At the same time that the interiors of these factories were emerging as bitter arenas of conflict between labor and capital, manufacturers often took great care to ensure that the exteriors of their buildings assumed a more appealing and elegant public guise. "In no class of buildings," observed contemporary historian John Chamberlain, was there a greater change in structure and design than in these new industrial edifices.[49] The factory was no longer simply viewed as a place to work, but also as a work of art. Instead of praising the city's natural splendors — its rivers, hills, parks, and trees — as was the custom of earlier years, city boosters described beauty in increasingly materialistic terms. They proudly pointed to "business houses of imposing appearance and unusual architectural beauty," and to the city's "manufactories which are costly and extensive."[50]

These changing attitudes toward factory architecture can be seen in the sharply diverging attitudes expressed by the editors of the Enquirer in 1847 and 1873. When the Mitchell and Rammelsberg Furniture Company erected the city's first six-story building in 1847, it was perceived by the Enquier as a symbol of arrogance — as a gargantuan structure which approached the heavens, not in tribute to God or man, but to Mammon. The newspaper blasted the factory and its owners for doing "much violence to our national patriotism by the contemptuous belittling of our Customhouse [built in the Classical style] sitting so squat and ignobly at its feet."[51] Twenty-six years later, however, when the company opened a new, even larger factory — designed by an architect specially brought over from England — the Enquirer praised the "handsome, spacious, and massive stone building" and remarked that visitors would "find great pleasure in examining the noble proportions of the edifice."[52]

In few industries was the attempt to link industrial development with artistic expansion more pronounced than in the brewing business. Major innovations in refrigeration, malting, and bottling procedures were developed in the 1870s and 1880s, and wealthy brewers combined these previously separately housed operations into a single massive factory. One brewery expert who reviewed the planning and attention that went into the design of these new structures noted that it was "not sufficient that a brewery should be equipped with all the latest apparatus and machinery." The building's designer also had to pay great attention to creating "a handsome architectural construction" which would stand as a tribute "to the good taste and to the wealth of owners."[53]

Following the damaging floods of 1884, the Foss-Schneider Brewery commissioned F. W. Wolff, Chicago's most prominent "brewers' architect," to design a building that would stand as one of the largest, most modern, and most beautiful breweries in the world —a building so beautiful that it would attract tourists from miles around. Not to be outdone by their competitor, the Gerke, Hauck, and Walker Brewing companies soon erected buildings that also had a pretense of being something more than mere factories. Although the increased centralization of production generated an enormous amount of resistance among brewery workers, it was the external beauty, the artistic façade of industrial expansion, which caught the eye and admiration of the general public. Indeed, many of the city's more cultivated citizens must have wondered how anyone laboring in such elegant buildings could complain of poor working conditions.[54]

The creation of elegant retail showrooms to display and sell finished products served as yet another means of enhancing the public image of industry. Although many manufacturers combined production and sale in one building — they used the upper floors for manufacturing and the lower floors for retail sales — the trend of the late 1870s was toward opening separate showrooms in the more fashionable areas of the city. Mitchell and Rammelsberg, the nation's largest furniture company in 1875, operated a factory near the shabby waterfront and a salesroom, built in the French Renaissance style, on fashionable Fourth Street. The latter, observed a local guidebook, was impressively decorated with "costly works of [imported] art."[55] Similarly, hat and fur manufacturer A. E. Burkhardt was lauded for his concern to beautify the inside as well as the outside of his showroom. "The internal arrangements," it was noted, comprised "all that modern art can do to render a salesroom elegant, luxurious and convenient."[56] Here, as elsewhere, the product of man's labor was separated from its increasingly tumultuous center of production and displayed for the public to view in peaceful and refined surroundings.

The growing separation between the worlds of employers and employees engendered by changes at the workplace and reflected in the language and imagery of urban progress was further exacerbated by the growing geographical isolation between the city's classes. Although a number of elites had abandoned the downtown areas in the late 1850s and 1860s, the introduction of inclined planes and electric cable cars which scaled the city's precipitate hills in the 1870s and 1880s and the expansion

(a)

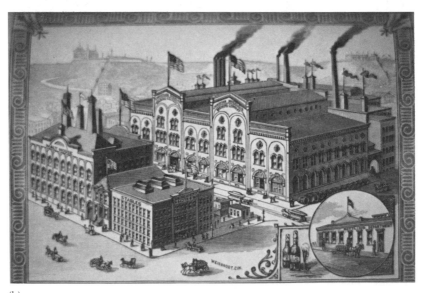

(b)

Figure 15 The Beautification of the Breweries.
(a) Gerke Brewing Co. (c. 1885); (b) Moerlein Brewing Co. (c. 1890). During the mid-1880s, a
number of brewers hired special architects to beautify the exterior of their new factories.
Courtesy of the Cincinnati Historical Society

of railroad and omnibus lines into distant suburban areas prompted greater numbers of manufacturers, merchants, and financiers to leave the fashionable but crowded East and West End areas for the "cleaner air and wider spaces of the hilltop suburbs of Clifton, Walnut Hills, Mount Adams, and Avondale."[57] Although a number of working-class families moved to the near hilltops, the bulk of the city's laboring population remained in the Basin area — some three, five, or ten miles away from the new elite residential districts.[58]

Whereas the domains of work and home and of rich and poor had once been located within a mile of each other, by the 1880s the spatial worlds of workers and employers grew increasingly distant from one another. This is not to romanticize the earlier "walking city" as a Golden Age of harmonious community life. It is, rather, to suggest that the possibilities for mutual understanding and cooperation between the classes, difficult in the best of times, appeared to diminish as the city's populace scattered throughout the valleys and hills of Cincinnati. Little wonder, then, that civic elites, who viewed their age as a time of increased progress and prosperity, were shocked and bewildered as workers slowly mounted new and occasionally violent campaigns to restore their vision of justice, independence, and equity to the new world of modern industry.

CHAPTER TEN

Confrontations With Capital: Economic Life and Working-Class Protest, 1873 – 1884

As Cincinnati experienced a temporary period of economic recovery that lasted from late 1878 until 1882, merchants and manufacturers optimistically proclaimed the end of hard times and the beginning of a new era of prosperity. Despite the prolonged years of depression, the value of annual production, even with a deflation in prices of 25 to 30 percent, increased by 33.5 percent between 1870 and 1880, and the total number of industrial employees rose by 46 percent. This picture of industrial growth, however, masked the enormous uncertainties and hardships which thousands of men and women experienced. Faced with declining wages and frequent periods of unemployment, Cincinnati workers increasingly questioned their employers' vision of the beneficent aspects of the new era of modern industry. Indeed, as greater numbers of wage earners moved from small shops to large factories and found their skills and chances for independence taking an ever downward turn, working-class perceptions of capital, government, and the possibilities for collective working-class action underwent marked transitions.

Making Ends Meet

While manufacturers, merchants, politicians, and civic elites gathered at the Industrial Expositions to praise the new era of modern industry, workers bitterly complained to reporters and state officials of the many hardships which they and their families were forced to endure. "Our wages have been reduced so much," said one group of cabinetmakers in 1877, "that we are compelled to suffer hunger in spite of hard work."[1] Asked that same year how he could support his wife and children on his meager five dollar weekly wage, an embittered cigarmaker spat out: "I don't live. I am literally starving. We get meat once a week, the rest of the time we have dry bread and black coffee."[2] Sounding a similar note, a Cincinnati bricklayer wrote to the Ohio Bureau of Labor Statistics (BLS) in 1879: "I know it is all a person can do, either as a journeyman or boss, to keep the wolf from the door. It was different in 1872, and even in 1860. In these days there was plenty of work and men were correspondingly happy and content, while now all is gloom."[3]

   The crises of the 1870s and 1880s produced enormous hardships, but they did not affect all Cincinnati workers in quite the same way. The ability to weather economic storms depended largely upon one's level of skill, the degree of mechanization and the division of labor at the point of production, and the general economic state of one's industry. Wages, as table 10.1 reveals, often varied within as well as between industries. Nor was it always clear that factories and machines were the primary causes of immiseration. Shoemakers and printers laboring in large establishments, for example, often earned higher wages and worked longer periods of time each year than their small-shop counterparts.[4] Nevertheless, although wages generally increased after the economic upswing of 1878, workers' earnings, regardless of skill, trade, or setting of employment, were consistently outpaced by the costs of food and housing.

   Cincinnati workers also found themselves faced with the dire prospects of long periods of unemployment or part-time work schedules. Between 1873 and 1877 — the most severe period of the depression — cabinetmakers, cigarmakers, shoemakers, and machinists repeatedly complained that few skilled members of their trades were able to secure steady employment for more than eight or nine months a year.[5] "Cincinnati is the poorest and most uncertain place I've ever worked," shoemaker Joseph Glenn remarked in July 1876. "A mechanic here will average about $10 a week for seven months in the year."[6] Although employment opportunities

Table 10.1 Changes in Food and Housing Costs and Weekly
Wages by Industry and Level of Skill: 1872–1881

	1872	1877	1881	Percentage of Change 1872–1881
Food (10 items)	$26.39	$26.90	$29.28	+11.0
Housing (Year)	$120.00	$115.85	$106.50	−11.2
Carriages:				
Blacksmith	18.00	9.50	13.00	−27.8
Trimmer	15.00	9.00	12.66	−15.6
Bodymaker	14.00	9.00	11.70	−16.4
Painter	14.00	7.50	9.60	−31.4
Blacksmith's Helper	9.00	7.50	6.72	−25.3
Furniture:				
Carver	21.50	9.50	12.24	−43.1
Woodworker	16.50	9.00	10.62	−35.6
Sawyer	16.50	7.50	9.78	−40.7
Varnisher	11.00	7.00	7.98	−27.5
Laborer	9.00	6.00	6.90	−23.3
Building Trades:				
Bricklayer	30.00	15.00	19.86	−33.8
Stonemason	21.00	—	17.58	−16.3
Plasterer	24.00	15.00	16.80	−30.0
Cigars:				
Hand Roller	19.50	10.00	15.00	−23.1
Machine Roller	—	6.00	11.70	—
Day Laborer	10.50	6.00	8.00	−23.8

SOURCE: Statistics were compiled from data contained in the *Annual Report of the Bureau of Labor Statistics*, 1877 – 1893; *Commercial*, July 29, 1877; *The Cincinnati Artisan*, April 1, 1878; *Enquirer*, January 1, 1872 – December 31, 1881.

improved as more factories resumed full-time production schedules after 1878, a survey conducted by the BLS that year revealed that 27 percent of the state's manufacturing workforce still labored only 39 to 49 weeks and 14 percent less than 38 weeks.[7]

It was the city's unskilled laborers who were most severely affected by the depression. Many laborers found themselves unable to procure jobs; the fortunate ones who did obtain work often found wages so low as to be insufficient to support an entire family. Although the City Council moved to ease the problems of widespread unemployment by instituting a series of public works projects, the number of positions created did not come close to filling the demand for jobs. Commenting on the widespread poverty and desperation of thousands of Cincinnati workers,

Superintendent of Streets — and former trades union leader — Larkin McHugh sadly observed in July 1876:

> I never saw the evidences of suffering I see now. We advertised for sixty hands to work on Columbia Avenue, and when I went out on the ground a thousand men stood waiting there to go to work. We had to employ two hundred of them. Every day a hundred men come to me to inquire if there is any prospect of getting work, and they keep coming. . . . The shops and mills that employ thousands are still — have been still for months, and thousands of little mouths cry daily for bread, and get none, because those whose place it is to provide them with bread can not get it for work, and they have not the wherewith to buy.[8]

Single unemployed males, unable to find jobs, often enlisted in the army of tramps who roamed the country and frequently sought shelter in police station houses and charitable institutions. In the past years, the *Enquirer* observed in 1876, the tramp element had become "a fixed institution" in Cincinnati.[9] Between dusk and dawn, city police stations were jammed with hundreds of people who, for want of housing, slept on the basement floor. Although many of these tramps were habitual "*lazzaronis*," the city's police chief explained, a goodly number were "worthy and honest homeless" men and women endeavoring to eke "out a miserable living by day, and returning at night to one of the numerous station houses for lodging."[10] Indeed, as times worsened, the number of station-house lodgers rose from 11,083 in 1866 to 60,875 in 1877.[11]

The early years of the depression also brought important changes in the nature of working-class family economies. The increased entry of women and children into the manufacturing sector in the 1870s

Table 10.2 Average Yearly Earnings, Expenses, and Savings Among Ohio Working-Class Families Generally Headed by Skilled Workers, 1874–1885

	1874	1877	1880	1883	1885
Number of Families	—	61	324	266	334
Average Family Size	4.0	4.9	4.8	5.1	4.9
Total Family Earnings	$572	$568	$681	$649	$623
Total Family Expenses	$504	$508	$552	$553	$567
Total Family Savings	$68	$60	$129	$96	$56
Expenses as a Percentage of Earnings	88.1	89.4	81.1	85.2	91.0

SOURCE: *BLS — 1877*, p. 306; *BLS — 1878*, pp. 250, 255; *BLS — 1880*, p. 249; *BLS — 1883*, p. 134; *BLS — 1885*, p. 94; *BLS — 1886*, pp. 220–21.

and 1880s was not caused simply by changes in production. Rather, with heads of households often unable to earn enough money to meet their monthly expenses, wives, daughters, and sons were often forced to enter the labor market in order to help make ends meet. While families headed by unskilled laborers had long been accustomed to such a necessity, hard times soon required skilled workers to adopt similar measures. "I believe that four-fifths of the men who now send their children out to labor," testified one Cincinnati printer before a United States Senate committee in 1883, "would not do it were their own compensation sufficient to provide for family expenses."[12] Yet, while skilled workers were often reluctant to send their families into the city's factories or clothing sweatshops, these supplementary wage earners contributed a vital 34 to 43 percent of the total family income between 1879 and 1882. Indeed, their earnings often meant the difference between minimal subsistence and enjoying at least a few minor amenities.

The statistics in table 10.2, however, provide only a partial indication of the importance that women and children played in helping to support their families. Had these surveys, which concentrated largely upon skilled workers, included a proportional number of families headed by semi- and unskilled workers, the percentage of working-class families with supplementary wage earners would have undoubtedly exceeded 50 percent of the total. For this latter group of families, the BLS noted in 1878, supplementary wage earners were an absolute necessity.[13]

Despite the increased reliance upon women and children, many Cincinnati working-class families endured the depression years living on the edge of debt. The existence of supplementary family wage earners did not signal an end to tight family budgets. Between 1874 and 1883, approximately 90 percent of the average earnings of families headed by *skilled* workers went toward paying for basic necessities: food, clothing, rent, fuel, and medical expenses.[14] What little income remained was either saved or spent on sundry indulgences like tobacco, beer, or family picnics. Yet, while some families did manage to save money each year, many others found themselves either breaking even or going into debt. When queried as to the difference between their yearly earnings and expenses, 49 percent of the families surveyed by the BLS in 1877, 36 percent in 1878, 33 percent in 1880, and 25 percent in 1882 replied that their expenses were either equal to or greater than their earnings.[15] Even periods of full employment, particularly for the families of unskilled workers, did not necessarily mean an end to debt. "Some of my fellow-laborers," remarked one local railroad

Table 10.3 Distribution of Annual Expenses Among Ohio Working-Class
Families Generally Headed By Skilled Workers, 1877–1885

	1877	1878	1879	1885
Number of Families	36	97	114	334
Total Family Earnings	$568	$517	—	$623
Total Family Expenses	$527	$492	$576	$567
Distribution of Expenses by Percent:				
Rent	18.2	16.0	13.6	16.8
Fuel	5.3	5.5	5.4	5.1
Meat & Groceries	50.4	46.5	46.2	44.2
Clothing, Shoes, & Dry Goods	16.1	17.4	17.0	20.5
Medical Expenses	—	4.7	4.0	4.5
Recreation	—	1.6	2.1	—
Education	—	1.8	1.3	—
Sundries	10.0	6.5	10.4	8.9
Total	100.0	100.0	100.0	100.0

SOURCE: *BLS — 1877*, p. 306; *BLS — 1879*, pp. 233–34; *BLS — 1881*, pp. 38–41; *BLS —
1882*, p. 348; *BLS — 1883*, pp. 118–19; *BLS — 1884*, p. 263; *BLS — 1886*, pp. 220–21.

laborer in 1878, "tell me they have spent and gone into debt fully $300
over their earnings the past five years, and have not lost a month's work in
that time."[16]

As budgets grew tighter, families often made ends meet either
by taking lodgers into their homes, moving to less expensive multifamily
dwellings, or, worst of all, relocating to the city's crowded and unsanitary
downtown tenements. When asked by a U.S. Senate committee to describe
the housing situation for "respectable working people" in Cincinnati, printer
W. H. Foster explained how even well-heeled families were forced to take
in boarders in order to meet monthly rental or mortgage payments. As for
the conditions of households headed by unskilled workers, Foster remarked,
"I have seen men so low that they had to shove a family of five or six
children and themselves, and perhaps their parents, and do their cooking
and all, in one room. They have a little trundle-bed to put all the children
in, and they shove it under the bed when not in use." It was conditions like
these, he insisted, that drove hard working, honest laborers to drink: "They
find no comfort at home, living in one room, and if they can get a few
cents they go and spend it in the saloon."[17] Indeed, between 1877 and
1882, the percentage of working-class families living in single-family homes
declined from 23 percent to 9 percent, while those inhabiting buildings
containing three or more families rose from 50 to 70 percent.[18]

Fashioning a Response: The Paths of Protest

While workers could readily agree that things were not right with the world, it was not so easy to reach a consensus on the causes of the economic distress. Even after many years of first hand experience, when Cincinnati workers were asked in 1885 to explain the central cause behind recent depressions, they offered a wide variety of explanations:

> Pressman: My opinion is, the depression is brought about by capitalists wanting to get rich too fast; also too much public stock gambling.
> Shoemaker: The needed reformation in our system of finance is the cause of depression in business.
> Machinist: Improved machinery; luxury in families of our business men, with money that ought to be paid for labor.
> Cigarmaker: Overproduction and the allowing of children to be employed in factories.
> Builder: It is my opinion that the foreign emigration to this country is too great for the amount of capital they bring with them. Stop flooding the country with foreign labor and times will be all right.[19]

With so wide a range of views, it is hardly surprising that there was no single working-class response to the problems engendered by the depression. Nevertheless, as the general conditions of work life and family economies grew increasingly similar in the 1870s and 1880s, workers began to fashion a number of common strategies aimed at halting the deteriorating conditions.

During the first several years of the depression, however, working-class protests and organizations went into a sharp period of decline. Between 1873 and 1877, most of the city's trade unions either dissolved or experienced a precipitate loss of members as workers abandoned their unions in a desperate quest to secure jobs at any pay and under any conditions. By the beginning of 1878, only 1,000 workers remained within the ranks of organized labor.[20] Those few unions which managed to survive this early period of distress found their power to oppose manufacturers or protect their crafts severely limited. "Owing to the depression condition of our trade," the leaders of Cincinnati Typographical Union No. 3 lamented in 1877, "this union is in no condition to demand justice of employers, or to enforce such demands, if made."[21] Similarly, Iron Molders' Union No. 4 was forced to suspend all union wage scales and work rules in order to prevent a wholesale defection of its remaining members.[22]

Not surprisingly, the strike fever which had gripped the city in the postwar era also subsided in the years between 1873 and 1877. Despite the sharp deterioration of their wages and working conditions, job-hungry workers launched only nine strikes — virtually all unsuccessful — between October 1873 and June 1877. This decline in strike activity, the BLS explained in 1878, was due not to "any spirit of contentment on the part of the workingmen," but to "their inability to maintain strikes, their poverty compelling acquiescence in a condition against which their spirit rebels."[23]

This period of relative quiescence came to a halt with the outbreak of the Great Railroad Strikes of 1877. On July 16, 1877, railroad workers on the Baltimore and Ohio lines in Martinsburg, West Virginia — angered by their second wage cut in eight months — uncoupled the engines in the local yards and announced that no trains would be allowed to enter or leave the city until the pay cut was rescinded. Outbreaks of violence soon ensued as local police and militia clashed with strikers in an unsuccessful effort to get the trains moving again. Pressured by the president of the Baltimore and Ohio Railroad, West Virginia Governor Henry M. Matthews wired a request to President Rutherford B. Hayes to send in federal troops to quell the "unlawful and domestic violence now existing at Martinsburg and at other points along the line."[24] Hayes, who had refused to dispatch troops into southern states to protect black citizens against protracted racial violence, moved to defend the property rights of the railroad by sending 300 armed troops to suppress the strike.

What had begun as a local action soon developed into a national struggle as railroad workers throughout the East, Midwest, and South joined the Martinsburg workers on strike. Like Governor Matthews, state officials in other regions responded to the workingmen's actions by sending in national guard units and federal troops to quell the strikes and prevent further outbreaks of violence. During the ensuing week, over 100 men were killed and hundreds wounded as strikers and their allies clashed with military forces in the country's first "national" strike.[25]

In Cincinnati, railroad workers on all local lines, explaining that they "felt bound to support the other men everywhere," joined the Baltimore and Ohio employees on strike.[26] Widespread working-class protest, which had virtually disappeared during the previous four years, was rekindled as Germans, Irish, black, and native-born wage earners, led by the city's socialists, organized several rallies and marches to denounce the railroads and defend the cause of their striking workers. Community support for the railwaymen ran so high that, when local militia units were ordered to gather at the city's railroad depot on July 21, they were "followed by a hissing, groaning, shouting crowd [of 2,000] who reviled the men who were marching to suppress the strikes."[27] Two days later, when firemen attempted to put out a blaze, set by striking workers, on the Ohio and Mississippi's wooden trestle bridge, they were met by a crowd of several hundred sympathetic citizens who cut their hoses "in no less than twelve sections."[28]

Outrage among workingmen ran so high, one reporter noted, that there was a danger that the strike would become general, "not only with the railroad men, but with all classes of laborers."[29] City streets, remarked gas works superintendent Andrew Hickenlooper, were filled "with a rabble that forcibly brought to mind the days of the French Commune."[30] Socialists urged wage earners to use only "lawful means to support the downtrodden, outraged, employees now on strike."[31] However, during a march in the city's factory district, demonstrators shouted warnings to manufacturers that they might burn down factories if employers continued to treat them unfairly. Fearing for the safety of their property, several dozen merchants and manufacturers donated $100 each to the police commissioner to enable him to hire and post an additional 300 armed guards in the downtown area.[32]

Although the strikes ended in Cincinnati on July 26, when railroad companies agreed to rescind all wage cuts, the week's events had a profound effect upon local workers. During the numerous rallies held that July, workers in a wide array of trades and industries began to speak of the inauguration of a new era in the history of labor and capital — one, explained shoemaker Emor Davis, which would "array the people and the industrial interests against the monopolists and money power."[33] Although many workers continued to view capital per se as a positive force which if properly used would benefit employers and employees alike, they believed that the new generation of capitalists, monopolists, and corporations used their power to oppress labor. "Virtue, honest, [and] useful lives of productive industry," exclaimed socialist leader William Haller, no longer meant "assurance of success."[34] The railroad strikes, exclaimed the city's cigarmakers, heralded the beginning of a "great struggle between the people and the monopolies."[35]

The course of action taken by railroad magnates and governmental officials during the strike also led Cincinnati workers to fear that capitalists had extended their corrupting tentacles into the halls of government and destroyed the neutrality of the state in the same way that they had destroyed the neutrality of capital. "Has it come to this," Peter Clark, a black high school principal and prominent socialist, asked an angry crowd of several thousand workers that July, "that the President of a private corporation can, by the click of a telegraphic instrument, bring State and National troops into the field to shoot down American citizens guilty of no crime of violence?"[36] By sending in troops to attack law-abiding citizens, declared one journeymen, President Hayes and various state officials had sided with capitalists "against the common interest of the people."[37] Even the editors of the *Enquirer* conceded that the "money power, prompted by their greed, have for years not only controlled the Congress of the United States, but the President, and have run both Houses in their interest."[38]

During the next several years, as the city's economy entered a period of prosperity — at least temporarily — Cincinnati workers embarked upon three distinct paths of action to remedy what they perceived as their deteriorating conditions as workers and citizens: socialism, trade unionism, and the Knights of Labor. Socialists, the most radical of these groups, were the first to benefit from the anger produced by the events of July.

Scores of German socialists arrived in Cincinnati in the late 1840s and 1850s, and in the early 1870s. They joined with several hundred Irish and native-born workers to form, successively, the International Workingmen's Association, the Workingmen's Social and Political Organization, and the Workingmen's Party of the United States. Unlike trade unionists, who generally advocated reformist solutions, socialists argued that true justice would only be achieved by a "radical change in the entire social fabric" of American life.[39] Despite the vast increase in the productive powers of modern industry, explained William Haller, the editor of the socialist weekly *Emancipator,* thousands of men and women were forced to beg for sufficient wages to sustain themselves and their families. "Capital under its present shape," he wrote in March 1877, "is a 'gorgon' that is swallowing the earnings of the great mass."[40] Simple reform measures would not alter the fundamental nature of injustice. "As long as the relation of employer and employee exists," Haller concluded, the wage earner would never obtain a fair "share of what his skill has helped to produce."[41]

While claiming that the "present mode of owning wealth is productive of gigantic evils," Haller and his fellow socialists insisted that industry, if "run under a different system," would "be beneficial to all."[42] It was the private ownership of industry, they believed, not industrialization per se, that produced the inequities of modern society. Avowing that "all legitimate property belonged to the producer," Cincinnati socialists called for radical political changes which would place all shops and factories "under the control of the Government as fast as practicable." Instead of serving the interests of a handful of wealthy capitalists, these new ventures, which would be "operated by free-cooperative trade unions," would pursue the "good of the whole people."[43]

During their various political campaigns of the mid-1870s, the Workingmen's Party — the political wing of the socialist movement — repeatedly called for the nationalization of all industries, the construction of municipally owned housing for the poor, the institution of an eight-hour work day, and various other reform measures. By early 1877, the party had succeeded in recruiting nearly 500 men from the ranks of the city's "Americans, Germans, Irish, Negroes, and half a dozen other nationalities" — but their political campaigns proved an abysmal failure.[44] Vilified by conservative newspaper editors, politicians, and clergymen as "the enemy of the true interests of the workingman, the declared foe of God and religion and human justice," the socialists rarely succeeded in garnering more than a few hundred votes at the polls.[45]

Yet, during the railroad strikes of 1877 and in the weeks thereafter, socialist denunciations of the repressive powers of corporations and the frequent collusion between politicians and industrial capitalists struck a responsive chord among thousands of men who had hitherto scorned the radical organization. Labor leaders and wage earners generally praised socialists for their support of the strikers and their steadfast insistence that workers employ peaceful methods to resolve the present situation. Socialist leaders, such as Haller, Clark, iron molder P. W. McIntyre, cigarmaker William Kemple, and saloon keeper Gustav Leubkert, urged their fellow citizens to support the Workingmen's Party in its efforts to put an end to a capitalistic system that made "dependence certain and absolute."[46]

The ensuing political campaign was one of the most dramatic of the depression era. Socialist leaders organized rallies and marches throughout the city and made intense efforts to recruit German, Irish, black, and native-born workers. For the "first time in the history of Hamilton County politics," remarked one astounded reporter, socialists were being "watched with serious interest both by the politicians and the people at large."[47] When the ballots were counted that October, the Workingmen's Party startled the political establishment by winning nearly 20 percent of the total vote. Indeed, the 9,000 votes received by most socialist candidates in Cincinnati far exceeded the success of socialist organizations in other major cities, such as New York, Chicago, and Milwaukee.[48]

The success of the budding socialist movement, however, was rapidly undermined by a number of factors. Troubled by the socialists' unexpected strength at the polls, politicians, newspaper editors, and ministers renewed the vituperative attacks upon the Workingmen's Party. Scores of articles and editorials appeared in the city's newspapers portraying socialists as "red-shirted and red-flagged" anarchists bent upon the violent destruction of the nation's republican institutions.[49] From the city's pulpits, such clergymen as Father J. F. Callaghan denounced the socialists as godless men bent upon creating "a revelry of hell on earth."[50]

Socialists were also attacked by trade unionists. Concerned with establishing themselves as the sole representatives of law-abiding workers, union leaders joined in the denunciation of radicalism. The shoemakers' union announced its "abhorence of 'Communism'" and pledged to observe strict "adherence to law and order."[51] The iron molders' local concurred that communists would find no sympathizers among its members.[52]

A bitter internal struggle over party strategy also hurt the socialists. The party's dominant German and Bohemian sections wanted to concentrate their efforts upon forging closer alliances with the city's trade unions. Its English-speaking section, however, argued for continuing the party's efforts at independent political action. Finding themselves on the losing side of the argument, the latter group, headed by Haller and printer H. T. Ogden, left the party, with many of them turning to the Greenback movement as an alternative. The mass defection of its English section gave further proof to antisocialist claims that the Workingmen's Party was a "foreign" movement devoid of true American support. Torn by internal dissension and external opposition, the socialist movement soon dwindled in size and influence. Although the party continued to run candidates in local and state elections throughout the 1880s, it rarely attracted more than 1 percent of the total vote.[53]

Disturbed by the radical language and demands of the socialists, thousands of Cincinnati workers embraced trade unionism as a more acceptable mode of protest. Unlike the socialists, trade unionists did not seek to overthrow the capitalist system. Rather, they attempted to impose limits upon the unfettered growth of the laissez-faire capitalism and to secure better wages, hours, and working conditions for their members.

"Trade Unionism," insisted iron molder Dan Thomas, was the "most practicable means at our command to induce capitalists to share with laborers a proportion of the benefits resulting from universal progress." Unions served as "as a necessary balance of the fabric of society, and without them men have reason to believe their standard of living would be gradually brought down to the level of chattel slaves."[54] At the same time, the trade union movement promised to revitalize republican principles by uplifting the masses. The advancement of the "whole industrial classes . . . in material comfort and security, and still more in intellectual and moral attainments," explained one unionist, would be "to the advantage of the whole community."[55]

The upswing in economic activity from late 1878 until early 1882 prompted Cincinnati workers to revive their dormant unions. Between 1878 and 1884, as workers formed over 100 unions, the number of active trade unionists leapt from 1,000 to 12,000 men and women.[56] This renewed movement toward unionization was particularly pronounced among those industries most affected by the recent growth of factory production. Approximately 63.1 percent of these new unions were organized by workers in industries which generally employed more than fifty people in their factories. Artisans in trades and industries whose shops employed less than fifty people organized 25.4 percent of the unions, while unskilled laborers formed 11.5 percent of the era's new organizations.[57] Although many of these unions were formed in preparation for strikes and lasted but a few months, the dramatic upsurge in labor organization nevertheless signaled that workers would not accept their employers' visions of industrialization without a battle.

The "revival of business interests," the *Enquirer* reported in October 1879, was quickly followed by a series of strikes led by wage earners "who a few months ago were pleading for work."[58] The greatest flurry of strike activity occurred among the city's small-shop artisans and those factory artisans working in trades with longstanding traditions of craft organization. Building tradesmen (the most active of all strikers), hand coopers, horseshoe blacksmiths, silver gilders, and leather craftsmen initiated 22 (26.5 percent) of the 83 strikes fought between 1878 and 1884. Printers, iron molders, cigarmakers, and shoemakers, although often laboring in large factories, nevertheless continued to battle for better wages and working conditions by launching 33 (39.7 percent) of the strikes. Factory artisans in the city's breweries, clothing, furniture, carriagemaking, and heavy-metalworking establishments accounted for an additional 15 strikes (18.1 percent), while unskilled laborers in meatpacking, textile, confectionary, and rope factories or in railroad, street car, and telegraph operations launched 13 battles (15.7 percent).

Long years of economic privation, however, led many Cincinnati workers to alter the focus of their grievances. Whereas the flush times of the late 1860s and early 1870s prompted numerous unions to extend their wage battle to include demands for greater control of workplace opertions, the vast majority of strikes in the late 1870s and early 1880s were aimed at securing better pay or resisting new wage cuts. Only 19 (22.9 percent) of the 83 strikes and lockouts initiated between 1878 and 1884 were fought over issues relating to the mechanization of production, the hiring of women, children and apprentices, the enforcement of union work rules, or demands for union recognition. Indeed, workers soon discovered that, while they were often able to force manufacturers to accede to their wage demands, they were markedly less successful in winning their battles for greater control over production. A report issued by the United States Commissioner of Labor in 1887 noted that, although Cincinnati union members won 71 percent of the wage strikes contested between 1881 and 1884, they succeeded in winning only 25 percent of their battles over non-wage-and-hour issues.[59]

The gulf between labor and capital widened as manufacturers

Table 10.4 Strikes and Lockouts in Cincinnati, 1873 – 1884

Year	Total	Primary Cause of Action	
		Wages and/ or Hours	Unionization and/ or Control of Work
1873	5	3	2
1874	2	1	1
1875	2	2	0
1876	3	2	1
1877	12	10	2
1878	5	4	1
1879	16	14	2
1880	5	4	1
1881	25	20	5
1882	12	9	3
1883	10	8	2
1884	10	5	5
Total	107	82	25

SOURCE: Strike and lockout data were drawn from the U.S. Commissioner of Labor, *Third Annual Report of the Commissioner of Labor, 1887. Strikes and Lockouts* (Washington, 1888), pp. 436–63, 660–63; *Annual Report of the Bureau of Labor Statistics, 1877–1884;* "Minute Books — IMU No. 4," 1–3, *passim;* "Minute Books — CTU No. 3," 1–2, *passim;* and sources cited in chapter 10 note 57.

reponded to this upsurge in unionization and strike activity by organizing their own associations. Although a number of industrial and trade bodies had been formed by manufacturers in the late 1850s and 1860s, they were generally viewed as temporary bodies which united employers against workers only for the duration of a strike. However, as trade unions grew more numerous and determined in their efforts to secure better wages and working conditions, manufacturers' organizations assumed a more permanent character. Not surprisingly, it was the manufacturers in the industries undergoing the greatest changes in production and ownership which were most active in forging new alliances. By the mid-1880s, employers in the furniture, carriage, brewing, publishing, pork, shoe, clothing, tobacco, iron, and textile industries had all joined local or national manufacturers' associations.[60]

Working-class confrontations with capitalists assumed a new degree of bitterness and violence in the 1870s as manufacturers frequently utilized local police, courts, and private guards to intimidate workers and break up strikes. In 1874, Cincinnati businessmen and civic leaders, alarmed by the rapid spread of crime and growing threat of violence, persuaded the Ohio legislature to end popular elections for the city's Board of Police Commissioners and to transfer control of all appointments to the Mayor's office. Determined to suppress the outbreaks of lawlessness and labor violence that swept much of the nation during the depression, Mayor George Johnston and his successors — all of whom came from the ranks of the city's wealthy manufacturers, merchants, or bankers — set out to professionalize the police force and create a new "perfect, complete, systematic organization, militarily disciplined and trained."[61]

During the following ten years, and particularly after the passage of a local riot act in March 1876, manufacturers and railroad managers repeatedly called upon the city's police to break up strikes and demonstrations. Strike leaders, although claiming that they were exercising their rights to free assembly and free speech, were promptly hauled off to court, where they were tried for inciting a riot.[62] When police — whose ranks were filled largely by men of working-class backgrounds — occasionally proved sympathetic to the workers' cause, a number of manufacturers and merchants responded by hiring private armed guards to patrol their factories and shops. Worried that striking workers would invade their factory and persuade nonstrikers to leave their jobs, stove manufacturers Albert Redway and Stephen Burton erected a 35-foot fence around their establishment in 1877 and hired armed guards to patrol its perimeter.

Although iron molders protested against the use of a private army to intimidate lawabiding citizens, local authorities turned a deaf ear to their complaint.[63]

Trade unionists also found their organizations coming under frequent attack from the city's religious leaders. "Trade Unions," the Reverend William Burnett Wright explained to the members of the Young Men's Christian Association in 1873, "care nothing about the the work their members perform." They were lawless and avaricious organizations that did little to "win sympathy for the working man."[64] Profoundly disturbed by the railroad strikes and demonstrations that swept the city in July 1877, one Methodist minister warned his congregation:

> All trade unions are monopolies of labor, and ought to be disbanded. They are the enemies of labor and business of the country, and ought not to be tolerated. . . . While a monopoly of capital leads to slavery, a monopoly of labor leads to conflagration, destruction, ruin, and murder. Of the two evils, by all means give us the former.[65]

Catholic priests, such as Father J. F. Callaghan and Archbishop John B. Purcell, while acknowledging that labor was not always treated as fairly as it ought to be, nevertheless condemned trade unions for following the "destructive and demoralizing" influence of communism, atheism, and internationalism.[66] Catholic employees and employers were urged to avoid conflict and be guided instead "by a Christian spirit which binds men together in a real brotherhood."[67] Even those ministers sympathetic to labor's cause, like the Reverend James Foster, spoke out against the frequent lawless excesses of trade unionists — specifically, the violence that often occurred during strikes. While supporting workers in their quest for decent wages, Foster also argued that, during any outbreak of violence, municipal authorities had an obligation to act forcibly to "protect capital against the encroachments of labor."[68] For those workingmen and women believing both in god and trade unions, such pronouncements must have caused severe inner turmoil.

The ability of trade unionists to launch collective struggles against the powers of capital was weakened not only by the opposition of clergymen, municipal authorities, and manufacturers, but also by a number of internal divisions within the working class itself. Despite the dramatic increase in union membership among artisans and factory workers, the overall effectiveness of labor protests was often limited by the fragmented nature of their organizations. The growing "specialization" of labor within the city's various industries was paralleled by the growing "specialization" of unions. Shoemakers, who found their trade radically altered by the growing reliance upon "team work" — the use of four or five specialists to perform distinct operations—organized a wide array of unions to represent the particular interests not merely of their trade, but also of their specific jobs. By the early 1880s, lasters, cutters, bottomers, upper cutters, finishers, Mackay operatives and stock cutters, and custom shoemakers had all formed their own unions. Similar trends also occurred within the city's furniture, printing, carriagemaking, cigar, metalworking, hardware, clothing, brewing, leather,and textile industries.

Rather than joining together in a single industrial union which would represent the interests of all factory workers, wage earners continued to fight their battles on a craft-by-craft or skill-by-skill basis. Since wages, working conditions, and craft traditions often greatly varied, strikes by one set of workers were often ignored or only loosely endorsed by other factory employees or by the industry's small-shop artisans. A strike by hand molders working in the city's cigar factories, for example, collapsed when factory (cigar) machine molders — who considered their wages fair at the time — failed to support their cause.[69] Only in 1879, when the city's furniture and brewery workers forged a temporary alliance among their industry's skilled, semi-skilled, and unskilled employees, did all workers within an industry join in a common struggle against manufacturers.[70]

Efforts to organize artisans, factory artisans, and factory laborers into common unions were also made more difficult by their persistent ethnic loyalties. While some Irish, German, and native-born workers joined together in trade unions, many of the city's building tradesmen, furniture workers, safemakers, cigarmakes, and tailors preferred to maintain a series of separate ethnically based organizations. Of the thirty unions filing for incorporation between 1873 and 1884, only eleven were organized as inter ethnic bodies; fifteen were made up solely of German workers, two of Irish workers, and one of black hod carriers.[71]

Throughout the 1870s and 1880s, social life in Cincinnati also continued to be heavily organized along ethnic and religious lines. Although the percentage of foreign-born residents dropped from 35.8 percent in 1870 to 24.1 percent in 1890, foreign-born parents and their children made up 69 percent of the population in 1890.[72] In addition to joining the Turner and Free Men's societies, first- and second-generation Germans — who constituted 57.4 percent of the population in 1890 —

formed numerous new associations such as the German Brotherhood, the German Woman's Association, and the German Mutual Relief Association. Irish residents also sought to maintain close ties with homeland kin by joining the Ancient Order of Hibernians, the Fenian Brotherhood, and the Irish National League of America. Similar associations were also forged by the city's Jewish, Italian, English, Scottish, French, and Swiss residents. With financially pressed unions often unable to help their members during periods of sickness or economic distress, these various social organizations —which offered their members mutual aid—emerged as important sources of security as well as camaraderie.[73]

As in ante-bellum years, these voluntary associations often diffused the class conflicts generated in economic life by joining men of all backgrounds in common social and political bonds. Like their counterparts in Troy, New York, Cincinnati workers often "found themselves increasingly cooperating with middle-class leaders in nationalist political movements."[74] The Irish National League — whose leaders included shoe manufacturer O. J. Cosgrave, clothing manufacturer Frank Quinn, Judge James Fitzgerald, printer Thomas Leonard, and shoe cutter Dennis Mahoney — urged their fellow countrymen to lay aside their class differences and join together in the more pressing struggle to liberate Ireland from English rule and restore to its people the "right to manage their affairs."[75] Members of the Turners, Free Men's, and German Pioneer Societies — whose ranks also included a wide array of manufacturers, merchants, clerks, politicians, skilled workers, and unskilled laborers — issued similar pleas which urged fellow Germans to join together and voice their opposition to the repressive policies being pursued by Bismarck's administration.[76]

The political arena, like social life, was crowded with issues which divided workers and turned their attention away from the problems of the workplace. Despite the economic crises generated by the depression, local party politics in the 1870s and 1880s continued to be dominated by such questions as Sunday-closing laws, temperance, the taxation of parochial schools, and the need to crack down on crime and vice. Irish voters were aggressively pursued by Democratic politicians who pledged their support for Fenian and Irish Land League struggles and promised more building contracts for loyal party members. German voters received similar guarantees of jobs and patronage appointments from the city's Republicans.[77] Party loyalties ran so high among workingmen that union meetings were occasionally disrupted by heated debates over which party — the Democrats, Republicans, or the new Greenback Party — represented the true interests of the city's wage earners. Indeed, one meeting of trade unionists had to be suspended when a lively political discussion between printer William Ogden (a Republican) and shoemaker H. C. Traphagen (a Democrat) ended in a fist fight.[78]

Determined to combat the various divisions which weakened the city's labor movement, a number of union leaders, drawn largely from the city's older artisanal trades — printers, blacksmiths, cigarmakers, shoe-makers, and building tradesmen — gathered at Eureka Hall on June 2, 1878, for the purpose of reviving the city's moribund Trades and Labor Assembly. Despite the recent upsurge in labor organization, they noted, Cincinnati workers remained "an army without organization." The increasingly common conditions of industrial life demanded common actions. Yet most workers continued to be guided by the isolated principles of "independent action." The "true aim of Trade Unionism — the improvement of the condition of its members, and that of the working class generally," they argued, could "only be effectively secured by the co-operation of all." Disavowing any taint of "Communism, Socialism, Nationalism or politics," these men announced the formation of a revived central labor association that would speak for and fight on behalf of the collective interests of all wage earners.[79]

During the next six year, as its membership increased from a dozen to over fifty unions, the TLA once again set out to raise money for striking workers, to organize the unorganized, and to promote closer ties between native- and foreign-born wage earners. The central labor body also moved to extend its "fraternal hand to the workers of our land and to all nations of the globe that struggle for the same independence" by joining the international Federation of Trades and Labor Unions in 1881 and helping to form the Ohio State Trades and Labor Association in 1883.[80] The TLA's newspapers, the *Exponent* and the *Unionist* — published in English and German — provided Cincinnati workers with information concerning local, state, and national labor struggles.

While the TLA pursued many of the same goals as its postwar predecessor, the growth of new modes of production and the increased opposition of manufacturers and their allies led the organization to develop new policies aimed at protecting workers against the "ever-growing encroachments of organized and consolidated capital."[81] The TLA began its new phase of opposition by advocating boycotts and arbitration as two important methods of reshaping the nature of working-class economic struggles with capitalists. Unlike strikes, which isolated a single union against the power of wealthy manufacturers, the boycott served as a means of drawing upon the combined strength of the entire working-class community.

Throughout the late 1870s and 1880s, striking workers frequently joined with the TLA in launching vigorous economic campaigns which urged workers to exercise their power as consumers by ceasing to do business with boycotted firms. The TLA also applied considerable pressure upon local merchants and shopkeepers. During an 1879 boycott of the *Gazette*, the city's most virulently anti-union paper, union printers and members of the TLA's Antagonizing Committee visited dozens of department store owners and distributed leaflets which called upon all "merchants, manufacturers, and businessmen who conduct establishments honestly," to withdraw "all patronage and support from a paper published by such an unworthy firm."[82] These traditional republican appeals to community justice were also bolstered by the warning that "any person or firm, who after due notice shall continue to advertise in said sheet," would be boycotted by every union in the city.[83] This action soon proved successful; declining advertising revenues led its publisher to accede to the union's demands. The boycott, remarked one union officer, succeeded in compelling "a respectful recognition which otherwise would not have been accorded."[84]

By asking the city's wage earners not to patronize boycotted firms or any establishments which continued to do business with them, the TLA managed to link their concerns as producers and consumers — of leisure as well as groceries — into a single powerful bond. Lists of saloons, beer halls, theaters, groceries, and dry goods stores which refused to honor boycotts were printed in local newspapers and circulated by leaflets throughout the entire city. Indeed, saloonkeepers, such as Louis Ertel and one Mr. Keebler, soon found their business going to rival establishments that displayed the red sign "Union Beer Sold Here."[85] These efforts to create new forms of mutual support, remarked one printer in 1881, were largely responsible for the "more fraternal feelings now exhibited between all branches of industry."[86]

Although boycotts often proved successful, TLA leaders urged wage earners to settle their disputes, whenever possible, by arbitration rather than by direct confrontations with capital. Finding that manufacturers were able to weather long strikes more easily than their financially pressed employees, the city's printers, building tradesmen, shoemakers, iron and steel workers, stove molders, and cigarmakers all effected arbitration agreements with their industry's manufacturers. Arbitration boards, which contained an equal number of representatives from both sides, were established to work out compromises between employers and employees. Like the city's printers and shoemakers, these unions pledged that strikes would be launched only "in extreme cases," or in instances where "arbitration has been offered and refused."[87]

While arbitration did not alter the fundamental nature of production, TLA leaders perceived the process as an important means of setting limits upon the virtually unrestricted character of laissez-faire capitalism. Arbitration, explained the cigarmakers' union, "entirely revolutionizes the old principles of Trade Unionism" by allowing labor and capital to meet on equal terms.[88] Although most of these arbitration agreements collapsed after only a few years — employers and employees found they could not in fact reach peaceful settlements — they nevertheless marked the beginning of a phase of trade unionism which would become particularly prominent at the turn of the century.[89]

The desire to create common bonds which united workers outside as well as inside the workplace also led TLA leaders to use leisure activities as a means of fostering greater mutuality and trust among wage earners. A special "Entertainment Committee" was instructed to "provide suitable entertainments from time to time, such as lectures, debates, readings, dramatic, musical, and literary entertainments, etc., for the instruction and edification of workingmen regardless of creed, color, or nationality."[90] The TLA also attempted to bring its "members together in a social manner" by sponsoring a series of annual picnics and fancy balls. Indeed, the picnic of May 1880, which attracted over 25,000 people, was the largest nonviolent interethnic gathering in the city's history. The success of the spring fete was repeated in December 1880, as several thousand German, Irish, and native couples met to drink and dance the night away at the TLA's winter ball.[91]

In addition to providing an outlet for fun and relaxation, these events also took on an overtly political character. Picnics were usually preceded by massive marches through the downtown factory areas. "Flags and banners that had been stowed away for year," reported one iron molder, were brought out for the occasion.[92] So, too, were placards and banners proclaiming "Eight Hours Work, Eight Hours Sleep, Eight Hours Play," "The Place for Children Is At School Not In The Factories," and "Ignorance Is Fostered By Long Hours of Labor." Numerous speakers exhorted workingmen, in both English and German, to cast aside petty jealousies and join in the common struggle against capital.[93]

Throughout the late 1870s and 1880s, the TLA and its members also moved to redefine their relationship to parties, politics, and the state. Although concerned that government was being steadily corrupted by the frequent collusion between capitalists and politicians, working-class leaders nonetheless clung to their faith in the purifying power of democratic politics. "A solid vote at the ballot box," the city's typographers insisted in 1881, was still the "most effective means of obtaining what tyrants will not give, and we believe the only available methods by which workingmen can obtain from the capitalistic class, that which is due them."[94]

Yet, while reaffirming their belief in republican politics, older trade unionists argued that the experiences of the early and mid-1860s had shown that labor's direct participation in party politics often did more harm than good. Divided party loyalties among union men served to weaken labor unity. TLA leaders also opposed the formation of independent workingmen's parties. Mainstream parties, they argued, had consistently "taken from the ranks of organized labor its best agitators, thus 'nipping in the bud' every independent political movement on the part of organized labor."[95] Moreover, once a union man "finally gets himself snugly ensconced in some good, fat, money making office," reflected one iron molder, "he forgets workingmen and the union altogether. There are also honorable exceptions to this class, but they are scarce."[96] Avowing that it was the "duty of all Union men to hold the cause of labor above and superior to party," TLA delegates meeting in October 1880 voted to exclude all politicians and office holders from "membership in this Assembly."[97]

During the ensuing years, the TLA channeled its energies into pressuring Democratic and Republican politicians to secure the "enactment and enforcement of needed laws in the interest of labor and the revocation of such as bear unjustly upon the industrial classes."[98] TLA lobbyists repeatedly met with local and state officials in the hope of trading votes for support of measures such as the prohibition of prison labor, the passage of minimum-wage legislation, factory safety laws, anti-coolie laws, and the long-desired eight-hour work day. Pre-election interviews were also arranged with local candidates and advertisements then placed in newspapers listing the names of those men, from the mayor down to ward officials, adjudged favorable to labor. With trade union membership rising to 12,000 by 1883, and with many local and state elections being determined by less than 3,000 votes, it is not surprising that TLA lobbyists often met with considerable success. "The results of the past elections," the city's printers boasted in December 1883, had plainly shown "that the united workingmen as a body represent an eminent power at the polls."[99]

Despite frequent successes, the TLA nevertheless suffered from a number of limitations which reduced its overall effectiveness within the laboring community. Although it often proclaimed the need to organize all wage earners, it was the city's older trade unions, ones with long-standing artisanal traditions — cigarmakers, printers, shoemakers, custom tailors, blacksmiths, iron molders, and building tradesmen — who continued to dominate the TLA's leadership and membership. Although factories had become the main setting of production, the semi- and unskilled workers in the city's largest establishments were conspicuously absent from the TLA's meetings, parades, and picnics. The organization, as the *Enquirer* noted in December 1880, was confined largely to the city's "better class of workingmen."[100]

TLA leaders and members also continued to ignore the plight of the growing number of female workers, as well as the small but significant number of black day laborers. While cigar, shoemaking, and typographical unions admitted a number of women into their organizations in the late 1870s and early 1880s, the vast majority of trade organizations persistently excluded them. Women, explained one iron molder, were not welcomed by most trade unions because they had driven "thousands of men" from the workshops, who were able to work, "and it is all on account of their services being obtained for a lesser rate of wages." Expressing an opinion shared by many male workers, he went on to say that he believed "in women attending to the household duties, and the men doing the outside work and providing for the family."[101] Thus, while greater numbers of workers found themselves faced with similar conditions of industrial exploitation, wage earners often remained divided along lines of craft, skill, industry, sex, and race.

It was amid this climate of working-class fragmentation that the Knights of Labor (KOL) emerged to offer wage earners an alternative solution to the common problems engendered by industrial distress. Organized in 1869 by a group of Philadelphia garment workers, the KOL occupied a middle ground between radical socialists and reform-oriented trade unionists. Although they accepted industrialization as the ruling force of production, they rejected the prevailing economic and social relations fostered by the acquisitive and competitive nature of industrial capitalism. Freedom and independence, explained Terence V. Powderly, the KOL's national leader, were synonymous with free labor. Yet, under the present system of production, men and women were forced to labor as virtual wage slaves. Unless something was done to halt the "recent alarming development and aggression of aggregated wealth," the KOL warned in 1878, it would "inevitably lead to the pauperization and hopeless degradation of the toiling masses."[102]

The evils of industrial capitalism, the KOL argued, could be overcome by the creation of a new industrial and moral order based upon the "nobility of labor" and the cooperation and harmony of all honorable producers. Rejecting strikes as measures that afforded only "temporary relief," Powderly called upon workers to abolish the wage system and to create in its place a series of "co-operative institutions, productive and distributive," which would "secure to the laborer the fruits of his toil."[103] In order to ensure that these cooperatives would be able to compete with private industry, the KOL urged that they be equipped with the latest labor-saving machinery and employ the most recent innovations in the organization of production. However, unlike other businesses, each worker would also be an owner; each man and woman would be an independent producer, not a "wage slave."

Unlike the city's TLA, Cincinnati's Knights endeavored to forge an organization which would represent all workers, regardless of sex, race, skill, trade, ethnicity, or religion. Only those people viewed as non-producers — lawyers, bankers, speculators, and those who made or sold liquor — were excluded from the organization. Beginning in 1877, when a group of shoemakers founded the city's first local assembly, the Knights set out to organize not only skilled workers, but also the unskilled factory laborers, female workers, black laborers, masters, and small manufacturers often ignored by local trade unionists. Between 1877 and 1884, as the KOL succeeded in forming 22 local assemblies, membership in the organization rose from 76 to 787 men and women. The Knights found their greatest support among the city's shoemakers, who founded nearly half of all the assemblies — including the female-dominated Lady Franklin Assembly. Carriagemakers, telegraph operators, safemakers, tailors, hair spinners and bristle combers, silver gilders, and tin, copper, and sheet metal workers also joined the KOL.[104]

In addition to advocating radical changes in the relations of production, the Knights also endeavored to create a new social and moral culture based upon "civic responsibility, education, a wholesome family life, temperance, and self-improvement."[105] Unlike trade unionists, who generally confined their joint social gatherings to semi-annual balls and picnics, the KOL advocated the creation of leisure institutions which would bring its diverse members together more frequently. In February 1881, shoemaker Joseph Glenn, rejecting the Victorian ideal of separate social spheres for men and women, urged the construction of a social hall that would serve as a "place of resort" and a "powerful lever . . . to thoroughly organize the mechanics of this city."[106] Such a building, he argued, would join the worlds of work and leisure by providing men and women with numerous rooms in which they could hold meetings, an auditorium designed for lectures and theatricals, a library, and a dining hall where they could enjoy inexpensive meals in the company of other producers. Glenn's dream was finally realized in November 1885, when the organization opened its first Knights of Labor Hall.[107] Yet, while the KOL continued to grow in number, it was not until the months following the May Day strikes of 1886 that their visions attracted the attention and support of thousands of Cincinnati wage earners.

While Knights, trade unionists, and socialists each offered answers to the problems plaguing the city's workers, the mass of Cincinnati wage earners did not always fashion their responses within the parameters of organized economic or political movements. Long years of economic distress and discontent occasionally led men and women to vent their anger and frustration in the form of spontaneous demonstrations. Whereas mass protest had taken the form of bank riots in 1842 and nativistic riots in 1855, discontent in 1884 was focused on the corruption of the political sphere and the inability of the government to mete out justice. Such frustrations, of course, were the result of a long-simmering situation. From the 1870s onward, Cincinnati politics gained the unenviable reputation as the most corrupt in the state. Close elections, reflected Ohio Governor Joseph B. Foraker, were frequently determined not by the votes of citizens but by stuffed ballot boxes, false counts, and secret deals between Democratic and Republican leaders.[108] "Party power," exclaimed one angered citizen, "ruled without proper check on the part of public authorities; and thus our society, and its political institutions, were constantly degraded."[109]

On the evening of March 28, 1884, following a rally held at Music Hall to protest against the light sentences given two murderers as a result of a political deal, several thousand workers sought to reassert notions of popular justice by marching upon and then burning down the county jail and courthouse. When local police were unable to quell the riot, Mayor Thomas Stephens quickly called upon the governor to send in the state militia. Within twenty-four hours, over 7,000 militia troops — most of them coming from other areas of the state — were posted around the city. Nevertheless, the depth of anger was so great that, for the next two evenings, thousands of Cincinnatians — shouting out cries that true justice would be served — marched down to the courthouse to battle with militiamen and police. By the time that the riot was finally suppressed on the morning of March 31, there were 35 dead and nearly 200 wounded.[110]

Newspaper editors endeavored to play down the class-oriented nature of the riots. The main perpetrators of the violence, they insisted, were the city's disreputable and shiftless "lumpenproletariat," not its honorable and lawabiding workingmen. Yet, an examination of the list of those killed, wounded, or arrested during the course of the riots reveals quite another picture. Of the 135 persons who can be identified, 95 (70.4 percent) came from the most "respectable" element of the laboring community — the men who worked in the city's small artisan shops and factories. Also included among these 95 men were two manufacturers and three shop foremen. As for the remaining rioters, 28 (20.7 percent) were listed as unskilled factory or day laborers, four as bartenders, two as clerks, and there were one jailer, one waiter, and one medical student. Only three persons (2.2 percent) were described as crooks or loafers.[111]

Although the riots were undoubtedly more an emotional than a considered protest against the seeming corruption of the state, working-class reactions to the summoning of the militia were not. Shortly after being ordered into action, Captain E. Potter Dustin, commanding officer of the German Garfield Rifle unit of the Ohio National Guard (ONG) — with headquarters at Workingman's Hall — notified the city police chief that he and his men unanimously "declined to assist in guarding the County Jail." They refused to take up arms against fellow workingmen.[112] Another local regiment reported that only 93 of its 400 members had obeyed the call to defend the courthouse. Those men who did turn out found themselves being cursed and pelted with assorted missiles by hostile onlookers.[113]

It was during moments like these that deep frustrations and cleavages often rose to the surface. For many workers, the use of the militia and its killing of several demonstrators confirmed earlier suspicions that the supposedly neutral republican forces of the state were being arbitrarily set against innocent workingmen. Similar uses of militia and federal troops during an iron workers' strike in 1874, the national railroad strikes of 1877, and a mine strike in Illinois and Ohio in 1883 had elicited great outrage on the part of Cincinnati workers. CTU No. 3 condemned such actions as "unwarrantable and unjustifiable." It also blasted the government for using troops "for the sole object of intimidating the working classes when compelled to strike to secure their just rights."[114] Consequently, it was not the

(a)

(b)

Figure 16 The Courthouse Riots of 1884.
(a) Hamilton County Courthouse before the riots (c. 1884); (b) and (c) Scenes of destruction;
(d) and (e) The Ohio militia patrols the barricades; (f) Despite the presence of the militia, local
citizens continued to assemble in front of the courthouse for several days.
Courtesy of the Cincinnati Historical Society

(c)

(d)

(e)

(f)

seeming lawlessness of local citizens that bothered the members of the TLA, but the seeming overkill and lawlessness of the state. "Past experience has demonstrated," read an angry declaration released by the typographers in April 1884, "time and again that the militia are organized with the view of intimidating the people, especially workingmen whenever their actions run counter to the interests of capitalists and corporations." Insisting that membership in the militia was "inconsistent with the duties and obligations of trade unionists," the printers requested all workingmen to withdraw from the Ohio National Guard "at the earliest day practicable."[115]

At their most important level, the courthouse riots represented a popular outcry and a search for order. Such a search was not, as one historian argues, confined largely to the middle and upper classes; the ranks of organized and unorganized labor were also involved.[116] The call for law and order, justice, the reformation of the state, and the reinstitution of an authentic republican government would soon emerge as the clarion call and unifying force of the Cincinnati working class.

CHAPTER ELEVEN

Law, Order, and Class Consciousness: The May Day Strikes of 1886

Declaring May 1, 1886, the inauguration of a new era in working-class history, some 340,000 workers throughout the nation walked off their jobs in an effort to force manufacturers to adopt a universal eight-hour work day. In Cincinnati, approximately 32,000 men and women — 35 percent of the city's laboring population — chose to discard longtime barriers of craft, skill, ethnicity, religion, race and sex and assemble in what was the most dramatic working-class protest of the nineteenth century: the May Day strikes.[1] At no time in the history of Cincinnati's working class did the process of politicization assume greater proportions than in the two-year period which followed the strikes.

For Cincinnati workers, the May Day strikes proved a unique and critical event, for they were led not by the traditional agents of working-class radicalism — well-established artisan unions — but by the ranks of the previously unorganized and disorganized factory workforce. Most particularly, the strikes marked the emergence of a new cadre of leaders — factory artisans and factory laborers—who worked among the city's massive and recently incorporated furniture, coffin, carriage, machine, and safe and lock factories.

Of the numerous factors contributing to the outbreak of strike activity, two were especially important: the emergence of a local language of law and order and the renewed national struggle for an eight-hour work day. While the latter provided Cincinnati workers with a common objective, the former served as a critical source of self-justification. Drawing upon republican ideology, traditional working-class notions of justice, the experiences gained at the workplace, and the civic language of law and order, workers created a new public language which merged the roles of *worker* and *citizen* in new and powerful ways. During the course of April and May, the tenets of law and order — usually preached by elites to workers — were appropriated, refashioned, and preached by workers to elites. More importantly, workers used *their* interpretations of law and order to unite all wage earners in a common crusade for justice, equity, and a more republican society.

The courthouse riots of March 1884 left many Cincinnati elites in a deep state of agitation and underscored their fears that the "Paris of America" contained as much of the seething turmoil and potential revolution as its European counterpart. Despite professions of dismay and vows of reform by politicians, the corruption which dominated local and state politics continued relatively unabated in the months following the March disorders.[2] Consequently, various Cincinnatians — fearful of further outbreaks of violence — gradually turned to law and order as a means of explaining and solving the problems which had shaken the very foundations of their society.

Cries for order and for the perservation of and adherence to law were by no means unique to the 1880s. They were sounded during the economic crises of the 1830s and 1840s, the nativistic riots of the 1850s, and the railroad strikes of 1877. Yet it was not until the aftermath of the courthouse riots that these sporadic cries were woven into a coherent and clearly articulated language, one which pervaded all levels of Cincinnati society and emerged as a central part of the city's political culture.

As the Monster Bank and Slave Power had once served as powerful metaphors of greater complexities, so too did the language of law and order serve as a shibboleth that marked deeper tensions. It endeavored to reduce the complexities and problems of industrialization to a comprehensible focal point: a crisis of authority. End political corruption and restore order and respect for law, and society would once again function properly.

The initial and most vocal articulation of this language came from the Committee of One Hundred. Formed in the wake of the courthouse riots, the committee consisted largely of the city's leading manufacturers, merchants, financiers, and landowners. The committee, dissatisfied with the slow progress of politicians, and angered by repeated incidents of election fraud and municipal corruption, in the autumn of 1885 organized as a permanent group dedicated to ending corruption and disorder.[3]

At the heart of the committee's preaching was a belief in the sanctity and redemptive powers of law. The crises of the past two decades, they argued, were not the result of industrialization. They had arisen due to a breakdown in the forces of law, order, and morality. Corruption and disorder did not, however, demand fundamental changes in political institutions. Their remedies lay in the restoration of proper respect for and adherence to law. As one of the committee's board of directors explained:

> I tell you, there is no man above the law. The law must be supreme; the law is sacred; it is our own making; it is not conceived above our heads by an oligarchy or an aristocracy, and put down amongst us by armed hands, to be carried out in our despite, whether we wish it or not; but it is ours.[4]

As numerous individuals and organizations joined in voicing their support of the committee, the language of law and order gradually permeated all levels of municipal life. Republicans translated popular discontent into a new political language and campaigned on a platform pledged to obliterate corruption and restore law and order.[5] The Law and Order League, a nativistic organization established late in 1885 and heavily supported by Protestant ministers and wealthy factory owners, merchants, and financiers, pledged itself to the cause of "good morals," proper modes of conduct, and the battle against sin, as well as to the "efficient enforcement of our laws relating to public order."[6] The German *Bund für Freiheit und Recht* (League for Freedom and Law), although organized in part as a response to the nativism and strict sabbatarianism advocated by the Law and Order League, nevertheless devoted its energies to rescuing society from the corruption bred by "parties, sects, corporations, etc., that constitute themselves into (illegitimate) authorities."[7] From the pulpits of the city's churches came sermons denouncing the corruption of politics by "gamblers, saloon keepers and other lawless men."[8]

The search for order, however, was not exclusively confined to the city's upper and middle classes. It was also a main concern of Cincinnati's laboring community. Several German trade unions, seeking to disassociate themselves from the ethnic stereotyping which frequently portrayed all Germans as incipient anarchists and communists, sought membership in local law and order societies.[9] The city's Trades and Labor Assembly (TLA), reluctant to allow capitalists to claim the language of law and order as their own, vowed to join the battle "against the corrupting power of outside politicians."[10] An audience of 2,000 Knights of Labor voiced their hearty approval of Master Orator Richard Trevellick's call for obedience to law and his warning that, in a democratic republic, there is "nothing so unsafe as to disobey the law."[11]

While Knights and trade unionists declared themselves advocates of law and order, their understanding of those terms often differed from that of civic elites. For workers, law was not simply an ideal of purity and means of protecting private property and public virtue. Rather, it was a potential agent for securing greater control over the adverse effects of industrialization — adversities often wrought by the actions of corrupt manufacturers and politicians. Industrialization, proclaimed the TLA's "Declaration of Principles for Agitation," demanded a "radical change in the relations between capital and labor," else the "technical progress in our industrial system should lead to the destruction of mankind." Such alterations could not "be brought about by economic changes alone." New laws were needed if workers were to "replace the present inequitable social system with one based upon equality, morality, and the nobility of all useful labor."[12] Organized labor ought to lobby for measures that would remedy the evils of the economic sphere.[13]

It was amid this general concern for law and order that the eight-hour movement assumed new dimensions. The national campaign for an eight-hour work day, begun in earnest after the Civil War, was resumed in October 1884, when the newly organized Federation of Trades and Labor Unions (FTLU) — the predecessor of the American Federation of Labor — called upon the nation's workers to lobby for the institution of a universal eight-hour work day to begin on May 1, 1886. During the next year and a half, wage earners in Cincinnati and throughout the nation were deluged with scores of FTLU circulars and speakers exhorting them to press forward on behalf of the eight-hour cause.[14]

Locally, the recent emphasis on law and order as a means of securing peaceful social and economic change gave new life and vigor to the eight-hour movement. An eight-hour day was seen as an important way in which law could be used to remedy a situation whereby workers had become the victims rather than the beneficiaries of industrialization. "The multiplication and use of labor-saving machines," argued the city's iron molders, "makes it our first duty to shorten the hours of labor, if we would share in the benefits of their introduction."[15] A reduction of two hours from the present ten-hour day, suggested cigarmaker Louis Benjamin, would act as a cure for overproduction and ease the perilous prospects of unemployment, impoverishment, and descent into the ever-growing army of tramps.[16]

In the months following the courthouse riots, state legislators were barraged by trade-union delegates who lobbied on behalf of an eight-hour bill. In April 1886, after several frustrating defeats, Ohio workers secured the object of their desire: the passage of an eight-hour law. The Haley bill, as it was popularly known, declared that as of May 1, 1886, "in any mechanical, manufacturing or mining business, a day's work, when the contract is silent upon the subject, or where there is no express contract, shall consist of eight hours."[17]

While the Haley bill marked an important victory for labor, it nevertheless contained several loopholes which appeared to render it virtually ineffective: it had no enforcement clause; it was restricted to three areas of labor; and it did not prohibit the introduction of special contracts, which could easily be drawn so as to circumvent the law.[18] The law also left several vital questions unanswered. Did an eight-hour day mean that men would work eight hours and receive the same pay as they had for a ten-hour day? Or would they work eight hours with a proportional decrease in wages?

Little guidance was forthcoming from the ranks of organized labor. Despite all the months of lobbying efforts, TLA leader Henry Askew lamented that there had been "no effort made by officers of this association looking to the universal adoption of their plan."[19] Although vigorously supporting the eight-hour law, boot and shoemakers, printers, and iron molders — three of the most militant unions — announced that they would not participate in any strike on its behalf. Without an enforcement clause, they argued, there was little likelihood that workers could win in a confrontation with employers. Moreover, declared iron molder's president P. F. Fitzpatrick, the "working people were not fully educated up to the movement, and it would be impossible to make it a success."[20]

The Knights of Labor also proved intractable in their opposition to a May Day strike. Like Fitzgerald, Grand Master Workman Terence V. Powderly held that workers were "not as yet educated in the movement, and a strike under such conditions must prove abortive."[21] When he discovered that many local assemblies had passed resolutions supporting a May Day strike, Powderly issued a secret circular prohibiting any local from participating in such an action.[22] Although local Knights organized a massive picnic on Saturday, May 1, in support of the hours' cause, they shared Powderly's contempt for the efficacy of strikes. Indeed, when the city's stonemasons ignored Powderly's injunction and went out on strike in early May, they were reprimanded by the district assembly and ordered to surrender the wage and hours benefits they had won during their struggle.[23]

Only the city's socialists and German trade unionists gave their active support to the eight-hour cause. These men and women began meeting in late April to organize a massive community-supported demonstration, planned for May 2, on behalf of the eight-hour work day. Yet, like their native counterparts, the Germans offered no plan of action to unite and coordinate possible strike actions.[24]

Despite the reluctance and ambivalence of more experienced labor leaders, the May 1 movement captured the imagination and support of thousands of Cincinnati workers. Much of the energy generated in the closing weeks of April came from new and unexpected sources: the ranks of previously unorganized artisans and unskilled laborers and the divided and unorganized men who worked in the city's large factories. While more experienced trade unionists remained aloof, these men and women rushed in unprecedented numbers to initiate new organizations. In the eleven days before May 1, the previously unorganized street pavers and rammers, laundresses, cartmen, leather workers, tanners and curriers, collarmakers, tailors, rangemakers, woodworking machinists, and machine molders all voted to unionize. Hundreds of other workers, while not establishing formal unions, organized craft, shop, and/or industrywide strike committees.

Never in the city's history had there been such a widespread movement toward labor organization and unionization. From mid-April onward, Workingman's Hall overflowed nightly with meetings of men and women discussing and planning the strategies and demands they would employ on May 1. "The workingman's unions," observed one somewhat astonished reporter, "are holding sessions and discussing the immediate future as they never did before."[25] The seemingly endless numbers of meetings, the formalization of demands, and the planning of strike activities provided a forum in which many men and women were able, for the first time in their lives, to assume a direct role in the mass organization and voicing of individual grievances. Although manufacturers and newspaper editors endeavored to attribute this spreading discontent to the agitation of a few radical malcontents, reporters and union leaders suggested otherwise. When told by a newspaperman that these meetings had been craftily orchestrated by the city's more established trade unions, one veteran labor leader responded: "The unions are not to be blamed. . . . Not a single union in this city has ordered one of these strikes. The shop organizations have undertaken them on their own responsibility."[26] "It was impossible," concurred a *Times-Star* reporter, "to find a trace to the effect that there were some half-dozen men who were furnishing the brains or backbone of the strike, and that the rest were following like a pack of sheep, or that there was any coercion."[27]

On Monday morning, May 3, following a weekend of labor rallies and speeches, some 12,000 workingmen and workingwomen, their varied demands not having been met, initiated the most massive and crippling series of strikes in the city's history. The clouds of smoke and sounds of machinery that usually emanated from the city's factories soon ceased as 15,000 workers left their jobs by the end of the first week; and

Figure 17 Cincinnati in 1886.
Courtesy of the Cincinnati Historical Society

by the end of the month, approximately 32,000 had participated in the strike. Cincinnati workers had virtually shut down the city. No freight-moved in or out of the city as the freight handlers walked off their jobs; the city's garbage lay uncollected as cartmen refused to work; restaurant-goers were inconvenienced as their waitresses deserted the dining hall in favor of the meeting hall; suburban residents had to find other means of transportation as streetcar workers abandoned their vehicles; laundry had to be done at home since laundresses refused to work at their previous wage and hour rates; virtually all the city's furniture and machine factories, carriage and wagon works, coffin factories, architectural iron works, starch factories, safe and lock works, clothing factories and sweatshops, and planing mills were shut down. Production and services in the nation's seventh largest manufacturing center had sputtered to a halt.[28]

This massive outpouring of strike fervor raises several important questions. How and why did so many previously unorganized workers join the strikes? How did they justify their actions? Who led the strikes? Three factors stand out as particularly important: the passage of the Haley bill, the ability of workers to defend their strikes by drawing upon the recent language of law and order, and the determination of many factory

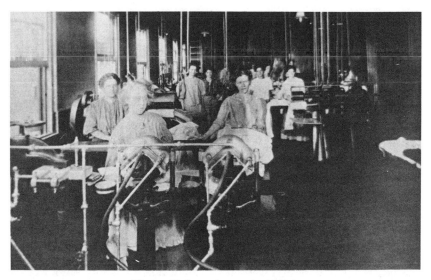

Figure 18 Laundresses (c. 1880s).
A number of workingwomen — including the city's laundresses, seamstresses, waitresses, and various factory workers — went out on strike on May 1, 1886.
Courtesy of the Cincinnati Historical Society

employees to remedy some of the ills of industrial capitalism. The popularity of the eight-hour cause, like that of the language of law and order, was due in large part to its ability to mean and offer different things to different people. Some workers saw it as a way to remedy the problem of overproduction. Others argued that it would help to alleviate unemployment.[29] Yet, virtually all agreed that its greatest appeal rested in the popular belief that an eight-hour day meant eight hours work at ten hours pay. After a decade of economic recession, there were few workers who could resist, as furniture worker Oscar Ameringer stated with appealing simplicity, the "cause of less work and more pay."[30]

With the passage of the Haley bill, individual desire was transformed into law. A wage earner now demanding an eight-hour day spoke as a citizen of the state seeking his lawful rights, not simply as a selfish worker. Manufacturers who refused to accede to the demand for eight hours (usually coupled with the additional "at ten hours pay") were violating their obligations as citizens. Law and order now *demanded* that they grant workers a shorter work day. When asked — during the first week in May — why he and his fellow workers were out on strike, one carriage worker responded: "We're out because we want eight hours of work and 20% increase of pay, what the law allows us." "But the law don't allow you anything," put in the *Times-Star* reporter. "Look here, none of that," was the reply a little savagely:

> The law says eight hours is a day's work, and we will see that it is a day's work and that we are paid for it. If the law said twelve hours was a day's work, the bosses would make us work that long, and you may be very sure they would pay us what we are getting now, a day's pay for a legal day's work.[31]

This sense that workers were the true agents of justice was further reinforced by the efforts of leading manufacturers, many of them members of the Committee of One Hundred or the Law and Order League, to circumvent the provisions and spirit of the Haley law. By the end of April, the common strategy adopted at the large factories was to switch over from a daily to an hourly wage scale and thus escape the strictures of the law.[32] There appeared to be little doubt among factory employees as to why these changes had been initiated. Workers at the Procter and Gamble factory — owned in part by William Gamble, a vice-president of the Law and Order League — insisted that the company had changed the pay agreement to "get around the eight-hour law and have their employees work for them sixty hours a week, as they are doing now."[33] This blatant attempt to circumvent the law only served to strengthen the factory workers' determination to press for their "legal rights."

An analysis of the residential and work patterns of 104 strike leaders indicates that the leadership of the May Day strikes came from what might be called the stable, grass-roots element of the working class.[34] The "new activists" — leaders of unions and strike committees formed during or just before the strikes — chosen to represent the city's unskilled laborers and factory workers were not the "outside agitators" that several manufacturers and newspaper editors claimed they were. Rather, they were men and women who had undergone more than a decade of training in their shops, trades, and factories.

In view of recent studies emphasizing the high geographical and occupational mobility of nineteenth-century American workers, Cincinnati strike leaders appear to be a distinctive and remarkable group.[35] Of the 91 men and women leading the new activists, 60.4 percent had worked in the city a minimum of ten years, 32.3 percent for fifteen years, and 20.8 percent for twenty years or more. These then, were the older, more respected workers of Cincinnati; men and women chosen for their experience and knowledge. More significantly, they were also workers who had entered the city's factories during the initial period of transformation from the world of manufacturing to the world of modern industry.[36]

Table 11.1 Profile of May Day Strike Leaders

	Number of People	Average Number of Years Listed in Directory	Average Number of Years Listed at Same Trade
New Activists:			
Factory Artisans & Factory Laborers:			
Officers:	19	10.6	8.5
Committee:	48	13.5	12.4
Total:	67	13.0	11.3
Unskilled Laborers:			
Officers:	18	13.5	11.2
Committee:	6	11.7	9.3
Total:	24	12.8	10.8
Established Union Leaders:			
Officers:	13	13.1	12.5

SOURCE: See chapter 11 note 34.

The May strikes were more varied in composition and extent than any other previous strike in local history. Indeed, their desire to secure their "legal rights" to fewer hours and better wages sparked an extraordinary number of new alliances among unskilled workers. The city's cartmen, led by Irishman John Nolan, German Leopold Leist, and black carter Lincoln Dahoney, joined together to found the Cincinnati Cartmen's Union. Similarly, day laborers, led by Thomas Campbell, Michael Condon, Alex Weizenecker, and John Metzner, also effected a new organization to represent the interests of unskilled workers, ethnicity notwithstanding. Unskilled female workers also joined the rush toward unionization and strike activity. Mary Henderson and Lena Graham, who had toiled in Cincinnati the past twelve and six years respectively, led the city's laundresses in their quest for a decent wage. They were joined, in turn, by a number of waitresses and seamstresses who issued similar demands for an eight-hour work day.[37]

While the immediate goals of many of these workers focused upon better wages and hours, for others, the strikes also served as a protest against the adverse effects of industrialization. The greatest number of new activists came from the ranks of those workers who had been most thoroughly schooled in the discipline of the new industrial order: factory artisans and factory laborers. Undaunted by the gloomy forecasts of most trade unionists, these men, led largely by factory artisans, met in unprecedented numbers during late April and early May to initiate new bonds of unity. Instead of organizing a series of different unions based upon varying levels of skill, these men formed vertical alliances which united all factory workers into a single factorywide or industrywide union.

As the large factory slowly rose to dominate the world of production, so, too, did it emerge in May 1886 as the critical focus of protest. The most militant and disciplined of the May strikes were mounted in those industries where methods of production, organization of labor, and forms of ownership and management had undergone the most rapid changes in the past decade: the furniture, carriage, coffin, safe and lock, and machine-making industries.

It was the city's most highly mechanized and usually incorporated factories that were the first targets of the spring strikes. The course of the furniture workers' strike in many ways typified those of the aforementioned industries. On April 26 and April 29, the Brunswicke and Balke Company and the Robert Mitchell Company — the two largest and most important factories in the industry (incorporated in 1879 and 1867 respectively) and the companies to whom other manufacturers looked to set the terms of a final settlement — were shut down. Although most of the city's furniture unions had dissolved during the recent depression, the workers in these two factories, in an unprecedented display of unity, quickly created factorywide organizations which voted to go out on strike for an eight-hour day and a 20 percent wage increase for *all* factory employees, regardless of skill.[38] For the next several days the entire furniture industry was abuzz as workers in virtually every factory initiated factorywide strike committees; these committees soon began meeting with each other until finally a central industrywide strike coordinating committee was formed and a uniform demand for the eight-hour day and a 20 percent wage increase was adopted. Workers pledged allegiance to one another and vowed not to return to work until all their demands had been met. The strength of these new organizations was soon evident: by the morning of May 4, the four to five thousand striking factory workers had shut down the industry.[39]

During the first week of its existence, the central strike committee attempted to oversee the actions of individual factory committees to ensure the maintenance of a uniform settlement. Workers were permitted to return to their factories only if the owners acceded to the published demands; consequently, as several owners began to reach agreements with workers during the first week of the strike, pressure was placed upon idle employers to settle or see their business taken over by local competitors.[40]

These new forms of unity, organization, and discipline were also adopted by the city's carriage workers. During the closing days of April, factory committees composed of union and nonunion blacksmiths, gear workers, body makers, trimmers, and packers were organized and a central industrywide strike committee formed. It agreed upon a uniform demand for an eight-hour day and a 20 percent increase for day workers and pieceworkers. By the afternoon of May 3, this infant alliance had succeeded in closing the city's lagest factories and all but two of its smaller shops.[41]

The carriage workers' strike, like that of the furniture workers, was led by men who had entered the factories just as the greatest transformations in production and ownership were taking place. The work patterns of thirteen key strike leaders show that they had labored in the city an average of 9.4 years and at their crafts for 8.8 years; 54 percent had worked in the city ten years or more. In all likelihood, these were men in a position to observe the relative decline of the artisan and the emergence of the new factory artisan.[42]

Cincinnati's coffin industry — the largest in the nation — was dominated by three factories: the Crane and Breed Company (400 workers), the largest in the world, the Cincinnati Coffin Company (330 workers), and the James Ritchey Company. All three were incorporated and heavily capitalized.[43] Although there were six other coffin factories in Cincinnati, the drive toward organizing and coordinating industrywide demands came from the workers at the three largest companies. After first organizing at the factory level, the coffin workers sent their representatives — men who averaged 11.5 working years and 8.0 craft years of experience — to a preliminary industrywide meeting on May 3, where an eight-hour day and 20 percent wage increase was adopted. On the following day, citing the actions of the furniture and carriage men as their inspiration, the coffin workers voted to form a permanent organization. "The coffinmakers," proclaimed a jubilant William Bennett, president of the new industrial association, "now not only act as employees of one factory, but all together."[44]

The situation of the safe and locksmiths, the employees of the second most highly worker-concentrated industry in the city, closely paralleled that of the coffin workers. Lacking any craft unions at the outset of the strike, workers at the world's two largest safe factories went out on strike on May 4 — but without having first coordinated their efforts with workers in other factories. Consequently, employers were presented with a series of varying demands. However, on the following day, the safemakers held a general meeting in which a central industrywide strike committee was elected and the eight-hour/20 percent demand was made on behalf of all factory employees. With wage earners at Hall's Safe and Lock factory leading the battle, the industry was completely shut down by the end of the week.[45]

These various groups of factory artisans and factory laborers also shared a common language which bridged two worlds: an older "artisanal" language and an emerging "industrial" language. Traditional artisan concepts of justice, honor, and fair wages were frequently relied upon as sources of self-affirmation.

Furniture workers, sounding a theme which had been used by countless artisans during the 1830s and 1840s, spoke of the need to strike in order to obtain a wage that would be "adequate to the decent support of many families."[46] It was this sense of reasonableness, of acting on behalf of one's family, and of pursuing their legal rights which bolstered the confidence of many wary strikers. "We have justice on our side," exclaimed one furniture man, "and our men are strong and firm as the rock of Gibraltar."[47] Asked when they would return to work, a half dozen employees of the Robert Mitchell Company replied: "Never! Not until he grants our demands. They are just and when Mr. Mitchell wants us to go to work, he will have to send for us."[48]

Once begun, the strike also became a matter of honor. When the Crane and Breed Company presented its workers with a wage proposal which they considered insulting, several employees angrily announced that "rather than sign away their manhood they would walk out of the shop."[49] Furniture men also spoke of the efforts of employers to rob them of their manhood by keeping them "at starvation wages."[50]

But industrialization had transformed the artisan language into one with new meaning and appeal. Concepts which had once been founded upon abstractions were now infused with an understanding of the vicissitudes of the local and national market economy. In justifying their wage and hour demands, factory workers pointed not only to the Haley law but also to the higher wages received by similar tradesmen in other cities. Drawing upon his work experiences in several eastern manufacturing centers, B. C. Keon, a furniture worker, insisted that the Cincinnati eight-hour/20 percent demand was not only just but also affordable: one needed simply to examine the recent shrinkage of wages, coupled with the expansion of furniture factories in the city, to see that proprietors were making substantial profits.[51] At the Procter and Gamble factory, one worker, when asked why he was striking, said that during the previous year the "firm's business was double that what it ever was, but we did not profit by it a cent. The firm got all the benefit." Procter and Gamble workers, he added, were now determined to redress that imbalance.[52] How this worker was able to assess the company's profits he did not say; but his conviction that factory owners were not sharing fairly in the benefits of industrialization strengthened his resolve and commitment to the strike.

Striking factory artisans and factory laborers also attempted to enlist the support of nonstrikers in their industries, as well as the general community, by staging a number of massive rallies and public demonstrations. Throughout the first weeks of May, the downtown area of Cincinnati was packed with thousands of men and women who suddenly found themselves parading through the streets which they had hitherto only walked on on their way to work. Waving banners and American flags and marching to the beat of fife and drum corps — all symbols of the fight for justice begun in 1776 — striking workers marched from shop to shop and from factory to factory in an effort to persuade their more reluctant co-workers to throw down their tools and join the strike procession.[53]

These efforts to use public demonstrations to induce the

uncommitted to join the action proved extraordinary successful. "A majority of our men were not in favor of a strike," remarked the secretary of the J. A. Fay Company, the city's largest machine-making factory. Yet, when striking machinists paraded through the factory district "and drums were beating, and crowds lined up the sidewalks," the employees were swept up "by the fever of excitement" and joined the men on strike.[54] Similarly, John Williams, a longtime employee of the Rothschild Furniture Company, stressed that initially he "was not in favor of the eight-hour basis"; however, when striking workers marched past his factory and shouted for his help, he decided to "go with the men," and even accepted a position as a strike marshall.[55]

The discipline, order, and sobriety stressed by factory owners were now used by factory employees to help enlist widespread community support for their cause. Strike leaders repeatedly emphasized the necessity for all members to maintain sobriety and order in all public actions; workers were cautioned to avoid barrooms, and strike marshalls were instructed to remove any intoxicated marchers.[56] The furniture workers, explained one strike leader, wanted "to show the public what furniture workers were, and demonstrate that a sober body of men could march through the streets without creating any disturbance or inciting any riot."[57] The hearty cheering of thousands of onlookers led various demonstrators to boast that their strikes were "backed by public sentiment."[58]

Factory workers were the most numerous and active of all strikers, but the city's unorganized and unskilled laborers were also swept along by the strike fever. The pick and shovel men, trench diggers, and granite workers — men usually considered the most unorganizable of all workers — displayed extraordinary unity and interest in the strikes. Although various groups of day laborers struck individually at first, between 2,500 and 4,000 striking unskilled men assembled at Workingman's Hall on May 5 to avow their determination to win an eight-hour day for all unskilled workers. The sense of mutual support ran so high that by the beginning of the second week of May, Irish, German, and black laborers overcame longstanding racial and ethnic antagonisms to form a Central Labor Union — the first such trades' council for unskilled workers in the city's history.[59]

Despite their fervor, the May Day strikes did not begin as a general strike aimed at securing equal benefits for all workers. Rather, the strikes were launched on an industry by industry, trade by trade, and sometimes, workplace by workplace basis, with each group often issuing different wage and hour demands. The new workers' alliances founded in April and early May might appear to have been powerful and radical, but they were associations which still tended to talk and act as particularistic interest groups rather than as a unified class. The supreme irony of the May Day strikes was that the impetus toward the creation of a common class identity — something workers had not achieved on their own — emerged in response to the actions of the city's municipal authorities, press, and manufacturers.

With the exception of two minor scuffles at the city's railroad yards and granite works, the May strikes were remarkably free from violence. Nevertheless, the two incidents, coming in the wake of the deaths in the Haymarket riot in Chicago, led Mayor Amor Smith — one of the city's leading candle and soap manufacturers — to call upon all citizens, employers and employees alike, to organize Committees of Safety "for keeping the peace and protecting property."[60] Striking workers responded to Smith's pleas by meeting in their local wards to form and join committees. Wage earners affirmed their obligations as citizens and promised to "cooperate with any city authorities in [the] suppression [of violence] at any or all times." However, not forgetting their other immediate concerns, they also adopted resolutions calling for an eight-hour day, liberal wages, and the submission of all classes to the laws of the state.[61]

Despite this working-class response, Smith — pressured by a number of local manufacturers and merchants who feared a possible repetition of the violence which had swept the city during the courthouse riots — called out the local militia on May 5. With Haymarket in mind, Smith also ordered the swearing-in of 1,000 special police in addition to the several hundred members of the Merchant's Police who had already volunteered their services. Two days later, although no new outbursts of violence had occurred, the Mayor wired a request to Governor Joseph B. Foraker for three additional militia regiments. By Sunday, May 9, several hundred troops had been stationed in the downtown industrial areas, while 1,400 men, eight gatling guns, and a battery of heavy artillery were kept at ready alert on the outskirts of the city.[62]

The presence of the military forces cheered Cincinnati's industrialists. Immediately following the troops' arrival, Captain W. G. Smith reported that the militia commanders were visited "by a number of Cincinnati's prominent businessmen, and they were unanimous in commending the State authorities for having at hand so large a force of troops."[63] The Chamber of Commerce, impressed by Smith's firm course of action, resolved to raise $25,000 to be placed at the Mayor's disposal for the recruitment and payment of special police.[64] The chamber's superintendent, Sidney Maxwell, although anticipating little violence, assured his mother that things were "so arranged to put down trouble if it should occur."[65]

By calling for the creation of committees of safety, bringing in the militia, and repeatedly playing upon fears of anarchy and violence, municipal authorities, with the help of newspaper editors, attempted to depoliticize the strikes. The main crisis, they argued, was not one of labor versus capital, but of law versus disorder, of the good citizen versus the anarchist. By interpreting the present situation in such a manner, the city's elites attempted to place wage earners in a difficult ideological predicament. While strike activities had served to bring men and women together as *workers* sharing, not only a common identity, but also common needs and enemies, possible threats of violence demanded that they place their role as workers in subordination to their obligations as *citizens* to defend the sanctity of law, order, and property. In other words, should *workers* engaged in a strike against employers be also and primarily *citizens*, who had a duty to abandon particularistic economic goals and protect the community from disorder, even if it means pitting worker against worker? In a time of crisis could the two roles be held simultaneously? Although this would not perhaps have been a serious dilemma for European workers, it was a major problem for an American working class steeped in the republican tradition.

Smith's actions in calling in the militia helped workers resolve any potential dilemmas. Far from intimidating or forcing workers to abandon their strikes, the Mayor's decision to bring in the militia was the catalyst which not only altered the immediate course of the strike; it also fostered the development and politicization of working-class consciousness during the next two years. The summoning of the militia produced strong reactions of outrage. Strikers and nonstriking workers alike demanded to know why Smith had brought in the troops when unions, strike committees, and committees of safety had repeatedly guaranteed that no violence would occur. Was it mere coincidence that the troops arrived on the weekend before many manufacturers had planned to reopen their factories in an effort to break the strikes? Was this not yet another attempt by corrupt capitalists and politicians to use the military power of the state to crush the workers' quest for justice?

The same workers who had, in the aftermath of Haymarket, issued sharp reprobations of anarchists, now passed similar resolutions denouncing the actions of municipal and state authorities. The most vehement and pointed of these attacks came from the embattled factory workers. Furniture men blasted the Mayor for "calling upon the military throughout the State, when no act of violence has been committed"; such a move was clearly intended as "an intimidation to those who know their demands to be just."[66] The carriagemakers agreed that the troops had been brought in "for the purpose of intimidating the workingmen on strike into breaking the eight-hour law passed by the General Assembly of Ohio" and proclaimed the workers, and not the municipal authorities, were the true representatives of law and order. They demanded that the Mayor and Governor either withdraw the troops "or move with them against manufacturers and contractors of Cincinnati who are breaking the eight-hour law."[67] The Trades and Labor Assembly also condemned the Mayor and Governor and maintained that their actions were "uncalled for by any evidence of danger to peaceable and law-abiding citizens."[68]

In a special meeting on May 6 between the Mayor and a delegation of labor leaders, Smith was asked if he planned to use the militia and police against the strikers. When he responded rather evasively that it was his responsibility to protect the rights of all men who wished to work, one strike leader interjected that he and his friends were willing to give a legal day's work of eight hours, but their bosses had disregarded the law and refused to allow them to do so. As eight hours was now a legal working day in Ohio, the worker demanded that Smith use the full power of his office to protect employees against manufacturers who sought to avoid their legal obligations.[69]

The holy obligations of law and order long preached by elites to workers were now being preached by workers to elites. As organization after organization continued to issue public denunciations of city and state officials, Mayor Smith endeavored to appease their anger by requesting a general meeting between himself and two representatives from each union and strike committee on May 13. The fears and uneasiness that lay behind this meeting, the concern over the growing unity of the working classes as the self-perceived vanguard of law and order, were reflected in the *Commercial Gazette*'s editorial printed on the eve of this meeting. The *Commercial Gazette*, the leading supporter of the Committee of One Hundred and the Law and Order League, now chose to ignore the sanctities it had once professed and argued that there was

No holy obligation upon anyone to accept the [Haley] law — none upon earth. The law is not a holy ordinance or a sacred thing, but a regulation that has no authority to back it, and that is introduced as an element of confusion and contention. There is nothing in the business of the country that requests it or will consent to it. It will not become the law of the land and rule of society, no matter what amount of striking is done. That it should be stuck up there like a tyrant's hat on a pole for people to confess slavery by making obeisance, is an impertinence and an absurdity.[70]

This remarkable interpretation found little support among the one hundred delegates who met with the Mayor. Whereas in their earlier meeting with Smith, workers had founded many of their arguments on the inherent rights of unions to regulate their own affairs, the events of the intervening week had produced a dramatic change in language and emphasis. By May 13, delegates insisted that they now acted, not as a diverse melange of workers, but as a law-abiding class pursuing the cause of justice. Unions which had been hesitant to participate in any May activities — molders, typographers and boot- and shoemakers, among others — now united as one force with strikers in confronting the Mayor.[71]

Strike leaders began the meeting by calling upon the Mayor and manufacturers to join them in fulfilling their duties as citizens by honoring the Haley law. A representative from the Crane and Breed factory reminded the Mayor that this law made eight hours a *legal* day's work; working people demanded that it be respected; and workers had, in an orderly and sober fashion, made a "grand demonstration for their rights according to law." He inquired whether the Mayor and Governor had "sent this crowd down upon us to intimidate us for the benefit of capital?" The chairman of the delegation, William H. Ogden, president of Typographical Union No. 3, explained that he considered himself a rather conservative man; he himself had preferred not to strike on May 1; however, those who did so could not be condemned for they were "simply obeying the law, and stood on legal ground."[72]

Each time that the Mayor attempted to move the debate away from the Haley law — away from the language of law and order — the worker delegation drew the discussion back in that direction. The president of the iron molders' union angrily accused local capitalists of having influenced the "Governor and Mayor to send the troops here to intimidate workingmen." By not insisting on the enforcement of an eight-hour day, the "authorities protected the men violating the laws of the State." "We claim," he added, "that troops should not have been brought here until the workingmen had called for them to make the capitalists obey the law."[73]

As the meeting drew to a close, the Mayor was asked if he would now disband the special police and militia. He refused to make any such commitment. The delegates responded by declaring that they would no longer tolerate outside intimidation; unions were stronger than ever, and union treasuries would guarantee that no man would be forced back to work by financial distress. Smith ended the meeting by expressing his pleasure at talking to so many representatives of "the working class," and suggested that he too "might one day be one them himself, for such change in fortune often occurred."[74]

Despite the Mayor's effort to appear unaffected, the meeting was an important victory for the strikers. By the following afternoon, Smith had ordered the disbanding of the special police and the return of the 3rd Regiment to Columbus; troops stationed in downtown factory districts were moved to the outskirts of the city.[75] More importantly, the meeting provided workers with a public forum which enabled them to formulate a common position around which wage earners could unite. Subsequent efforts by manufacturers to undermine the workers' avowed position as "true citizens" proved futile.[76]

The sense of working-class unity and legitimacy created at the meeting on May 13 was reflected in the shops and factories throughout the city. Men and women who had been reticent to act during the early days of May now went out on strike in pursuit of their "legal rights." Similarly, workers who had reached earlier compromise settlements went out on strike and once again demanded that employers adopt an eight-hour work day.[77]

The victories achieved in the public sphere against the Mayor were soon duplicated in the economic sphere against manufacturers. The continued militancy of many strikers, coupled with the settlement of labor disputes by competitors in other cities, imposed great pressure on local manufacturers to reach rapid settlements with their work force. By the third week of May, as workers' succeeded in winning many of their demands, the estimated number of strikers had dropped from between 20,000 and 30,000 to approximately 5,000.[78]

By and large, the city's factory artisans and factory laborers won the greatest gains. Carriage workers, wishing to settle their struggle before strike funds ran out, offered manufacturers a compromise proposal: they still insisted on an eight-hour day, but they were willing to take a 10 percent rather than a 20 percent raise. Manufacturers quickly accepted the offer. Machinists and safemakers also secured concessions from employers.

Nearly 90 percent of the workers at the city's eighteen leading machine-making factories and 100 percent of all safemakers had secured shorter hours, higher wages, or both from manufacturers.[79]

The battle between furniture workers and employers was the most bitter and protracted of the May strikes. The Furniture Exchange, and particularly its cadre of large factory owners, had employed private police, militia, and friendly newspaper editors in an attempt to intimidate workers and force them back into the factories. Although strike action against the most powerful company — the Robert Mitchell Company — was not resolved until the middle of June, of the 28 firms settling by June 7, 26 (92.9 percent) agreed to adopt an eight-hour day: 22 (78.6 percent) granted a 10 percent wage increase; and 2 (7.1 percent), a 20 percent increase. The two remaining firms compromised on a nine-hour day with some wage increase.[80]

The only factory group which did not secure any concession was the coffin makers. The industrywide strike committee was unable to resist efforts by owners to entice individual workers back into the factories. By May 15, virtually all coffin workers had returned to work at the same hours and wages as before the strikes.[81]

While there is insufficient information to draw precise correlations between factory ownership and longevity of strikes, there is enough data to indicate that the most extended struggles occurred not in the smaller, privately owned shops and factories, but in the large incorporated firms. Of the owner-identifiable furniture factories which held out into late June, 62.5 percent were corporately owned. The chief protagonist, not surprisingly, was the Robert Mitchell Company. Mitchell eventually settled the strike by agreeing to a fifty-five hour week at sixty hours' pay. Although this was less than they had originally hoped for, workers nevertheless regarded it as a victory against a company which had vowed never to compromise with its employees.[82]

The same pattern of resistance by incorporated firms also held true in the machine-making industry. While, overall, 77.8 percent of the key factories acceded to demands for an eight- or nine-hour day, only 57.1 percent of the incorporated firms did so. Indeed, the only factories to refuse any wage or hour concessions were incorporated firms.[83] One might also speculate that the coffin workers failed largely because their craft was one of the most heavily incorporated of any major Cincinnati industry: 66.7 percent of all coffin factories in 1886 were so owned.[84]

As to the general gains secured during April, May, and early

June, an analysis of 17,337 workers affected by the strikes indicates that 11.8 percent won a reduction in hours without any reduction in pay, while 59.6 percent received some partial wage/hour settlement. Thus, a total of 71.4 percent of these men and women secured some material benefits as a result of their strikes.[85] The spirit of common success and unity engendered by the strike attained its final dramatic moment at the TLA picnic on June 20. Ten thousand workers and their families — natives and immigrants, blacks and whiles — joined in celebrating the victories of May.[86]

There are many levels on which we can explore the significance and meaning of the May Day strikes. As a fight for material advancement and a power struggle between labor and capital, the spring protests were the most widespread and successful of the decade.[87] Yet at a more important level, the May strikes provided workers with a common experience which helped inaugurate new bonds of unity both within and among trades and industries. Before the May strikes, there were few forces which acted to bind the majority of Cincinnati workers in the self-conscious pursuit of common class goals. Different rates of mechanization, organization of labor, diminutions of skills, and possibilities for advancement had often served to particularize and fragment working-class interests and weaken any sense of common identity. Ethnicity, religion, race, and gender presented additional barriers to class unity.

Under the impact of May, a new sense of class was forged within the working community. From the ranks of the unorganized there evolved new energies, new leaders, and new unions. As the strikes progressed, fragmented interest-group consciousness gradually centralized into industrywide consciousness. Nevertheless, despite this internal evolution, it was the force of external events which precipitated the transformation from a series of working classes to a single working class.

Throughout the nineteenth century, Cincinnati wage earners had generally accepted the propriety of separate spheres of action. A person participated in the economic sphere of production as a *worker*, but he or she participated in the supposedly classless political sphere of government as a *citizen*. Even as workers increasingly lost control over the former sphere, they retained their claims to independence and equal rights in the latter. The Mayor's decision to call in the militia, as far as many workers were concerned, violated this principle of the separation of spheres of activity. Smith's actions, as workers so dramatically declared at the meeting on May 13, had violated the supposedly classless and neutral authority of the state by placing market needs on a higher plane than law. Whereas during late April and early May, workers—with the exception of the city's socialists — generally spoke of grievances against particular employers rather than employers as a class, in the aftermath of the militia, they began to speak in terms of classes and class coercion. As in 1877, 1883, and 1884, workers charged that capitalists and municipal authorities had conspired to set the forces of government against law-abiding citizens. The laws of the state, complained one irate strike representative, had not been "impartially enforced without fear or favor to class or condition." The Mayor and Governor had used their powers "to coerce the law-abiding class into submission to another class who were in open rebellion against the law."[88]

What differentiated these from earlier protests, however, was the ability of labor activists to appropriate, refashion, and use the language of law and order as a means of uniting mutually suspicious groups of wage earners into a single, self-conscious class. During the course of the May strikes, the language which had so thoroughly dominated civil society over the past year and a half was transformed so as to provide Cincinnati workers with a common vocabulary, common cause, and common perception of the role which the working class was to play in the city's political life.

From the perspective of the strikers, lawlessness and corruption threatened to overwhelm law and order. What could be done when state authorities conspired with lawbreakers? Ironically, workers chose to follow a path similiar to the one suggested several weeks earlier by Committee of One Hundred spokesman H. Wilson Brown. Lecturing on the remedies for political corruption, Brown reminded his audience that when all else failed they should never forget that the "people are the power, and the politicians are but a small part of this great community; the power is lodged in the people, and if the people are ready to exercise that power and assert their rights, I believe we can remedy this thing."[89]

In trying to uphold the Haley law, workers had demonstrated, they believed, that they were law-abiding citizens while the capitalists were not. Consequently, if republican government was to be restored to its proper equilibrium, then it was incumbent upon workers to enter the political sphere as a class — as the law-abiding class — in the pursuit of justice and obeisance to law. The roles of *worker* and *citizen* would be fused until such time as the political sphere was purged of its corruption.

The political consciousness stirred by the strikes, the organizations formed in the process, and the language which emerged from confrontations with the Mayor and manufacturers combined to form the basis of a new political party — one which would soon become the most powerful third party in nineteenth-century Cincinnati politics. Profiting from the lessons of May, the United Labor Party — a self-professed party of law and order — embarked upon a struggle for control, not simply of the workplace, but of society as well.

CHAPTER TWELVE

Workers On the Edge:
The Rise and Fall
of the United Labor Party

At no time in the history of Cincinnati's working class were the worlds of work and politics more closely linked than in the two years following the May Day strikes. Although these strikes did not end all the internal divisions which had long plagued the working class, the political consciousness generated during the spring struggles led a wide array of workers to embark upon a united campaign to create a new and more just industrial world. Cincinnati wage earners, declaring themselves to be the legitimate representatives of law and order, conjoined the roles and concerns of worker and citizen in one powerful organization — the United Labor Party (ULP). During its subsequent campaign, the ULP fashioned a radical political program which sought to alter the nature of the state, the economy, and the role which workers were to play in remedying the evils of both.

Of the many factors which contributed to the initial rise of the ULP in Cincinnati, three stand out as particularly important: the unprecedented organization and centralization of labor in the months following the May strikes; the gradual return of economic prosperity; and the widespread popularity of Henry George, the ULP's chief national spokesman.

The organizing fires, ignited during the spring, continued to burn strongly throughout the summer and autumn of 1886. Thousands of factory workers, small-shop artisans, building tradesmen, and unskilled laborers, flushed with a new spirit of unity, vowed to affiliate with one of the city's three swelling central labor associations: the Amalgamated Council of Building Trades (ACBT), the Central Labor Union (CLU), and the Knights of Labor (KOL). The building tradesmen — traditionally among the most narrowly craft-minded and politically conservative workers in Cincinnati — were roused by a massive series of wage strikes in the summer of 1886 to form the industrywide Amalgamated Council of Building Trades. By November, just a few months after its formation, the ACBT represented some sixteen construction unions and 17,000 men and was the largest central labor group in Cincinnati.[1] The city's socialistic-oriented German trade unionists sought to press the demands and spirit of May in more radical directions by organizing a Central Labor Union in July 1886 — one distinct from that forged by unskilled workers in May. Within a matter of months, the CLU had attracted over a half a dozen artisans', factory workers', and unskilled laborers' unions to its ranks.[2]

The chief beneficiary of the May Day strikes was the Knights of Labor. Nationally, the Knights experienced an astronomical rise in membership as a result of the eight-hour strikes — from 110,000 members in 1885 to over 700,000 by the end of 1886. In Cincinnati, membership in District Assembly No. 48 swelled from a meager 619 men and women in fourteen local assemblies in July 1885 to 6,533 members in fifty-four locals in July 1886 and 16,926 members in ninety-one locals by July 1887.[3] From May 1886 until the end of 1888, the KOL, although frequently outnumbered by the ACBT, ruled as the most powerful and respectable labor organization in Cincinnati.

In light of the KOL's steadfast opposition to the May strikes, it seems ironic that the Knights should have appealed to so many workers. In the weeks following the spring conflicts, many Cincinnati workers attributed their recent success to the ability of wage earners to move beyond the narrow confines of trade unionism and unite, irrespective of skill, in new factory- and industrywide organizations. As numerous workers called for continued joint participation in a common labor body which would represent and pursue the interests of a wide array of wage earners, the KOL — its anti-strike policy notwithstanding — emerged as the logical vehicle for forging such a new alliance. Indeed, the KOL was the only labor organization that was truly working class in character, for, as we have seen earlier, it sought to unite all workers—small-shop artisans, factory workers, day laborers, men, women, whites, blacks, Protestants, Jews, Catholics, the native-born and the foreign-born — into one central association.[4]

The Knights also benefited from a number of factors external to the labor movement. The fears engendered by the Haymarket affair and the possibility that socialists and anarchists might gain a receptive ear among Cincinnati workers led various civic leaders and community groups to legitimize the seemingly more conservative KOL as being the only true representative of the honest and law-abiding members of the working class. Anti-labor newspapers, which had scorned the KOL in earlier years, now honored it for its ability to reconcile the demands of labor with the higher responsibilities of citizenship. Unlike socialists, anarchists, or communists, explained the *Times-Star*, the KOL was devoted to improving the "conditions of the workingmen by all lawful and reasonable means . . . while respecting the rights of others."[5]

Local clergymen, eager to halt declining church attendance and fearing a further loss of parishioners to less godly radicals, frequently praised the Knights in their sermons and invited district assembly leaders to speak at church gatherings. The Reverend E. F. Pember, a Universalist minister, lauded the Knights and insisted that they were "knights indeed, well worthy to wear the brightest crown, so long as they are manly and just."[6] Temperance advocates, such as the Rev. R. H. Leonard, were similarly eloquent in their support of the local organization and its national leader, Terence V. Powderly, a strong foe of Demon Rum.[7] Close personal friendships with District Master Workman Hugh Cavanaugh led a popular Irish Catholic priest, the Rev. John Mackay, and the Rev. Melanchon C. Lockwood, a Baptist minister, to praise the Knights as religious, honorable, and law-abiding men. This new public recognition and acceptance of the Knights by various clergymen apparently proved to be mutually beneficial: it helped to attract religious workers to the Knights and the Knights to the churches of pro-labor ministers.[8]

Increased membership in the KOL, the ACBT, the CLU, the TLA, and various unions also coincided with the return of economic prosperity in the spring and summer of 1886. After decades of falling prices and frequent business failures, manufacturers and merchants joyously reported that they had earned greater profits in 1886 than during any year since the Civil War. The May strikes notwithstanding, production, employment, and sales figures all showed sharp increases during the year. Flushed with their recent good fortune, businessmen confidently predicted that Cincinnati would soon return to its ante-bellum position as the Queen City of the West.[9]

Wage earners had even greater reason to be gladdened by such good tidings. Years of recession and deflation had steadily eroded the real income and savings of large numbers of working-class families. Between January 1884 and December 1885 — the period just before the May Day strikes — food and housing costs in Cincinnati fell approximately 21.5 percent and 10.6 percent respectively, but the average wages of small-shop artisans, factory workers, and day laborers plummeted from 20 to 30 percent. Of the city's major craft and industrial workers, only printers, pattern makers, tanners, and custom tailors received wage increases during that period.[10]

The optimism expressed by the city's business community was matched by the fervid determination of various wage earners to secure their fair share of the new prosperity. It was this widespread effort to achieve economic "justice" which led many workers and unions to affiliate with one or more of the city's labor councils. The greatest enrollment spurts in the KOL, the ACBT, and the CLU almost invariably came during the course of protracted wage disputes.[11] Indeed, by the autumn of 1886, after several months of prolonged strike activity, Cincinnati had become one of the most heavily unionized cities in the nation. Depending upon whose estimates one chooses, between 31.5 and 50 percent of the city's manufacturing workforce belonged to some formal labor organization.[12] Nevertheless, the growth of the KOL, the ACBT, and the CLU did not necessarily produce harmony and accord among the working class. Ethnic and political divisions continued to drive a serious wedge into the laboring community. The German and socialist-dominated CLU and the predominantly Irish and native-born ACBT frequently clashed over the best means to pursue economic and political justice in the aftermath of the May strikes.[13]

Although internal divisions and hostilities remained, the divergent strands of Cincinnati's working community were pulled together in the autumn and winter of 1886 as several thousand workers, influenced by the writings of political economist Henry George, the rapid national growth of the United Labor Party, and the "lessons" learned during the previous spring, joined to inaugurate a new political crusade which sought to redirect the course of industrialization along a more equitable and just path of development.

The United Labor Party was organized in New York City in the summer of 1886, and its candidate for mayor, Henry George, shocked the political establishment by finishing a strong second to the Democratic incumbent, Abram S. Hewitt. George campaigned on a platform which called for sweeping land reform, the nationalization of all means of transportation, communication, and natural monopolies (gas, oil, minerals, etc.), more homes for workers, and an endorsement of home rule for Ireland. He won the enthusiastic support of Irishmen, Germans, Americans, Catholics, Protestants, socialists, Knights, and trade unionists throughout New York. Inspired by George's program, workers in cities and towns across the nation soon abandoned traditional party ties and established local ULP organizations.[14]

In Cincinnati, a small group of workers, led by the CLU, began meeting that autumn to lay the groundwork for a local party organization. At the ULP's first formal meeting in mid-November, the CLU, aware of the attacks that would befall any organization led by socialists, offered control of party leadership to District Master Workman Hugh Cavanaugh. As the recently acknowledged agents of law and order among the working class, the Knights' participation and leadership, the CLU reasoned, would help legitimize and promote greater public acceptance of the new party.[15] Although the Knights had generally avoided direct participation in independent party politics, Cavanaugh quickly accepted the offer. His decision was motivated not only by ideological considerations, but also by a fear of losing control of the city's labor movement to the fledgling American Federation of Labor (AFL). While the Knights were the overwhelming choice of newly organized unions, they were increasingly being attacked by the city's more established trade unionists — men who formed the core of the rival AFL. They criticized the Knights for their conservative political policies and for their policy of accepting men and women whom other unions, as the Secretary of Cincinnati Typographical Union No. 3 bitterly explained, had "either been compelled to expell" or whom they "could not admit to membership on account of their non-union proclivities."[16] When the AFL and its local ally, the Ohio State Trades Assembly, voted to endorse the ULP at their conventions that fall, Cavanaugh, sensing which way the political winds were blowing, decided to move to the forefront of the leadership of the ULP.[17]

Led by a coalition of leaders from the Knights, the CLU, the Henry George Clubs, and various trade unions, the ULP's executive committee called upon all law-abiding citizens to join their battle to "fight for the substantiation and realization of those rights which the great character of American freedom guarantees for us all, which, however, the two great national parties have hitherto ignored."[18] During the next several weeks, Cincinnati was deluged with leaflets, posters, and newspaper advertisements urging workingmen to attend the party's initial citywide convention in December and its countywide convention in January. Between five and eight hundred delegates, who represented a wide spectrum of the laboring community, responded to these appeals and gathered at Workingman's Hall in December and January to write a platform for the party and to plan for the coming national convention to be held in Cincinnati in February. In light of the limited success of workingmen's parties since the Civil War and the political tensions which had traditionally divided workers, the coalescing of so large and diverse a body of workers requires some explanation.

In Cincinnati, and throughout the nation, the ULP's initial appeal was greatly enhanced by Henry George's decision to serve as the party's national spokesman. George was admired by conservatives and radicals, Catholics and Protestants, native-born and foreign-born. He was one of the few people who could, and did, prompt the CLU, the ACBT, and the KOL in Cincinnati to suspend mutual enmities and pursue a common course. Socialists, although they regarded George as a confused bourgeois theorist, viewed his attacks on private property in land as a major step toward socialism.[19] Although Irish wage earners generally shied away from participation in radical working-class parties (they preferred instead to channel their energies into organizations which promoted the cause of Irish nationalism and land reform, such as the Irish Land League, the Irish Repeal Association, and the Fenian Brotherhood), they warmly supported George — a man who had consistently spoken out on behalf of the Irish crusade and against English landlordism.[20] Similarly, George's call for land reform and his close personal friendship with Grand Master Workman Powderly, earned him the backing of the city's Knights of Labor — whose ranks included large numbers of Irish workers — as well as the support of reform organizations such as the Greenbackers, Free Soil Societies, Anti-Monopoly Leagues, and Land and Labor Clubs.[21]

Uniting behind the banner of George's new party, these diverse groups of wage earners met frequently during the winter of 1886 – 1887 to forge a political organization which would offer concrete solutions to the problems plaguing the city and the nation. Merging the experiences of the workplace with aspects of socialism, the producers' ethic, the labor theory of value, republican ideology, Christian millenarianism, and the teachings of Henry George, the ULP fashioned a radical program which sought to end economic and political corruption and to redirect the course of industrialization. The genius of this new party, however, lay not in the nature of its demands, but in its ability to frame radical goals within the context of a political language grounded in everyday, seemingly conservative American values; a language which used the dominant beliefs, sentiments, and aspirations of working-class culture as the basis for launching a radical assault against what ULP delegates perceived as the antidemocratic forces of society. Appeals to citizenship, democracy, and God — appeals which had long been used by ruling elites to defuse working-class radicalism — were appropriated and refashioned by the ULP and used to attract supporters and legitimize the party's call to action.

　　Dissociating themselves from foreign thinkers and foreign radicalism, ULP convention delegates drew upon the American writings of Henry George to expose what they saw as the true crises afflicting the nation's citizens. Despite the vast increase in industrial and agricultural wealth, the party platform proclaimed, a "general discontent prevails on the part of wealth-producers. Farmers are suffering from a poverty which has forced them to mortgage their estates. . . . Laborers are sinking into greater and greater dependence."[22] How had such a corrupted world come into being? Why was there so much poverty and inequality amid such great economic progress? ULP delegates, borrowing heavily from George's *Progress and Poverty*, pointed to an inequitable system of distribution, land monopoly, and the corruption of democratic politics as the three principal causes of distress.

　　It was the unequal distribution of the benefits of industrialization, and not industrialization itself, the ULP argued, which brought misery and poverty to so many honest workers. Instead of sharing the advantages of industrial growth with "society at large," industrial capitalists had used "beneficient inventions" as a "means of oppression of the people and the aggrandizement of wealth and power."[23] These same corrupt persons also sought to monopolize control of "God's gift to all" — the land. The critical shortages of homes for honest working-class families and the "crowding of many of our people into narrow tenements at enormous rents, while a large part of the area of the city" remained as yet unbuilt upon, were due solely to the scandalous greed of land monopolists. By not permitting undeveloped lands to be put to productive use, these men had acted "to deprive labor of natural opportunities for employment, thus filling the land with tramps and paupers and bringing about an unnatural competition which tends to reduce wages to starvation rates and to make the wealth producer the industrial slave of those who grow rich by his toil."[24]

Harking back to the themes and arguments which had appeared in the aftermath of the courthouse riots and during the May Day strikes, party delegates declared that these "evils" were further compounded by the capitalists' success in using their power to corrupt the law making agents and agencies of government. Legislators, operating under the influence of corruptionists and in "defiance of public welfare," had repeatedly passed laws "almost exclusively for the benefit either of those who are already rich or those who are seeking to become so by means that have nothing in common with honest industry."[25] Democrats and Republicans had abrogated their responsibilities as citizens by adopting laws which established "class distinctions founded upon wealth."[26]

If law could be used to corrupt one world, so, too, could it be used to fashion another. The delegates to the conventions in December, January, and February disclaimed any desire to return to an illusory golden age of agrarianism or simple commodity production. They reasoned that, although industrialization was an inevitable process, industrial capitalism was only one of several possible paths of development. The ULP rejected the acquisitive individualism fostered by industrial capitalism and offered citizens a more "republican" alternative path of economic development — a cooperative industrial commonwealth in which the benefits accruing from land and industry would be applied "to the promotion of the health, comfort, education and recreation of its people."[27]

The ULP proposed to inaugurate the creation of such a new world by offering a seemingly simple yet radical solution to contemporary problems — George's Single Tax. In order "to extirpate poverty," George had explained, "to make wages what justice commands they should be, the full earnings of the laborer, we must therefore substitute for the individual ownership of land a common ownership."[28] Rather than urging the direct confiscation of land, a measure bound to be denounced as socialistic, George and his party proposed that the government simply appropriate the profits derived from increased land values. Let the government, he suggested, impose a uniform tax upon all land regardless of whether it was developed or not. The Single Tax was essentially a land-use fee which would be paid by the renter directly to the government rather than to landlords or speculators. Although the actual mechanisms of the Single Tax were never clearly delineated, George implied that the tax would be determined according to the prevailing market demand for property. In other words, the new property taxes would be equal to the rental value that any piece of land could command. If, for example, a manufacturer was willing to pay the government $10,000 for the use of a plot of land, then the original owner would either have to pay a tax equal to that amount or give up the right to the use of that property for a year.[29]

The Single Tax in effect nationalized the ownership of land, yet it did so within a democratic context. Land monopoly, according to George, threatened the very fabric of American life and defied God's intention to provide His creatures with a "right to sufficient land for self support."[30] Therefore, republican and Christian principles *demanded* that citizens act to abolish this evil. The Single Tax would restore justice by transfering the unearned profits of rent and land speculation back to the community as a whole. Speculators, faced with the prospect of having to pay high taxes on non-income-producing lands, would be forced to sell or build upon their holdings. This, in turn, would eventually lead to the construction of more factories and homes and thereby alleviate the problems of unemployment and urban congestion. The elimination of usurious rents would also reduce production costs and thereby bring higher wages to workers and greater profits to employers. "This distribution of land," party delegates proclaimed in February 1887, "would gradually make us a nation of independent freeholders, instead of, as we are rapidly drifting, a nation of landlords and tenants."[31] Moreover, the Single Tax would generate sufficient funds to end the need for all other taxes (thus the popular title, Single Tax). Its revenues would meet the cost of governmental operations, then only 5 percent of the Gross National Product, and leave a surplus which would be returned to the people in the form of new railroads, telegraphs, schools, libraries, hospitals, museums, and parks.

Party delegates also condemned laissez-faire government as inconsistent with the modern needs of democracy and insisted that the people required an active state which, acting in accordance with the designs of God and the Founding Fathers, would directly involve itself in furthering the interests of the majority of its citizens. To this end, the ULP demanded that all transportation and communication systems and natural monopolies be taken out of the hands of private corporations and placed under the ownership and control of the government. Once again, the party justified these attacks upon traditional property rights within the context of familiar American democratic principles. The ULP was not preaching socialism, party delegates declared. It was simply attempting to pass laws, which in accordance with the "self-evident truths proclaimed by the founders of this Republic," would "bring about a just and liberal administration of public affairs."[32] The party platform also pressed for the abolition of convict labor, the payment of equal wages for equal work without distinction of sex, the more vigorous enforcement of factory and tenement safety and sanitary laws, a graduated income tax, compulsory arbitration of labor disputes, the direct election of United States senators, the prohibition of the use of private armies by corporations, and the establishment of agricultural and industrial cooperatives."[33]

While similar in many respects to earlier workingmen's parties, the ULP nevertheless perceived itself as something more than just another labor party. All party delegates repeatedly declared themselves to be the true vanguard of the forces of law, order, Christianity, and republican justice. The ULP, they avowed, was a party which sought to expand traditional notions of party politics by combining the responsibilities of worker and citizen into a new and more powerful identity: the middle class. In an age whose popular heroes included such persons as Andrew Carnegie and John D. Rockefeller, the ULP called upon the heroes of an earlier era, workers and farmers — the backbone of the middle class — to set the republic on a new and more virtuous path. As the national party chairman, A. J. Streator explained:

> We are not the friends of anarchy — we are the opponents of anarchy. We are in favor of government and of law. We are the middle class of society who meet here — not the extremely rich or the extremely poor. We stand on middle ground. We have come here to organize and save this government from the extremes of one and the robbery of the other.[34]

Echoing Streator's remarks, the Rev. M. C. Lockwood insisted that party delegates had gathered, "not to wave a red flag, not cry revolution," but to inaugurate "reform in the political life of the nation." Praising them for their moderation and commitment to law, Lockwood went on to say:

> You are not gathered here to make sweeping condemnations of all rich men, nor to declare war on your country's institutions. . . . We represent the middle classes. There are fast becoming two classes in this country — the extremely rich and the extremely poor. We wish to prevent the encroachments of both.[35]

As men and women who stood between the extremes of unbridled wealth and dire poverty, the worker/citizens who composed this "new" middle class claimed to represent the vast majority of the American people. They were not a class in the most narrow economic sense. Rather, the ULP envisioned the new middle class (which they would lead) as a *universal* class which would act in the interests of *all* society; one which would reconstruct the industrial world so as to create a new harmonious whole.

This was not mere campaign rhetoric designed to win votes. The experiences of the previous spring, as well as a longstanding tradition of confrontation with corrupt politicians and capitalists, had convinced many Cincinnati workers they they were indeed the only true law-abiding class; the one class who, through its new role as the vanguard of the middle class, could and would act to restore the American traditions of justice, virtue, independence, and commonwealth. Once in power, the ULP — unlike the mainstream parties — would serve the "will of the people" by working to abolish all laws which gave to any class of citizens advantages, either "judicial, financial, industrial, or political," which were not equally shared by all others.[36] The ultimate benefactor of their policies, party leaders avowed in true republican fashion, was not the individual worker, but the American state. All "class distinctions founded upon wealth" would be ended by the ULP and replaced by government policies that sought to promote the "social equality" of all citizens.[37]

By insisting that the middle class was a universal class which could act on behalf of all classes, the ULP came closer to being an indigenous American proletarian movement than any previous workingmen's movement. The ULP disclaimed any taint of radicalism, but it advocated measures which, if they had been adopted, would have dramatically altered traditional notions of property rights and the relationships among government, business, and the economy.

On March 19, 1887, after several months of intensive organizing efforts, the Cincinnati ULP — led by a coalition of the KOL, the CLU, Henry George Clubs, socialists, and trade unionists — reconvened to nominate a full slate of candidates for the municipal elections to be held on April 4. Harking back to the experiences of May 1886, convention delegates called for the election of a mayor who would obey the laws of the state rather than one, like Amor Smith, who attempted to "overawe the workmen in their attempts to better their condition by an inexcusable use of the state militia." The party demanded that henceforth all city officers be salaried (in order to reduce the lure of bribery); that an eight-hour day be adopted for all public-works employees; that the city assume ownership and control of all street railroads, telegraph and telephone services, natural monopolies; and that a more efficient Board of Public Health be appointed to supervise the cleaning of city streets and tenements.[38]

Whatever its seeming tensions and contradictions, the ULP succeeded in attracting a wide array of Cincinnati workers. Unlike the artisan-dominated workingmen's parties of the past, the ULP drew its greatest support from the same group of workers who had played the prominent role during the May Day strikes — factory artisans and factory laborers. An examination of the occupational backgrounds of 168 leading ULP activists — men who either served on the party's central or ward committees, served as officers at party rallies, or were nominated for public office — reveals that factory workers constituted 57.7 percent of party activists. Carriage workers John Leonard and Theodore Ludwig, machinists Rudolf Bosshardt and Thomas Burke, and furniture workers William Kronauge and William Smith all pledged that the men who had restored order and justice to the city's economic sphere the spring before would now do the same for its political sphere. They were joined in their quest by scores of factory workers who belonged to the city's shoemaking, printing, iron molding, clothing, and cigarmaking unions, and by numerous unskilled laborers, such as teamster George Williams, drayman Daniel Wheaton, and day laborers Charles Rouse and Joseph Rooney. The party also attracted supporters from the ranks of the city's clerks, small manufacturers, merchants, and professionals.

The ULP's desire to demonstrate that it was truly the party of the middle class and that it could represent the interest of people of different occupations and ethnicities was most apparent in its selection of candidates for the April elections. The nominees for the ten major municipal offices included three factory artisans, two small-shop artisans, one clerk, one grocer, and three lawyers (one of whom had risen from the ranks of Cincinnati Typographical Union No. 3). Five of these men came from families of German descent, three from families of Irish descent, and two from long-term native-born families.[39] Party activists, like party candidates, also cut across ethnic as well as class lines. Judging from surnames, 37.3 percent of the 168 ULP activists came from German backgrounds and 21.7 percent from Irish backgrounds. These were men, the party proudly boasted, who had spent most, if not all, of their working lives in Cincinnati. They were men who came from the hardest working and most respectable elements of the middle class; men who were intimately acquainted with the problems and needs of the city and its residents.[40]

Table 12.1 Occupational Breakdown of United Labor Party Activists:
December 1886 – November 1887

Occupation	n	%	
Small-Shop Artisans:	27	*16.1*	
Building Tradesmen	11		
Custom Tailors	5		
Blacksmiths	4		
Harnessmakers	3		
Broommakers	2		
Tanners	1		
Ship Caulkers	1		
Factory Artisans & Laborers:	97	*57.7*	
Shoemakers	25	Furniture Workers	5
Printers	18	Engineers & Boilermakers	5
Carriage Workers	11	Iron & Rolling Mill Workers	3
Cigar Workers	10	Coffin Worker	1
Machinists	9	Brewery Worker	1
Iron Molders	8	Bookbinder	1
Semi- & Unskilled Nonfactory Workers:	11	*6.5*	
Railroad Workers	4		
Teamsters	2		
Day Laborers	2		
Fireman	1		
Porter	1		
Waiter	1		
Commercial Workers:	8	*4.8*	
Clerks	4		
Bookkeepers	2		
Collector	1		
Canvasser	1		
Manufacturers:	9	*5.4*	
Pumps	1	Printing	1
Brushes	1	Sheet Iron	1
Tinware	1	Confectionary	1
Machinery	1	Marble Monuments	1
Merchants:	7	*4.2*	
Grocers	3		
Hotel Owner	1		
Saloon Owner	1		
Liquor Store Owner	1		
Retail Shoe Store Owner	1		
Professionals:	9	*5.4*	
Lawyers	5		
Doctors	3		
Minister	1		
Grand Totals	*168*	*100.0*	

Note: These activists represented several levels of party leadership: party candidates, citywide officers, and ward officers. My original list included the names of 211 men (no women held formal office in the ULP). I was able to identify with absolute certainty the occupations of 168 activists.

In setting out to recruit rank-and-file support for the party's platform and candidates, the ULP launched a campaign which, unlike the spontaneous activities of the previous spring, was marked by an extraordinary effort to organize at the grass roots and by concerted attempt to unite the worlds of work, leisure, and politics. From December through April, United Labor clubs were organized in all 25 wards, officers were elected, constitutions were drawn up, weekly meetings and rallies were held, and party members were asked to canvass their neighborhoods to solicit written pledges of support for candidates. Lists of new supporters were immediately fowarded to the central campaign headquarters at Workingman's Hall. In this way, the party leaders were kept constantly apprised of its strong and weak areas.[41]

While the greatest emphasis was placed upon neighborhood organizing, the party also took its campaign directly to the workplace. ULP candidates and activists delivered lunchtime speeches at hundreds of shops and factories throughout the city. Men and women were encouraged to ignore differences of craft, skill, and ethnicity and to participate in party rallies and marches as shop or factory units. They were also urged to leave their jobs on election day to help in last minute campaign efforts.

These efforts to politicize the workplace met with notable success in the days just before the election. Workers at dozens of shops and factories met and voted to endorse the ULP on behalf of all workers at their establishment. The most numerous and enthusiastic responses came from those working in the city's large factories — particularly those factories which had been struck during the previous spring. The 675 men and women at Hall's Safe and Lock Company, the 500 employees of the Hiram Davis carriage factory, the workers at the J. W. Foley Iron Foundry, and several hundred other factory workers declared April 4, election day, a "workers' half-holiday" and announced their intention to devote their labor to the cause of the ULP.[42] Craft organizations such as the machinists, stove foundry workers, hod carriers, and brassworkers, also issued statements supporting ULP candidates.[43]

Although the ULP adopted many of the outward forms of the Democratic and Republican parties, it nevertheless endeavored to alter the meaning and significance of traditional party activities. The party's ward organizations, its numerous committees, and its frequent rallies and public demonstrations operated at several levels. At the most obvious, they served to persuade people to vote for one party rather than another. Yet, at another level, they gave workers an opportunity to enhance their feelings of self-esteem by proving that they could make a difference in the world by participating in an organization which held the betterment of society, not the party, as its primary goal. Writing to Powderly in 1883 of the untapped passion that lay within the working class, Henry George observed:

> There is a widespread consciousness among the masses that there is something radically wrong in the present social organization . . . . The failure of all previous labor organizations to accomplish much, or to force their issues to politics seems to me to have been due to their failure to urge anything radical enough and large enough to satisfy this feeling or arouse opposition.[44]

For many workers, participation in the ULP was a means to relieve the alienation of factory life and to restore a sense of mutual trust and personal recognition. Hundreds of workers could, and did, hold positions of importance within the party. Each of the 25 ward organizations offered men a chance to serve as a United Labor Party officer, committee representative, convention delegate, or nominee for public office. The citywide party organization offered further opportunities for the ordinary wage earner to bask in a moment of public honor. At each major gathering, several dozen of the party faithful, many of them from the rank and file, were rewarded for their services by being appointed honorary vice presidents and given seats of honor upon the main platform.[45]

The ULP also provided an outlet for religious energies. Like many workers of the Gilded Age, Cincinnati men and women discovered in the labor movement, and especially the United Labor Party, a concern for Christian brotherhood and justice which they did not find in the city's established churches. "I have tried for years," noted one party member, "to find that enthusiasm in religion which I know animated the founders of Christianity, but never succeeded until the Anti-Poverty cause [an offshoot of the Henry George Clubs] awoke within me that wonderful enthusiasm of humanity."[46] Numerous party members rejected traditional churches as insensitive to their needs and chose instead to hold their own Sunday services at Druid Hall, services which addressed themselves to moral and political questions of immediate concern to the working class.[47] The ULP also warmly welcomed pro-labor ministers such as M. C. Lockwood and E. P. Foster into the party hierarchy. They were frequently called upon to deliver the opening prayers, as well as several keynote addresses, at party gatherings. Lockwood preached what party members wished to hear: the ULP was composed of God-fearing men who used the Lord's words as their guiding light.[48] Moved by the spirit of one of Lockwood's more evangelical orations, E. T. Fries, a bookkeeper, reminded party members that theirs was not just a political campaign; it was a "holy crusade."[49]

At yet another level, the ULP sought to unite the concerns of the workplace, the obligations of citizenship, and the need for enjoyment and excitement. Party gatherings were often gala and festive affairs. Members were given weekly opportunities to participate in dramatic evening torchlight rallies, to march in massive weekend parades, to listen to the martial tunes played by bands hired to enliven outdoor meetings, or simply to partake in the beer and conversation which flowed freely at most party gatherings. Here, then, was an organization in which leisure assumed a very political meaning, and was used for the purpose of helping to improve one's life both outside and inside the workplace.[50]

While leisure, religion, and ideology all contributed to the growth and appeal of the ULP, party fortunes were also aided by a tremendous rise of labor discontent between the autumn of 1886 and the spring of 1887. In particular, the months from January to April 1887 — the crucial period in the party's development — saw a strong resurgence of strike activity. In late March 1887, the leaders of the ACBT, frustrated by the refusal of contractors to accept union wage demands — particularly since this was a period of anticipated prosperity for builders — initiated a series of strikes against their employers and denounced their so-called allies within the Democratic Party for not coming to their aid. Aware of the potential votes that the ACBT could provide, the ULP's nominating convention named Wiliam H. Stevenson, president of the bricklayers' union, and Joseph Nicholas, a carpenter and Master Workman of KOL Local Assembly No. 280, as its candidates for mayor and director of the city infirmary. The building trades unions in turn — which had hitherto played only a minor role in party affairs — announced their unconditional support of Stevenson, Nicholas, and the entire ULP ticket.[51]

The coincidence of labor militancy and political support for the ULP occurred in several other trades and industries. Over 6,000 workers, as table 12.2 indicates, participated in strikes during the weeks just before and after the election. Machinists, stove molders, safe workers, carriage makers, iron workers, and typographers, all involved in contract negotiations or strikes in March and April, pledged to vote the ULP line.[52]

As election day approached and wage negotiations assumed an increasingly feverish pitch, so too did the ULP's campaign. Rallies were held in one or more wards each evening; candidates and party leaders

Table 12.2 Strikes and Lockouts in Cincinnati,
August 1886 – June 1888

Year/Month	Number of Strikes	Number of Striking Workers
1886		
August	1	780
September	4	408
November	1	640[a]
December	1	1,000
1887		
January	3	120[a]
February	1	150
March	5	718[a]
April	16	5,365[a]
May	9	1,500[a]
June	3	60[a]
July	5	640
August	5	192[a]
September	3	407[a]
October	1	—
November	4	68[a]
December	1	—
1888		
February	1	2,500
March	1	300
April	4	1,760[a]
May	1	440
June	1	2,200
Partial Totals	76	19,248[b]

SOURCE: Strike statistics were compiled from the following sources: *Enquirer, Commercial Gazette,* and *Times Star,* August 1, 1886 – June 30, 1888; *Annual Report of the Bureau of Labor Statistics,* 1886 – 1889; "Minute Book of the Cincinnati Typographical Union No. 3," 1 – 2, *passim;* U.S. Bureau of Labor, *Third Annual Report. Strikes and Lockouts* (Washington, 1888), pp. 470 – 83, 661 – 62.

[a] Complete totals for these strikes were not available; figures only include known number of strikers.

[b] This figure underestimates the actual number of strikers (see note a).

toured the city and gave speeches in English and German; ethnic associations, such as the Irish Land League and the Turnerverein, were visited; and personal canvassing was stepped up. On March 30, just four days before the election, the party announced that it had already received 11,000 written pledges of support and expected more to come.[53] The peak of the campaign came on Sunday, April 2, during the party's last demonstration and rally. Parading yet again behind the symbols of 1776 — fife and drum corps and American flags — some 10,000 men, women, and children slowly proceeded from the public theater of the streets to the private theater of Music Hall, the city's main palace of culture and entertainment. As they dramatically marched unit by unit into Music Hall, Knights, CLU, and ACBT members, trade unionists, and assorted shop and factory workers were all given rousing ovations by the already assembled crowd. Party spokesman once again urged workers to cast out the corruptionists and the lawless and to vote for "men whom the lust of office can not move; whom the spoils of office can not corrupt."[54]

Of course, not all Cincinnatians were equally excited about the United Labor Party. Its self-perceived role as the party of the middle class and the purveyor of law and order aroused considerable resentment from a number of quarters. The ULP, insisted various business leaders, was not led by honest American workingmen, but by foreign rabble rousers "without any understanding of our institutions." Extortion of higher wages, not justice, was the party's ultimate goal.[55] Fearing the devastating effects a ULP victory might have upon the business community, Cincinnati's most powerful manufacturers and corporations reportedly threw their full financial and political support behind the Republican incumbent mayor, Amor Smith.[56]

Republican and Democratic newspapers were particularly scathing in their attacks upon the ULP. The *Commercial Gazette* blasted the ULP as an "amalgam of Anarchism, Know-Nothingism and Prohibitionism that was truly pathetic."[57] The newspaper singled out Lockwood for special vilification and accused him of being a "political preacher" who brazenly violated constitutional principles regarding the separation of church and state.[58] The *Volksblatt* said that the ULP was little more than an agent of the Democratic Party; it urged German voters to stand by their old friends in the Republican Party.[59] The Democratic-oriented *Enquirer* responded to the ULP threat by reducing its coverage of party activities in the weeks before the election.

While both Republicans and Democrats joined in condemning the ULP as a class-oriented party, the Democrats, with their traditionally strong roots in the labor movement, stood the most to lose from a successful ULP campaign. Democratic leaders initially attempted to meet the problem by employing the familiar tactic of political co-optation. They endorsed a number of ULP candidates running for city council and ward offices and expected that the ULP would agree to withdraw from the mayoralty race and support the Democratic nominee. When the ULP leaders refused to make such a deal, Democratic leaders, fearing new rivals more than old, threw their support behind Smith.[60]

On April 4, election day, Cincinnatians were gripped by an atmosphere "even more exciting than in a Presidential campaign." City streets were swollen with thousands of workers who "seemed to have full confidence in the success of their ticket."[61] At 2 A.M. on April 5 Stevenson led Republican Smith by ten votes and appeared to be headed toward victory. However, when the final votes were tallied, workingmen discovered that the Republican-Democratic-capitalistic alliance had proved too formidable a combination. Although Stevenson carried 12 of the city's 25 electoral wards and received 5,459 more votes than the Democratic candidate, he was 682 votes short of victory. Smith polled 17,998 votes to Stevenson's 17,317 — the largest vote ever garnered by a third party in Cincinnati. The same pattern of narrow defeat was repeated in the other nine major citywide contests. ULP candidates consistently won several thousand more votes than Democratic candidates but suffered close losses at the hands of their Republican opponents.

However, the ULP fared well at the ward level. Of 25 contested positions, nine ULP candidates were elected to the city council, seven to the board of education, nine as assessors, and ten as constables. All told, the ULP carried 69 (42.1 percent) of the city's 164 election precincts; the Republicans carried 83 precincts (50.6 percent), and the Democrats carried 12 (7.3 percent).[62] Although losing the mayoralty race, ULP leaders nevertheless basked in the relative success of their maiden campaign. Come next fall, they promised, they would sweep Democrats and Republicans out of office, once and for all.

Despite these optimistic predictions, the ULP soon entered a period of rapid decline. Total votes for major offices in subsequent elections dropped from 17,317 votes (36.7 percent of the total) in April 1887 to 11,121 (17.1 percent of the total) in November 1887, to 3,115 (8.0 percent of the total) in April 1888, and to a bare 932 (1.2 percent of the total) for the party's presidential candidate in November 1888. By the beginning of 1889, the ULP had ceased to exist.

There were a number of reasons for the gradual decline and demise of the ULP. In the weeks following the election in April 1887, the ULP found itself in a predicament which had haunted workingmen's parties throughout the century: how to sustain commitment to radical principles and at the same time gain power through electoral politics? This tension was manifested most dramatically in the split among ULP moderates, conservatives, and radicals. Although they maintained a united front during the party's initial campaign, their often uneasy alliance broke down under the strain of charting a future course of action.

During the following months, party moderates and conservatives became convinced that the election had been lost because Democrats and Republicans were able to portray the ULP as a class-based party that stood as the political offshoot of the Haymarket riots. In fact, the ULP *was* a class-based party. Although Stevenson and his fellow candidates received some votes from small manufacturers, merchants, and professionals, the bulk of their support came from the city's working-class wards.[63] Instead of moving to solidify and expand their support among workers, KOL and ACBT representatives argued that the path to future political victory lay in removing all taints of radicalism and in broadening the party's appeal and acceptance among the middle class. Moving to dissociate themselves from socialists and radical land theorists (Single Tax supporters), the Cincinnati executive committee voted in May to change the party's name to the Union Labor Party, the name adopted by the national convention in February 1887. The decision to alter names, explained Hugh Cavanaugh, was made in order to reaffirm the party's strict adherence and commitment to principles of law and order. "Socialism and other isms antagonistic to American institutions," he promised, would have "no place in Union Labor party."[64]

More significant than the change in name was the decision to enlarge the constituency and alter the platform of the "new" party. In addition to courting the city's middle class, the party opened its summer conventions to Grangers, Greenbackers, Prohibitionists, soldiers' organizations, and any other group willing to unite under the Union Labor Party banner.[65] The brush with success and the lure of future victory also led the party to abandon the increasingly controversial Single Tax. Although party leaders had tried to cloak the measure in democratic guise, clergymen, newspaper leaders, Republicans, Democrats, and a number of trade unionists blasted the measure for what it was: an attempt to nationalize private property. Hence, in order to avoid further attacks by the more "respectable" members of the community, party delegates to the convention in July 4 dropped the Single Tax from their platform. The convention still supported most of the economic planks adopted in January and February. However, it downplayed them and turned instead toward a renewed emphasis on the restoration of law and order as the single most effective solution for economic and political distress.[66]

These decisions to change the name, composition, and focus of the labor party met with reactions of outrage on the part of Germans, socialists, and radical land theorists. They accused the executive committee of using the "same manipulating methods of machine politicians that destroyed the character of the old political parties."[67] By welcoming reformers and courting middle-class voters with little understanding of labor's problems, they argued, the Union Labor Party had forsaken its position as the party "of the toiling masses." Ambition had proved greater than principle.[68]

The men refused to join in the campaign to rename their party and continued to operate under the banner of the United Labor Party. Socialists and Georgites, insisting that *they* were "fighting only for a grand principle, not for public office," demanded the inclusion of the Single Tax as the price for their support of the Union Labor Party.[69] As one ULP stalwart stated: "I wouldn't give a cent for a party without a land plank in its platform."[70] The old ULP forces held a separate state convention in July 1887. Political reform, they agreed, would have little real meaning without an effective program of land reform. The latter, not the former, would serve as the foundation of a new and more just society.[71]

The political divisions that tore the ULP alliance apart in Cincinnati were repeated at the New York convention in August 1887. When socialist delegates pressed for the nationalization of all instruments of production, as well as land, George, fearful of antagonizing moderate voters, responded by expelling them from the party. There was "no alternative," he explained to a friend, "other than to consent to have the movement ranked as a socialistic movement or to split with the socialists."[72] In New York, Cincinnati, and other ULP strongholds, Irish and moderate and consevative native-born workers quickly rallied around George and the new Union Labor Party, while Germans, socialists, and land theorists struggled to keep the United Labor Party alive.[73]

Despite their many differences, the leaders of the ULP still preferred to ally with the Union Labor Party rather than with the Democrats or Republicans. Hence they agreed to suspend hostilities and accepted an invitation to participate in the Union Labor Party's nominating convention on August 30. Although they were still unwilling to endorse a land platform, Union leaders attempted to heal recent wounds by appointing printer William B. Ogden, a known socialist, as chairman of the convention. Ogden was also selected as one of the party's nominees for state legislator. Similarly, several other CLU and Henry George Club leaders were chosen to run for minor state and county offices. In an effort to lure black voters away from the Republicans, the Union Labor Party nominated Alfred R. Paige, a waiter and president of the Fifth Ward Colored Union Labor Club, for the state legislature.[74]

The party once again launched a massive campaign during the statewide elections that autumn. Yet, despite their hard efforts, Union Labor Party attempts to attract more working-class and middle-class voters to their cause proved unsuccessful. The Republican gubernatorial candidate, Joseph B. Foraker, polled 30,040 votes (46.2 percent of the total), as compared to 23,338 votes (35.9 percent) for the Democratic candidate, 11,121 votes (17.1 percent) for the Union Labor Party candidate, and 525 votes (0.8 percent) for the Prohibitionist candidate. Although the Union Labor candidates for the Ohio Senate and House received as many as 15,000 votes, their Republican and Democratic rivals averaged 30,000 and 19,500 votes respectively. Not one Union Labor candidate was elected to any county or state office.[75]

The abysmal failure that November spread depression and resentment among many Union Labor Party leaders. "When I went around yesterday morning, I was confident we could win," remarked William Stevenson. "Well, it's all right. If the workingmen of this city want to put chains around their necks and be stamped upon by their enemies, all right. They deserve to be slaves." John Schrage, the party's candidate for county solicitor, complained that workingmen "went like a flock of sheep against us where we expected they would stand the strongest."[76]

Not all party leaders were so distraught. Several pointed toward the more positive aspects of the election. "When a great party of 14,000 or 15,000 is enrolled under the standard," reflected the editors of the labor daily, *United Labor Age*, "there is no reason that it should be disbanded."[77] Echoing similar sentiments, shoemaker Edward Harris asked: "Do you think with a vote of 15,000 we intend to disband? No Sir. The Labor party has come to stay. We can stand several defeats, and we will still be undismayed."[78]

It was the party's pessimists, however, who were to make the most prescient forecasts. "The tide is against us," concluded a forlorn Hugh Cavanaugh. "There is no chance for a Labor party here. A Labor ticket next spring will not poll over 5,000 votes. We needed one victory to hold our men together."[79]

The party did not collapse as quickly as Cavanaugh feared. Union Labor Party clubs continued to meet and build organizations at the grass roots throughout the winter and spring of 1887–1888. Nevertheless, by November 1888, the Union and United Labor Parties were but mere shadows in the world of party politics. Gone was the sense of drama and excitement that had once characterized the ULP. As the fervor, memories, and anger produced by the May Day strikes continued to fade, so, too, did the prospects of the United and Union Labor Parties.

After so dramatic and promising a rise, how can we explain the rapid and total collapse of the ULP? First, there were the deep-seated political divisions between radicals and conservatives. In addition, there was the misguided strategy of trying to court middle-class voters rather than to build a stronger base of support among the party's more likely working-class constituents. Despite its efforts to modify its platform, the Union Labor Party was unable to attract substantial numbers of middle-class voters, for they still perceived the party as too radical.

There were also a number of external pressures which brought about the party's collapse. The Cincinnati Union and United Labor Parties, like their counterparts in New York, faced the combined opposition of mainstream parties, clergymen, and capitalists. In the months following the election of April 1887, Democrats and Republicans continued to join forces to defeat ULP candidates and moved to co-opt party leaders and to assimilate moderate party demands into their own platforms.[80] The ULP also came under assault from numerous local clergymen and the Catholic Church. Unable to dissuade parishioners and priests from joining the labor party, New York's Catholic hierarchy persuaded the Pope to excommunicate George's chief party lieutenant, the Rev. Edward McGlynn. Fearing the worst for themselves, sympathetic clergy, Irish voters (in New York and Cincinnati), and important national party spokesmen like Patrick Ford, editor of the influential *Irish World*, abandoned the ULP and sided with the church.[81]

The most important reason for the parties' dissolution ran much deeper than any of these factors. The rise of the United Labor Party had reflected a general discontent over the course of industrialization. It collapsed because there were unresolvable cleavages within the party and within the labor movement over the relationship between the individual worker and the industrial system and over the type of action needed to guarantee a more just and equitable future for American workers.

The steady decline of the Union Labor Party after the elections of November 1887 was paralleled and hastened by the gradual disintegration of the party's central force—the Knights of Labor. While United and

Union men fought Democrats and Republicans and each other for control of the political sphere in the summer, autumn, and winter of 1887-1888, the Knights were engaged in a death battle with trade unionists and their organ, the American Federation of Labor, for control of the economic sphere. The stakes were high, for the victor would determine the path which labor would follow into the twentieth century.

The battle between the KOL and the AFL was essentially one over competing visions of the relationship between the worker and the industrial world. At the heart of the Knights' vision was a belief that the die for the new industrial world had not yet been cast. The United States, insisted Powderly and his adherents, was still an *industrializing*, not a fully industrial nation. Consequently, American workers still had the power to alter the final course of industrialization. Although they often drew upon agrarian views propounded by Jefferson, the Knights were by no means a "backward looking" organization. They simply used the honored and cherished language and values of the past as a guide for the future. The Knights were not opposed to industrialization *per se*. Rather, they were opposed to industrial capitalism; they were opposed to its tendency to deprive men and women of their dignity and independence by reducing them to the role of "wage slaves."[82]

The Knights rejected wage strikes, such as those advocated by the AFL, as measures which simply served to perpetuate a corrupt economic system. They offered workers an alternative to the allegedly demeaning and selfish world of industrial capitalism — cooperation, solidarity, and the creation of a new moral order. Producer cooperatives, they insisted, would free men and women from the degrading and inequitable influences of capitalistic production and allow them to share in the true benefits brought by industrialization and new labor-saving machinery. Only under such a system could independence and industrialization coexist.

The initial rush toward joining the KOL in the spring and summer of 1886 had less to do with what the Knights actually were than with popular hopes of what they might be. Workers apparently envisioned the Knights as an organization which would continue to battle, and battle successfully, against employers. "During the flood-tide of 1886 – 1887," reflected the labor newspaper editor, John Swinton, "tens of thousands rushed into the Order with a vague expectation that it would somehow bring them immediate advantages; that it would at once shorten their hours, raise their wages, improve their condition, and subdue their adversaries."[83]

The fervor of the May strikes was sufficient to attract thousands of Cincinnati workers to the Knights, but it was not sufficient to hold them there. Workers were disgruntled with District Assembly No. 48's failure to support wage strikes, its inability or unwillingness to pursue the needs of skilled craftsmen, its continued recruitment and acceptance of trade union apostates, its laxity in defending workers against the onslaughts of manufacturers' associations, and its unpopular stance on behalf of temperance — banning the sale or distribution of alcohol at any Knight function. Thus, the machinists, iron molders, coopers, brewers, building tradesmen, and other trade unionists gradually abandoned the Knights during the summer, autumn, and winter of 1887 – 1888 in favor of a more militant course of action, action often taken in association with the AFL.[84]

Unlike Powderly and the Knights, Samuel Gompers and the AFL conceded the inevitablity of wage labor and industrial capitalism as the ruling forces of modern economic life. "The fact is being fast forced upon the consciousness of the wage-workers of this continent," Gompers wrote in 1888, "that they are a distinct and particularly permanent class of modern society; and, consequently, have distinct and permanent common interests."[85] Practical trade unions, not visionary organizations like the Knights, were needed to establish "normal permanent relations between capitalists and laborers."[86] Preaching "pure and simple" wage unionism, Gompers argued that the best long-range strategy for labor was to press for immediate increases in pay and decreases in working hours. Continual economic improvements gained through wage strikes, he insisted, would make "men more dissatisfied with unjust conditions and readier to battle for the right."[87]

It was Gompers, not Powderly, who generated the most excitement and enthusiasm among Cincinnati workers in the early months of 1888. In late January and early February, the city's most prominent trade unions, inspired by the preachings of the AFL, joined together to form a new trade-union-oriented city labor council: the Congress of Amalgamated Labor of Cincinnati and Vicinity (CALC).[88] The leaders of Cincinnati Typographical Union No. 3 predicted that the new organization was "destined in the near future to become a power such as was never before felt in this city."[89]

District Assembly No. 48 quickly acted to join the CALC.[90] Nevertheless, the move came too late. Disenchantment with the Knights had grown too strong. The final death blow to the fortunes of the KOL came during the shoemakers' lockout in February and March 1888. In the belief that Cavanaugh and other KOL leaders had betrayed them, 1,500 male and 1,000 female shoemakers — the largest and most important trade within the District Assembly — refused to obey the District Master Workman's order to return to their jobs. The conflict was finally settled in late March, but only after the direct intervention of Powderly and the Roman Catholic Church. Father Mackay, a close friend of Cavanaugh, pleaded with his parishioners — many of them members of the shoemakers' assembly — to trust the District Workman and return to work. The embittered shoemakers did so, but they denounced their District Assembly and sought membership in the more radical assembly led by Thomas Skeffington in Massachussetts. The most important result of the lockout, however, was the KOL's loss of control over the one industry it had dominated for years. "A month ago," Cavanaugh wrote to Powderly, in early March, "our Order was recognized in every shoe factory. Today it is 'Free Shop.' "[91]

The dissension which rocked the ranks of the shoemakers soon spread to the city's lock and safemakers. On Tuesday, March 27, 1888, thirty blacksmiths walked off their jobs at Hall's Safe and Lock Company to protest against the recent practice of laying off old hands and replacing them with cheaper new workers. Within several days, the blacksmiths were joined by 300 workers from the factory's other twenty-three departments. Cavanaugh ordered the men back to work. While most obeyed, a large number of anti-Cavanaugh men continued to stay out. Once again, Cavanaugh succeeded in ending the strike, but at the cost of splitting his organization and losing control over yet another industry.[92] KOL membership suffered a precipitate decline after the winter of widespread discontent. Membership in the District Assembly dropped from 13,250 in October 1887, to 7,866 in April 1888, to 4,502 in August 1888, and to only several hundred by the beginning of 1889. Cavanaugh resigned in September 1888.[93]

The bitter struggles over charting an economic course of action were also carried into the political sphere. At the county conventions in March 1888 and again at the national conventions in May (held in Cincinnati), Union and United Labor Party leaders met in a desperate final attempt to reach a compromise which would unite the two factions. The parties were able to agree upon a number of radical demands for governmental regulation of railroads and the nationalization of all natural monopolies and communication facilities. However, they remained unalterably divided over two issues: the Single Tax and the question of teaching technical education in public schools.

For Union and United Labor Party faithful, the conflicts over the Single Tax and technical education extended far beyond the realm of party politics. The debates over these two issues revealed two distinct visions of the relations of workers to the industrial world and their future in American society. The leaders of the Union Labor Party, drawn largely from the KOL, saw American workers forever standing on the edge of an industrializing world. It was a world in which the individual could still rely upon hard work and perseverance to preserve independence, foster mobility, and escape from the adverse effects of the industrializing system. Spokesmen of the United Labor Party, drawn from the city's socialists and more militant trade unionists, saw American workers as having crossed the threshold into a new industrial world. While *individuals* might still continue to rise in society, the vast majority of American workers — as well as their children and grandchildren — would remain a distinct and permanent wage-earning class. Consequently, it was necessary to abandon the older artisanal mentality and adopt a new outlook.

These different visions were most clearly articulated during the debates over the Single Tax. Like the eight-hour day, much of the initial appeal of the Single Tax lay in its apparent promise to bring vast benefits to all workers. Yet, as Cincinnati wage earners began to question the ultimate effects of the Single Tax upon their personal situations, earlier enthusiasm turned to dismay. Union men expressed a fear that its adoption would undermine the most basic of all working-class family goals: homeownership. The return of prosperity in 1886 and 1887 was accompanied not only by higher wages, but also by a sharp increase in the number of new mortgages taken out in Cincinnati: from 430 in 1885 to 776 in 1886, and 1,386 in 1887.[94] Although it is impossible to provide any precise analysis of new mortgage holders, it does seem likely that a good percentage came from the ranks of the working class. By 1890, 26.1 percent of all residents living in the areas beneath the city's hilltops — areas inhabited largely by the city's working-class population — either owned or were paying off mortgages on homes.[95]

Nevertheless, while homeownership continued to soar, so too did local property taxes. In September 1886, taxes were assessed at 2.02 percent of the property's market value — a rate exceeded only in Chicago. Within the next two years, property taxes rose by nearly 50 percent. This rapid increase in taxes was followed by an equally rapid decline in the issuance of new mortgages: from 1,386 in 1887 to 278 in 1888.[96]

The institution of the Single Tax, Union Labor men argued,

would make the prospects of homeownership even more remote. With all taxes abolished except land taxes, the city, they reasoned, would be forced to levy extraordinarily high property taxes. While such a measure might be a minor burden to wealthy capitalists, it would prove a disaster to the average working-class family. Workers, barely able to afford monthly mortgage payments as it was, would be forced to sell their homes if taxes rose substantially. Homeownership, then, would become a luxury available only to the rich. Moreover, the vagueness of the Single Tax made it unclear whether a family would be forced to leave its home if a manufacturer offered to pay the city a higher tax for the use of the land than the family could afford.[97]

The appeal to preserve middle-class values, which had united men in earlier months, now served to tear them apart. Union Labor Party leaders continued to proclaim homeownership as the "highest result of free institutions."[98] Clinging to the republican strain of ante-bellum free labor ideology, which equated property ownership with independence, Union delegates rejected the Single Tax precisely because it threatened the immediate and future independence, mobility, and middle-class aspirations of the average American worker. The Union leader S. F. Norton explained his party's unbending position on the matter as follows:

> The Union party will not admit the single tax plan of the United Labor Party. Yes, that is known as the Henry George idea. On everything else except that they agree with us. That single land tax idea antagonizes our theory that a homestead should be exempt from taxation. We believe that every man should have at least that much of the world's goods exempt from taxation, attachment, and execution. That idea is directly antagonistic to the George land tax scheme, which taxes everyone, and makes the taxes on the workingman's little cottage just the same as on the $100,000 palace of the millionaire across the street.[99]

Furthermore, argued another delegate, by creating enormous financial pressure to build upon undeveloped lands, the Single Tax would cause a vast reduction in the amount of fallow land available for future homesteading. In so doing, workingmen would have their safety valve cut off and would thereby be sentenced to a life of urban labor with little chance for real independence.[100]

The United Labor Party leaders turned away from these older notions of independence and individualism and insisted that the working class, not the individual worker, ought to be the focus of all party actions.

"We are working for the masses," declared the party's national spokesman, the Rev. Edward McGlynn, at the May convention, "and we want to do what is best for them."[101] The greatest need for the mass of workers lay less in guaranteeing access to homeownership than in providing adequate housing for the thousands of families forced to live in unhealthy and decrepit tenements. Only when workingmen finally awoke to the realities of the new industrial world would they come to see the wisdom of the Single Tax. Like their Union counterparts, United men remained adamant in their refusal to compromise on this point. As one delegate remarked: "I don't want to give up the idea of the single land-tax plank, and if we don't withdraw from that, I don't see how there can be a combination."[102]

The conflict over technical education in public schools also revolved around conflicting ideas concerning the ability of the worker to extricate himself from the detrimental effects of industrialization. The Union Labor Party county convention in March 1888 called for "compulsory eduction, free school books and enough school hours to accommodate our children." However, the delegates voiced strong opposition to turning public schools into "workshops by the introduction of technical and manual training."[103] Manual training in schools, argued Edward Davis, a former party chairman, was not intended to produce better citizens; it was intended to make scabs of American youth. "The tendency of trade schools," one workingman had explained several months earlier, "has been, and always will be, to reduce wages. Boys who half learn trades in three months, will work much cheaper than men who have spent years at them."[104]

The few United Labor Party men at the convention were quick to take the other side of the argument. "We have," responded William Ogden, "a nation of dissatisfied workers, and I favor the system of manual training." With apprenticeship breaking down, he stressed, technical education in the public schools was one of the few ways to free future generations of workers from their dependence upon manufacturers to teach them the "mysteries" of the trade. Ogden and the United Labor Party contingent were voted down 160 to 108.[105] Continuing the debate several days later at their own county convention, United Labor Party delegates announced their refusal to compromise with the Union Labor Party on this issue.[106]

As was the case with the land tax, the debate over technical education reflected growing concerns over recent developments within the economic sphere. In July 1886, eighteen of the city's leading manufacturers joined together to establish the Technical School of Cincinnati. It was founded as an alternative to public high schools and would "furnish practical instruction in the use of tools, freehand, mechanical and architectural drawing, combined with mathematics, science, and English branches of a high school course."[107] The ultimate goal of the school, noted its prospectus, was to train youth for the "occupations which many of the pupils must prepare to enter."[108] Yet clearly, such a school was not born solely out of altruism. Manufacturers, by training young people in a program of their own design, would be able to instill the kind of discipline that they desired and, more importantly, remove apprenticeship from the control of the unions.

This was the threat to which the United Labor Party adherents were responding. Implicit in the Union position was a fear that public education — the training ground for good and virtuous citizens — would be used to create a permanent working class. Yet, implicit in the United Labor Party's response was an understanding that schools were already being used to fashion a particular kind of working class. Only by placing technical education in the public sphere could workers hope to remove it from the influence of capitalists.[109]

Unable to resolve their differences, the two parties parted ways after the May conventions. Several months later, however, desperate for United Labor Party support, local Union Labor Party leaders agreed to include the Single Tax in their new platform. It was too late. Frustrated by internal divisions and repeated losses at the polls, many Union and United Labor Party leaders deserted in the summer and autumn of 1888 to the Democrats, Republicans, and Prohibitionists. "I for one," explained former United Labor Party leader C. S. Walker, "believe that the line of our advance still lies in acting with the Democratic Party. We have all seen how our most radical ideas have been warmly received in Democratic meetings during the last campaign, and how we were listened to as friends."[110]

Although the Union Labor Party ran a full ticket in November, it received less than 1 percent of the total vote. The attempts to redirect the development of industrial capitalism, to alter the role of the state, and to merge the role of worker and citizen had come to an end for a time.

Whatever their shortcomings, the Union and United Labor Parties left behind an important legacy. Party campaigns directed Cincinnati workers toward an assault upon the very foundations of industrial capitalism. By calling for the nationalization of railroads, telegraphs, and all natural monopolies, party members challenged the most sacred principle of capitalism: the sanctity of private property. Although ULP leaders steadfastly denied any intentions to nationalize industry, the radical implications of their programs were clear to most capitalists. If the state interfered with property rights in one sector of the economy, it ultimately could do so in other sectors. But what must have been most frightening to capitalists and their allies was that the proponents of this movement did not perceive themselves as socialists or communists, but as "middle-class" Americans.

The collapse of the Union and United Labor Parties did not signal the complete demise of working-class activisim. The ideas and organizations fostered between the fall of 1886 and the autumn of 1888 were soon redirected toward new political and economic campaigns. Although many party leaders either abandoned the political arena or moved into mainstream politics, a small number of labor party faithful sought to preserve the ULP's vision of a cooperative industrial commonwealth through participation in the National Party (1889) and the Populist Party (1891, 1894).[111]

While some continued the political crusade, many more Cincinnati workers, disillusioned by the failure of independent political action, turned to trade unionism — modeled along the lines advocated by the AFL — as the central vehicle for working-class action and protest. In June 1889, the leaders of the ACBT, CLU, AFL, Congress of Amalgamated Labor, and the remaining members of the KOL agreed to put aside their various disagreements and organize a new citywide labor association: the Central Labor Council (CLC). Incorporating many of the themes enunciated by the ULP, the CLC's "Preamble and Declaration of Principles" declared:

> There can be no harmony between capital and labor under the present industrial system, for the simple reason that capital in its modern character, consists very largely of rents, interests and profits wrongfully extorted from the producer, who possesses neither the land nor the means of production, and is therefore compelled to sell his arms, brains, or both, to the possessor of the land and means of production, and at such prices as an uncertain and speculative market may allow.[112]

Although the CLC was able to attract several thousand wage earners to its ranks, the question which plagued the organization was how to remedy this situation. With radicals, moderates, and conservatives persistently clinging to their own distinctive solutions, the CLC soon found itself split apart by the same ideological tensions and diverging visions which had shattered the Union and United Labor Parties.[113]

Looking back over the course of 100 years of working-class life in Cincinnati, we see that industrialization did not ultimately produce a single working-class identity or response to its varied problems. During the first three quarters of the nineteenth century, the uneven development of industrial capitalism often acted to divide Cincinnati's working class into a series of working classes — each pursuing its own special needs. However, by the late 1870s and 1880s, as the nature of ownership, production, and working conditions grew increasingly similar across all industries, wage earners of different skills, trades, and industries began forging new economic, social, and political alliances that often extended well beyond the workplace.

Class consciousness, however, was not the automatic result of a capitalistic system or changing modes of production. Despite the increased similarities and hardships of work life, Cincinnati wage earners of the 1870s, 1880s, and 1890s often found themselves divided by competing social, ethnocultural, and political loyalties — loyalties which, at times, superseded the new class bonds being forged in and outside the workplace. Even when workers were able to unite and pursue a course of common action, they were frequently plagued by a number of highly divisive questions: Should workers direct their struggles at obtaining short-term reforms or should they fight for long-term radical change? Should workers cooperate with mainstream parties or should they remain aloof from party politics? Was individual perseverance the best path to success and upward mobility or was collective class action needed to achieve any meaningful gains?

Despite the number of common ties which bound them, Cincinnati workers of the 1890s, as well as those of the early twentieth century, continued to remain deeply divided between those who spoke of successfully negotiating the edges of an industrializing world and those who saw the edge forever crossed.

APPENDIX

Cincinnati's Fourteen Leading Industries (1841–1890) Broken Down By Component Trades

These trade headings were the ones used in the census reports of Charles Cist, the Cincinnati Chamber of Commerce, and the United States Bureau of the Census. Trades were often subdivided and listed according to their product or products.

I. BOOTS AND SHOES
  boots and shoes — general
  lasts and separables
  findings
  uppers

II. BREWING
  beer
  malt

III. CARRIAGES AND WAGONS
  carriages
  wagons
  cars and omnibuses
  spokes
  wheelwrighting

IV. CLOTHING
  clothing— general
      — men's
      — women's
  tailors
  cloaks
  shirts and stockings
  stocking weavers
  caps
  hatters
  millinery and lace
  gloves and mittens
  corsets
  men's furnishings

V. CONSTRUCTION
   brickmasons and plasterers
   carpenters and builders
   painters and glaziers
   stair builders
   stonemasons
   stucco workers
   roofers
   plumbers
   gas fitters
   sash blind doors
   paper and paper hanging

VI. FURNITURE
   furniture — general
   coffins
   upholsterers
   bedsteads
   cabinets
   chairs
   desks
   billiard tables
   pianos
   mattress and spring beds

VII. HARDWARE
   grates
   hot air furnaces
   scales and balances
   agricultural implements
   safes, locks, and vaults
   edge tools
   brand, stamps, and chisels
   bolts, nuts and washers
   planes
   saws
   screw plates
   type foundries
   wire works
   cutlery and surgical tools
   stoves
   nails
   railroad chairs and spikes
   seal presses
   stencils and brands

   hardware
   files
   squares and bevels
   saws
   stone cutters' tools
   carpenters' tools
   tanners' tools
   forges
   refrigerators
   architectural iron works
   washing machines

VIII. IRON AND STEEL
   rolling mills
   railing and wrought iron
   iron, bar, and sheet
   perforated iron
   forged iron

IX. MACHINERY
   agricultural machinery
   fire engines and hydraulic
     apparatus
   engine shops
   machinery — general
   planing machinery
   boilers
   die sinking
   model and pattern makings
   printing presses
   bloc, spur, and pumps
   gasometers
   mills — portable
   sewing machines
   cotton and wool machines

X. MEAT PROCESSING
   slaughtering
   beef curing
   pork curing
   sausages
   tongues
   minced meat
   beef and pork packing

XI. METAL WORKING
   bell and brass foundries

copper, tin, and sheet iron
britannia ware
lead and lead pipes
coppersmithing
XII. PRESSING AND COOKING
chemicals
varnish
glue
lard and stearine
perfumes
patent medicines
ground spices and drugs
paints
starch
soap and candles
castor oil
linseed oil
vitriol oil
lubricating oil
white lead
tallow rendering

fertilizers
grease and tallow
lime
matches
blacking
explosives
flavoring extracts
baking and yeast powders
XIII. PRINTING AND
        PUBLISHING
copperplate printers
job printers
publishers
stereotypers
lithographers
book binding and blank books
newspapers
XIV. TOBACCO
tobacco — general
cigars
cigarettes

Abbreviations

BLS	*[Ohio] Bureau of Labor Statistics*
CHS	Cincinnati Historical Society
CHSB	*Cincinnati Historical Society Bulletin*
HCIR, HCC	Hamilton County Incorporation Records, Hamilton County Courthouse
HPSOB	*Historical and Philosophical Society of Ohio Bulletin*
OAHQ	*Ohio Archaeological and Historical Quarterly*
PLHCC	Public Library of Hamilton County and Cincinnati
UCL	University of Cincinnati Library

Notes

Introduction

1. A detailed account of strikes, labor violence, and class conflict during this era can be found in *Report of the Committee of the Senate Upon the Relations Between Labor and Capital, Testimony Taken By the Committee*, 5 vols. (Washington, 1885); Robert V. Bruce, *1877: Year of Violence* (Indianapolis: Bobbs-Merrill, 1959); Jeremy Brecher, *Strike* (San Francisco: Straight Arrow Books, 1972); P. K. Edwards, *Strikes in the United States 1881 – 1974* (New York: St. Martin's Press, 1981); Melvyn Dubofsky, *Industrialism and the American Worker* (Arlington Heights: AHM Publishing Company, 1975); Richard O. Boyer and Herbert M. Morais, *Labor's Untold Story* (New York: Cameron Associates, 1955).

2. See for example Alan Dawley, *Class and Community: The Industrial Revolution in Lynn* (Cambridge: Harvard University Press, 1976); Paul Faler, *Mechanics and Manufacturers in the Early Industrial Revolution: Lynn, Massachusetts, 1780 – 1860* (Albany: State University of New York Press, 1981); John T. Cumbler, *Working-Class Community in Industrial America: Work, Leisure, and Struggle in Two Industrial Cities, 1880 – 1930* (Westport: Greenwood Press, 1979); Carl Siracusa, *A Mechanical People: Perceptions of the Industrial Order in Massachusetts, 1815 – 1880* (Middletown: Wesleyan University Press, 1979); Paul E. Johnson, *A Shopkeeper's Millennium: Society and Revivals in Rochester, New York, 1815 – 1837* (New York: Hill and Wang, 1978); Daniel J. Walkowitz, *Worker City, Company Town: Iron and Cotton-Worker Protest in Troy and Cohoes, New York, 1855 – 1884* (Urbana: University of Illinois Press, 1978); Howard B. Rock, *Artisans of the New Republic: The Tradesmen of New York City in the Age of Jefferson* (New York: New York University Press, 1979); Susan E. Hirsch, *Roots of the American Working Class: The Industrialization of Crafts in Newark, 1800 – 1860* (Philadelphia: University of Pennsylvania Press, 1978); Bruce Laurie, *Working People of Philadelphia, 1800 – 1850* (Philadelphia: Temple University Press, 1980).

1. Forging a Republican World

1. C. E. Cabot, "The Carters in Early Ohio. A Glimpse of Cincinnati in Its First Quarter Century," *The New England Magazine* (May 1899) 20:347 – 48.

2. Ibid., 349 – 50.

3. Donna Largent Streifthau, "Cincinnati Cabinet- and Chairmakers, 1819 – 1830," Ph.D. diss., Ohio State University, 1970, pp. 110 – 13; George Valentine to Brother, July 18, 1819, Valentine Letters, CHS.

4. Daniel Drake, *Natural and Statistical View, or Picture of Cincinnati and the Miami County* (Cincinnati, 1815), pp. 133 – 40; James Hall, *The West: Its Commerce and Navigation* (Cincinnati, 1848), pp. 265 – 66; Thomas Senior Berry, *Western Prices Before 1861: A Study of the Cincinnati Market* (Cambridge, Mass., 1943), pp. 3 – 4.

5. Charles Cist, *Cincinnati in 1841: Its Early Annals and Future Prospects* (Cincinnati, 1841), pp. 13 – 14, 76 – 77.

6. Drake, *Natural and Statistical View*, p. 26.

7. Nearly 40 percent of the city's residents came from the mid-Atlantic region, 18 percent from New England, 12 percent from border states, and 6 percent from Ohio. Maurice Neufeld, "Three Aspects of the Economic Life of Cincinnati from 1815 to 1840," *OAHQ* (January 1935) 44:70 – 71; Walter Glazer, "General Population Characteristics," p. 2. The 1820 Cincinnati Data Bank Collection, CHS.

8. Quoted in Hugh McCulloch, *Men and Measures of Half a Century* (New York, 1888), p. 40; Henry A. and Mrs. Kate B. Ford, *History of Cincinnati, Ohio* (Cincinnati, 1881), pp. 146 – 70; Reverend John H. Lamott, *History of the Archdiocese of Cincinnati 1821 – 1921* (Cincinnati, 1921), pp. 30 – 39, 116; Ann Deborah Michael, "The Origins of the Jewish Community in Cincinnati 1817 – 1860," *CHSB* (Fall-Winter 1972) 30:155 – 58.

9. Daniel Drake, *Notes Concerning Cincinnati* (Cincinnati, 1810), p. 30.

10. *Williams' Cincinnati Directory and Business Advertiser, for 1849 – 1850* (Cincinnati, 1849), p. 10; Glazer, "Population Characteristics," p. 3.

11. Henry Melish, *Travels in the United States of America in the Years 1806 and 1807, and 1809, 1810, & 1811*, 2 vols. (Philadelphia, 1812), 2:127.

12. *Cincinnati Directory for 1819*, pp. 29, 33 – 34, 48 – 50, 101; Benjamin Drake and Edward Mansfield, *Cincinnati in 1826* (Cincinnati, 1827), pp. 64 – 66.

13. Henry B. Fearon, *A Narrative of a Journey of Five Thousand Miles Through the Eastern and Western States of America* (London, 1818), pp. 233 – 34.

14. Drake and Mansfield, *Cincinnati in 1826*, pp. 60 – 66. The growth of manufacturing before 1826 is described in *Cincinnati Directory for 1819*, pp. 48 – 51; Reverend Charles Frederic Goss, *Cincinnati, The Queen City*, 4 vols. (Cincinnati, 1912), 2:327 – 34; Drake, *Natural and Statistical View*, pp. 142 – 47; J. Leander Bishop, *A History of American Manufactures from 1608 to 1860*, 3 vols. (Philadelphia, 1864), 2:144, 217 – 18, 243.

15. James Matthew Morris, "The Road To Trade Unionism: Organized Labor in Cincinnati To 1893," Ph.D. diss., University of Cincinnati, 1969, pp. 6 – 11; Richard T. Farrell, "Cincinnati, 1800 – 1830: Economic Development Through Trade and Industry," *Ohio History* (Autumn 1968) 77:115, 126 – 27; Roger W. Clark, "Cincinnati Coppersmiths," *CHSB* (October 1965) 23:256 – 72; Henry W. Meyer, *Memoirs of Buggy Days* (Cincinnati, 1965), pp. 5 – 15; Cincinnati Typographical Union No. 3, *125th Anniversary Celebration Commemorating the Foundation of the Cincinnati Typographical Union No. 3* (Cincinnati, 1971), n.p.; Streifthau, "Cincinnati Cabinet- and Chairmakers," *passim*.

16. Cabot, "The Carters," p. 350.

17. Fearon, *Narrative*, p. 228.

18. William Anthony Rengering, "Early Germans in Cincinnati and Biographical Studies of Four Representative Men," M.A. thesis, University of Cincinnati, 1951, pp. 20 – 21.

19. Cincinnati *Western Spy*, September 7, 1811; Richard C. Wade, *The Urban Frontier. Pioneer Life in Early Pittsburgh, Cincinnati, Lexington, Louisville, and St. Louis* (Chicago, 1959), pp. 117 – 19, 124 – 28.

20. Quoted in Wade, *Urban Frontier*, p. 172.

21. *Independent Press and Freedom's Advocate,* January 16, 1823; also see George Valentine to Brother, October 3, 1819, Valentine Letters, CHS.

22. Drake and Mansfield, *Cincinnati in 1826,* p. 65; Fearon, *Narrative,* p. 228; I. T. Fray, *Ohio in Homespun and Calico* (Richmond: Garrett and Massie, 1942), pp. 80–83.

23. Virginia Raymond Cummins, compiler, *Hamilton County, Ohio. Court and Other Records,* 4 vols. (Cincinnati, 1966), 1:66–69; 2:111–12.

24. *Western Spy,* April 6, 1811; Drake and Mansfield, *Cincinnati in 1826,* pp. 60–66; Morris, "Road to Trade Unionism," pp. 7–8; Streifthau, "Cincinnati Cabinet- and Furniture Makers," p. 15; William T. Utter, *The Frontier State 1803–1825* (Columbus, 1942), pp. 248–49.

25. Cabot, "The Carters," p. 347.

26. Frances Trollope, *Domestic Manners of the Americans* (New York, 1949, orginally published in 1832), p. 116.

27. Melish, *Travels,* 2:128.

28. Statistics computed from information contained in Glazer, "General Population Characteristics," pp. 2–3, and Walter Glazer "A Percentage of Wealth Owned By Deciles of Cincinnati Property-Holders, 1799–1865," The 1820 Cincinnati Data Bank Collection, CHS.

29. Cabot, "The Carters," p. 349; Fearon, *Narrative,* pp. 227–30; Melish, *Travels,* 2:128; Neufeld, "Three Aspects of Economic Life," p. 77; Edgar Winfield Martin, *The Standard of Living in 1860: American Consumption on the Eve of the Civil War* (Chicago: University of Chicago Press, 1942), pp. 423, 429; Cincinnati *Gazette,* April 16, 1866.

30. Food prices are based upon eight basic items likely to be purchased by working-class families regardless of the economic climate: flour, wheat, potatoes, pork, sugar, coffee, cheese, and butter. The addition of five more working-class staples — beans, bacon, lard, rice, and soap — does not alter the previous results in any appreciable manner. The price of these thirteen items rose 58.4 percent between 1825 and 1860. Food prices were taken from the *17th Annual Report of the Bureau of Labor Statistics for the Year 1893* (Norwalk, Ohio, 1894), pp. 798–806. The prices of basic foods in Cincinnati during this period increased faster than the national average. U.S. Department of Commerce, *Historical Statistics of the United States: Colonial Times to 1970,* 2 vols. (Washington, 1975), 1:186, 201; Berry, *Western Prices,* pp. 91–135; 545–96.

31. Wage figures were drawn from the following sources: Cincinnati *Enquirer, Gazette, Nonpareil,* and *Times,* January 1830 through May 1, 1861; *Gazette,* April 19, 1866; *The Cincinnati Artisan,* April 1, 1878; Morris, "Road to Trade Unionism," pp. 6–108; Daniel Aaron, "Cincinnati, 1818–1838: A Study of Attitudes in the Urban West," Ph.D. diss., Harvard University, 1942, pp. 54, 81–84.

32. For a more detailed analysis of the standard of living question see Steven Joseph Ross, "Workers On the Edge: Work, Leisure, and Politics in Industrializing Cincinnati, 1830–1890," Ph.D. diss., Princeton University, 1980, pp. 276n–78n.

33. Economic development and the growth of class divisions in eastern cities are discussed in Bruce Laurie, *Working People of Philadelphia, 1800–1850* (Philadelphia, 1980); Susan E. Hirsh, *Roots of the American Working Class: The Industrialization of Crafts in Newark, 1800–1860* (Philadelphia, 1978); Diane Lindstrom, *Economic Growth in the Philadelphia Region, 1810–1850* (New York: Columbia University Press, 1978); Alan Dawley, *Class and Community: The Industrial Revolution in Lynn* (Cambridge, 1976).

34. Timothy Flint, *Recollections of the Last Ten Years in the Valley of the Mississippi,* edited by George R. Brooks (Carbondale and Edwardsville, Ill., 1968, originally published in 1826), p. 33.

35. *Cincinnati Directory for 1819,* pp. 51–53; Harvey Hall, *The Cincinnati Directory for 1825* (Cincinnati, 1825), p. 112; *History of Hamilton County* (Cincinnati, 1891), pp. 61–64; Utter, *Frontier State,* pp. 240–41.

36. Cabot, "The Carters," pp. 347–50; Wade, *Urban Frontier,* pp. 54–56; Farrell, "Cincinnati, 1800–1830," pp. 77, 111–14; Curtis P. Nettles, *The Emergence of a National Economy*

1775–1815 (New York: Holt, Rinehardt and Winston, 1962), pp. 304–8; Berry, *Western Prices,* pp. 14 – 15, 16 – 27; James Miller, "The Steamboat as a Factor in the Transportation and Industrialization in Cincinnati 1800 – 1850," M.A. thesis, University of Cincinnati, 1967, pp. 97–100.

37. Marilyn Melton Larew, "The Cincinnati Branch of the Second Bank of the United States and Its Effects On the Local Economy, 1817 – 1836," Ph.D. diss., University of Maryland, 1978, pp. 70 – 71, 95 – 97; Hall, *The West,* pp. 105 – 88; Joseph Nimmo Jr., *The Commercial, Industrial and Transportation Interests of the City of Cincinnati* (Washington, D.C., 1881), pp. 7, 11 – 12; Berry, *Western Prices,* pp. 4–5, 11 – 14, 22 – 25, 329. For a general description of trade and credit patterns between western and eastern cities see Lewis E. Atherton, *The Pioneer Merchant in Mid-America* (Columbia, Mo., 1939), pp. 49 – 76.

38. Berry, *Western Prices,* pp. 29 – 35, 42 – 57, 71 – 81; Wade, *Urban Frontier,* pp. 70 – 71.

39. Larew, "Second Bank of the United States," pp. 70–72, 95–97; Farrell, "Cincinnati 1800 – 1830," pp. 115 – 116; Miller, "Steamboat in Transportation and Industrialization," pp. 18 – 28.

40. Drake and Mansfield, *Cincinnati in 1826,* p. 77; Farrell, "Cincinnati 1800–1830," pp. 125 – 28; Streifthau, "Cincinnati Cabinet- and Furniture Makers," pp. 184, 196.

41. Nettles, *Emergence of a National Economy,* pp. 277–79; Berry, *Western Prices,* pp. 160 – 63.

42. Drake and Mansfield, *Cincinnati in 1826,* pp. 67 – 68, 82; Cabot, "The Carters," p. 350; Farrell, "Cincinnati 1800 – 1830," p. 113; Berry, *Western Prices,* pp. 10 – 11.

43. Drake and Mansfield, *Cincinnati in 1826,* pp. 82 – 83.

44. Larew, "Second Bank of the United States," pp. 70–72, 95; Berry, *Western Prices,* pp. 75 – 78, 328 – 29. Records for the Cincinnati branch of the Bank of the United States indicate that 80 percent of the money loaned in 1817 went to merchants while only 1 percent went to artisans and manufacturers. Larew, "Second Bank of the United States." p. 280.

45. Quoted in Drew McCoy, *The Elusive Republic. Political Economy in Jeffersonian America* (Chapel Hill: University of North Carolina Press, 1980), p. 14.

46. Flint, *Recollections,* p. 277.

47. Rowland Berthoff, "Independence and Attachment, Virtue and Interest: From Republican Citizen to Free Enterpriser, 1787 – 1837," in Richard Bushman et al., *Uprooted Americans: Essays to Honor Oscar Handlin* (Boston: Little, Brown, 1979), p. 114.

48. Quoted in Farrell, "Cincinnati 1800 – 1830," p. 118.

49. Richard T. Farrell, "Cincinnati in the Early Jacksonian Era, 1816 – 1834: An Economic and Political Study," Ph.D. diss., Indiana University, 1967, pp. 76 – 86; Berry, *Western Prices,* pp. 173–77; Larew, "The Second Bank of the United States," pp. 76–77, 280–81; Maurice Neufeld, "The Queen City of the West: Cincinnati From 1815 to 1840," M.A. thesis, University of Wisconsin, 1932, pp. 11 – 15, 90 – 92. Between 1819 and 1820 the total percentage of BUS loans to artisans and manufacturers rose from 5.9 percent to 16.0 percent. Larew, "Second Bank of the United States," p. 280.

50. *Liberty Hall and Commercial Gazette,* August 17, 1819, September 22, 29, 1817; Farrell, "Cincinnati 1800 – 1830," pp. 115 – 16; *Cincinnati Directory for 1849-1850,* pp. 12 – 13; Utter, *Frontier State,* p. 261; Wade, *Urban Frontier,* pp. 56 – 58.

51. Larew. "Second Bank of the United States," pp. 146–239; Wade, *Urban Frontier,* pp. 58 – 59; Miller, "Steamboat in Transportation and Industrialization," pp. 50 – 52.

52. Drake and Mansfield, *Cincinnati in 1826,* pp. 59, 72–75; Cist, *Cincinnati in 1841,* p. 253.

53. Miller, "Steamboat in Transportation and Industrialization," p. 28.

54. Drake and Mansfield, *Cincinnati in 1826,* pp. 64–66.

55. Workforce statistics were computed from data in Ibid., pp. 60 – 66. For the

relationship between artisans and steamboat production see William F. Gephardt, *Transportation and Industrial Development of the Middle West* (New York, 1909), pp. 69–81; Miller, "Steamboat in Transportation and Industrialization," pp. 31–54.

56. *Liberty Hall*, June 28, 1820; *Cincinnati Pioneer* (April 1874) 3:13–16; Larew, "Second Bank of the United States," pp. 197–203, 285; Farrell, "Cincinnati 1800–1830," pp. 118–19; Wade, *Urban Frontier*, pp. 162–75.

57. *Cincinnati Directory for 1819*, pp. 44; Morris, "Road to Trade Unionism," pp. 6–21; Aaron, "Cincinnati 1818–1838," pp. 81–84, 91–96; Wade, *Urban Frontier*, pp. 212–17.

58. Streifthau, "Cincinnati Cabinet- and Chairmakers," pp. 67, 99–105, 113–14.

59. Ibid., pp. 130–33; also see Clark, "Cincinnati Coppersmiths," pp. 258–64.

60. The elite 10 percent increased their holdings to 54.2 percent of the assessed wealth in 1817, 55.1 percent in 1838, and 67.1 percent in 1860, while the wealth of the bottom 50 percent steadily declined to 8.8 percent in 1817, 8.1 percent in 1838, and 2.4 percent in 1860. Statistics were compiled from information in Glazer, "Percentage of Wealth," The 1820 Cincinnati Data Bank, CHS.

61. Glazer, "Cincinnati in 1840," pp. 120–22, 233–37. For a further analysis of wealth and property holdings during this era see Irwin F. Flack, "Who Governed Cincinnati? A Comparative Analysis of Government and Social Structure in a Nineteenth Century River City: 1819–1860," Ph.D. diss., University of Pittsburgh, 1978, pp. 67–81.

62. Alexis de Tocqueville, *Journey to America*, translated by George Lawrence (New Haven, 1960), p. 217.

63. Drake, *Natural and Statistical View*, pp. 61–62; Department of the Interior, *Report On the Social Statistics of Cities*, 2 vols. (Washington, D.C., 1887), 2:358–60.

64. The extensive collections of maps and city directories at the CHS were particularly helpful in shaping my understanding of early spatial development. Other sources which were especially useful are Drake, *Natural and Statistical View*, pp. 59–61, 349–50; Reverend Charles Frederic Goss, *Cincinnati the Queen City 1788–1912*, 4 vols. (Cincinnati, 1912), 1:41–70, 86–89, 91–174; Fords, *History of Cincinnati*, pp. 42–81; Glazer, "Cincinnati in 1840," pp. 48–52, 132–37, 225–27.

65. *The Cincinnati Pioneer* (April 1874) 3.20; George Puchta, "Autobiography of George Puchta," p. 1, Special Collections, PLHCC; Streifthau, "Cincinnati Cabinet- and Chairmakers," pp. 45–183, 265–74.

66. Quoted in Charles Theodore Greve, *Centennial History of Cincinnati*, 2 vols. (Chicago, 1904), 1:465.

67. Drake and Mansfield, *Cincinnati in 1826*, pp. 30, 44–46.

68. Trollope, *Domestic Manners*, p. 43.

69. Tocqueville, *Journey to America*, pp. 262, 264.

70. The Cincinnati Fire Department Records, 1819–1950, housed at the CHS, contain a wealth of information concerning the early workings of volunteer fire companies and their relationship to the economic, social, and political life of the city. Further information concerning the members and workings of these early companies can be found in Kathleen J. Kiefer, "Flying Sparks and Hooves: A Prologue," *CHSB* (Summer 1970) 28:83–102; Kathleen J. Kiefer, "A History of the Cincinnati Fire Department in the Nineteenth Century," M.A. thesis, University of Cincinnati, 1967, pp. 14–103; Clyde W. Park, *The Cincinnati Equitable Insurance Company: Oldest Fire Insurance Company West of the Alleghenies* (Cincinnati, 1954), pp. 4–106.

71. Donn Piatt, *Some Historical Notes Concerning the Cincinnati Fire Department* (Cincinnati, n.d.), p. 1.

72. Mayors Mark Taylor (1851–1853), David Snellbaker (1853–1855)—both former union leaders—and Nicholas Thomas (1857–1859) all served as fire company officers during the 1830s. Similarly, political leaders such as David Disney, Thomas Spooner, Joseph Ross, Jacob

Piatt, and scores of others, devoted several years of service to the volunteer companies. "Minute Books," Cincinnati Fire Department Records, CHS; Fireman's Protective Association, *Cincinnati Fire Department,* pp. 3–103; Goss, *Cincinnati the Queen City,* 1:181–82.

73. Goss, *Cincinnati the Queen City,* 1:95; Cist, *Cincinnati in 1841,* pp. 155–94; Blanche M. G. Linden, "Inns to Hotels in Cincinnati," *CHSB* (Summer 1981) 39:127-52; Nancy Ray Siegel, "A Matter of Public Welfare: The Temperance Movement in Ante-Bellum Cincinnati," M.A. thesis, University of Cincinnati, 1971, pp. 18–19.

74. Flint, *Recollections,* pp. 37, 296n; Drake and Mansfield, *Cincinnati in 1826,* pp. 36–37.

75. *The Cincinnati Directory for the Year 1829* (Cincinnati, 1829), pp. 487–88; Henry Howe, *Historical Collections of Ohio,* 3 vols. (Columbus, 1891), 2:29–32; Neufeld, "Three Aspects of Economic Life," p. 75; Wade, *Urban Frontier,* pp. 79–83.

76. Neufeld, "Queen City of the West," pp. 103–4; Farrell, "Cincinnati in the Early Jacksonian Era," pp. 177–78.

77. Neufeld, "Queen City of the West," p. 113; Wade, *Urban Frontier,* pp. 78–79. For more in-depth analyses of who ruled Cincinnati see Flack, "Who Governed Cincinnati?" pp. 168–96, 202–34; Farrell, "Cincinnati in the Early Jacksonian Era," pp. 176–87.

78. Quoted in Coggeshall, "History of the Press," p. 10, CHS.

79. Quoted in Andrew H. Hickenlooper, "Personal Reminiscences," Andrew Hickenlooper Papers, CHS, 2:288.

80. Trollope, *Domestic Manners,* 1:73.

81. For descriptions of July 4th rituals between 1788 and 1841 — for workers as well as the community at large — see *Cincinnati Pioneer* (July 1874–July 1875) 4-5:5-17; Cist, *Cincinnati in 1841,* pp. 159–60, 184; Streifthau, "Cincinnati Cabinet- and Chairmakers," pp. 252–53; Fords, *History of Cincinnati,* p. 222.

82. John Broadfoot Smith, "Oration, July 5, 1819," quoted in Streifthau, "Cincinnati Cabinet- and Chairmakers," p. 252.

83. Drake and Mansfield, *Cincinnati in 1826,* pp. 88–89, 22.

2. Cracks in the Republic

1. C. F. Arfwedson, *United States and Canada in 1832, 1833, and 1834,* 2 vols. (London, 1834), 2:126.

2. *Liberty Hall,* March 23, 1830; Maurice F. Neufeld, "Three Aspects of the Economic Life of Cincinnati From 1815 to 1840," *OAHQ* (January 1935) 44:68–73.

3. Donna Largent Streifthau, "Cincinnati Cabinet- and Chairmakers, 1819–1830," Ph.D. diss., Ohio State University 1970, pp. 82–85, 181–82, 280.

4. Augustus Roundy to Nehemiah Roundy, June 3, 1838, Letters of Augustus Roundy, CHS.

5. Ibid., May 7, 1845; January 12, 1839.

6. Ibid., May 7, 1845.

7. The growth and impact of internal improvements upon Ohio's economy are best detailed in Henry N. Scheiber, *Ohio Canal Era: A Case Study of Government and the Economy, 1820–1861* (Athens, Ohio, 1969), and Thomas Senior Berry, *Western Prices Before 1861: A Study of the Cincinnati Market* (Cambridge, 1943).

8. Scheiber, *Ohio Canal Era,* pp. 106–7, 212–46; Francis P. Weisenburger, *The Passing of the Frontier, 1825–1850* (Columbus, 1941), pp. 91–92, 106–15.

9. Benjamin Drake and Edward Mansfield, *Cincinnati in 1826* (Cincinnati, 1827), p. 22; Scheiber, *Ohio Canal Era*, p. 90; Michel Chevalier, *Society, Manners, and Politics in the United States*, ed. John W. Ward (Garden City, New York, 1961, originally published in 1839), p. 204

10. Scheiber, *Ohio Canal Era*, pp. 9–11, 187–225; Berry, *Western Prices, passim*.

11. Scheiber, *Ohio Canal Era*, pp. 205, 232; Charles Cist, *Sketches and Statistics of Cincinnati in 1859* (Cincinnati, 1859), p. 346.

12. Weisenburger, *Passing of the Frontier*, pp. 63–64, 78–84; Scheiber, *Ohio Canal Era*, pp. 198–223; Berry, *Western Prices*, pp. 247–85.

13. Scheiber, *Ohio Canal Era*, pp. 48, 70–74, 124–26, 190; Weisenburger, *Passing of the Frontier*, pp. 94–96.

14. Scheiber, *Ohio Canal Era*, pp. 371–79; Berry, *Western Prices*, pp. 410–24, 438–41; Neufeld, "Economic Life 1815 to 1840," p. 77.

15. Drake and Mansfield, *Cincinnati in 1826*, p. 71.

16. Ibid., pp. 76–79; Richard T. Farrell, "Cincinnati, 1800–1830: Economic Development Through Trade and Industry," *Ohio History* (Autumn 1968) 77:120–23; Berry, *Western Prices*, pp. 318–54.

17. Charles Cist, *Cincinnati in 1841: Its Early Annals and Future Prospects* (Cincinnati, 1841), p. 49; Farrell, "Cincinnati, 1800–1830," pp. 114–15; Carl John Abbott, "The Divergent Development of Cincinnati, Indianapolis, Chicago, and Galena, 1840–1860: Economic Thought and Economic Growth," Ph.D. diss., University of Chicago, 1971, p. 66.

18. Cist, *Cincinnati in 1841*, p. 49; Richard Wade, *The Urban Frontier* (Cambridge, 1959), p. 308.

19. "Cincinnati Chamber of Commerce," October 14, 1839, I, n.p., Cincinnati Chamber of Commerce Collection, CHS; also see Wade, *Urban Frontier*, p. 205; Berry, *Western Prices*, pp. 15–16; Irwin Flack, "Who Governed Cincinnati? A Comparative Analysis of Government and Social Structure in a Nineteenth-Century River City: 1819–1860," Ph.D. diss., University of Pittsburgh, 1978, pp. 53–57.

20. Harvey Hall, *The Cincinnati Directory for 1825* (Cincinnati, 1825), p. 111; Cist, *Cincinnati in 1841*, p. 43.

21. Cist, *Cincinnati in 1841*, p. 236.

22. Edward Mansfield, *Annual Report of the Commissioner of Statistics to the General Assembly of Ohio, for the Year 1857* (Columbus, 1858), p. 25.

23. Cist, *Cincinnati in 1841*, pp. 54–55.

24. Ibid., pp. 54–55, 247–52. The development and expansion of the city's "new" industries is discussed in Robert Moore, *Autobiographical Outlines of a Long Life* (Cincinnati, 1887), pp. 45–61; George A. Wing, "The Development of an Industrial Base for the Cincinnati Machine-Tool Industry, 1817–1860," *CHSB* (April 1965) 23:88–103; James R. Miller, "The Steamboat as a Factor in Transportation and Industrialization in Cincinnati, 1800–1860," M.A. thesis, University of Cincinnati, 1967, pp. 55–76; Isaac Lippincott, *A History of Manufactures in the Ohio Valley to the Year 1860* (Chicago, 1914), pp. 95–103.

25. Charles Cist, *Sketches and Statistics of Cincinnati in 1851* (Cincinnati, 1851), pp. 278–88; Berry, *Western Prices*, pp. 215–46.

26. Moore, *Autobiography*, pp. 33, 35, 36.

27. Quote from interview with E. W. Vanduzen, in *110th Anniversary of the Commercial Tribune* (Cincinnati, 1904), n.p.; Moore, *Autobiography*, pp. 35–68; J. Leander Bishop, *A History of American Manufactures From 1608 to 1860*, 3 vols. (Philadelphia, 1864), 2:310, 395.

28. Drake and Mansfield, *Cincinnati in 1826*, p. 64; Cist, *Cincinnati in 1841*, p. 54.

29. Streifthau, "Cabinet and Chairmakers," pp. 213, 222, 206; also see Donna L. Streifthau, "Fancy Chairs and Finials: Cincinnati Furniture Industry, 1819–1830," *CHSB* (Fall-

Winter 1971) 29:172 – 97; Jane E. Sikes, *The Furniture Makers of Cincinnati 1790 to 1849* (Cincinnati, 1976).

30. Timothy Whiting, "Letter Copy Book — Shoe Store, 1839 – 1846," Timothy Whiting Collection, CHS.

31. Quote from Augustus Roundy to Nehemiah Roundy, June 3, 1838, Roundy Letters, CHS; also see Henry Castles, "Account Book, 1829 – 1844," Henry Castles Collection, CHS; Whiting, "Letter Copy Book," CHS; Robert W. Lovett, "Augustus Roundy's Cincinnati Sojourn, 1838 – 1845," *HPSOB* (Fall-Winter 1972) 30:155 – 82.

32. Cist, *Cincinnati in 1841*, p. 57; Lippincott, *History of Manufactures*, pp. 90 – 92, 168. For a more detailed description of the subcontracting and putting-out systems see Christine Stansell, "The Origins of the Sweatshop: Women and Early Industrialization in New York City," in Michael H. Frisch and Daniel J. Walkowitz, eds., *Working Class America. Essays on Labor, Community, and American Society* (Urbana: University of Illinois Press, 1983), pp. 78 – 103.

33. Walter Sutton, "Cincinnati as a Frontier Publishing and Book Trade Center 1796 – 1830," *OAHQ* (April 1947) 56:119 – 40; William T. Coggeshall, "How the Parlor Magazine is Printed: With Some Account of the Art," *Parlor Magazine* (January 1854) 2:5 – 14, 68 – 78; Cist, *Cincinnati in 1851*, pp. 232 – 34.

34. Quotation from W. T. Coggeshall, "History of the Press. The Cincinnati Press and Its Conditions 1793 – 1850," (scrapbook of articles published by the author in the 1850s), p. 7, CHS; Coggeshall, "Parlor Magazine," pp. 10 – 12, 68 – 78; Cincinnati Typographical Union No. 3, *125th Anniversary . . . of the Cincinnati Typographical Union No. 3* (Cincinnati, 1971), n.p.

35. CTU No. 3, *125th Anniversary*; Streifthau, "Fancy Chairs and Finials," pp. 171 – 79; John R. Commons, David J. Saposs, Helen L. Sumner, E. B. Mittelman, H. E. Hoagland, John B. Andrews, and Selig Perlman, *History of Labour in the United States*, 4 vols. (New York: Augustus M. Kelley, 1966, originally published in 1918), 1:352 – 53; James Matthew Morris, "The Road to Trade Unionism: Organized Labor in Cincinnati to 1893," Ph.D. diss., University of Cincinnati, 1969, pp. 21 – 53; *People's Paper*, September 22, 1843; *Enquirer*, Feb. 22, 1844.

Price books issued by journeymen and masters during this period are a particularly valuable source for tracing the changing price structures, methods of payment, and grievances of the trade. See *The Cincinnati Cabinet-Makers' Book of Prices, for Manufacturing Cabinet Ware* (Cincinnati, 1830); *The Book of Prices of the United Society of Journeymen Cabinet Makers for the Manufacture of Cabinet Ware* (Cincinnati, 1836); *The Book of Prices of the House Carpenters and Joiners of the City of Cincinnati. Adopted Monday, January 4, 1819* (Cincinnati, 1835); *The Book of Prices of the House Carpenters and Joiners of the City of Cincinnati. . . . Carefully Revised and Enlarged, February 1844 by Louis H. Shally* (Cincinnati, 1844).

36. Streifthau, "Cabinet and Chairmakers," pp. 42 – 171, 290 – 91; Sikes, *Furniture Makers*, passim; CTU No. 3, *125th Anniversary*; *Weekly Atlas*, December 7, 1854; Morris, "Road to Trade Unionism," pp. 28 – 31, 51.

37. Drake and Mansfield, *Cincinnati in 1826*, pp. 65 – 66; Cist, *Cincinnati in 1841*, pp. 54, 56.

38. Coggeshall, "Parlor Magazine," p. 70; Cist, *Cincinnati in 1851*, pp. 232 – 34.

39. *Enquirer*, February 22, 1844; for changing trade conditions see *Liberty Hall*, August 9, 1825; *Cincinnati Advertiser and Ohio Phoenix*, June 22, 1831; *The Book of Prices of the House Carpenters and Joiners . . . Revised 1844*.

40. (St. Louis) *Commercial Bulletin and Monthly Literary Register*, December 18, 1835, quoted in Commons et al., *History of Labour*, 1:353; CTU No. 3, *125th Anniversary*.

3. The Decline of Commonwealth

1. David Henry Shaffer, *The Cincinnati, Covington, Newport, and Fulton Directory for 1840* (Cincinnati, 1839), p. 478.

2. One study of of social mobility among 167 artisans, manufacturers, merchants, and professionals who remained in Cincinnati between 1820 and 1840 found that 29 percent experienced some upward mobility, 58 percent remained at the same level, and 13 percent suffered a decline in fortune. These statistics tend to overestimate the extent of mobility since they do not take into account the large numbers of dissatisfied and unsuccessful men who left Cincinnati. Walter Stix Glazer, "Cincinnati in 1840: A Community Profile," Ph.D. diss., University of Michigan, 1968, pp. 246 – 48.

3. *Constitution and By-Laws of the General Trades' Union, of the City of Cincinnati and Vicinity* (Cincinnati, 1836), p. 3.

4. Walter Glazer, "A Percentage of Wealth Owned By Deciles of Cincinnati Property-Holders, 1799 – 1865," The 1820 Cincinnati Data Bank, CHS.

5. See chapter 1, nn. 30 – 32. Additional information on wages and living expenses between 1830 and 1844 was drawn from the *Enquirer, People's Paper, Elevator*, and William Thomson, *A Tradesman's Travels, in the United States and Canada, in the Years 1840, 41, 42* (Edinburgh, 1842), p. 136.

6. James Matthew Morris, "The Road to Trade Unionism: Organized Labor in Cincinnati to 1893," Ph.D. diss., University of Cincinnati, 1969, pp. 14 – 19; William Baillie, *Josiah Warren: The First American Anarchist* (Boston: Small, Maynard, and Co., 1906), pp. 9 – 24.

7. *Cincinnati Chronicle and Literary Gazette*, October 23, 1830, quoted in Richard Wade, *The Urban Frontier* (Cambridge, 1959), p. 213.

8. Morris, "Road to Trade Unionism," p. 26 – 37.

9. The expansion of commercial and industrial capitalism and the rise of working-class protest in eastern cities during the late eighteenth and early nineteenth centuries are analyzed in Eric Foner, *Tom Paine and Revolutionary America* (New York: Oxford University Press, 1976); Anthony F. C. Wallace, *Rockdale. The Growth of an American Village in the Early Industrial Revolution* (New York: W. W. Norton, 1972), Gary Lawson Browne, *Baltimore in the Nation 1789 – 1861* (Chapel Hill: University of North Carolina Press, 1980); and the sources cited in the Introduction, n. 2.

10. *Gazette*, January 30, 1841; January 22, 27, 1842; Francis P. Weisenburger, *Passing of the Frontier 1825 – 1850* (Columbus, 1941), p. 87.

11. *Cincinnati Advertiser and Ohio Phoenix*, January 13, 1841.

12. Ibid., November 5, 1834.

13. *Enquirer*, November 3, 1843.

14. *Cincinnati Advertiser and Ohio Phoenix*, June 22, 1831; *Working Man's Friend*, July 16, 1836.

15. Commons, et al., *History of Labour in the United States* (New York, 1966), 1:352 – 53.

16. Cincinnati Typographical Union No. 3, *125th Anniversary . . . of the Cincinnati Typographical Union No. 3* (Cincinnati, 1971), n.p.; Morris, "Road to Trade Unionism," pp. 28 – 32.

17. *The Book of Prices of the United Society of Journeymen Cabinet Makers of Cincinnati for the Manufacture of Cabinet Ware* (Cincinnati, 1836), n.p.

18. *Cincinnati Advertiser and Ohio Phoenix*, June 22, 1831.

19. Vanduzen interview, *110th Anniversary of the Commercial Tribune* (Cincinnati, 1904), n.p.

20. *Liberty Hall*, August 9, 1825.

21. *Constitution of the GTU*, pp. 3 – 4, 9; Morris, "Road to Trade Unionism," pp. 33 – 37.

22. Augustus Roundy to Nehemiah Roundy, February 3, 1840, Letters of Augustus Roundy, CHS.

23. *Gazette*, May 20, 1840.

24. Frederick Gerstaecker, *The Wanderings and Fortunes of Some German Emigrants*, trans. by David Black (Cincinnati, 1856), p. 103; Augustus Roundy to Nehemiah Roundy, May 7, 1845, Roundy Letters, CHS.

25. *Liberty Hall*, May 4, 1829.

26. Vanduzen interview, *110th Anniversary Commercial Tribune*.

27. Frederick Gustorf, *The Uncorrupted Heart. Journal and Letters of Frederick Julius Gustorf 1800 – 1845*, edited and translated by Fred and Gisela Gustorf (Columbia, Missouri, 1969), p. 25.

28. Peter Schmitt, "Autobiography of a German Blacksmith," pp. 7 – 8, CHS. Further information on the changing nature of family economies can be found in George Henshaw, "Memoirs of George Henshaw," pp. 7 – 9, George Henshaw Collection, CHS; Gersteacker, *Wanderings*, p. 103; Pauline Rehfuss Esselborn, *Recollections of Pauline Rehfuss Esselborn, 1844 – 1925* (Private Printing, n.d.), pp. 4 – 5; Roundy Letters, CHS.

29. Joel Brown to Anson G. Willey, February 26, 1843, "Minute Book of the Franklin Reading Room and Library and Mutual Instruction Institute," Special Collections, UCL.

30. *People's Paper*, January 29, 1845; *Gazette*, March 1, 1840; *Enquirer*, February 6, March 9, 10, 16, 1843.

31. David Snellbaker, 1836, quoted in Morris, "Road to Trade Unionism," p. 34; Augustus Roundy to Nehemiah Roundy, June 3, 1838, Roundy Letters, CHS; *Elevator*, February 26, 1842.

32. *Gazette*, April 27, 1840.

33. *Enquirer*, September 22, 1841.

34. *Elevator*, December 18, 1841, April 9, 1842; *Enquirer*, September 22, 1841.

35. Thomson, *Tradesman's Travels*, p. 166.

36. *Ohio Statesman*, January 13, 1842. Further descriptions of the riots can be found in the *Gazette, Enquirer, and Daily Republican*, January 11 – 14, 1842.

37. *Gazette*, March 17, 1842; *Elevator*, February 26, 1842.

38. Of the sixteen candidates whose place of birth could be determined, twelve were native-born and four foreign-born.

39. *Gazette*, April 5, 1842.

40. Party leaders moved into the Democratic and Whig organizations in relatively equal proportion. During the spring elections of 1843 and 1844, David Snellbaker, Mark Taylor, Edward Inskip, J. Y. Armstrong, William Conn, and David Griffey all ran for office on the Democratic ticket; D. E. A. Strong, N. Speer, George Runyan, T. McClean, and John Young ran as Whigs. *Enquirer*, October 3, 1842; *Gazette*, April 8, 1843; *People's Paper*, April 4, 1844; April 9, 1845.

41. *Enquirer*, October 17, 1843.

42. Ibid., October 4, 1843.

43. Hugh McCulloch, *Men and Measures of Half a Century* (New York, 1888), p. 57.

44. *Enquirer*, October 4, 1843.

45. Ibid., September 22, 1843.

46. For the uses of republican rituals and symbols see Ibid., October 10, 1843; April 1, June 28, 1845; *Enquirer*, October 20, November 2, 1843; March 5, August 6, September 25, 1844; *Gazette*, July 3, 1845.

47. J. G. A. Pocock, *The Machiavellian Moment: Florentine Political Thought and the*

Atlantic Republican Tradition (Princeton: Princeton University Press, 1975); J. G. A. Pocock, "Virtue and Commerce in the Eighteenth Century," *Journal of Interdisciplinary History* (Summer 1972) 3:119–34; Caroline Robbins, *The Eighteenth-Century Commonwealthman: Studies in the Transmission, Development, and Circumstance of English Liberal Thought from the Restoration of Charles II until the War with the Thirteen Colonies* (Cambridge: Harvard University Press, 1959); Joyce Appleby, *Economic Thought and Ideology in Seventeenth-Century England* (Princeton: Princeton University Press, 1978).

48. Rowland Berthoff, "Independence and Attachment, Virtue and Interest: From Republican Citizen to Free Enterpriser, 1787–1837," in Richard Bushman, et al., eds., *Uprooted Americans. Essays to Honor Oscar Handlin* (Boston, 1979), pp. 106–7.

For the development of republican ideology at the national and local levels see Gordon Wood, *The Creation of the American Republic, 1776 – 1787* (Chapel Hill: University of North Carolina Press, 1969); Drew McCoy, *The Elusive Republic. Political Economy in Jeffersonian America* (Chapel Hill, 1980); Robert E. Shallope, *John Taylor of Caroline: Pastoral Republican* (Columbia: University of South Carolina Press, 1980); Daniel Walker Howe, *The Political Culture of the American Whigs* (Chicago: University of Chicago Press, 1959); Foner, *Tom Paine;* Laurie, *Working People of Philadelphia;* Dawley, *Class and Community;* Faler, *Mechanics and Manufacturers.*

49. Berthoff, "Independence and Attachment," pp. 117–18.

50. James Underwood, *An Address by James Underwood and the Proceedings of the Festival Held in the City of Cincinnati, January 29, 1840* (Cincinnati, 1840), p. 8.

51. *Gazette*, November 4, 1840; Benjamin P. Aydelott, *"The Intelligent Mechanic." Introductory Address Delivered and Published By Request of an Association of Mechanics* (Cincinnati, 1839), p. 29. On the redefinition of the producing classes also see *Enquirer*, September 22, 1841; *Daily Republican*, March 15, 1842.

52. *Gazette*, November 4, 1840.

53. James Hall, *The West: Its Commerce and Navigation* (Cincinnati, 1848), p. 313.

54. *Gazette*, November 4, 1850.

55. Timothy Walker, *Annual Discourse Delivered at the Ohio Historical and Philosophical Society at Columbus on the 23rd of December 1837* (Cincinnati, 1838), p. 16

56. *Western Literary Journal and Monthly Review* (January 1845) 1 180

57. *Elevator*, February 26, 1842.

58. Ibid., December 25, 1841.

59. Quoted in Morris, "Road to Trade Unionism," p. 34.

60. *Elevator*, March 5, 1842; *People's Paper*, August 21, 1843.

61. *Elevator*, December 18, 1841.

62. Ibid., November 13, 1841.

63. *Constitution of the GTU*, p. 3.

64. *Nonpareil*, April 29, 1852.

65. *Elevator*, January 15, 1842.

66. *Enquirer*, September 22, 1841.

67. Quoted in Daniel Aaron, "Cincinnati, 1818–1838: A Study of Attitudes in the Urban West," Ph.D. diss., Harvard University, 1942, pp. 95–96; *People's Paper*, January 22, 1844.

68. *Elevator*, December 25,1841.

4. The New City

1. Bruce Laurie, Theodore Hershberg, George Alter, "Immigrants and Industry: The Philadelphia Experience," in Theodore Hershberg, ed., *Philadelphia: Work, Space, Family, and Group Experience in the Nineteenth Century* (New York: Oxford University Press, 1981), p. 114.

2. Quoted in J. Leander Bishop, *A History of American Manufactures From 1608 to 1860*, 3 vols. (Philadelphia, 1868), 3: 463. Biographical information on Greenwood's life and career was drawn from M. Joblin, *Cincinnati Past and Present: Or, Its Industrial History, As Exhibited in the Life-Labors of Its Leading Men* (Cincinnati, 1872), pp. 101 – 5; Allen Johnson and Dumas Malone, eds., *Dictionary of American Biography*, 10 vols. (New York: C. Scribner's Sons, 1960), 4:592 – 93; Charles Cist, *Sketches and Statistics of Cincinnati in 1851* (Cincinnati, 1851), pp. 195 – 96; Charles Cist, *Sketches and Statistics of Cincinnati in 1859* (Cincinnati, 1859), pp. 278 – 82.

3. Ele Bowen, *Rambles in the Path of a Steam Horse* (Philadelphia, 1855), p. 387.

4. As late as 1890, immigrants and their native-born children made up 69.0 percent of the city's population. Census Office, *Compendium of the Eleventh Census: 1890* (Washington, 1897), pp. 720 – 21.

5. These statistics were compiled from data contained in Glazer, "Cincinnati in 1840," pp. 261 – 73; Carl John Abbott, "The Divergent Development of Cincinnati, Indianapolis, Chicago, and Galena, 1840 – 1860: Economic Thought and Economic Growth," Ph.D. diss., University of Chicago, 1971, pp. 94, 464 – 67; Irwin F. Flack, "Who Governed Cincinnati? A Comparative Analysis of Government and Social Structure in a Nineteenth Century River City: 1819 – 1860," Ph.D. diss., University of Pittsburgh, 1978, pp. 55, 65n; Census Office, *Ninth Census — Volume I. The Statistics of the Population of the United States* (Washington, 1872), p. 783.

6. Census Office, *Statistics of the United States: 1860*, p. xviii; Census Office, *Report of the Manufactures of the United States at the Tenth Census (June 1, 1880)*, 2 vols. (Washington, 1883), 2:379 – 80; Abbott, "Divergent Development," pp. 189 – 90; *Ninth Census*, 1:783.

7. *Ninth Census*, 1:783.

8. Peter Schmitt, "Autobiography of a German Blacksmith," pp. 1 – 8, CHS; Pauline Rehfuss Esselborn, *Recollections of Pauline Rehfuss Esselborn 1844 – 1925* (private printing, n.d.), pp. 4 – 5; Sister Mary Edmund Spanheimer, "Heinrich Armin Ratterman, German-American Author, Poet, and Historian, 1832 – 1923," Ph.D. diss., The Catholic University of America, 1937, pp. 15 – 16; Kenneth David Roseman, "The Jewish Population of America, 1850 – 1860: A Demographic Study," Ph.D. diss., Hebrew Union College, 1971, p. 93; Leonard Koester, ed., "Early Cincinnati and the Turners," *HPSOB* (January 1949) 7:19 – 20.

9. *Never Despair: A Tale of the Emigrants. Founded on Fact* (New York, 1837), p. 11. Statistics on the distribution of wealth were taken from Walter Glazer, "A Percentage of the Wealth Owned by Deciles of Cincinnati Property-Holders, 1799 – 1865," The 1820 Cincinnati Data Bank Collection, CHS.

10. Cist, *Cincinnati in 1851*, pp. 278 – 88; Cist, *Cincinnati in 1859*, pp. 240, 345 – 46; Cincinnati Chamber of Commerce, *Annual Report of the Cincinnati Chamber of Commerce, 1843 – 1873* (hereafter cited as *Chamber Report*) Thomas Senior Berry, *Western Prices Before 1861: A Study of the Cincinnati Market* (Cambridge, 1943), pp. 327 – 32, 476 – 80; Harry N. Scheiber, *Ohio Canal Era: A Case Study of Government and Economy 1820 – 1861* (Athens, Ohio, 1969), pp. 324 – 37.

11. Scheiber, *Ohio Canal Era*, pp. 220 – 31, 271 – 306; Berry, *Western Prices*, pp. 83 – 94; Sherry O. Hassler, " 'The Great Disturbing Cause' and the Decline of the Queen City," *HPSOB* (July 1962) 20:173 –80; Tod Jordon Butler, "The Cincinnati Southern Railway: A City's Response to Relative Commercial Decline," Ph.D. diss., Ohio State University, 1971, pp. 17 – 155; E. M. Coulter, *The Cincinnati Southern Railroad and the Stuggle for Southern Commerce 1865 – 1872* (Chicago: American Historical Society, 1922), pp. 5 – 63.

12. William Chambers, *Things As They Are in America* (London and Edinburgh, 1854), p. 151.

13. *Chamber Report — 1890*, p. 95; Cist, *Cincinnati in 1841*, p. 49.

14. William Smith, *Annual Statement of the Trade and Commerce of Cincinnati Including a General View of the Present Position and Future Prospects of the City* (Cincinnati, 1855), p. 12.

15. Ibid., pp. 9 – 25; *Manufactures of the U.S. in 1860*, pp. xliv – ccvii; *Report of the Manufactures: 1880*, 2:xxvi – xxvii; *Enquirer*, July 10, 1887.

16. *Gazette*, April 10, 1846.

17. The top 10 percent of the manufacturing firms in 1850 and 1870 were determined on the basis of the value of annual production, the number of employees, and the amount of capital invested as listed in the federal manuscript manufacturing census for those years. The 126 leading firms of 1850 — which were owned by 339 individuals — generally employed at least fifty people, produced an annual product worth $50,000, and maintained a total capital investment of $20,000. The 218 leading firms of 1870 employed at least 75 people, produced $130,000 worth of goods, and had a total capital investment of $55,000 or more. For a more elaborate description of the methodology used to select these firms, see Ross, "Workers On the Edge," pp. 143 – 44.

18. For similar arguments regarding the persistence and prosperity of small shops amid the growth of large manufactories see Hershberg, ed., *Philadelphia*, pp. 43 – 119; Raphael Samuel, "Workshop of the World: Steam Power and Hand Technology in mid-Victorian Britain," *History Workshop* (Summer 1977) 3:6–72; William Sewell, "Social Change and the Rise of Working-Class Politics in Nineteenth-Century Marseille," *Past and Present* (November 1974) 65:78.

19. *Western General Advertiser*, June 25, 1845.

20. Information concerning the utilization of primary and secondary sources of motive power was taken from the "Manufacturing Schedule, Hamilton County, Ohio," 1850 and 1870.

21. Chambers, *Things As They Are*, p. 152.

22. *Western General Advertiser*, December 11, 1844, December 12, 1845; Cist, *Cincinnati in 1859*, pp. 257 – 326.

23. "Manufacturing Schedule, Hamilton County, Ohio," 1850 and 1870; *Ninth Census*, 1:783.

24. For wage scales see "Manufacturing Schedule, Hamilton Co., Ohio," 1850, 1870. The hazardous conditions of Cincinnati's factories are most vividly described in the annual reports of the Ohio Bureau of Labor Statistics (beginning in 1877) and those of the Department of Inspection of Workshops, Factories, and Public Buildings (beginning in 1884).

25. Address of Edward Mansfield, in *Report of the First Annual Fair of the Ohio Mechanics' Institute, Held At Cincinnati, On the 30th and 31st May, and 1st June* (Cincinnati, 1838), p. 27 (Annual Reports of mechanics' fairs are hereafter cited as *OMI*).

26. John D. Craig, *An Address Delivered at A Meeting of the Citizens of Cincinnati, Convened for the Purpose of Forming A Mechanics' Institute* (Cincinnati, 1829), p. 11.

27. These efforts to redefine manufacturing were not unique to Cincinnati. Manufacturers and capitalists throughout the United States expressed similar aims and sentiments. The only major difference was in the timing of these ideological pronouncements — a timing which was generally determined by the city's stage of industrial development. Rowland Berthoff, "Independence and Attachment, Virtue and Interest: From Republican Citizen to Free Enterpriser, 1787 – 1837," in Richard Bushman, et al., *Uprooted Americans. Essays to Honor Oscar Handlin* (Boston, 1979), pp. 106 – 24; John Kasson, *Civilizing the Machine: Technology and Republican Values in America, 1776 – 1900* (New York: Penguin Books, 1977); Daniel Howe, *The Political Culture of American Whigs* (Chicago, 1979); Carl Siracusa, *A Mechanical People: Perceptions of the Industrial Order Massachusetts 1815 – 1880* (Middletown, Connecticut, 1979); Sean Wilentz, "Whigs and Bankers," *Reviews in American History* (September 1980) 8:344 – 50.

28. George Kendall, *A Sketch of the History of the Ohio Mechanics' Institute and a Statement of its Present Condition* (Cincinnati, 1853), p. 16; *Gazette*, November 7, 1843.

29. Craig, *Address*, p. 10.

30. *OMI — 1838*, p. 28.

31. Cist, *Cincinnati in 1841*, p. 236.

32. *OMI — 1858*, p. 132.

33. *Articles of Association, Constitution, and By-Laws of the Association for Practical Science, Cincinnati, Ohio* (Cincinnati, 1847), p. 26.

34. *OMI — 1838*, pp. 27 – 28, 35.

35. Address by Flanders, in *OMI — 1858*, p. 133.

36. *OMI — 1838*, pp. 28, 36.

37. *OMI — 1850*, p. 6; *OMI — 1839*, pp. 28 – 29.

38. Cist, *Cincinnati in 1851*, pp. 388, 306.

39. *Nonpareil*, October 31, 1850.

40. *OMI — 1850*, p. 6.

41. James Underwood, *An Address By James Underwood and the Proceedings of the Festival Held in the City of Cincinnati, January 29,1840* (Cincinnati, 1840), p. 10; *Elevator* February 19, 1842; *Scientific Artisan*, May 7, 1859; U.T. Howe, *An Address Delivered to the Members of the Ohio Mechanics' Institute, at its Eighth Annual Fair* (Cincinnati, 1845), p. 17.

42. See, for example, *Cincinnati Directory for 1840* (Cincinnati, 1840), p. 478; *Liberty Hall and Commercial Gazette*, April 1, 1841; *Gazette*, April 16, 1841; January 16, 1845; *Commercial*, April 15, 1852, January 13, 1853.

43. Howe, *Address to 8th OMI Fair*, pp. 17, 19. The opening and closing addresses of the OMI exhibitions are the most revealing sources for observing the changing perceptions of the mechanic and his role in society.

44. *OMI — 1838*, p. 3; "Constitution of the Ohio Mechanics' Institute," in "Minute Book of the Ohio Mechanics' Institute," (September 13, 1841) 23:24, Special Collections, UCL.

45. "Minute Book — OMI," (November 7, 1850), vol. 1; Ibid, I, n.d., p. 3. Manufacturers also created a School of Industry in 1868 for the "training of girls to industrial employment by which they may be fitted to earn their living." Hamilton County Incorporation Records, May 21, 1868, vol. 2, County Recorder's Office, Hamilton County Courthouse.

46. *OMI — 1855*, p. 1.

47. *OMI — 1839*, p. 3.

48. Elaborate descriptions of all entries, prizewinners, and the layouts of the exhibitions are contained in the annual reports of the OMI Fairs.

49. Donald Smith, "Classicism in Nineteenth-Century Cincinnati Architecture," pp. 1 – 12, CHS; Charles Cellarius, "Milestone in Cincinnati's Architecture," pp. 1 – 9, CHS; Talbot Faulkner Hamlin, *The Pageant of America* (New Haven: Yale University Press, 1920), pp. 124 – 25; James Marston Fitch, *American Building: The Forces That Shape It* (Boston: Houghton Mifflin Co., 1948), pp. 49 – 59; Talbot Faulkner Hamlin, *Greek Revival Architecture in America* (New York: Oxford University Press, 1949), *passim*; Leland M. Roth, *A Concise History of American Architecture* (New York: Harper and Row, 1979), pp. 52 – 125.

50. Hugh McCulloch, *Men and Measures of Half A Century* (New York, 1888), p. 43. For descriptions, drawings, and photographs of early classical buildings in Cincinnati see Smith, "Classicism in Cincinnati," pp. 3 – 9; Cellarius, "Milestone," pp. 7 – 9; Carl M. Becker and William H. Daily, "Some Architectural Aspects of German-American Life in Nineteenth Century Cincinnati," *HPSOB* (January 1962), 20:75 – 79; Cist, *Cincinnati in 1851*, pp. 108, 116 – 17, plate between 192 – 93; Goss, *Cincinnati: The Queen City*, 2:135, 177, 182, and plate between 196 – 97.

51. McCulloch, *Men and Measures*, p. 43; also see Cist, *Cincinnati in 1841*, pp. 40 – 41.

52. Cist, *Cincinnati in 1841*, p. 237.

53. Ibid., p. 238; William B. Sherwood to Lois Sherwood, October 6, 1848, in Sherwood Collection, CHS.

54. Cist, *Cincinnati in 1851*, p. 71.

55. Carl Condit, *American Building: Materials and Techniques from the First Colonial Settlements to the Present* (Chicago: University of Chicago Press, 1968), pp. 43 – 45; Carl Condit, *American Building Art: The Nineteenth Century* (New York: Oxford University Press, 1960), pp.

17 – 22; John A. Kouwenhoven, *The Arts in Modern American Civilization* (New York: W. W. Norton, 1967), pp. 48 – 63.

    56. Cist, *Cincinnati in 1841*, p. 42; Cist, *Cincinnati in 1851*, pp. 72 – 73.

5. Inside the Workplace

    1. The industries in table 5.1 were selected on the basis of their long-term continuity as the leading employing industries of nineteenth-century Cincinnati. Unlike the tables presented in chapter 4, all related trades and branches of a particular industry are herein grouped under one general category. That is, technologically and skill-related endeavors such as stove, safe, vault, and bolt and nut shops, for example, were placed under the single category of Hardware. Changing industrial classifications were based upon shifts in shop size, wages, capitalization, the ratio of labor costs to capital investment as a percentage of the total value of the annual product, the amount of money expended on machinery per operative, and changes in the organization of labor within an industry. A complete listing of the component trades within each industry can be found in Appendix A.

    2. Although building tradesmen continued to ply their crafts in traditional ways for most of the century, they were nevertheless affected by industrialization. The emergence of housing contractors and subcontractors (middle men with little or no training who often displaced the master craftsmen), the introduction of factory-made wooden work, and the use of "wood-butchers" on construction sites later in the century altered the nature of ownership and control in the trade. Yet, despite these changes, building tradesmen were generally quite successful in maintaining their customs, high wages, and control over work longer than any other major group of workers. Steven Joseph Ross, "Workers On the Edge: Work, Leisure, and Politics in Industrializing Cincinnati, 1830 – 1890," Ph.D. diss., Princeton University, 1980, pp. 153 – 56; Philip D. Jordan, *Ohio Comes of Age 1873 – 1900* (Columbus, 1943), 330, 332; *Second Annual Report of the Bureau of Labor Statistics for the Year 1878* (Columbus, 1879), pp. 172 – 76, 234 (hereafter cited as *BLS*); *BLS — 1882*, pp. 31 – 36; Robert A. Christie, *Empire in Wood: A History of the Carpenters' Union* (Ithaca, 1956), *passim*; Henry C. Bates, *Bricklayers' Century of Craftsmanship* (Washington, 1955), *passim*; James M. Motely, "Apprenticeship in the Building Trades," and Solomon Blum, "Trade-Union Rules in the Building Trades," in Jacob Hollander and George E. Barnett, eds., *Studies in American Trade Unionism* (New York, 1906), pp. 261 – 320.

    3. *BLS — 1877*, pp. 192 – 93.

    4. *BLS — 1894*, p. 104.

    5. *BLS — 1878*, p. 303.

    6. Oscar Ameringer, *If You Don't Weaken* (New York, 1940), p. 44.

    7. Charles Cist, *Cincinnati in 1841: Its Annals and Future Prospects* (Cincinnati, 1841), pp. 54 – 58; U.S. Bureau of the Census, *Report on Manufacturing Industries — 11th Census, 1890. Part 2: Statistics of Cities* (Washington, 1895), pp. 142 – 57; [J. W. Leonard], *The Centennial Review of Cincinnati: One Hundred Years* (Cincinnati, 1888), pp. 75 – 76.

    8. *First Annual Report of the Commissioner of Statistics, to the General Assembly of Ohio, for the Year 1857* (Columbus, 1858), p. 27; Cincinnati Chamber of Commerce, *Eighth Report of the Chamber of Commerce for the Year 1856* (Cincinnati, 1857), p. 20 (hereafter cited as *Chamber Report*).

    9. The following sources were particularly useful in charting the transformation of the furniture industry after 1840: Charles Cist, *Sketches and Statistics of Cincinnati in 1851* (Cincinnati, 1851), pp. 200 – 8; Charles Cist, *Sketches and Statistics of Cincinnati in 1859* (Cincinnati, 1859), pp. 290 – 95; Charles Cist, *The Cincinnati Miscellany, or Antiquities of the West: and Pioneer*

History and General and Local Statistics (February 1845) 1:145 – 46; Western General Advertiser, March 12, April 30, August 18, 1845; Cist's Weekly Advertiser, April 26, 1847; George Henshaw, "Reminiscences of the Henshaw Family From England to America," Henshaw Collection, CHS; William Chambers, Things As They Are in America (Edinburgh, 1854), pp. 151 – 53; Henry Ashworth, A Tour of the United States, Cuba, and Canada (London, 1861), p. 123; J. Leander Bishop, A History of American Manufactures from 1608 to 1860, 3 vols. (Philadelphia, 1868), 2: 465 – 66; Donald C. Pierce, "Mitchell and Rammelsberg: Cincinnati Furniture Makers, 1847 – 1881," M.A. thesis, University of Delaware, 1976, pp. 8 – 87.

10. Gazette, January 1, 1850.

11. Nonpareil, February 11, 1851.

12. In addition to the sources mentioned in note 9, see U.S. Census Office, "Census of the United States, Manufacturing Schedules, Hamilton County, Ohio," 1850; Moritz Busch, Travels Between the Hudson and the Mississippi 1851–2, translated and edited by Norman H. Binger (Lexington, 1971), p. 140; "Special Report of Mr. George Wallis. Presented to the House of Commons by Command of Her Majesty, in Pursuance to Their Address of February 6, 1854," in Nathan Rosenberg, editor, The American System of Manufactures: The Report of the Committee on the Machinery of the United States 1855 and the Special Report of George Wallis and Joseph Whitworth (Edinburgh, 1969), p. 294.

13. Isabella Lucy Bird, The English Woman in America (Madison, 1966), pp. 122–23; also see Chambers, Things As they Are, p. 152; Rosenberg, ed., American System, p. 294.

14. U.S. Census, "Manufacturing Schedule," 1850, 1870.

15. Chamber Report — 1878, p. 116; Chamber Report—1881, p. 36.

16. See Table 5.2. For changes in market demand and production during the depression see Chamber Report — 1873, pp. 104 – 05; Chamber Report — 1877, p. 110; Chamber Report — 1878, p. 116.

17. BLS — 1877, p. 228.

18. A. N. Marquis, ed., The Industries of Cincinnati (Cincinnati, 1883), pp. 141 – 42; also see A History of the Manufactures of Cincinnati: Being an Index to the Principal Manufactories (Cincinnati, 1870), p. 77. Although the main purpose of these local "puff" books was to promote the grandeur of Cincinnati's manufacturers and manufacturing intrerests, they are nevertheless a valuable source for describing the organization of work, the layout of factories, the number of workers employed, the nature of supervision, and the changing patterns of company ownership and control.

19. Enquirer, August 27, 1873; BLS — 1878, p. 144.

20. BLS — 1877, p. 299.

21. Chamber Report — 1883, p. 157; also see Chamber Report — 1887, p. 165.

22. Carrol D. Wright, "Report On the Factory System of the United States, in Report of Manufactures — 1880, p. 17.

23. Report on Manufacturing Industries — 1890, pp. 142 – 57.

24. Ninth Census, Volume III. Statistics of Wealth and Industry of the United States (Washington, 1872), pp. 714 – 15; Report of Manufactures—1880, pp. 393–95; Edward P. Duggan, "Machines, Markets, and Labor: The Carriage and Wagon Industry in Late Nineteenth-Century Cincinnati," Business History Review (Autumn 1977) 51:310 – 12; Chamber Report — 1888/1889, pp. 154 – 55; Cincinnati Federal Writers' Project, They Built A City: 150 Years of Industrial Cincinnati (Cincinnati, 1938), pp. 211 – 18. In 1870, Cincinnati carriage manufacturers controlled 1.6 percent of the national market; by 1887 they controlled 11.3 percent. [Leonard], Centennial Review, p. 59.

25. Cincinnati Carriage Exhibitors, The World's Carriage Building Center (Cincinnati, 1893), p. 11.

26. Henry W. Meyer, Memories of the Buggy Days (Cincinnati, 1965), pp. 5 – 65; Andrew Morrison, The Industries of Cincinnati: Manufacturing Establishments and Business Houses

(Cincinnati, 1886), pp. 97, 108; [Leonard], *Centennial Review*, pp. 58 – 59; John Endebrock, "History of the Sechler and Company, Cincinnati, Ohio," CHS.

27. See Table 5.2

28. Marquis, *Industries of Cincinnati*, p. 213; [Leonard], *Centennial Review*, p. 59; Charles Theodore Greve, *Centennial History of Cincinnati and its Representative Citizens*, 2 vols. (Chicago, 1904), 2:998 – 1001.

29. *BLS — 1878*, p. 132; *BLS — 1890*, pp. 160 – 62; Duggan, "Carriage and Wagon Industry," pp. 317 – 18.

30. *BLS — 1887*, p. 9.

31. Walter Sutton, *The Western Book Trade: Cincinnati as a Nineteenth-Century Publishing and Book-Trade Center* (Columbus, 1961), pp. 3 – 276; V. C. Stump, "Early Newspapers of Cincinnati," *OAHQ* (April 1925) 34:169 – 83; Cincinnati Typographical Union No. 3, *Centennial Booklet 1946* (Cincinnati, 1946), n.p.; C.T.U. No. 3, *125th Anniversary Celebration . . . of Cincinnati Typographical Union No. 3* (Cincinnati, 1971), n.p.. For an excellent overview of the transformation of the printing industry see Ava Baron, "Woman's 'Place' in Capitalist Production: A Study of Class Relations in the Nineteenth Century Newspaper Printing Industry," Ph.D. diss., New York University, 1981.

32. William T. Coggeshall, "How the Parlor Magazine is Printed," *Parlor Magazine* (January 1854) 2:10; *The Cincinnati Pioneer* (April 1874) 3:21 – 22; *Gazette*, August 21, 1846; *Commercial*, December 25, 1856.

33. *Nonpareil*, September, 3, 1852; also see *BLS — 1878*, p. 210; CTU No. 3, *125th Anniversary*, n.p.; Typothetae of Cincinnati, *Report of the Committee on the Cost of Printing. Presented to the Typothetae of Cincinnati, August 9, 1888* (Cincinnati, 1888), pp. 20 – 24.

34. Oscar Harpel, *Harpel's Typograph or Book of Specimens* (Cincinnati, 1870), p. 11.

35. Ibid., p. 13.

36. *Manufactures of the U.S. — 1860*, cxxxix; CTU No. 3, *125th Anniversary*, n.p.; Jordan, *Ohio Comes of Age*, p. 415; "Minute Book of the Cincinnati Typographical Union No. 3," vol. 2, January, 17, 24, February 7, 1886; "Record Book of the Corresponding Secretary of Cincinnati Typographical Union No. 3," January 26, 1886, 164 – 65 (These records are housed in the offices of the International Typographical Union No. 3, Cincinnati, Ohio). Changes in composing and presswork are also described in Baron, "Woman's Place," pp. 82 – 88, 105 – 58. For information concerning the general impact of linotype machines, see George E. Barnett, "The Introduction of the Linotype," in John R. Commons, ed., *Trade Unionism and Labor Problems* (Boston, 1905), pp. 250 – 73.

37. *BLS — 1878*, p. 210; *BLS — 1882*, p. 31; *A Study of the History of the International Typographical Union 1852 – 1963*, 2 vols. (Colorado Springs, 1964), 1:267. The changing nature of the printing trade and its effects on artisans are discussed in the annual proceedings of the International Typographical Union: *Report of the Proceedings of the Annual Session of the International Typographical Union* (printed in different cities each year).

38. C.T.U. No. 3, *Souvenir of the Fall Festival Labor Day, September 24, 1900* (Cincinnati, 1900), n.p.; also see Baron, "Woman's Place," pp. 87 – 104.

39. Harpel, *Typograph*, pp. 3, 13.

40. Coggeshall, "Parlor Magazine," *Parlor Magazine*, 2:10; *Gazette*, August 21, 1846; Walter Sutton, "Cincinnati as a Frontier Publishing and Book Trade Center 1796 – 1830," *OAHQ* (April 1947) 56:117 – 43; Cist, *Cincinnati in 1859*, p. 320.

41. Cist, *Cincinnati in 1859*, pp. 320 – 21; *Times*, December 21, 1858.

42. Coggeshall, "Parlor Magazine," *Parlor Magazine* (February 1854) 2:72, 70. The inner workings of the city's publishing houses and the development of new technologies (like stereotyping) are discussed in Ibid., 69–78; Coggeshall, "Parlor Magazine," *Parlor Magazine* (January 1854) 2:10 – 14; Cist, *Cincinnati in 1851*, pp. 232 – 35, 240 – 41; Cist, *Cincinnati in 1859*, pp. 317 – 25; Charles H. McMullen, "The Publishing Activities of Robert Clarke and Company, of

Cincinnati, 1858 – 1909," *The Papers of the Bibliographical Society of America* (1940) 34:315 – 26; *BLS — 1878*, p. 213; *Report on Manufacturing Industries — 1890*, pp. 142 – 57.

Although several newspapers occasionally advertised for women to work as compositors and pressworkers, they made little entry into this branch of the trade until the end of the nineteenth century.

43. Cist, *Cincinnati in 1859*, p. 321; Coggeshall, "Parlor Magazine," *Parlor Magazine* (February 1854) 2:73 – 76.

44. U.S. Census, "Manufacturing Schedules," 1880.

45. "Minute Books — CTU No. 3," vols. 1 – 2, *passim*; CTU No. 3, *Souvenir — 1900*, n.p.; Baron, "Woman's Place," pp. 134 – 45, 158 – 66. The rising costs of setting up a job shop, as well as other printing establishments, are delineated in Typothetae of Cincinnati, *Cost of Printing*, pp. 12 – 27; *The Cincinnati Type Foundry Company's Specimen and Price List* (Cincinnati, 1870); *The Sixteenth Annual Specimen Book and Catalogue of Machinery From the Cincinnati Type Foundry* (Cincinnati, 1885).

46. *BLS — 1878*, pp. 210 – 12.

47. Cist, *Cincinnati in 1851*, p. 176.

48. Cist, *Cincinnati in 1859*, p. 259. For many years John Commons and Blanche Hazzard reigned as the main historians of the trade. Their work has been recently challenged by a number of historians. Alan Dawley, *Class and Community: The Industrial Revoltion in Lynn* (Cambridge, 1976); Paul Faler, *Mechanics and Manufacturers in the Early Industrial Revolution: Lynn, Massachusetts, 1780 – 1860* (Albany, 1981).

49. Busch, *Travels*, p. 140.

50. Bruce Laurie and Mark Schmitz, "Manufacture and Productivity: The Making of an Industrial Base, Philadelphia, 1850 – 1880," in Theodore Hershberg, ed., *Philadelphia* (New York: Oxford University Press, 1981), p. 59.

51. *Western General Advertiser*, April 22, 1846.

52. Cist, *Cincinnati in 1851*, pp. 175 – 80; Cist, *Cincinnati in 1859*, pp. 259 – 60; *Enquirer*, October 9, 1843; *Western General Advertiser*, December 24, 1845; Robert W. Lovett, "Augustus Roundy's Cincinnati Sojourn, 1838 – 1845," *CHSB* (October 1961) 19:258; Isaac Lippincott, *A History of Manufactures in the Ohio Valley to the Year 1860* (Chicago, 1914), pp. 176 – 77.

53, *Chamber Report — 1860*, p. 15.

54. See table 5.2

55. *BLS — 1877*, p. 192.

56. George Puchta, "Autobiography of George Puchta," p. 2, Puchta Collection, Special Collections, PLHCC.

57. D. J. Kenny, *Illustrated Cincinnati: A Pictorial Handbook* (Cincinnati, 1875), p. 239.

58. *BLS — 1878*, p. 190; *BLS — 1877*, p. 198; Jessie B. Adams, *The Shoe Industry in Cincinnati* (Cincinnati, 1921), p. 6; Writer's Project, *They Built a City*, pp. 157 – 59.

59. See table 5.2

60. *BLS — 1877*, p. 194, 193; Cist, *Cincinnati in 1851*, p. 178.

61. *BLS — 1878*, p. 192; *BLS — 1877*, p. 197.

62. *Enquirer*, January 22, 1871; *Report on Manufacturing — 1890*, pp. 142 – 57; Morrison, *Industries of Cincinnati*, p. 101.

63. *Iron Molders' Journal*, January 10, 1887.

64. *Report of Manufactures — 1880*, xxvi – xxvii; Morrison, *Industries of Cincinnati*, p. 97; *BLS — 1887*, p. 216.

65. In particular see David Brody, *Steelworkers in America: The Non Union Era.* (Cambridge, 1960); Peter Temin, *Iron and Steel in Nineteenth Century America: An Economic Inquiry* (New York, 1964); David Montgomery, *Workers' Control in America: Studies in the History of Work, Technology, and Labor Struggles* (New York, 1979); Daniel J. Walkowitz, *Worker City, Company*

Town: Iron and Cotton-Worker Protest in Troy and Cohoes, New York, 1855 – 1884 (Urbana, 1978); Eric Hosbawm, "The Labour Aristocracy in Nineteenth-Century Britain," in Hobsbawm, *Labouring Men: Studies in the History of Labour* (New York: Doubleday, 1967), pp. 321 – 70.

66. The expansion and centralization of the metalworking trades is described in J. Leander Bishop, *A History of American Manufactures From 1608 to 1860*, 3 vols. (Philadelphia, 1864), 3:462 – 64; *Gazette*, September 26, 1846; Cist, *Cincinnati in 1841*, pp. 245 – 52; Cist, *Cincinnati in 1851*, pp. 189 – 99, 213 – 18, 225; Cist, *Cincinnati in 1859*, pp. 240 – 45, 278 – 90, 298 – 303; Robert Moore, *Autobiographical Outlines of a Long Life* (Cincinnati, 1887), pp. 45 – 64; *Western General Advertiser*, September 9, 1844; *Chamber Report — 1856*, p. 20; George Wing, "The Development of an Industrial Base for the Cincinnati Machine-Tool Industry, 1817 – 1860," *CHSB* (April 1965) 23:85 – 103; George Wing, "The History of the Cincinnati Machine-Tool Industry," Doctor of Business Administration diss., Indiana University, 1964.

67. *Iron Molders' Journal*, July 31, 1873.

68. David M. Gordon, Richard Edwards, Michael Reich, *Segmented Work, Divided Workers: The Historical Transformation of Labor in the United States* (Cambridge and New York, 1982), pp. 79 – 92; also see Laurie and Schmitz, "Manufacture and Productivity," in Hershberg, *Philadelphia*, pp. 56 – 58; Bruce Laurie, George Alter, and Theodore Hershberg, "Immigrants and Industry: The Philadelphia Experience, 1850 – 1880," in Ibid., pp. 102 – 3.

69. William Huston Chartener, "The Molders' and Foundry Workers' Union: A Study in Union Development," Ph.D. diss., Harvard University, 1952, pp. 121 – 211.

70. *Iron Molders' Journal*, December 31, 1870. The changing nature of the molders' craft is described in Frank T. Stockton, *The International Molders' Union of North America* (Baltimore, 1922); James Cebula, *The Glory and Despair of Challenge and Change: A History of the Molders' Union* (Cincinnati, 1976), pp. 1 – 49; "Minute Books of the Iron and Machine Molders' Union No. 4," vols. 1 – 4, 1859 – 1880 (vols. 1 – 2 in CHS; vols. 3 – 4 in International Molders and Allied Workers' Headquarters, Cincinnati, Ohio).

71. Laurie and Schmitz, "Manufacture and Productivity," p. 57; William H. Buckler, "The Minimum Wage in the Machinists' Union," in Jacob H. Hollander and George E. Barnett, eds., *Studies in American Trade Unionism* (New York, 1906), pp. 114 – 16.

72. Buckler, "Machinists' Union," pp. 115 – 116; The rise of the city's machine-tool industry is detailed in Wing "Cincinnati Machine-Tool Industry," *passim*; Wing, "Development of Machine-Tool Industry," pp. 85 – 103; Frederick V. Geier, *The Coming of the Machine-Tool Age — The Tool Builders of Cincinnati* (New York, 1949); Nathan Rosenberg, "Technological Change in the Machine Tool Industry, 1840 – 1910," *Journal of Economic History* (December 1963) 23: 414 – 43.

73. Buckler, "Machinists' Union," pp. 115 – 16.

74. *Technical Education. Extracts from Addresses Delivered by Hon. John Fehrenbatch, Prof. Thomas Norton, Prof. Thomas H. French Jr., and Dr. John B. Peaslee, in Cincinnati, Ohio, June 22, 1887* (Cincinnati, 1887), p. 3.

75. Harry Braverman, *Labor and Monopoly Capital: The Degradation of Work in the Twentieth Century* (New York: Monthly Review Press, 1974), p. 212.

76. These ratios were determined by dividing an industry's labor costs and capital investment by the total value of the industry's annual product. The latter percentage (capital/value of annual product) was then divided by the former (labor costs/value of annual product), thereby yielding the ratios shown in the table. Unless one were to control for inflation and deflation across time, comparing capital:labor ratios on a decade-by-decade basis yields the most accurate representation of the growth of capital-intensive industries.

77. Henry Ford, *My Life and Work* (New York, 1922), p. 81; Siegfried Giedion, *Mechanization Takes Command* (New York, 1948), pp. 77 – 79.

78. Carl M. Becker, "Evolution of the Disassembly Line: The Horizontal Wheel and the Overhead Railway Loop," *CHSB* (July 1968) 26:277 – 78; R. Douglas Hurt, "Pork and Porkopolis," *CHSB* (Fall 1982) 40:191 – 99; Louis C. Hunter, *Studies in the Economic History of the*

352   5. Inside the Workplace

Ohio Valley: Seasonal Aspects of Industry and Commerce Before the Age of Big Business: The Beginnings of Industrial Combination (New York, 1970), pp. 41 – 43.

79. J. S. Buckingham, *The Eastern and Western States of America*, 2 vols. (London, 1842), 2:394.

80. Cist, *Cincinnati in 1851*, p. 278. Cincinnati's meat products were sold throughout the United States, Europe, Central America, and Latin America. Lippincott, *Manufactures in the Ohio Valley*, pp. 178 – 79; Henry A. and Mrs. Kate B. Ford, *History of Cincinnati, Ohio* (Cincinnati, 1881), pp. 328 – 30.

81. Harriet Martineau, *Retrospect of Western Travels*, 2 vols. (New York, 1838), 2:45.

82. Quoted in Fords, *History of Cincinnati*, pp. 328 – 29.

83. Quotation from Charles Mackay, *Life and Liberty in America: or Sketches of a Tour in the United States and Canada in 1857 – 8*, 2 vols. (London, 1859), 1:126 – 27; Chambers, *Things As They Are*, pp. 155 – 56; Richard G. Arms, "From Disassembly to Assembly. Cincinnati: The Birthplace of Mass Production," *HPSOB* (July 1959) 17:198; Becker, "Evolution of the Disassembly Line," p. 278; Giedion, *Mechanization*, p. 216; *Gazette*, November 15, 1845; Writers' Project, *They Built A City*, pp.77 – 85; Hurt, "Pork and Porkopolis," pp. 199 – 202.

84. *Gazette*, Match 3, 1843.

85. *Gazette*, March 18, 1843.

86. Quoted in Arms, "From Disassembly to Assembly," p. 17.

87. Becker, "Evolution of the Disassembly Line," pp. 278 – 79; Busch, *Travels*, pp. 147 – 48.

88. *Gazette*, November 25, 1862; Arms, "From Disassembly to Assembly," p. 202; Giedion, *Mechanization*, p. 95.

89. U.S. Census, "Manufacturing Schedules," 1850, 1870, 1880; *Report on Manufacturing — 1890*, pp. 142 – 57. The perfection of new machinery is described in Giedion, *Mechanization*, pp. 228 – 40; Leopold Steigert, *Manufacturer of Steigert's Patent Meat Choppers* (Cincinnati, n.d.); Writer's Project, *They Built A City*, pp. 89 – 91; John Commons, "Labor Conditions in Slaughtering and Meat Packing," in Commons, ed., *Trade Unionism*, pp. 222 – 49.

90. *BLS — 1877*, p. 259; Hunter, *Economic History of Ohio Valley*, pp. 42 – 43, 94; for the early seasonal character of employment see Augustus Roundy to Nehemiah Roundy, May 7, 1845, Letters of Augustus Roundy, CHS.

91. Procter and Gamble Company, *Into a Second Century with Procter and Gamble* (Cincinnati, 1944), pp. 7 – 10; Richard R. Deupree, *William Cooper Procter (1862 – 1934) Industrial Statesman* (New York, 1951), p. 13; Cist, *Cincinati in 1859*, p. 264.

92. *Chamber Report — 1876*, p. 26; *Chamber Report — 1886*, p. 124; *Chamber Report — 1891*, p. 169. On the development of steam rendering, see G. M. Weber and C. L. Alsbery, *The American Vegetable-Shortening Industry: Its Origins and Development* (Palo Alto, 1934), pp. 8 – 9; Writers' Project, *They Built A City*, pp. 99 – 130.

93. Procter and Gamble, *Second Century*, p. 10; Deupree, *William Procter*, pp. 129 – 30; Alfred Lief, *The Moon and the Stars, The Story of Procter and Gamble and Its People* (Cincinnati, 1958), p. 9; Cist, *Cincinnati in 1859*, p. 266.

94. *BLS — 1878*, p. 202; *BLS — 1877*, pp. 243.

95. Lief, *Moon and Stars*, pp. 13 – 15; *Chamber of Commmerce — 1887*, p. 124. In 1890 Procter and Gamble's operations, including their suburban Ivorydale factories, were incorporated at $6.5 million. The Ivorydale factories, built after a fire destroyed the Central Avenue plant in 1884, were the world's largest producers of soap, candles, and glycerine.

96. Cist, *Cincinnati in 1859*, p. 264; also see *Commissioner of Statistics — 1857*, pp. 28 – 29.

97. *Times*, March 26, 1858; Cist, *Cincinnati in 1859*, p. 269; Greve, *Centennial History*, 2:1003 – 4; [International Publishing Company], *Manufacturers and Merchants*, p. 160.

98. [International Publishing Co.], *Manufacturers and Merchants*, p. 186; Greve, *Cen-*

tennial History, 2:898 – 99; Cist, Cincinnati in 1859, pp. 269, 308 – 13; William J. Comley and
W. D. Eggville, Ohio: The Future Great State. Her Manufacturers and a History of Her Commercial Cities Cincinnati and Cleveland (Cincinnati and Cleveland, 1875), p. 188; Chamber Report —
1870, p. 87; Chamber Report — 1880, p. 167; Weber and Alsbery, Vegetable-Shortening Industry,
pp. 19 – 20.

99. Laurie and Schmitz, "Manufacture and Productivity," p. 63; Puchta, "Autobiography of Puchta," p. 2, PLHCC; [Henry Castles], "Account Book for Bootmaker, 1829 – 1844,"
CHS; Timothy Whiting, "Letter Copy Book, 1836 – 1846," CHS.

100. For the early development of outwork and contracting in eastern cities see Laurie
and Schmitz, "Manufacture and Productivity," pp. 62 – 64; Bruce Laurie, Working People of
Philadelphia, 1800–1850 (Philadelphia, 1980), pp. 13–14, 23–25; Christine Stansell, "The Origins
of the Sweatshop: Women and Early Industrialization in New York City," in Daniel Walkowitz
and Michael H. Frisch, eds., Working-Class America: New Essays on Labor, Community, and American
Society (Urbana, 1983), pp. 78 – 103; John R. Commons, "The Sweating System in the Clothing
Trade," in Commons, ed., Trade Unionism, p. 317.

101. Commissioner of Statistics — 1860, p. 25; Lippincott, Manufactures in the Ohio
Valley, pp. 168–69; "Report of George Wallis," in Rosenberg, ed., American System of Manufactures,
p. 253; Francis P. Weisenberger, The Passing of the Frontier, 1825–1850 (Columbus, 1941), p. 85;
Chamber Report — 1860, p. 19.

102. Cist, Cincinnati in 1859, p. 271; [Leonard], Centennial Review, p. 87; Commissioner
of Statistics — 1860, p. 26.

103. Stansell, "Origins of the Sweatshop," p. 83.

104. Ibid., pp. 7 – 18; Cist, Cincinnati in 1841, p. 57; Joel Seidman, The Needle Trades
(New York: Farrar and Rinehart, 1942), pp. 14 – 32; Robert Ernst, Immigrant Life in New York
City 1825 – 1863 (New York: Columbia University Press, 1949), pp. 17 – 18.

105. "Report of Wallis," in Rosenberg, ed., American System, pp. 252 – 53; BLS —
1880, pp. 262 – 64; Ann Deborah Michael, "The Origins of the Jewish Community in Cincinnati
1817 – 1860," M.A. thesis, University of Cincinnati, 1970, pp. 114 – 22; William A. Greenbaum,
"A Study of the Economic Activity of Cincinnati Jewry Prior to the Civil War," M.A. thesis,
Hebrew Union College, 1957, pp. 31 – 37; Kenneth David Roseman, "The Jewish Population of
America 1850 – 1860: A Demographic Study of Four Cities," Ph.D. diss., Hebrew Union College,
1971, p. 93.

106. Western General Advertiser, July 30, 1845; Cist, Cincinnati in 1851, pp. 184,
219 – 20, 242 – 43, 258 – 61; Cist, Cincinnati in 1859, pp. 271, 306, 330, 332, 336; Lippincott,
Manufactures in Ohio, pp. 90–91.

107. People's Paper, November 20, 1844.

108. Enquirer, April 12, 1853.

109. "Report of Wallis," in Rosenberg, ed., American System, p. 253.

110. Cist, Cincinnati in 1859, p. 367.

111. Ibid., pp. 366, 271, 367 – 68, and advertisements following 368. The impact of
the sewing machine upon the clothing industry is also discussed in William Smith, Annual Statement
of the Trade and Commerce of Cincinnati Including a General View of the Present Position and Future
Prospects of the City (Cincinnati, 1855), p. 9; Commissioner of Statistics — 1858, pp. 34–38; Scientific
Artisan, August 19, 1858, November 12, 1859; Chamber Report — 1860, p. 19; Manufactures of
the U.S. — 1860, lxxxii – lxxxvii.

112. The expansion of the postwar ready-to-wear clothing industry is described in
Seidman, Needle Trades, pp. 15 – 16, 33, 54 – 55; Moses Rischin, The Promised City: New York's
Jews 1870 – 1914 (New York: Harper and Row, 1970), p. 62; BLS — 1878, pp. 226 – 29; BLS —
1889, pp. 36 – 47; BLS — 1892, pp. 355–56; M. Joblin, Cincinnati Past and Present (Cincinnati,
1872), 243 – 46, 317 – 18, 321 – 23; Greve, Centennial History, pp. 164 – 65, 780 – 82; Marquis,
Industries of Cincinnati, p. 124; [International Publishing Company], Manufacturers and Merchants,

p. 114; Ohio Department of Inspection of Workshops, Factories and Public Buildings, *Annual Report of the Department of Inspection of Workshops, Factories, and Public Buildings*, see volumes 1884–1892.

113. *Report on Manufacturing — 1890*, pp. 142 – 57; for wage differentials see U.S. Census, "Manufacturing Schedules," 1880.

114. *BLS — 1894*, pp. 63, 58. The rise of the sweating system in eastern cities during the late nineteenth century is more fully explored in ibid., pp. 57 – 67; Mabel Hurd Willett, "Women in the Clothing Trade," in Commons, ed., *Trade Unionism*, pp. 371 – 79; Commons, "Sweating System," in ibid., pp. 316 – 335; Rischin, *Promised City*, pp. 61 – 68; Seidman, *Needle Trades*, pp. 55 – 63.

115. *BLS — 1894*, pp. 58, 67.

116. Ibid., pp. 65 – 66; also see *Enquirer*, December 8, 1887. The impact of the sweating system upon family and gender relations is explored in Stansell, "Origins of the Sweatshop," pp. 78 – 83, 91 – 97.

117. *Report on Manufacturing — 1890*, pp. 142 – 57.

118. Herbert Gutman, "Work, Culture, and Society in Industrializing America," *American Historical Review* (June 1973) 78:566.

119. *Report on Manufacturing — 1890*, pp. 142 – 57.

120. Ibid.; U.S. Census, "Manufacturing Schedules," 1870, 1880.

121. "Minute Books — IMU No. 4," vols. 1 – 4, *passim*.

122. Quoted in Laurie, Hershberg, and Alter, "Immigrants and Industry," p. 100.

123. The only major exception to this general rule occurred in the textile industry where wages remained low despite the high level of mechanization. *Report on Manufacturing — 1890*, pp. 142 – 57; Ross, "Workers On the Edge," p. 220. Similar conclusions regarding the relationship between mechanization and wages are also presented in Laurie and Schmitz, "Manufacture and Productivity," pp. 66 – 88; Laurie, et al., "Immigrants and Industry," pp. 96 – 106.

124. An extensive listing of Cincinnati unions, arranged by industry, trade, and ethnicity, can be found in James Matthew Morris, "The Road to Trade Unionism: Organized Labor in Cincinnati to 1893," Ph.D. diss., University of Cincinnati, 1969, pp. 373 – 431.

6. World Grown Apart: Economic Struggles

1. *Gazette*, March 19, 1868.

2. *Enquirer*, March 22, 1847.

3. Ibid., February 11, 1847.

4. Journeymen's daily wages rose from approximately $1.25 in 1842 to $1.75 in 1850, while those received by unskilled laborers rose from $1 to $1.25. Data for wages, food and housing costs were drawn from sources cited in chapter 1, notes 30 – 31. Additional information concerning the costs of room and board was taken from *Nonpareil*, August 24, 1850, May 1, 1851; *Gazette*, April 19, 1866; Augustus Roundy to Nehemiah Roundy, May 7, 1845, Roundy Letters, CHS; Walter Stix Glazer, "Cincinnati in 1840: A Community Profile," Ph.D. diss., University of Michigan, 1968, p. 115; Edgar Winfield Martin, *The Standard of Living in 1860: American Consumption on the Eve of the Civil War* (Chicago, 1942), pp. 423, 429.

5. *Cist's Weekly Advertiser*, March, 14, 1849.

6. *Enquirer*, March 17, 1853.

7. Journeymen's wages increased from approximately $1.75 in 1850 to $2.25 in 1860;

laborers' earnings rose from $1.25 to $1.30. The cost of room and board rose from $4.50 a week in 1850 to $5.75 a week in 1860. In addition to the sources mentioned in note 4, see *Gazette*, April 19, 1866.

8. *Nonpareil*, August 23, 1852.

9. These statistics were compiled from information contained in Walter Glazer, "A Percentage of the Wealth-Owned By Deciles of Cincinnati Property Holders, 1799 – 1865," The 1820 Cincinnati Data Bank Collection, CHS; Glazer, "Cincinnati in 1840," pp. 120–22, 233–37. A slightly different breakdown in the distribution of wealth is presented in Irwin Flack, "Who Governed Cincinnati? A Comparative Analysis of Government and Social Structure in a Nineteenth Century River City, 1819 – 1860," Ph.D. diss., University of Pittsburgh, 1978, pp. 33 – 128, 216 – 94.

10. Fred and Gisela Gustorf, eds., *The Uncorrupted Heart: The Journal and Letters of Frederick Julius Gustorf 1800 – 1845* (Columbia, Mo., 1969), pp. 24 – 25.

11. Charles Reemelin, *Life of Charles Reemelin* (Cincinnati, 1892), p. 42.

12. Cincinnati Typographical Union No. 3, *125th Anniversary Celebration . . . of Cincinnati Typographical Union No. 3* (Cincinnati 1971), n.p.; Ethelbert Stewart, "A Documentary History of the Early Organizations of Printers," in Department of Commerce and Labor, *Bulletin of the Bureau of Labor Statistics* (September 1905) 60:930.

13. *Enquirer*, April 28, September 17, 1853.

14. In exchange for their monthly dues of twenty-five cents, the members of the journeymen tanners' union received two dollars a week (for up to three months) during times of sickness or physical disability. If the member died, his widow was given a lump sum of cash to cover funeral expenses and help her through her travails. "Constitution of the United Tanners of Cincinnati," Hamilton County Incorporation Records, February 6, 1854, 1:116 – 17, County Recorder's Office, Hamilton County Courthouse, Cincinnati, Ohio. For further examples of the benevolent functions of local unions see ibid., 1:125, 162, 206; "Minutes of the Iron and Machine Molders' Union No. 4," July 1860 – November 1866, vol. 1, Records of the Iron and Machine Molders' Union No. 4, CHS.

The county incorporation records are mislabeled as "Church Records" by the County Recorder's Office. Henceforth they will be cited as Hamilton County Incorporation Records (HCIR). I am grateful to Laura Chace of the Cincinnati Historical Society for bringing these files to my attention.

15. *Enquirer*, March 22, 1847.

16. Ibid., February 11, 1847.

17. Ibid., October 4, 1843.

18. Of the thirteen strikes fought around wage and hour issues, two were led by tailors and carpenters, and the rest by printers, bricklayers, plasterers, bakers, cabinetmakers, shoemakers, woodturners, iron molders, and cotton factory operatives. Printers also went out on strike in 1846 to enforce their control of the union wage scale. Nine of the decade's reported strikes occurred between 1843 and 1845. Strike data were compiled from information contained in local newspapers and James Matthew Morris, "The Road To Trade Unionism: Organized Labor in Cincinnati To 1893," Ph.D. diss., University of Cincinnati, 1969, pp. 30 – 108.

19. *Enquirer*, March 27, 1847.

20. Ibid., March 30, 1847.

21. Ibid., June 6, 1849.

22. The uses of republican symbols and rituals are described in *Enquirer*, October 20, November 2, 1843; March 5, August 6, September 25, 1844; July 7, 1845; *People's Paper*, September 22, October 10, 1843; April 1, June 28, 1845; *Gazette*, July 3, 1845; October 13, 1846.

23. *People's Paper*, December 14, 1843.

24. *Nonpareil*, August 25, 1852.

25. C.T.U. No. 3, *125th Anniversary*, n.p.; *Nonpareil*, November 4, 25, 1850; *Enquirer*, September 25, 1852.

26. "United Tanners," February 6, 1854, 1:116, HCIR; *Enquirer*, May 7, 1852; February 27, April 26, 28, 1853.

27. *Constitution and By-Laws of the Mechanics' and Manufacturers' Exchange of Cincinnati, Adopted March 1859* (Cincinnati, 1859), pp. 5, 6. Information concerning the composition of the Exchange can be found in the *Enquirer*, March 17, 23, April 10, 1859; *Times*, March 13, April 4, 1860.

28. *Nonpareil*, August 27, 1850.

29. Forty unions were organized between 1850 and 1857 and 27 between 1858 and 1861. The most intense spurts of unionization occurred during periods of favorable market conditions: 19 unions were organized in 1853 and 11 in 1859. Information concerning union activities was drawn from the following: *Enquirer, Nonpareil, Gazette, Times*, January 1850 through April 30, 1861; Hamilton County Incorporation Records, 1:*passim*; Morris, "Road to Trade Unionism," 70–106, 113.

30. *Enquirer*, April 12, 1853; *Nonpareil*, December 17, 1852; Morris, "Road to Trade Unionism," pp. 79–83.

31. *Enquirer*, November 24, 1853.

32. "Minute Book — IMU No. 4," 1, July 21, August 4, 1860. For an excellent breakdown of unionization across time and trades see Morris, "Road to Trade Unionism," pp. 381–431.

33. Germans also formed a number of central bodies such as the German Trades' Union Society (1844), German Labor Reform Agency (1850), and German Laborers' Society (1851); local representatives also attended the National Conventions of German Workers held during the early 1850s. *People's Paper*, December 19, 1844; *Nonpareil*, October 19, 24, 1850; March 13, 1851.

The rise of ethnic-based craft unions is partially described in Morris, "Road to Trade Unionism," pp. 45–108, 389–431. For correlations between craft and ethnicity see table 5.5.

34. *Times*, April, 21, 1858. Early immigrant traditions of working-class radicalism are described in Herbert Gutman, *Work, Culture, and Society in Industrializing America* (New York, 1977), pp. 3–78; Clifton K. Yearly Jr., *Britons in American Labor* (Baltimore: The Johns Hopkins University Press, 1957), *passim*; Carl Wittke, *Refugees of Revolution: The German Forty-Eighters in America* (Westport: Greenwood Press, 1970), pp. 6–176; Friedrich A. Sorge, *Labor Movement in the United States*, edited by Philip S. Foner and Brewster Chamberlain (Westport: Greenwood Press, 1977, originally published in 1907), pp. 52–98; Edith Abbott, *Historical Aspects of the Immigration Problem* (Chicago: University of Chicago Press, 1926), *passim*.

35. *Nonpareil*, October 1, 1851.

36. Of the 25 strikes initiated by journeymen, nine were led by building tradesmen, four by printers, three each by furniture workers and coopers, two by shoemakers, and one by bakers, machinists, tailors, and hatters. Of the 10 strikes initiated by unskilled workers, three were led by building trades laborers, two each by railroad laborers and omnibus drivers, and one by barbers, waiters, and female hat trimmers.

37. These six strikes were led by journeymen in trades where employers had initiated the decade's most radical changes in traditional production. Four strikes were launched by printers and one each by shoemakers and furniture workers.

38. "Constitution and By-Laws of the Cincinnati Typographical Union No. 3," in "Minute Book of the Cincinnati Typographical Union No. 3," vol. 1, insert on first page, Headquarters, International Typographical Union Local No. 3, Cincinnati.

39. "Plan of Apprenticeship, Adopted by the Cincinnati Typographical Union, February 15, 1851," flyer contained in "Membership Book," CTU No. 3, ITU No.3 headquarters; CTU No. 3, *125th Anniversary*; Morris, "Road to Trade Unionism," pp. 87–90; *Nonpareil*, November 4, December 11, 1850. For a general overview of local and national efforts to gain greater control over the trade during this period see Executive Council, International Typographical Union, *A*

Study of the International Typographical Union 1852–1963, 2 vols. (Colorado Springs: International Typographical Union, 1964), 1:157–62; Stewart, "Early Organizations of Printers," pp. 929–41, 981–87.

     40. *Nonpareil,* April 8, 1851; *Enquirer,* September 25, 1852; Morris, "Road to Trade Unionism," pp. 90 – 95. A copy of the 1853 "Scale of Prices" can be found in Stewart, "Early Organizations of Printers," pp. 1021 – 24.

     41. *Daily Columbian,* November 26, 1853.

     42. *Gazette,* November 26, 28, 1853.

     43. *Enquirer,* November 27, 1853.

     44. Ibid.; *Gazette,* December 8, 1853.

     45. *Enquirer,* November 30, 1853; also see ibid., November 26, 27, 1853.

     46. *Enquirer,* December 4, 1853.

     47. Ibid., November 30, 1853; Morris, "Road to Trade Unionism," pp, 94 – 95.

     48. *Enquirer,* March 13, 17, 1853; Morris, "Road to Trade Unionism," pp. 84 –86.

     49. *Enquirer,* December 11, 1853; April 1, 1854.

     50. Ibid., December 1, 1853.

     51. Ibid., December 4, 1853.

     52. *Herald,* quoted in *Enquirer,* March 22, 1847.

     53. *Christian Advocate and Journal,* quoted in *Quaker City,* July 7, 1849, and cited in Commons et al., *History of Labour,* 1:571.

     54. *Enquirer,* March 3, 1852.

     55. Ibid., September 28, 29, 1846; September 18, 19, 1850; December 2, 1851; July 22, 1858; *Gazette,* September 29, 1846; August 8, 1853; *Times,* April 21, 1858; March 21, 1860.

     56. *Nonpareil,* October 16, 1852.

     57. L. A. Hine, *A Plea For Harmonic Education* (Cincinnati, 1856), p. 184.

     58. *Commercial,* July 20, 1855.

     59. *Times,* October 21, 1857. For an overview of the economic crisis see Herbert F. Koch, "The Panic of 1857 and its Effects in Ohio," M.A. thesis, University of Cincinnati, 1951, pp 77 – 111, 132 – 92.

     60. *Times,* March 25, 1859; also see *Enquirer,* March 17, 23, 1859; Morris, "Road to Trade Unionism," pp. 104 – 7.

     61. *Enquirer,* April, 5, 1859.

     62. Ibid.

     63. See the daily reports of strike activities in the *Enquirer, Commercial,* and *Times,* March 17 – April 16, 1859.

     64. *Enquirer,* April 9, 10, 1859; *Times,* April 11, 14, 16, 1859.

     65. *Nonpareil,* January 24, 1852.

     66. *Enquirer,* December 11, 1853.

     67. *Nonpareil,* January 24, 1852.

     68. "Constitution of the Journeymen Tailors' Co-Operative Association," printed in the *Nonpareil,* September 11, 1850. The history of earlier cooperative ventures is recounted in Arthur E. Bestor Jr., *Backwoods Utopias: The Sectarian and Owenite Phases of Communitarian Socialism in America: 1663 – 1829* (Philadelphia: University of Pennsylvania Press, 1950), p. 239; John Humphrey Noyes, *History of American Socialism* (New York: Hilary House Publishers, Ltd., 1961, originally published in 1870), pp. 369 – 73; Morris, "Road to Trade Unionism," pp. 27, 56 – 63, 379.

     69. *Nonpareil,* December 12, 1852; *Enquirer,* April 28, September 17, 1853; Morris, "Road to Trade Unionism," pp. 80 – 83.

     70. Morris, "Road to Trade Unionism," pp. 63 – 70, 379; *Western General Advertiser,* March 1, 1844; *Nonpareil,* August 2, 1850; January 1, 24, 1852; *Enquirer,* December 11, 16, 1853; *Times,* August 18, 1860.

71. John R. Commons, et al., *A Documentary History of American Industrial Society*, 10 vols. (Cleveland, 1911), 8:309–14; *Cist's Weekly Advertiser*, March 14, 1849; *Nonpareil*, May 1, 31, June 28, 1850; Records of Partnership, 1:6, 24, County Recorder's Office, Hamilton County Courthouse.

72. *Enquirer*, October, 10, 1849, also see *Gazette*, June 11, 1849; *Nonpareil*, October 10, 1849; Records of Partnership, 1:15, HCC.

73. *Nonpareil*, May 2, 1850.

74. *"What is Association?" Tract No. 1. Cincinnati Branch of the American Union of Associationalists* (Cincinnati, n.d.), p. 1.

75. Glazer, "Cincinnati in 1840," p. 219.

7. World Grown Apart: Social and Political Lives

1. Eugene H. Roseboom, *The Civil War Era, 1850–1873* (Columbus, 1944), p. 226.

2. The expansion and segmentation of leisure pursuits are discussed in Richard Wade, *The Urban Frontier* (Chicago, 1959), pp. 100–157; Daniel Aaron, "Cincinnati, 1818–1838: A Study of Attitudes in the Urban West," Ph.D. diss., Harvard University, 1942, pp. 389–424; Francis P. Weisenburger, *The Passing of the Ohio Frontier 1825–1850* (Columbus, 1941), pp. 119–43; Charles Cist, *Sketches and Statistics of Cincinnati in 1851* (Cincinnati, 1851), pp. 157–61; Charles Cist, *Sketches and Statistics of Cincinnati in 1859* (Cincinnati, 1859), pp. 192–98; Thomas William Nightingale, "A History of Physical Education, Sport, Recreation and Amusement, in Cincinnati, Ohio in the Nineteenth Century," Ph.D. diss., Ohio State University, 1979, pp. 10–148; Reverend Charles Frederick Goss, *Cincinnati, the Queen City 1788–1912*, 4 vols. (Cincinnati, 1912), 1:446–53; Blanche M. G., Linden, "Inns to Hotels in Cincinnati," *CHSB* (Summer 1981) 39:127–52; Margaret King, *Memories of the Life of Mrs. Sarah Peters*, 2 vols. (Cincinnati, 1889), 2:38–39, 266–67. Local newspapers also contained daily columns describing the various commercial and associational activities available to residents.

3. Hugh McCulloch, *Men and Measures of Half a Century* (New York, 1888), p. 40. The "New England Society of Cincinnati" was organized in 1845 "to cherish the memory and perpetuate the principles of the original settlers of New England." Louis L. Tucker, "The New England Society of Cincinnati," *HPSOB* (July 1962) 20:215. In addition to the sources mentioned in the preceding note, the New England influence on social life is also described in Sister M. Evangeline Thomas, *Nativism in the Old Northwest* (Washington: The Catholic University of America, 1936), pp. 51–57, 72–73.

4. *Enquirer*, April 5. 1859.

5. Ibid., June 30, 1853.

6. *Constitution of the Great Council, and code of laws for the Government of Subordinate Tribes of the Order of Red Men for the State of Ohio* (Cincinnati, 1856), p. 28, 38.

7. Cornelius Moore, *The Craftsman and Freemason's Guide* (Cincinnati, 1853), p. 267. Council leaders were generally chosen from the city's leading manufacturers and merchants. Lists of the officers and members of Cincinnati's lodges can be found in *One Hundredth Anniversary, Cincinnati Council #1. Royal and Select Masons 1827–1927* (Cincinnati, 1927); *Proceedings of the Grand Lodge of the Most Ancient and Honorable Fraternity of the Free and Accepted Masons of the State of Ohio* (Columbus, 1857); *By Laws of Nova Cesarea Lodge #2. With a History of Its*

Organization, and Rules and Regulations of the General Lodges of Ohio (Cincinnati, 1873); Hamilton County Incorporation Records, 1, HCC.

8. Although supportive of religious doctrine, workers often criticized the conservative and hypocritical tendencies of religious institutions. The editors of the *Nonpareil*, for example, were particularly critical of the Episcopalian church which "embraces more of the aristocrats and monopolists of society than any other sect. . . . They accumulate the proceeds of the people's labor without the least scruple, [and] grind the toiler to the lowest notch of life." *Nonpareil*, May 20, 1850; also see L. A. Hine, *Hine's Lecture on the Highest Steeple. Rejoinder to the Reverend C. B. Boynton delivered in Center Hall, Sunday, December 14, 1851* (Cincinnati, 1851).

The radical uses of religion by working-class leaders is discussed in more depth in Bruce Laurie, *Working People of Philadelphia, 1800–1850* (Philadelphia, 1980); Herbert Gutman, *Work, Culture, and Society in Industrializing America* (New York, 1977), pp. 79–117.

9. *Christian Advocate and Journal*, quoted in *Quaker City*, July 7, 1849, and cited in Commons, *History of Labour*, 1:571.

10. *Catholic Telegraph and Advocate*, October 23, 1852.

11. Information concerning the links between religious revivals and economic activity can be found in *Minutes of the 54th Anniversary of the Miami Association of Regular Baptists* (Cincinnati, 1852), pp. 7, 21; *Ibid. — 1857*, pp. 16–17; *Ibid. — 1858*, pp. 14–15; *Ibid — 1859*, pp. 12–14; Walnut Hills Congregational Church, *Annual Reports*, 1856–1860; Joseph Emery, *Thirty-Five Years Among the Poor and the Public Institutions of Cincinnati* (Cincinnati, 1887), pp. 148–55, 183–84; August Roundy to Nehemiah Roundy, June 9, 1845, Augustus Roundy Letters, CHS; *People's Paper*, March 19, 1845; *Times*, March 1857–January 1859.

12. *Enquirer*, April 4, 1859.

13. "Minutes of the Board of Directors," March 1, 1853, 1:310, 309, Ohio Mechanics' Institute Collection, Special Collections, UCL.

14. *Letter of the Session of the Central Presbyterian Church, Cincinnati, Upon the Fashionable Amusements of the Day* (Cincinnati, 1859), p. 1; *Minutes of the Cincinnati Annual Conference of the Methodist Episcopal Church* (Cincinnati, 1858), p. 17; *Baptist Minutes — 1850*, p. 7; *Baptist Minutes — 1854*, p. 14; *One Hundred and Fifty Years of Presbyterianism in the Ohio Valley, 1790–1940* (Cincinnati, 1941), p. 61; *Manual of the Vine Street Congregational Church and Society, Cincinnati, Ohio* (Cincinnati, 1878), p. 15.

15. "Minute Book — Board of Directors," January 7, 1847, 1:175, OMI Collection, UCL. The efforts of large manufacturers to sustain the OMI in the wake of declining artisanal participation are described in Ibid., p. 170, 176; July 4, 1842, 1:56–57; December 11, 1843, 1:87; August 21, 26, 1854, 1:360–62; *Elevator*, January 22, 1842; *Enquirer*, March 13, 1854; *Gazette*, March 14, 1855; Dana B. Hamel, "A History of the Ohio Mechanics' Institute Cincinnati, Ohio," Doctor of Education diss., University of Cincinnati, 1962, pp. 18–23, 38–44.

16. *Nonpareil*, October 23, August 31, 1850.

17. *Gazette*, February 14, 1844.

18. Ibid., September 20, 1843. Civic elites took great pride in contrasting their harmonious volunteer companies to the rowdy and contentious companies of Philadelphia. For a description of the latter see Bruce Laurie, "Fire Companies and Gangs in Southwark: The 1840s," Allen F. Davis and Mark H. Haller, eds., *The Peoples of Philadelphia: A History of Ethnic Groups and Lower Class Life, 1790–1940* (Philadelphia: Temple University Press, 1973), pp. 71–87.

19. Donn Piatt, *Some Historical Notes Concerning the Cincinnati Fire Department* (Cincinnati, n.d.), p. 1.

20. These lists, which extend back to the 1820s, reveal the changing class composition of the city's volunteer companies. The Cincinnati Fire Department Records, 1819–1950, CHS; also see Kathleen J, Kiefer, "A History of the Cincinnati Fire Department in the Nineteenth Century," M.A. thesis, University of Cincinnati, 1967, pp. 47–48; Fireman's Protective Association,

History of the Cincinnati Fire Department (Cincinnati, 1895), pp. 58 – 96; *Gazette*, April 25, 1840, September 20, 1843; *Nonpareil*, December 22, 1852; *Annual Reports of the Chief Engineer of the Cincinnati Fire Department — 1854 - 1857* (this last source lists the occupations of all company members).

21. *Nonpareil*, January 9, 1851; January 10, May 13, 31, 1852; *Times*, May 5, 1858; June 17, 27, July 1, 1859; April 28, June 9, 18, 1860.

22. "Records of the Independence Fire Engine and Hose Company #2," August 5, 1850, 7:157, Cincinnati Fire Department Records, CHS.

23. Ibid., September 3, 1849, p. 145.

24. Ibid., September 4, 1848, p. 97.

25. Clyde W. Park, *The Cincinnati Equitable Insurance Company: Oldest Fire Insurance Company West of Alleghenies* (Cincinnati, 1954), p. 96.

26. *Report on the Re-Organization of the Fire Department of Cincinnati* (Cincinnati, 1853), p. 7. When asked about the merits of the new paid fire company, Greenwood replied: "It never gets drunk. It never throws brickbats, and the only drawback connected with it is that it can't vote." Park, *Equitable Insurance Company*, p. 105.

The growing ineffectiveness of fire companies and the ensuing campaign to abolish them are described in Ibid., pp. 71 – 106; Fireman's Protective Association, *History of Fire Department*, pp. 97 – 103; Kiefer, "History of Fire Department," pp. 50 – 87; Kathleen J. Kiefer, "Flying Sparks and Hooves: Prologue," *CHSB* (Summer 1970) 28:87 – 105; Geoffrey Giglierano, "'A Creature of Law': Cincinnati's Paid Fire Department," *CHSB* (Summer 1982) 40:79 – 99.

27. *Western Washingtonian and Sons of Temperance Record*, October 17, 1846. For the history of the temperance campaign in Cincinnati and its successes and limitations in attracting working-class support see Jed Dannenbaum, "Drink and Disorder: Temperance Reform in Cincinnati, 1841 – 1871," Ph.D. diss., University of California, Davis, 1978; Jed Dannenbaum, "The Crusader: Samuel Cary and Cincinnati Temperance," *CHSB* (Spring 1975) 33:137 – 51; Nancy Ray Siegel, "A Matter of Public Welfare: The Temperance Movement in Antebellum Cincinnati," M.A. thesis, University of Cincinnati, 1971.

28. Dannenbaum, "Drink and Disorder," pp. 48 – 49, 59 – 60. Of the 144 Sons of Temperance members active between 1844 and 1850, 43 percent were artisans, 2 percent semi- or unskilled workers, 24 percent professionals, 19 percent shopkeepers, 9 percent commercial employees, 1 percent government employees, and 2 percent had no occupation listed. Ibid., pp. 49, 60.

29. *Nonpareil*, August 27, 1851.

30. Ibid., October 14, 1850.

31. "Constitution of the United Tanners," 1, February 6, 1854, HCIR, HCC.

32. Commons, et al., *American Industrial Society*, 8:314.

33. *Gazette*, March 27, 1844; *Nonpareil*, September 20, 1851.

34. *Times*, January 27, 1859; Alvin Harlow, *The Serene Cincinnatians* (New York, 1950), pp. 266 – 67.

35. Francis and Theresa Pulszky, *White, Red, Black. Sketches of American Society in the United States During the Visit of Their Guests*, 2 vols. (New York, 1853), 1:291.

36. Quoted in William A. Baughin, "Nativism in Cincinnati Before 1860," M.A. thesis, University of Cincinnati, 1963, p. 54n. This is the best study of nativism in ante-bellum Cincinnati.

37. *Times*, June 19, 1848.

38. Gustorfs, *Journal of Frederick Gustorf*, p. 28.

39. Isabella Lucy Bird, *The English Woman in America* (Madison: University of Wisconsin Press, 1966, originally published in 1856), p. 118. The changing demographic composition of the Over-the-Rhine area is analyzed in Peter M. Harsham, "A Community Portrait: Over-the-Rhine, 1860," *CHSB* (Spring 1982) 40:66 – 71.

40. *Enquirer*, August 30, 1868.

41. Frederick Gerstaecker, *The Wanderings and Fortunes of Some German Emigrants* (Cincinnati, 1856), p. 108. By 1850, four of the city's ten daily newspapers and four of its seventeen weeklies were published in German. Cist, *Cincinnati in 1851*, pp. 74–75.

42. Joseph Michael White, "Religion and Community: Cincinnati Germans, 1841–1870," Ph.D. diss., University of Notre Dame, 1980, p. 57.

43. In 1850, approximately 67 percent of the city's Germans and their native-born children were Catholics, 30 percent Protestants, and 3 percent Jews. Ibid., p. 51; *Presbyterian of the West*, March 2, 1848.

44. Quoted in Guido Andre Dobbert, "The Distintegration of an Immigrant Community: The Cincinnati Germans, 1870–1920," Ph.D. diss., University of Chicago, 1965, p. 78. The regional composition of the city's Germans is also described in White, "Religion and Community," p. 42.

For the development and varied nature of German community life in Cincinnati see Carl Wittke, "The Germans of Cincinnati," *HPSOB* (January 1962) 20:3–14; Wilbur D. Jones, "Some German Societies of a Century Ago," *HPSOB* (January 1962) 20:38–43; Cincinnati Freie Presse, *100 Jahre Deutsches Wort und Deutcher Gang im Schoenen Cincinnati* (Cincinnati: Cincinnati Freie Presse, 1935); Henry John Groen, *A History of the German-American Newspapers of Cincinnati Before 1860* (Columbus, 1945); Diane Shaver, "The Mid-Nineteenth Century German Immigration Movement into the United States," M.A. thesis, University of Cincinnati, 1960, pp. 1–130; Henry A. and Mrs. Kate Ford, *History of Cincinnati, Ohio* (Cleveland, 1881), pp. 127–42; Goss, *Cincinnati the Queen City*, 2:9–20.

There is also an extensive literature that charts the rise of the city's large and important German-Jewish community. Ann Deborah Michael, "The Origins of the Jewish Community in Cincinnati 1817–1860," *CHSB* (Fall-Winter 1972) 30:155–82; Stephen G. Mostov, "A 'Jerusalem' on the Ohio" The Social and Economic History of Cincinnati's Jewish Community, 1840–1875," Ph.D. diss., Brandeis University, 1981, *passim*; Morris U. Schappes, ed., *A Documentary History of the Jews in the United States 1665–1875* (New York: Schocken Books, 1971), pp. 223–35.

45. H. A. Ratterman, *Early Music in Cincinnati. An Essay Read Before the Literary Club, November 9, 1879* (Cincinnati, n.d.), pp. 5–6. The growth of saloons and beer-hall life is described in William L. Downard, *The Cincinnati Brewery Industry: A Social History* (Athens, Ohio, 1973), pp. 5–27, 64–77.

46. Bird, *English Woman*, p. 120.

47. Leonard Koester, "Early Cincinnati and the Turners," *HPSOB* (January 1949) 7:22.

48. Quoted in Wittke, "Germans of Cincinnati," p. 12.

49. Koester, "Cincinnati and the Turners," p. 21. For the development and growth of the Turners in Cincinnati and throughout the nation see Cincinnati Central Turner, *The First Hundred Years 1848–1948* (Cincinnati, 1948); Carl Wittke, *Refugees of Revolution: The German Forty-Eighters in America* (Westport, Conn., 1970), pp. 147–220; Wittke, "Germans of Cincinnati," pp. 10–12; A. E. Zucker, ed., *The Forty-Eighters: Political Refugees of the German Revolution of 1848* (New York: Columbia University Press, 1950), pp. 43–156; *Nonpareil*, October 18, 1852; September 29, 1852; *Enquirer*, October 10, 1854.

50. Jones, "Cincinnati German Societies," p. 40. Further information concerning the radical activities of the Freemen can be found in Wittke, *Refugees of Revolution*, pp. 122–46; 161–220; Zucker, ed., *Forty-Eighters*, pp. 111–81; Lloyd D. Easton, "German Philosophy in Nineteenth-Century Cincinnati — Stallo, Conway, Nast, and Willich," *HPSOB* (January 1962) 20:24–28; Jones, "Cincinnati German Societies," pp. 39–43.

51. *Enquirer*, February 15, 1853; also see *Times*, December 14, 1858; August 20, 1860.

52. Wittke, *Refugees of Revolution*, p. 124; *Enquirer*, February 15, 1853.

53. *Enquirer*, February 15, 1853.

54. *Baptist Minutes — 1854*, p. 13.

55. Rufus King to Mrs. Sarah Peters, June 15, 1855, 2:47, Rufus King Papers, CHS.

56. For a complete listing of the Turner membership rolls see the Records of the Cincinnati Central Turner Society, 1850–1948, CHS.

57. "Association of Freemen of Cincinnati," 1, April 14, 1852, HCIR. These incorporation records also contain a complete listing of the officers of several dozen German voluntary associations. See Hamilton County Incorporation Records, 1, May 6, 1844–April 1861, HCC.

58. *Irish National Independence. An Address, Delivered Before the Citizens of Cincinnati, At the First Public Meeting of the 'Emmet Club,' of that City, Held 28th February 1848* (Cincinnati, 1848), p. 6.

59. *General Report of the Cincinnati Executive Committee For Irish Relief* (Cincinnati, 1847), p. 3; this pamphlet includes an extensive list of the committee's leaders, members, and contributors. For other important Irish cross-class alliances see *Reading For Irishmen. An Old But Good Document. Daniel O'Connell and the Committee of the Irish Repeal Association of Cincinnati* (Cincinnati, 1843); Jeremiah O'Donovan, *A Brief Account of the Author's Interview with His Countrymen . . . . During His Travels Through Various States of the Union in 1854 and 1855* (Pittsburgh, 1864), pp. 344 – 53; *Gazette*, January 21, 1850; *Enquirer*, July 17, 1855; Hamilton County Incorporation Records, 1, *passim*, HCC.

60. *Irish National Independence*, p. 3. Accounts of Irish associational life can be found in Sister Mary Edward Clark, "The Contribution of the Irish Immigrant to the Early Growth and Development of Ohio 1758–1860," M.A. thesis, Catholic University, 1945, pp. 27–49; Virgil A. Rogers, "The Irish in Cincinnati, 1860–1870: A Typical Experience," M.A. thesis, University of Cincinnati, 1972, pp. 11 – 22, 47 – 79; Reverend John H. Lamott, *History of the Archdiocese of Cincinnati 1821–1921* (New York, 1921), *passim*; Robert Francis Hueston, *The Catholic Press and Nativism 1840–1860* (New York: Arno Press, 1976), pp. 15–31; *Nonpareil*, July 30, 1852; October 30, 1852; *Enquirer*, July 17, 1855; March 18, 1859.

61. *Catholic Telegraph and Advocate*, September 24, 1853.

62. Cist, *Cincinnati in 1851*, p. 83. Cincinnati's Catholic population increased from approximately 10 percent in 1831 to 22 percent in 1839, and nearly 40 percent by 1860. Of the county's three largest Protestant denominations, Methodists made up 20 percent of the population in 1850 and 24 percent in 1860; Presbyterians 20 percent in 1850 and 13 percent in 1860; and Baptists 12 percent in 1850 and 7 percent in 1860. Dannenbaum, "Drink and Disorder," pp. 15 – 16; *Eighth Census of the United States. Statistics of the United States in 1860* (Washington, 1866), pp. 441 – 46; Glazer, "Cincinnati in 1840," pp. 130 – 31.

63. Quoted in James Campbell, "The Catholic Church and the Model City Area," p. 28, Special Collections, UCL.

64. *The [eye] Opener No. 1. The Nature and Obligations of an Oath as Taught by the Church of Rome* (Cincinnati, 1852), p. 4.

65. *Nonpareil*, September 15, 1852.

66. *Catholic Telegraph*, February 12, 1862; also see ibid., December 15, 1860. Conflicts over public and parochial schools are discussed in F. Michael Perko, "The Building Up of Zion: Religion and Education in Nineteenth-Century Cincinnati," *CHSB* (Summer 1980) 38:97 – 104; Nancy R. Hamant, "Religion in the Cincinnati Schools 1830 – 1900," *HPSOB* (October 1963) 21:239 – 42; Thomas, *Nativism in the Old Northwest*, pp. 42–46, 107–8; Baughin, "Nativism in Cincinnati," pp. 30–43, 50–67, 156–59.

67. *Report of the Committee of the Board of Trustees and Visitors on Text Books: On the Introduction into the Common Schools of Different Versions of the Bible, Rendered by the Majority and the Minority, August 31, 1852* (Cincinnati, 1852), p. 8.

68. Reverend Charles B. Boynton, *Oration Delivered on the Fifth of July 1847, Before the Native Americans of Cincinnati* (Cincinnati, 1847), p. 20.

69. The preeminent role of ethnocultural issues in Cincinnati politics during the 1840s and early 1850s is discussed in Baughin, "Nativism in Cincinnati," pp. 44 – 169; Glazer, "Cincinnati in 1840," pp. 72 – 83, 253 – 54; Dannenbaum, "Drink and Disorder," pp. 61 – 161;

Reverend Alfred G. Stritch, "Political Nativism in Cincinnati, 1830–1860," *Records of the Catholic Historical Society of Philadelphia* (September 1937) 48:227 – 63; Goss, *Cincinnati the Queen City*, 2:179 – 205; Thomas, *Nativism in the Old Northwest*, pp. 18 – 159.

70. The political struggles over temperance are analyzed in Dannebaum, "Drink and Disorder," pp. 61 – 205; Jed Dannenbaum, "Immigrants and Temperance: Ethnocultural Conflict in Cincinnati, 1845 – 1860," *Ohio History* (Spring 1978) 87:125 – 39; also see sources in note 27.

71. *Twenty-Sixth Annual Report of the Trustees and Visitors of the Common Schools of Cincinnati — Year Ending 30 June 1855* (Cincinnati, 1855), p. 15.

72. Bitter battles between Catholics and Protestants over the direction of the city's public schools flared up again during the municipal elections of 1853 as local citizens lined up to vote for what was popularly known as the "Pope's Ticket" or the "Anti-Catholic Ticket." In addition to the sources mentioned in note 66, see H. H. Barney, *Report on the American System of Graded Free Schools, to the Board of Trustees and Visitors of Common Schools* (Cincinnati, 1851), pp. 4 – 71; Rufus King, *Report to the State Commissioner of Schools, On the History and Condition of Public Schools in Cincinnati, December 1859* (Cincinnati, 1859), pp. 8 – 9; Edwin H. Zeydell, "The Teaching of German in Cincinnati, An Historical Survey," *HPSOB* (January 1962) 20:30 – 33.

73. *Address of the American Republican Association of Hamilton County* (Cincinnati, 1845), p. 12.

74. Boynton, *Oration*, pp. 7, 24. The fundamental tenets of the American Protestant Association are outlined in American Protestant Association Liberty Lodge No. 2 Cincinnati, *Constitution, By-Laws, Rules, and Regulations of the Liberty Lodge No. 2 of the American Protestant Association, of the State of Ohio, Instituted July 1853* (Cincinnati, 1856).

75. *Dollar Weekly Times*, July 13, 1854.

76. *Enquirer*, October 15, 1854.

77. *Dollar Weekly Times*, October 19, 1854. The rise and fall of the American (Know-Nothing) Party in Cincinnati is most thoroughly detailed in Baughin, "Nativism in Cincinnati," pp. 44 – 169.

78. Percentages were compiled from statistics contained in the *Annual Reports of the Board of Directors of the City Infirmary — 1854 – 1861*. Immigrants were also blamed for the sharp increase in crime during the 1840s and 1850s. Dannenbaum, "Immigrants and Temperance," pp. 127 – 28.

79. Quoted in Stritch, "Political Nativism in Cincinnati," p. 253; also see *Catholic Telegraph*, January 7, 1854.

80. *Times*, September 4, 1848.

81. Ibid., September 10, 15, 1858.

82. *Nonpareil*, August 29, 1850; *Enquirer*, August 25, 1854; *Times*, October 5, 1857; June 10, 15, 1858.

83. *Constitution, By-Laws, and Rules of Order of the Washington Council, No. 1 of the Order of United American Mechanics of the State of Ohio* (Cincinnati, 1847), p. 3. For an excellent analysis of Philadelphia's OUAM see Laurie, *Working People of Philadelphia*, pp. 174 – 77.

84. *Constitution of Washington Council, OUAM*, p. 4.

85. *Nonpareil*, June 26, 1850.

86. Ibid. Journeymen drawn to the OUAM generally came from the trades most seriously affected by the influx of foreign labor. Of the seventeen artisans who held leadership positions during this period, five worked in the metal trades, four in the furniture industry, three in the building and printing trades, and one each in the clothing and shoemaking industries. The names of OUAM leaders were drawn from local advertisements and various newspaper stories.

87. These men either contributed to OUAM lodges or were listed as marshalls at OUAM balls and July 4th celebrations. Several interesting descriptions of OUAM activities and leaders can be found in the following: *Nonpareil*, May 1, June 20, 26, July 22, 24, 25, 1850; February 18, 24, April 3, 8, July 4, 1851; *Enquirer*, September 24, 1853.

88. *Enquirer*, August 25, 1854.

89. *Nonpareil,* May 1, 1850; *Constitution of Washington Council,* p. 19; also see *Constitution, By-Laws and Rules of Order of Mechanics' Council No. 4, of the Order of United American Mechanics, of the State of Ohio. Instituted 20 October 1848* (Cincinnati, 1850).

90. *Nonpareil,* July 24, 1850.

91. Ibid., August 27, September 13, 1850.

92. Ibid., August 23, 1850.

93. Ibid., September 6, 1850.

94. Ibid., October 9, 1850.

95. Ibid., August 29, September 6, 1850.

96. The LLRP's campaign and the subsequent efforts of Democrats to co-opt party leaders are described in the *Nonpareil* and *Enquirer,* August 23 – October 15, 1850. For brief biographies of Taylor and Snellbaker see *Cincinnati's Mayors* (Cincinnati, 1957), pp. 19–22.

97. Rufus King to Mrs. Sarah Peters, June 16, 1855, 2:47, King Papers, CHS. For a more extensive description of the riots see William A. Baughin, "Bullets and Ballots: The Election Day Riots of 1855." *HPSOB* (October 1963) 21:267–72.

98. The changing nature of local and state politics between 1854 and 1861 are analyzed in Baughin, "Nativism in Cincinnati," pp. 170–203; Charles Reemelin, *Life of Charles Reemelin* (Cincinnati, 1892), pp. 122–29; Dannenbaum, "Drink and Disorder," pp. 162–89; Stritch, "Political Nativism," pp. 272–78; Thomas, *Nativism in the Old Northwest,* pp. 160–244; William E. Van Horne, "Lewis D. Campbell and the Know-Nothing Party in Ohio," *Ohio History* (Autumn 1967) 76:202–21; J. F. Bell to Thomas B. Stevenson, January 26, 1856; Charles Anderson to Thomas B. Stevenson, February 6, 1856, Thomas B. Stevenson Collection, CHS. For a more general overview of national politics during this era see Eric Foner, *Free Soil, Free Labor, Free Men: The Ideology of the Republican Party Before the Civil War* (New York: Oxford University Press, 1970).

99. *Times,* March 10, 1860; also see Ibid., March 9–20, 1860; *Enquirer,* March 11, 17, 1860.

100. *Enquirer,* March 27, 1860.

101. *Times,* March 8, 1860.

102. *Enquirer,* May 15, 1860.

103. Ibid., January 5, 1861; also see *Times,* December 22, 1860; February 6, 1861; *Gazette,* January 5, 1861.

104. *Times,* January 7, 1861. The cross-ethnic composition of the party is most fully described in ibid., February 18, 1861.

105. *Gazette,* February 18, 1861.

106. Ibid.; *Times,* February 16, 1861; *Enquirer,* February 18, 1861.

107. *Gazette,* March 3, 1861.

108. *Times,* April 4, 1861.

109. Ibid., February 18, 19, 1861; *Enquirer,* January 5, 1861.

110. Lists of the party's ward leaders provide an excellent indication of its diverse ethnic appeal. *Times,* February 14, 15, 16, March 3, 19, 21, 26, 1861.

111. *Enquirer,* February 14, 1861.

112. CTU No. 3, *125th Anniversary; Times,* April 15, 1861; *Gazette,* April 17, 20, 1861; Fords, *History of Cincinnati,* p. 108.

8 Fighting For Union

1. George C. Ware to Frederick Cushing, May 1861, George C. Ware Papers, CHS.

2. Charles Cist, quoted in Henry Howe, *Historical Collections of Ohio,* 2 vols. (Cincinnati, 1902), 1:767.

3. *13th Annual Statement of the Cincinnati Chamber of Commerce, for the Commercial Year Ending 31 August 1861* (Cincinnati, 1861), p. 5.

4. Ibid., pp. 5–49; *Chamber Report — 1862*, pp. 5–46; *Annual Message of the Mayor and Reports of the City Departments of the City of Cincinnati for the Year Ending April 14, 1862* (Cincinnati, 1862), p. 4; "Memoirs of George Henshaw," p. 19, George Henshaw Collection, CHS.

5. George Blanchard to the *Boston Transcript*, June 17, 1861, in Blanchard Scrapbook, George Blanchard Collection, CHS.

6. *Times*, January 11, 13, 1862.

7. Blanchard to *Boston Transcript*, June 17, 1861, Blanchard Collection, CHS; *City Reports — 1861*, pp. 359–64; *City Reports — 1862*, pp. 351–78; *City Reports — 1863*, pp. 331–57.

8. *Enquirer*, July 16, 1862; Leonard Harding, "The Cincinnati Riots of 1862," *CHSB* (October 1967) 25:229–39.

9. Colonel A. E. Jones, *The Financial and Commercial Statistics of Cincinnati. The Past and Present* (Cincinnati, 1871), p. 14.

10. *Chamber Report — 1863*, p. 8.

11. Ibid., p. 20. For an analysis of changing market conditions between 1862 and 1865 see *Chamber Reports 1863 – 1866*; "Henshaw Memoirs," pp. 20 – 21; Henry Clyde Hubbert, *The Older Middle West 1840 – 1880* (New York: Appleton-Century Co., 1936), pp. 220–21.

12. *Times*, May 11, 1864.

13. Ibid. For a general description of labor activities during the war, see James Matthew Morris, "The Road To Trade Unionism: Organized Labor in Cincinnati to 1893," Ph.D. diss., University of Cincinnati, 1969, pp. 109 – 47, 208 – 21.

14. *Chamber Report — 1864*, p. 6.

15. Jones, *Financial and Commercial Statistics*, pp.14, 15.

16. Changing residential patterns between the late 1850s and early 1870s are described in Sidney D. Maxwell, *The Suburbs of Cincinnati* (Cincinnati, 1870); Steven Joseph Ross, "Workers On the Edge: Work, Leisure, and Politics in Industrializing Cincinnati, 1830–1890," Ph.D. diss., Princeton University, 1980, pp. 30 – 40, 54 – 74.

17. Boston *Daily Evening Voice*, November 3, 1865, quoted in David Montgomery, *Beyond Equality: Labor and the Radical Republicans 1862 – 1872* (New York: Alfred A. Knopf, 1967), pp. 90–91.

18. *Volksblatt*, July 15, 1865.

19. *The Plunder of Labor* (Cincinnati, 1865), pp. 25–26.

20. *Enquirer*, August 23, 1867.

21. *Constitution and By-Laws of the Carpenters' and Joiners' Union of the City of Cincinnati* (Cincinnati, 1865), p. 3.

22. *Constitution of the Shipcarpenters' and Caulkers' International Union* (Cincinnati, 1865), p. 3.

23. Twelve of the journeymen's strikes were initiated by building tradesmen, four each by iron molders and furniture workers, three by shoemakers, two by blacksmiths, and one each by carriagemakers, cigarmakers, coopers, printers, and tanners. As for the city's unskilled laborers, two strikes were led by street car drivers, and one each by coal cart drivers, gas stoke workers, stevedores, and colored waiters. Printers and molders each fought one strike over demands for union recognition and greater jurisdiction over work rules.

Strike data were compiled from information in the *Enquirer, Times, Commercial*, and *Gazette*, January 1, 1864–December 31, 1867; "Minutes of the Iron and Machine Molders' Union No. 4," 1, January 1, 1865–December 31, 1867, Records of the Iron and Machine Molders' Union No. 4, CHS; "Letter Book of the Corresponding Secretary of Cincinnati Typographical Union No.

3," January 1, 1864 – December 31, 1867, ITU No. 3 Headquarters, Cincinnati, Ohio; Morris, "Road To Trade Unionism," pp. 113–47.

24. *Enquirer*, June 20, 1866.

25. *Ibid.*, February 24, 1866.

26. The development of these national labor bodies is discussed in Montgomery, *Beyond Equality*, pp. 90–196, 458–61; Gerald Grob, *Workers and Utopia: A Study of Ideological Conflict in the American Labor Movement 1865 – 1890* (Chicago: Quadrangle Books, 1969), pp. 11–33; John R. Commons, et al., *History of Labour in the United States*, 4 vols. (New York, 1966), 2:33–102.

27. *Times*, May 11, 1864.

28. *Enquirer*, November 8, 1865. These efforts to promote greater unity between skilled and unskilled workers are described in *Commercial*, September 19, 1864; "Minute Book — IMU No. 4," 1, April 6, May 21, September 24, 1864; *1st Annual Report of the Ohio Bureau of Labor Statistics For the Year 1877* (Cincinnati, 1877), p. 33 (hereafter cited as *BLS*).

29. *Commercial*, April 6, 1865; also see *Enquirer*, March 29, 30, 31, April 1, 1865; *BLS — 1885*, p. 34.

30. *Commercial*, April 6, 1865; *Times*, November 8, 1865; *Enquirer*, December 2, 1865.

31. Quoted in Executive Council, International Typographical Union, *A Study of the History of the International Typographical Union 1852 – 1963*, 2 vols. (Colorado Springs, 1964), 1:274.

32. *Iron Molders' Journal*, January 10, 1875.

33. Michael F. Holt, *The Political Crisis of the 1850s* (New York: John Wiley and Sons, 1978), p. 190.

34. These arguments were not unique to Cincinnati. Workingmen throughout the nation advanced similar pleas in the defense of the eight-hour cause. Marion Cotter Cahill, *Shorter Hours: A Study of the Movement Since the Civil War* (New York, 1932), pp. 31–40, 69–71, 94–152; Montgomery, *Beyond Equality*, pp. 230–334; Commons, et al., *History of Labour*, 2:86–110.

35. *Enquirer*, November 8, 1865.

36. *Times*, February 24, 1866.

37. *Enquirer*, February 24, 1866.

38. Montgomery, *Beyond Equalilty*, p. 239.

39. *Enquirer*, November 8, 1865.

40. *Gazette*, November 8, 1865. Local merchants and manufacturers opposed the bill on the grounds that it would drive businesses out of Ohio. *Commercial*, February 19, March 9, 1866.

41. *Volksfreund*, July 16, 1865.

42. *Volksblatt*, July 15, 1865.

43. *Enquirer*, December 2, 1865.

44. *Fincher's Trade Review*, September 30, 1865, quoted in Morris, "Road to Trade Unionism," p. 213.

45. *Times*, February 22, 1866; *BLS — 1878*, pp. 266–67.

46. *Enquirer*, March 16, September 7, 1867.

47. Ibid., September 7, 1867.

48. *Commercial*, September 13, 1867.

49. *Enquirer*, September 13, 1867; also see ibid., September 7, 10, 1867.

50. These efforts to recruit German, Irish, and black voters are most fully described in the columns of the city's newspapers for September and early October 1867.

51. *Enquirer*, September 16, October 6, 14, 1867; Cahill, *Shorter Hours*, pp. 69–71.

52. *Enquirer, Commercial,* and *Gazette,* March 20 – April 10, 1868; Morris, "Road to Trade Unionism," pp. 220 – 21.

53. *Gazette,* July 17, 1868; *Enquirer,* August 22, 1868. Frederick Oberkline and J. B. Lodge soon joined Neal in the Republican Party, while Larkin McHugh, Frederick Jenny, and Ansil Robinson went over to the Democrats.

54. Morris, "Road to Trade Unionism," pp. 221 – 34.

55. Montgomery, *Beyond Equality,* p. 215.

56. Andrew Hickenlooper, "Personal Reminiscences," 2:242, Andrew Hickenlooper Collection, CHS; also see ibid., 1:9 – 23.

57. *Enquirer,* March 8, 1866.

58. The shifting loyalties of the city's German voters are described in *Volksfreund,* August 13, 1868; *Enquirer,* August 25, 1868. For Irish political allegiances see *Enquirer,* August 8, September 27, 30, October 1, 6, 13, 1868; September 22, 25, 26, 1870. For black voters see ibid., September 21, 27, 1870; *Times,* August 19, 27, 1870; *Commercial,* April 3, 1870.

59. Harry Jebsen, "Cincinnati's Protestant Clergy in Social and Political Reform 1865 – 1915," M.A. thesis, University of Cincinnati, 1966, pp. 21 – 23; Nancy R. Hamant, "Religion in the Cincinnati Schools 1830 – 1900," *HPSOB* (October 1963) 21:242 – 49; Janet A. Miller, "Urban Education and the New City: Cincinnati's Elementary Schools, 1870 – 1914," *Ohio History* (Spring 1979) 88:152 – 72; Joseph B. Foraker, *Notes of a Busy Life,* 2 vols. (Cincinnati, 1917), 1:105 – 106; Reverend John H. Lamott, *History of the Archdiocese of Cincinnati 1821 – 1921* (Cincinnati, 1921), pp. 279 – 80; Hickenlooper, "Personal Reminiscences," 2:434; *Enquirer,* June 6, 1869; September 26, 1871; February 27 – April 10, 1872; *Commercial,* April 5, 1870.

60. Democratic victories also meant more Irish appointments to the police force and other municipal jobs, while Republican victories brought similar results for German and black supporters. Celeste Estelle Anderson, "The Invention of the 'Professional' Municipal Police: The Case of Cincinnati, 1788 – 1900," Ph.D. diss., University of Cincinnati, 1979, pp. 191 – 94; *Enquirer,* February 24, 1866; September 27, 1867; September 30, October 1, 6, 13, 1868; November 5, 1873; *Times,* August 19, 1870; Barbara Musselman, "The Quest for Collective Improvement: Cincinnati Workers, 1893 to 1920," Ph.D. diss., University of Cincinnati, 1975, pp. 2 – 3, 40 – 41.

61. *Enquirer,* May 8, 1869.

62. The TLA appointed a series of standing committees charged with encouraging unionization among unorganized workers and resolving differences between local unions. *Enquirer,* May 24, 1870; *Times,* August 15, 17, 21, 1870; *Catholic Telegraph,* August 22, 1870. A list of the various unions formed during this period can be found in Morris, "Road to Trade Unionism," pp. 381 – 432; *BLS — 1877,* pp. 32 – 33.

63. "Minute Books — IMU No. 4," 2, January 25, 1868.

64. Ibid., 2, December 15, 1866; June 18, 1867; January 28, 1868; *9th Proceedings of the International Iron Molders' Union* (Philadelphia, 1868), p. 13; "Letter Book — CTU No. 3," December 7, 1867, May 1, 1869, November 20, 1870, January 18, 1871.

65. L. A. Hine, *Hine's Quarterly* (July 1869) 1:193.

66. Jones, *Financial and Commercial Statistics,* p. 15. The growth of factory production is also described in George Blanchard to the *Boston Transcript,* June 25, 1865, Blanchard Collection; Carl M. Becker, "Miles Greenwood," in Kenneth W. Wheeler, ed., *For the Union: Ohio Leaders in the Civil War* (Columbus: Ohio State University Press, 1968), pp. 281 – 302; *110th Anniversary of the Commercial Tribune* (Cincinnati, 1904), n.p. (see article on shoemaking by Harry L. Manss).

67. See tables 4.5 and 5.2.

68. *New York Times,* February 22, 1869, quoted in Montgomery, *Beyond Equality,* p. 26.

69. These figures were drawn from information contained in the Hamilton County Incorporation Records, 1–3, County Recorder's Office, Hamilton County Courthouse. The ensuing impact of changing forms of ownership and control of industry are more thoroughly discussed in chapter 9.

70. The Mitchell and Rammelsberg and Procter and Gamble companies were incorporated in 1867 at an approved capital stock of $2 million and $800,000 respectively. The Cincinnati Stationary Engine and Hydraulic Works was incorporated in 1871 at $1 million. Hamilton County Incorporation Records, 2, March 18, November 19, 1867; 3, October 6, 1871.

71. *Enquirer*, June 9, 1869; August 17, 1870; May 22, 1871; also see *Times*, March 10, 1866.

72. Morris, "Road to Trade Unionism," pp. 144–47.

73. In the period between January 1, 1868 and October 1, 1873, seven strikes were initiated by iron molders, six by shoemakers, two by printers, and one each by cigarworkers, tailors, coopers, steamboat carpenters, building tradesmen, coal heavers, telegraphers, and gas stokers. Strike data were compiled from information contained in the *Enquirer, Commercial, Gazette,* and *Times* January 1, 1868–October 1, 1873; Morris, "Road to Trade Unionism," pp. 115–47; "Minute Books — IMU No. 4," 2 – 3, January 1, 1868 – October 1, 1873; "Letter Book — CTU No. 3," January 1, 1868 – October 1, 1873; "Minute Books — CTU No. 3," 1, June 3, 1871 – October 1, 1873.

74. *Iron Molders' Journal,* July 31, 1873.

75. The changing nature of production in these industries is described in chapter 5.

76. *Times*, March 22, 1866.

77. Further descriptions of these strikes can be found in Morris, "Road to Trade Unionism," pp. 131, 137 – 40; and the "Minute Books" of IMU No. 4 and CTU No. 3, *passim.*

78. Union printers were represented by CTU No. 3. Stove and holloware molders joined IMU No. 3, machine molders joined IMU No. 4, and bench and flask molders joined IMU No. 122.

79. *Times,* March 22, 1866. These work rules, complained the editors of the *Enquirer,* were "of the most stringent character . . . . [and] practically denied proprietors any authority in or control over the details of the business in which they have risked their capital and reputations as businessmen." *Enquirer,* July 19, 1874.

80. The "Minute Books" of the molders and printers provide a wealth of information concerning the formulation and enforcement of union work rules, the daily activities of shop committees, the planning and carrying out of strikes, and the changing number of craftsmen coming in and out of Cincinnati. Similar efforts by molders and printers in other parts of the country to govern the daily workings of the trade are discussed in Commons, et al., *History of Labour,* 2: 48–56, 58–61; Daniel J. Walkowitz, *Worker City, Company Town: Iron and Cotton-Worker Protest in Troy and Cohoes, New York, 1855–1884* (Urbana, 1978), pp. 81–218.

81. Social activities included frequent picnics, steamboat excursions, annual balls, organized baseball teams, and the establishment of reading rooms and union libraries. *Enquirer,* June 14, 21, 1866; July 7, 1867; "Minute Books — IMU No. 4," 1, June 20, 1866, March 2, 1867; 3, August 7, 1869, April 3, 1874. For the ethnic composition of the trade in 1870, see U.S. Census Office, *Ninth Census — Vol. I. The Statistics of the Population of the United States* (Washington, 1872), p. 783.

82. These percentages were compiled from the membership lists contained in the "Minute Books" and the "Letter Book" of the molders and printers, and, from unionization figures listed in the *Enquirer,* December 13, 31, 1870; January 15, 1871.

83. "Minute Books — CTU No. 3," 1, July 14, 1874.

84. *Enquirer,* April 2, 1869. The changing nature of the shoemaking industry is described in chapter 5. For KOSC activities in other parts of the nation, see Commons, et al.,

History of Labour, 2:76–79; Alan Dawley, *Class and Community: The Industrial Revolution in Lynn* (Cambridge, 1976), pp. 175–219.

85. *Enquirer*, October 3, 1869; Morris, "Road to Trade Unionism," pp. 113–18.

86. Morris, "Road to Trade Unionism," pp. 125–27, 140–44. See table 5.2 for the growth of factory production.

87. *Enquirer*, January 22, 1871.

88. *Commercial*, March 2, 16, 1873; *Enquirer*, April 24, 27, 1873; Morris, "Road to Trade Unionism," pp. 117–18; *Statistics of Population — 1870*, p. 783.

89. German cigarmakers, whose ranks included a large number of socialists, urged tradesmen to recruit women into their unions. Native-born cigar workers generally opposed the idea, arguing that manufacturers would use female employees to undercut male wages. *Enquirer*, October 2, 1869 – March 18, 1870; January 29, 1871; Morris, "Road to Trade Unionism," pp. 140–44; *BLS — 1877*, pp. 199–201; *Statistics of Population — 1870*, p. 783.

90. An extensive listing of the various unions within each of the city's major industries can be found in Morris, "Road to Trade Unionism," pp. 381–429.

91. Ibid., pp. 126–27; *Enquirer*, May 30, June 1, 1872.

92. Augusta Lewis to John P. Young, November 20, 1870, "Letter Book — CTU No. 3." For local prejudice against black printers see Atlanta Typographical Union No. 48 to CTU No. 3, November 1870, in ibid.; *Enquirer*, June 9, 1870.

93. *Enquirer*, June 22, 1872.

94. *Enquirer*, February 28, 1871.

95. *Iron Molders' Journal*, April 30, 1873.

96. Ibid., February 10, 1873.

97. *Times*, April 25, 1869, February 20, 1861; "Incorporation Records of the Arbeiter Bund," May 19, 1864, 1:343, HCIR; Moses King, *King's Pocket-Book of Cincinnati* (Boston, 1879), p. 9.

98. Hickenlooper, "Personal Reminiscences," 1:138; *Commercial*, October 23, 25, 1873; *Enquirer*, October 4, 26, 1873; Morris, "Road to Trade Unionism," pp. 112–13, 155; Andrew Morrison, *The Industries of Cincinnati* (Cincinnati, 1886), pp. 41–42.

99. See the "Minute Books" and "Letter Book" of the molders and printers, October 1873 – December 1885.

9. City of Modern Industry

1. *Enquirer*, January 20, 1880.

2. Ibid., March 15, 1874. For a general description of changing economic conditions during this period see *Annual Statement of the Chamber of Commerce — 1873–1885*.

3. *Chamber Report — 1878*, quoted in *Annual Report of the Secretary of State, To the Governor of the State of Ohio, for the Year 1878* (Columbus, 1879), p. 615.

4. Ibid.; *Chamber Report — 1879*, quoted in *Report of Secretary of State — 1879*, pp. 675–76.

5. *Annual Report of the [Ohio] Bureau of Labor Statistics for the Year 1878* (Columbus, 1879), p. 32.

6. Hamilton County Incorporation Records, 1–5, County Recorder's Office, HCC. Some 4,069 Ohio manufacturing establishments were incorporated between 1851 and 1873 at a total capital stock of $882 million. In the twelve years following the onset of the depression, 6,852

firms were incorporated with an authorized stock of $2 billion. *Report of Secretary of State—1885*, p. 230.

7. Of the 127 firms comprising the manufacturing elite of 1850, 45 were family operations, 34 small partnerships, and 48 multipartnered companies. In 1880, 73 of the top 318 manufacturing operations were owned by single families, 78 by small partnerships, and 167 (52.5 percent) by corporations or multipartnered companies. The top 10 percent of the city's factories in 1880 generally employed over 75 workers, produced at least $50,000 worth of goods, and were capitalized at more than $90,000. Information and data concerning Cincinnati incorporations were gathered from the Hamilton County Incorporation Records, 1–5, HCC, and the *Report of Secretary of State*, 1865–1890.

8. *Manufacturers of the United States in 1860, Compiled from the 8th Census* (Washington, 1865), xviii; *Report on Manufacturing Industries—11th Census 1890. Part II: Statistics of Cities* (Washington, 1895), p. 3.

9. See table 4.4 for the career patterns of earlier manufacturing elites. For a more thorough examination of persistence rates among the city's leading manufacturing firms see Steven Joseph Ross, "Workers On the Edge: Work Leisure, and Politics in Industrializing Cincinnati, 1830–1890," Ph.D. diss., Princeton University, 1980, pp. 239–55.

10. Hamilton County Incorporation Records, 3–4, HCC. These records provide an invaluable source of information concerning the changing patterns of ownership and the interlocking nature of corporate control in Cincinnati. Incorporation listings include the names of a company's main investors, its total capital stock, and the date filed for incorporation.

11. *BLS—1878*, p. 302.

12. A. N. Marquis, *The Industries of Cincinnati* (Cincinnati, 1883), pp. 205, 141–142, 231. Information concerning the growing tendency of industrial capitalists to transfer control over production to factory superintendents was obtained from the local histories of manufacturers and manufacturing firms cited in table 4:4.

13. *Enquirer*, August 23, 1877. The evolution of the carriage industry is described in chapter 5.

14. "Manufacturing Schedules, Hamilton County, 1880."

15. *BLS—1887*, p. 9.

16. *Thirteenth Annual Report of the Commissioner of Labor, 1898. Hand and Machine Labor*, 2 vols. (Washington, 1899), 1:171–73, 34–37.

17. Ibid., pp. 36–37.

18. Cincinnati Carriage Exhibitors, *The World's Carriage Building Center* (Cincinnati, 1893), p. 10.

19. Henry W. Meyer, *Memories of Buggy Days* (Cincinnati, 1965), p. 70

20. Some 63.9 percent of all cigarmakers in 1880 labored in factories employing more than fifty people as compared to 17.3 percent in 1870. The figures in table 9.2 include cigarette and tobacco as well as cigar workers.

21. *BLS — 1877*, p. 204. Hand rollers were paid an average weekly wage of $10 in 1877 as compared to $6 for machine mold workers.

22. The mechanization of the cigar trade and the increased employment of women and children are discussed in *Enquirer*, August 29, 1877; November 11, 1886; *Times-Star*, March 18, 1884; *BLS—1877*, pp. 199–201; *BLS—1878*, p. 169; *BLS—1882*, p. 181.

23. *Scientific Artisan*, September 1, 1878.

24. *BLS—1878*, pp. 301–2.

25. Ibid., p. 276.

26. *Iron Molders' Journal*, October 10, 1875.

27. *4th Annual Report of the Commissioner of Labor 1888. Working Women in Large Cities* (Washington, 1889), p. 72. This report provides a wealth of information concerning the

9. City of Modern Industry 371

employment patterns, earnings, ethnic backgrounds, marital status, and living conditions of Cincinnati's workingwomen. Percentages of female employees were compiled from the *Manufactures of the U.S. — 1860*, pp. 453–56; *Report on Manufacturing — 1890*, pp. 142–57.

28. *BLS — 1887*, p. 9; "Manufacturing Schedules, Hamilton County, 1880."

29. *BLS — 1878*, p. 302.

30. William Jungst, *Are the Aims of Socialism Justifiable or Not? An Essay, Delivered Before the "Popular Science Society"* (Cincinnati, 1875), p. 7.

31. *BLS — 1878*, p. 301. See BLS reports for 1877–1885 for further information on the decline of traditional systems of apprenticeship.

32. *BLS — 1879*, p. 250.

33. *Ninth Census — 1870*, p. 557; *Report on Manufacturing — 1890*, p. 3.

34. *Chamber Report — 1891*, p. 83.

35. *Enquirer*, July 10, 1887.

36. *BLS — 1887*, p. 216.

37. *Report of Manufactures — 1880*, 2:xxvi–xxvii; *Enquirer*, July 10, 1887; Andrew Morrison, *The Industries of Cincinnati: Manufacturing Establishments and Business Houses* (Cincinnati, 1886), pp. 97–111.

38. For a general history of the expositions, as well as a description of its exhibits, activities, halls, speeches, and Board of Directors, see *Annual Report of the General Committee of the Cincinnati Industrial Exposition* (Cincinnati, 1870–1888); Philip D. Speiss, "The Cincinnati Industrial Expositions (1870–1888): Propaganda or Progress?" M.A. thesis, University of Delaware, 1970; Philip D. Speiss, "Exhibitions and Expositions in Nineteenth-Century Cincinnati," *CHSB* (Fall 1970) 27:171–92. Numerous guidebooks containing listings and pictures of exhibits can be found in the Cincinnati Industrial Exposition Collection at the CHS.

39. *Exposition Report — 1870*, p. xvi.

40. Ibid., p. xxxviii; Ibid — *1873*, p. 53.

41. *Exposition Report — 1874*, p. 24.

42. *Exposition Report — 1879*, p. 67.

43. *Exposition Report — 1875*, p. 50.

44. *Enquirer*, September 22, 1870.

45. *Exposition Report — 1874*, p. 20.

46. *Exposition Report — 1872*, p. 7.

47. *Scientific Artisan*, January 6, 1878. Far from being unique to Cincinnati, these changing attitudes toward machines and progress swept the entire nation during the last quarter of the nineteenth century. Descriptions of industrial expositions and discussions of a national movement toward the creation of an aethestics of machinery can be found in John F. Kasson, *Civilizing the Machine: Technology and Republican Values in America 1776–1900* (New York, 1976), pp. 137–234; Leo Marx, *The Machine in the Garden* (New York: Oxford University Press, 1967); John A. Kouwenhoven, *The Arts in Modern American Civilization* (New York, 1967), pp. 18–34, 190–93.

48. Samuel Williams, "Notes of Samuel Williams Concerning the History of Cincinnati, Religion, and Famous Women," p. 20, CHS; John Chamberlain, *A Century of Cincinnati* (Cincinnati, 1880), p. lxv; Donald Smith, "Classicism in Nineteenth-Century Cincinnati Architecture," p. 13, CHS; Charles F. Cellarius, "Milestones in Cincinnati's Architecture," pp. 9–15, CHS; John Maas, *The Gingerbread Age: A View of Victorian America* (New York: Rinehart, 1957), pp. 14, 158; Talbot Faulkner Hamlin, *The Pageant of America* (New Haven: Yale University Press, 1920), pp. 153, 188. Additional information concerning the changing size, structure, and design of the city's buildings was obtained from various photographs, lithographs, guide books, and street directories contained in the Cincinnati Historical Society.

49. Chamberlain, *Century of Cincinnati*, p. lxv.

50. Sidney D. Maxwell, *The Suburbs of Cincinnati* (Cincinnati, 1870), p. 9; D. J. Kenny, *Illustrated Cincinnati. A Pictorial Hand-Book of the Queen City* (Cincinnati, 1875); Morris King, *King's Pocket-Book of Cincinnati* (Boston, 1879).

51. *Enquirer*, August 23, 1847.

52. Ibid., August 27, 1873.

53. Quoted in William L. Downard, *The Cincinnati Brewing Industry. A Social and Economic History* (Athens, Ohio, 1973), p. 42.

54. Ibid., pp. 35–49, 52–62; *Enquirer*, January 9, 1887.

55. Kenny, *Illustrated Cincinnati*, p. 158; Donald C. Pierce, "Mitchell and Rammelsberg: Cincinnati Furniture Makers 1847–1881," M.A. thesis, University of Delaware, 1976, pp. 72–85.

56. Kenny, *Illustrated Cincinnati*, p. 158. For descriptions and lithographs of various showrooms and factories see Ibid., pp. 137–293.

57. [Seventh Street Congregational Church], "Memorial to the Church and Society of the Vine Street Congregational Church," December 2, 1882, Vine Street Congregational Church Collection, CHS.

58. Changes in transportation facilities and residential patterns are discussed in Daniel Hurley, *Cincinnati the Queen City* (Cincinnati, 1982), pp. 75–88; Zane L. Miller, *Boss Cox's Cincinnati: Urban Politics in the Progressive Era* (New York, 1968), pp. 3–55; Ross, "Workers On the Edge," pp. 54–75.

10. Confrontations with Capital

1. *Enquirer*, August 6, 1877.

2. *Cigarmakers' Journal*, May 1877, quoted in Robert V. Bruce, *1877: Year of Violence* (Chicago, 1970), p. 66.

3. *Third Annual Report of the Bureau of Labor Statistics for the Year 1879* (Columbus, 1880), p. 242.

4. *Report On Manufacturing Industries—11th Census, 1890. Part II: Statistics of Cities* (Washington, 1895), pp. 142–57; U.S. Census Office, "Census of the United States, Manufacturing Schedule, Hamilton County, 1880."

5. *BLS—1877*, pp. 29, 111–12, 193, 197, 204; *BLS—1878*, p. 190; *BLS—1879*, p. 225.

6. *Enquirer*, July 25, 1876.

7. *BLS—1878*, pp. 12–13.

8. *Enquirer*, July 30, 1876.

9. Ibid., November 9, 1876.

10. *Annual Report of the Chief of Police for the Ten Months Ending 31 December 1872*, in *Annual Reports of the City Departments of the City of Cincinnati for the Year 1872* (Cincinnati, 1873), p. 38.

11. *City Reports—1866*, p. 35; *City Reports—1877*, p. 97.

12. *Report of the Committee of the Senate Upon the Relations Between Labor and Capital, and Testimony Taken by the Committee*, 5 vols. (Washington, 1885), 1:589.

13. *BLS—1878*, pp. 22–23.

14. See sources in table 10.3

15. *BLS — 1877*, p. 310; *BLS — 1879*, pp. 230 – 31; *BLS — 1880*, p. 259; *BLS —*
1881, pp. 47, 67; *BLS — 1882*, p. 233; *BLS — 1883*, pp. 118 – 19, 134.

16. *BLS — 1878*, p. 244.

17. *Report of Senate Upon Labor and Capital*, 1:409.

18. *BLS — 1877*, p. 310; *BLS — 1881*, pp. 38 – 41; *BLS — 1883*, pp. 145 – 47.

19. *BLS — 1885*, pp. 140 – 47.

20. *Report of Senate Upon Labor and Capital*, 1:411. Union membership throughout
the nation decreased from 300,000 in 1870 to 50,000 in 1876. Bruce, *1877*, pp. 15, 17.

21. "Minute Book of Cincinnati Typographical Union No. 3," 1, November 9, 1877,
ITU No. 3 Headquarters, Cincinnati, Ohio.

22. "Minute Book of Iron Molders' Union No. 4." 4, November 17, 1877; August 28,
October 2, 1875; and passim (volumes 3 – 4 are in the International Molders and Allied Workers'
Union Headquarters, Cincinnati, Ohio). CTU No. 3 was also forced to suspend union work rules
and wage scales during this period.

23. *BLS — 1879*, p. 15.

24. *Martinsburg Independent*, July 21, 1877, cited in Bruce, *1877*, p. 84.

25. For a more complete analysis of the national impact of the railroad strikes see
Ibid., pp. 28 – 291; Jeremy Brecher, *Strike* (San Francisco, 1972), pp. 1 – 24.

26. *Enquirer*, July 25, 1877.

27. Ibid., July 22, 1877.

28. Ibid., July 24, 1877.

29. Ibid., July 22, 1877.

30. Andrew H. Hickenlooper, "Personal Reminiscences," 2:204, Hickenlooper Papers,
CHS.

31. *Enquirer*, July 23, 1877.

32. Ibid., July 24, 1877; Hickenlooper, "Personal Reminiscences," 2:204. For a more
thorough description of local working-class responses to the railroad strikes see Cincinnati *Eman-*
cipator, July – August 1877; James Matthew Morris, "The Road to Trade Unionism: Organized
Labor in Cincinnati to 1893," Ph.D. diss., University of Cincinnati, 1969, pp. 162 – 70, 239 – 40.

33. *Enquirer*, July 23, 1877.

34. Ibid., February 12, 1876.

35. Ibid., July 25, 1877.

36. *Emancipator*, July 28, 1877. Clark, disillusioned with the increasingly conservative
direction taken by the Republican Party, left that organization and became one of the city's leading
socialists. For a more detailed history of this remarkable man, see Reverend William J. Simmons,
Men of Mark: Eminent, Progressive, and Rising (New York, 1968), pp. 374 – 83; Herbert G. Gutman,
"Peter H. Clark: Pioneer Negro Socialist, 1877," *Journal of Negro Education* (Fall 1965) 34:413 –
18; Lawrence Grossman, "In His Veins Coursed No Bootlicking Blood: The Career of Peter H.
Clark," *Ohio History* (Spring 1977) 86:79 – 95.

37. *Emancipator*, July 23, 1877.

38. *Enquirer*, July 25, 1877.

39. *Emancipator*, March 24, 1877. By the beginning of 1877, Cincinnati socialists
maintained three sections: German, Bohemian, and English (the smallest of the three). Ibid., March
27, 1877.

40. *Emancipator*, March 24, 1877.

41. Ibid., March 31, 1877.

42. Ibid., March 24, 1877.

43. *Enquirer*, February 6, 1874; *Emancipator*, August 12, June 30, 1877. For more
detailed explorations of contemporary socialist thought see William Jungst, *Are the Aims of Socialism*
Justifiable or Not? An Essay Delivered Before the Popular Science Society (Cincinnati, 1875); William
Jungst, *The Social Task of the United States of America* (Cincinnati, 1876); William Haller, "*German*

Socialism in America." A Reply to an Article in the North American Review, for April and May 1879 (Cincinnati, 1879).

44. *Enquirer*, December 23, 1873; July 31, 1876. For Irish and black involvement in the socialist cause see Ibid., January 29, August 19, November 18, 1877.

45. *Catholic Telegraph*, June 20, 1872; also see *Times*, December 12, 1873; *Commercial*, December 23, 29, 1873. The political activities of the socialists are detailed in Morris, "Road to Trade Unionism," pp. 234–39.

46. *Enquirer*, August 12, 1877.

47. Ibid., August 11, 1877.

48. Ibid., September 20, October 11, 1877; John R. Commons, et al., *History of Labour in the United States* (New York, 1966), 2:277.

49. *Enquirer*, October 2, 1877; *Commercial*, December 29, 1877.

50. *Commercial*, October 2, 1877.

51. *Iron Molders' Journal*, June 30, 1878.

52. Ibid.; also see Commons, et al., *History of Labour*, 2:282.

53. Morris, "Road to Trade Unionism," pp. 242–58. For an account of the socialists' "trial" of William Haller and his allies, see *Enquirer*, July 28, 1879.

54. *Enquirer*, February 21, 1881.

55. Ibid.

56. *Report of Senate Upon Labor and Capital*, 1:411.

57. These statistics were compiled from information contained in the *Enquirer* and *Gazette*, January 1, 1878 through December 31, 1881; Hamilton County Incorporation Records, 3–4, 1878–1881, County Recorder's Office, HCC; Morris, "Road to Trade Unionism," pp. 381–431.

58. *Enquirer*, October 2, 1879.

59. U.S. Commissioner of Labor, *Strikes and Lockouts — 1887*, pp. 436–61, 660–63.

60. Major manufacturers' associations were formed in the following industries: tobacco (1869), furniture (1873), brewing (1877), building trades (1878), and boot and shoe (1880).

61. George Lindemann, "Police Matters. An Address, Delivered Before the Police Force of Cincinnati, Ohio 1876," CHS; also see *City Reports — 1873*, p. 53; *City Reports — 1874*, p. 7.
    The changing nature, composition, and political character of the police force during this period is analyzed in Celestine Estelle Anderson, "The Invention of the 'Professional' Municipal Police: The Case of Cincinnati, 1788–1900," Ph.D. diss., University of Cincinnati, 1979, pp. 159–370; George M. Roe, *Our Police: A History of the Cincinnati Police Force, From the Earliest Period Until the Present Day* (Cincinnati, 1890), pp. 47–148.

62. For several particularly interesting episodes, see *Enquirer*, December 29, 1873; August 11, 16, 1876; *Times*, August 1, 31, 1876; October 20, 1879. A copy of the riot law, passed on March 24, 1876, can be found in *Enquirer*, July 27, 1876.

63. *Iron Molders' Journal*, January 10, 1876; July 31, 1884; *Emancipator*, June 30, 1877. For a description of the ethnic and class composition of the police force, see Anderson, "Municipal Police," pp. 188–93, 204–15; *Annual Reports of the Police Commissioner*, in *City Reports*, 1873–1884.

64. *Commercial*, March 19, 1873.

65. *Gazette*, July 30, 1877.

66. *Enquirer*, October 2, 1877.

67. *Catholic Telegraph*, August 2, 1877.

68. *Commercial*, August 14, 1882. The attitudes of local clergymen and religious leaders toward labor and capital are analyzed in Sister Mary S. Connaughton, *The Editorial Opinion of the Catholic Telegraph in Cincinnati on Contemporary Affairs and Politics 1871–1921* (Washington,

1943), pp. 132 – 202; Harry Jebsen, "Cincinnati Protestant Clergy in Social and Political Reform 1865 – 1915," M.A. thesis, University of Cincinnati, 1966, pp. 34 – 62; Morris, "Road to Trade Unionism," pp. 151 – 52.

69. *Enquirer*, March 2, 1880.

70. These strikes are described in the *Enquirer*, September 22 through October 24, 1879; *Times*, December 20, 1879; Morris, "Road to Trade Unionism," 171 – 72; Hermann Schluter, *The Brewery Industry and the Brewery Workers' Movement in America* (Cincinnati, 1910), pp. 100 – 1; William L. Downard, *The Cincinnati Brewing Industry: A Social and Economic History* (Athens, Ohio, 1973), pp. 100 – 2.

71. Hamilton County Incorporation Records, 3 – 5, HCC.

72. Department of the Interior, *Compendium of the 11th Census: 1890. Part III* (Washington, 1897), pp. 720 – 21.

73. The following sources were particularly useful in describing the development of ethnic and religious associations: Carl Wittke, "The Germans of Cincinnati," *HPSOB* (January 1962) 20:9 – 11; Guido A. Dobbert, "The Disintegration of an Immigrant Community: The Cincinnati Germans, 1870 – 1920," Ph.D. diss., University of Chicago, 1965, pp. 7 – 55; Barnett Brickner, "The Jewish Community of Cincinnati: Historical and Descriptive," Ph.D. diss., University of Cincinnati, 1935, pp. 13 – 42; Thomas N. Brown, *Irish-American Nationalism 1870 – 1890* (Philadelphia: J. B. Lippincott, 1966); Reverend Charles Frederic Goss, *Cincinnati The Queen City 1788 – 1912*, 4 vols. (Cincinnati, 1912), 1:467 – 511; 2:9 – 52, 461 – 65; Henry A. and Mrs. Kate B. Ford, *History of Cincinnati, Ohio* (Cleveland, 1881), pp. 212–22; Hamilton County Incorporation Records, 3 – 5, HCC.

74. Daniel Walkowitz, *Worker City, Company Town* (Urbana, Illinois, 1978), p. 165.

75. "Constitution of the Irish National League of America, adopted April 27, 1883," reprinted in *Address of George W. Houck, President, Dayton Branch of the Irish National League of America* (Dayton, Ohio, 1886), p. 113. For further information concerning local participation in the Fenian Brotherhood, Irish Land League, and Friendly Sons of St. Patrick see *Enquirer*, July 24, 1876; February 20, 1880; February 7, 10, 14, 1881; *76th Annual Banquet of the Friendly Sons of St. Patrick of Cincinnati* (Cincinnati, 1944).

76. Dobbert, "Disintegration of Immigrant Community," pp. 46, 152 – 57; "Membership Books of the Central Turner Association of Cincinnati," 1873 – 1884, Turner Society Records, CHS; Hamilton County Incorporation Records, 1 – 4, HCC.

77. Nancy R. Hamant, "Religion in the Cincinnati Schools 1830 – 1900," *HPSOB* (October 1963) 21:242 – 49; F. Michael Perko, "The Building Up of Zion: Religion and Education in Nineteenth-Century Cincinnati," *CHSB* (Summer 1980) 38:108 – 11; Jebsen, "Cincinnati's Protestant Clergy," pp. 21 – 23; Foraker, *Notes of a Busy Life*, 1:105 – 6; Reverend John H. Lamott, *History of the Archdiocese of Cincinnati 1821 – 1921* (Cincinnati, 1921), pp. 279 – 80; Hickenlooper, "Personal Reminiscences," 2:434; Cincinnati *Daily Gazette* and Cincinnati *Catholic Telegraph, The Persecution of Catholics in the United States* (Cincinnati, 1873).

Working-class divisions over temperance and patronage appointments are described in *Enquirer*, March 3, 1879; February 7, 10, March 3, 1881; Barbara Musselman, "The Quest for Collective Improvement: Cincinnati Workers, 1893 to 1920," Ph.D. diss., University of Cincinnati, 1975, pp. 2 – 3, 40 – 41.

78. *Enquirer*, February 20, 1885.

79. "Minute Books — IMU NO. 4," 4, June 15, 1878.

80. "Minute Books — CTU No. 3," 2, November 1, 1885; June 1, 1884; *Report of the First Annual Session of the Organized Trades and Labor Unions of the United States, Held in Pittsburgh, Pa., December 15, 16, 17, 18, 1881* (n.p., n.d.); *BLS — 1885*, p. 34.

81. "Minute Books — CTU No. 3," 2, November 1, 1885.

82. Ibid., 1, October 5, 1879.

83. Ibid., 1, November 2, 1879.

84. Corresponding Secretary to Officers and Delegates of the Trades and Labor Assembly, December 29, 1880, "Letter Book of the Corresponding Secretary of CTU No. 3."

85. *Iron Molders' Journal*, July 31, 1881; Antagonizing Committee of the TLA to CTU No. 3, February 9, 1884, "Letter Book — CTU No. 3."

86. *Enquirer*, February 21, 1881. Descriptions of other major boycotts can be found in Ibid., March 2, 5, 8, 9, 10, 1880; Downard, *Cincinnati Brewing Industry*, pp. 101 – 4; "Letter Book — CTU No. 3," December 29, 1880; February 9, 1884; *Iron Molders' Journal*, July 31, 1881; *The Unionist*, March 30, 1883; "Minute Books — CTU No. 3," 1, April 6, 1884.

87. "Minute Books — CTU No. 3," 1, August 14, 1881; *Enquirer*, July 26, 1877.

88. *Enquirer*, February 15, 1880.

89. For the formation of early arbitration boards see *Enquirer*, July 26, 1877; April 2, 9, 1881; January 1, June 5, 1884; "Minute Books — IMU No. 4," 4, April 1, 1876; *BLS — 1882*, pp. 31 – 36; *BLS — 1889*, pp. 233 – 42; Morris, "Road to Trade Unionism," pp. 182, 185, 197.

90. "Minute Books — CTU No. 3," 1, September 7, 1884.

91. "Minute Books — IMU No. 4," 4, April 17, 1875; *Iron Molders' Journal*, May 31, 1880; *Enquirer*, May 22, November 22, December 14, 1880; Morris, "Road to Trade Unionism," pp. 203 – 3.

92. *Iron Molders' Journal*, May 31, 1880.

93. Ibid., May 31, 1881; May 31, 1882; *Enquirer*, June 2, 8, 9, 1884.

94. "Minute Book — CTU No. 3," 1, April 10, 1881.

95. Ibid., 2, November 1, 1885.

96. *Iron Molders' Journal*, May 31, 1871.

97. "Minute Books – CTU No. 3," 1, September 5, October 3, 1880.

98. *Enquirer*, February 21, 1881.

99. "Minute Books — CTU No. 3," 1, October 7, 1883. For the development of lobbying and pressure group tactics see Ibid., 1, April 6, 1879; October 7, December 2, 1883; December 7, 1884; February 1, 1885; *Enquirer*, August 27, 1880; April 9, 1881; *The Unionist*, March 30, 1883; Morris, "Road to Trade Unionism," pp. 203 – 4, 227 – 29.

100. *Enquirer*, December 14, 1880.

101. *Iron Molders' Journal*, March 31, 1885. The entry of women into various unions is discussed in *BLS — 1879*, p. 359.

102. Quoted in Terence V. Powderly, *Thirty Years of Labor 1859 to 1889* (Philadelphia, 1890), p. 128. The general aims and policies of the KOL are discussed in Ibid.; Terence V. Powderly, *The Path I Trod* (New York, 1940); Gerald Grob, *Workers and Utopia. A Study of Ideological Conflict in the American Labor Movement 1865 – 1900* (Chicago, 1961), pp. 34 – 59; Normal J. Ware, *The Labor Movement in the United States 1860–1895: A Study in Democracy* (New York: D. Appleton and Co., 1929), pp. 22 – 376; Leon Fink, *Workingmen's Democracy: The Knights of Labor and American Politics* (Urbana: University of Illinois Press, 1983).

103. Powderly, *Thirty Years*, p. 129.

104. Jonathan Garlock, *Guide to the Local Assemblies of the Knights of Labor* (Westport, Conn., 1982), pp. 380 – 81; Jonathan Garlock and N. C. Builder, "Knights of Labor Data Bank: User's Manual and Index to Local Assemblies," *Knights of Labor Assemblies 1879 – 1889*, Inter-University Consortium for Political Research (Ann Arbor, 1973); Morris, "Road to Trade Unionism," pp. 199 – 201, 430 – 31.

105. Fink, *Workingmen's Democracy*, p. 8; also see Susan Levine, "Labor's True Woman: Domesticity and Equal Rights in the Knights of Labor," *Journal of American History* (September 1983) 70:323 – 39.

106. *Enquirer*, February 14, 1881.

107. *Journal of United Labor*, December 10, 1885.

108. Foraker, *Notes of a Busy Life*, 1:213 – 14.

109. Charles Reemelin, *Life of Charles Reemelin* (Cincinnati, 1892), p. 257.

110. By the morning of April 4, the death toll had risen to 51 men. Descriptions of the events leading to the courthouse riots, as well as the riots themselves, were drawn from the following sources: J. S. Tunison, *The Cincinnati Riot: Its Causes and Results* (Cincinnati, 1886); Hickenlooper, "Personal Reminiscences," 2:458 – 520; *The Great Cincinnati Riots. Being the Only Correct History of that Most Lamentable Outbreak in Ohio's Greatest City, Because of the Villainous Verdict of the Berner Jury* (Philadelphia, 1884); James H. Rodabaugh, "The Cincinnati Riot of 1884," *Museum Echoes* (December 1959) 32:91–94; W. Laird Kleine, "Anatomy of a Riot," *HPSOB* (October 1962) 20:234 – 44; *History of the First Regiment of Infantry. Ohio National Guard* (Cincinnati 1905), pp. 5–8, 59–62; John A. Johnson, *On the Roof of Europe Behind the Guardsman's Rifle* (Covington, Kentucky, 1920), pp. 65 – 95; Mortimer D. Leggett, *The Military and the Mob: A Paper Read Before the Ohio Commandry of the Military Order of the Loyal Legion of the United States* (Cincinnati, 1884); *Enquirer, Commercial Gazette, Times Star,* March – April 1884; *John Swinton's Paper,* April 6, 13, 1884.

111. Workers — particularly those living in the poorest areas of the city — were often excluded from the city directories. Nevertheless, 135 (67.2 percent) of the 201 casualties mentioned in newspaper reports had their occupation and address listed in the city directories of 1882, 1883, or 1884. Had there not been so many misspellings of German names or so many commonly held names, like John Miller, the number of identifiable workers would have been significantly greater. This suggests that rioters represented a more stable portion of the working-class community than newspapers and city officials were apt to admit.

112. *Enquirer,* March 30, 1884.

113. Johnson, *On the Roof,* p. 79.

114. "Minute Books — CTU No. 3, " 1, July 1, 1883; also see Ibid., 1, September 2, 1883; *Emancipator,* July 22, 23, August 4, 1877; Herbert G. Gutman, "An Iron Workers' Strike in the Ohio Valley, 1873 – 1874," *Ohio History Quarterly* (October 1959) 68:353 – 70.

115. "Minute Books — CTU No. 3, " 1, April 6, 1884; *Commercial Gazette,* April 7, 1884. Further reactions to the militia can be found in *Enquirer,* April 1, May 22, 1884; Hickenlooper, "Personal Reminiscences," 2:520.

116. Robert Wiebe, *The Search For Order 1877 – 1920* (New York: Hill and Wang, 1967).

11. Law, Order, and Class Consciousness

1. The figure of 340,000 was estimated by *Bradstreets* and that of 32,000 by the Ohio Bureau of Labor Statistics. *Bradstreets,* May 15, 1886, cited in Gerald A. Grob, *Workers and Utopia. A Study of Ideological Conflict in the American Labor Movement 1865–1900* (Chicago, 1969), pp. 74 – 75; *10th Annual Report of the Bureau of Labor Statistics for the Year 1886* (Columbus, 1887), p. 52.

For accounts of May Day activities in other cities see Jeremy Brecher, *Strike* (San Francisco, 1972), pp. 25 – 50; Marion Cotter Cahill, *Shorter Hours: A Study of the Movement Since the Civil War* (New York 1932), pp. 155 – 59.

2. J. S. Tunison, *The Cincinnati Riot: Its Causes and Results* (Cincinnati, 1886), p. 72; Reverend Charles Frederic Goss, *Cincinnati the Queen City 1788–1912,* 4 vols. (Cincinnati, 1912), 1:255 – 56; Joseph B. Foraker, *Notes of a Busy Life,* 2 vols. (Cincinnati, 1917), 1:213 – 29; Zane

Miller, *Boss Cox's Cincinnati: Urban Politics in the Progressive Era* (New York, 1968), pp. 61–62; Philip Jordan, *Ohio Comes of Age 1873–1900* (Columbus, 1943), pp. 198–202.

3. The formation, teachings, and membership of the committee are described in *Constitution of the Committee of One Hundred* (Cincinnati, 1885), pp. 1–8; *Public Meeting of the Committee of One Hundred . . . In the Odeon, February 11, 1886* (Cincinnati, 1886), pp. 1–15; Andrew H. Hickenlooper, "Personal Reminiscences," 2:552–55, Andrew Hickenlooper Papers, CHS; George Augustine Thayer, *The First Congregational Church of Cincinnati, A Historical Sketch* (Cincinnati, 1917), p. 43; Miller, *Boss Cox*, p. 71.

4. *Proceedings of the Association of the "Committee of One Hundred" held in the Odeon Friday Evening, March 26, 1886* (Cincinnati, 1886), p. 23.

5. Miller, *Boss Cox*, pp. 74–78; Christopher B. Hett, "Political Boss of Cincinnati: The Era of George B. Cox," M.A. thesis, Xavier University, 1968, pp. 8–11; Reverend Charles Frederic Goss, *Cincinnati the Queen City, 1788–1912*, 4 vols. (Cincinnati, 1912), 1:264–65.

6. *The Citizens' Law and Order League of Hamilton County* (n.p., n.d.); *Minutes of the Cincinnati Annual Conference of the Methodist Church for the Year 1886* (Cincinnati, 1886), pp. 99–101; *Address of the Bund für Freiheit und Recht* (Cincinnati, 1886), pp. 5, 7; Thayer, *First Congregational Church*, pp. 41, 43. A published list of 85 members of the Law and Order League contains the names of many of the city's large factory owners, merchants, bankers, and other prominent capitalists; 29.4 percent of these names were also found on the 1880 leading manufacturers' list. There was only one labor leader included in the membership roles. *The Citizens' Association to Promote the Observance of Law and Order in Cincinnati, List of Members, November 12, 1885* (Cincinnati, n.d.).

7. *Address of the Bund*, pp. 3, 4–15; Charles Reemelin, *Life of Charles Reemelin* (Cincinnati, 1892), p. 266; *Enquirer*, April 1, May 31, 1886; *Times-Star*, April 6, 1886. By June 1886, membership in the Bund was estimated to be 16,986. *Commercial Gazette*, June 3, 1886.

8. Thayer, *First Congregational Church*, p. 41. Clergymen also saw appeals to law and order as a means of halting moral decay and declining church attendance; see *Minutes of the 85th Anniversary of the Miami Association of Regular Baptists* (Cincinnati, 1883), pp. 7–8, 12, 21–24; *Baptist Minutes — 1884*, pp. 8–9; *Minutes of the Cincinnati Annual Conference of the Methodist Episcopal Church* (Cincinnati, 1884), pp. 90–96; *Methodist Minutes — 1886*, pp. 95–101; *One Hundred Years of Presbyterianism in the Ohio Valley 1790–1940* (Cincinnati, 1941), pp. 150–52; Harry Jebsen, "Cincinnati's Protestant Clergy in Social and Political Reform 1865–1915," M.A. thesis, University of Cincinnati, 1966, pp. 48–71; *Discussions of the Inter-Denominational Congress in the Interest of City Evangelization* (Cincinnati, 1886).

9. *Enquirer*, April 1, 1886.

10. "Declaration of Principles of Agitation," Cincinnati Trades and Labor Assembly, in "Minute Book of the Cincinnati Typographical Union No. 3," 2, November 1, 1885.

11. *Enquirer*, April 18, 1886.

12. "Declaration of Principles," "Minute Book — CTU No. 3," 2," November 1, 1885.

13. Ibid., 1, September 7, December 7, 1884; February 1, March 1, 1885; 2, November 1, 1885; *The Unionist*, March 30, 1883; James Matthew Morris, "The Road to Trade Unionism: Organized Labor in Cincinnati to 1893," Ph.D. diss., University of Cincinnati, 1969, pp. 260–61.

14. Terence V. Powderly, *Thirty Years of Labor, 1859 to 1889* (Columbus, 1889), pp. 180–81, 492; Stuart Bruce Kaufman, *Samuel Gompers and the Origins of the American Federation of Labor 1846–1896* (Westport: Greenwood Press, 1973), pp. 151–53; Cahill, *Shorter Hours*, pp. 40–49, 152–55; "Minute Book — CTU No. 3," 1, November 2, 1884; *Enquirer*, April 28, 29, 1886; *Commercial Gazette*, April 29, 1886.

15. *Iron Molders' Journal*, July 31, 1885.

16. *Commercial Gazette*, May 2, 1886.

17. Revised Statutes of Ohio, section 4365, quoted in *BLS — 1890*, p. 40.

18. In March 1884, Hamilton County legislator William Peet introduced a bill that

would have made it a misdemeanor, punishable by a fine of $100 to $500, for any employer to work his employees more than eight hours per day. The Peet bill, as well as three similar measures, were all voted down by Republican legislators. *Times Star*, March 28, 1884; *Commerical Gazette*, April 11, 1886; Joseph B. Foraker Scrapbooks, 8:10 – 11, CHS.

19. *United Labor Age*, quoted in *Enquirer*, February 5, 1887; also see *BLS* — *1886*, p. 39.

20. *Proceedings of the 17th Annual Convention of the Iron Molders' Union of North America* (London, Ontario, 1886), p. 9.

21. Powderly, *Thirty Years*, p. 493.

22. Ibid., pp. 495 – 96.

23. *Enquirer*, May 6, 1886. For local KOL views on the May Day strikes see Ibid., May 7, 1886.

24. *Enquirer*, April 26, May 3, 1886; *Times Star*, April 26, 1886. The eight-hour cause received the endorsement of the Bund in late March. *Enquirer*, April 1, 1886.

25. *Times Star*, April 19, 1886.

26. Ibid., May 1, 1886. State Labor Commissioner Larkin McHugh, a former Cincinnati union leader, reported in 1886 that "many of the best organized trades gave it [the strikes] the cold shoulder." *BLS* — *1886*, p. 39.

27. *Times Star*, April 27, 1886.

28. *Enquirer*, May 5, 8, 9, 1886.

29. *Times Star*, May 22, 1886; *Commercial Gazette*, April 26, 1886.

30. Oscar Ameringer, *If You Don't Weaken* (New York, 1940), p. 44. This conviction that shorter hours meant more pay was shared by numerous workers around the country. Robert A. Christie, *Empire in Wood. A History of the Carpenters' Union* (Ithaca, New York, 1956), pp. 47 – 48, 60.

31. *Times Star*, May 4, 1886.

32. Ibid., April 21, 28, 1886; *Enquirer*, April 30, May 1, 2, 1886.

33. *Times Star*, April 28, 1886.

34. My original list of strike leaders included the names of 129 men and women mentioned in local newspaper reports. Using the city directories, I was able to trace the residential work patterns of 104 (80.6 percent) people. This in itself is a significant indication of the stability and relative importance of these leaders, for workers were usually among the first groups to be excluded from city directories. Factory artisan and factory laborer activists generally included machinists, heavy metal workers, boilermakers, safe workers, carriage workers, furniture workers, coffin workers, and coopers laboring in large establishments. Those listed as unskilled laborers included railroad freight handlers, pavers and rammers, cartmen, barbers, laundresses, seamstresses, and general day laborers.

35. For studies of worker mobility in other nineteenth-century cities, see Stephan Thernstrom and Richard Sennett, eds., *Nineteenth-Century Cities: Essays in the New Urban History* (New Haven: Yale University Press, 1969); Stephan Thernstrom, *Poverty and Progress: Social Mobility in a Nineteenth-Century City* (Cambridge: Harvard University Press, 1964); Stephan Thernstrom, *The Other Bostonians: Poverty and Progress in the American Metropolis, 1880 – 1970* (Cambridge: Harvard University Press, 1973); Peter R. Knights, *The Plain People of Boston, 1830 – 1860: A Study in City Growth* (New York: Oxford University Press, 1971); Alan Dawley, *Class and Community: The Industrial Revolution in Lynn* (Cambridge, 1976); Stuart M. Blumin, *The Urban Threshold: Growth and Change in a Nineteenth-Century American Community* (Chicago: University of Chicago Press, 1976); Clyde and Sally Griffen, *Natives and Newcomers: The Ordering of Opportunity in Mid-Nineteenth-Century Poughkeepsie* (Cambridge: Harvard University Press, 1978).

36. Of these 91 new activists, 11.5 percent had worked at the same shop ten years or more, and 5.2 percent for twenty years or more. Moreover, at least 8.3 percent were shop foremen

at the time of the strikes. These are all minimum figures; in only a handful of cases did the city directory list the shop a man worked in. Therefore it is likely that long-term shop, as well as craft, stability was a characteristic shared by a large number of these workers.

37. During the first eleven days of May, new unions were organized by barbers, cracker bakers, undertaker carriage drivers, grocery clerks, seamstresses, waitresses, laundresses, and pick and shovel men.

38. *Times-Star*, April 29, 1886; *Enquirer*, April 30 – May 1, 1886. Thirteen furniture companies were incorporated between 1863 and 1874, and 26 firms between 1875 and May 1886. Even if one shifts the base years, the general pattern remains the same: 1863 – 1873, 13 incorporations; 1873 – 1884, 23 incorporations. An analysis of furniture strike leaders shows that the average activist worked in Cincinnati an average of 9.5 years and at the same occupation an average of 8.5 years. Incorporation statistics were taken from the Hamilton County Incorporation Records, 1 – 6, County Recorder's Office, HCC.

39. *Enquirer, Commercial Gazette*, and *Times Star*, April 30 – May 4, 1886.

40. By the end of the first week of May, a conditional settlement had been agreed to by many of the smaller manufacturers: shorter hours and higher wages would be granted provided large firms did likewise.

41. *Enquirer, Commercial Gazette*, and *Times Star*, April 28 – May 8, 1886.

42. Incorporation statistics show that 89.5 percent of all carriage company incorporations occurred between 1872 and May 1886. Hamilton County Incorporation Records, 1 – 6, HCC.

43. Crane and Breed was incorporated in 1882 with an initial capital stock of $500,000; James Ritchey Company was incorporated the same year at $100,000; the Cincinnati Coffin Company was incorporated in 1872 at $100,000. HCIR, 5, November 2, 1882; 3, November 18, 1872.

44. *Enquirer*, May 5, 1886.

45. *Enquirer*, May 5, 7, 1886. Strike leaders in this trade averaged 20.2 working and 18.8 craft years in Cincinnati. By the mid-1880s, Cincinnati was the largest safe manufacturer in the United States. *BLS—1887*, p. 217.

46. Interview with John Techtel, *Commercial Gazette*, May 2, 1886.

47. *Times Star*, May 12, 1886.

48. Ibid., May 20, 1886.

49. *Enquirer*, May 4, 1886.

50. Ibid., May 4, 1886. Working-class concepts of masculinity and manhood are discussed in David Montgomery, *Workers' Control in America* (Cambridge: Cambridge University Press, 1979), pp. 9 – 31.

51. *Commercial Gazette*, May 2, 1886. Similar attempts to link wage demands to national market conditions are described in Ibid., May 25, 1886; *Enquirer*, April 21, May 11, 22, 1886; *Times Star*, May 12, 1886.

52. *Times Star*, April 28, 1886.

53. *Enquirer, Commercial Gazette*, May 5, 1886.

54. *Times Star*, May 20, 1886.

55. Ibid.

56. Ibid., May 5, 1886.

57. *Enquirer*, May 7, 1886.

58. Ibid.; also see May 5, 1886.

59. Ibid., May 5, 10, 1886; *Commercial Gazette*, May 6, 1886.

60. *Enquirer*, May 6, 1886. The actions taken by railroad and granite workers are described in Ibid., May 4, 5, 6, 7, 1886; *Times Star*, May 3, 1886; *Commercial Gazette*, May 6, 8, 1886.

61. *Enquirer*, May 7, 1886; also see Hickenlooper, "Personal Reminiscences," 2:600 – 1.

62. *Annual Report of the Adjutant General for the Year 1886* (Columbus, 1887), pp. 76, 78–79, 90; *BLS — 1886*, p. 52; "Journal of the Board of Councilmen," June 1, 1886, 9:607 (journals are kept at the Cincinnati City Hall); *Enquirer*, May 7, 1886; *Commercial Gazette*, May 7, 1886.

63. *Adjutant General Report — 1886*, p. 89.

64. "Minutes of the Cincinnati Chamber of Commerce," May 7, 1886, 3:378, CHS.

65. Sidney Maxwell to Diana Maxwell, May 11, 1886, Sidney Maxwell Papers, CHS.

66. *Enquirer*, May 9, 1886.

67. Ibid., May 11, 1886.

68. Ibid., May 14, 1886.

69. *Commercial Gazette*, May 7, 1886.

70. Ibid., May 12, 1886.

71. Information concerning the Mayor's meeting of May 13 was drawn from Ibid., *Enquirer*, and *Times Star*, May 14, 1886.

72. *Enquirer*, May 14, 1886.

73. Ibid.

74. Ibid.

75. *Adjutant General Report — 1886*, p. 73; *Enquirer*, May 15, 1886.

76. *Enquirer*, May 25, 1886.

77. Ibid., May 20 – June 7, 1886; *Times Star*, May 21 – June 18, 1886; *Commercial Gazette*, May 23, 29, 1886.

78. *Times Star*, May 17, 1886.

79. *Enquirer*, May 12, 13, 14, 16, 23, 24, 1886; *Times Star*, May 23, 25, 1886; *Commercial Gazette*, May 19, 1886.

80. These statistics were compiled from daily newspaper reports; for the most comprehensive settlement list, see *Times Star*, June 8, 1886.

81. *Enquirer*, May 13, 15, 1886.

82. Of the twelve major longterm holdouts ("major" as identified by the press), I was able to identify the ownership patterns of eight firms: one was privately owned, two controlled by partners, and five by corporations. On the Mitchell settlement, see *Times Star*, June 12, 14, 1886.

83. I was able to identify the owners of fourteen of the eighteen key firms: one was privately owned, six were partnerships, and seven corporations.

84. There were nine coffin manufactories in May 1886, six of which were incorporated (with an average capitalization of $208,333).

85. These statistics are taken from the figures published in the U.S. Bureau of Labor, *Third Annual Report, Strikes and Lockouts* (Washington, 1888), pp. 468–83; they were compiled in Morris, "Road to Trade Unionism," p. 294n. The government figure of 17,337 represents less than 50 percent of the total number of workers affected by the strikes.

86. *Enquirer*, June 21, 1886; *Times Star*, June 21, 1886.

87. U.S. Bureau of Labor, *10th Annual Report of the Commissioner of Labor, 1894, Strikes and Lockouts*, 2 vols. (Washington, 1896), 1:26.

88. *BLS — 1886*, p. 53.

89. *Second Public Meeting of Committee of One Hundred of Cincinnati, in the Odeon, February 25, 1886* (Cincinnati, 1886), pp. 15–16.

12. Workers on the Edge

1. *Enquirer*, July 30 – August 30, 1886; James Matthew Morris, "The Road to Trade Unionism: Organized Labor in Cincinnati to 1893," Ph.D. diss., University of Cincinnati, 1969, p. 316.

2. *Enquirer*, August 30, November 12, 1886; *Iron Molders' Journal*, November 30, 1886; Barbara L. Musselman, "Working-Class Unity and Ethnic Division: Cincinnati Trade Unionists and Cultural Pluralism," *CHSB* (Summer 1974) 34:125; "Minute Book of the Central Labor Union," October 21, 1886 – November 30, 1886, Records of the Cincinnati Central Labor Union, Special Collections, UCL.

3. *Record of the Proceedings of the Eighth Regular Session of the General Assembly, held at Philadelphia, Pa., September 1 – 10, 1884*, p. 796; *Proceedings — 1885*, p. 173; *Proceedings — 1886*, p. 326; *Proceedings — 1887*, p. 1847.

4. *Enquirer, Commercial Gazette*, May 1, 1886 – December 31, 1886; *Proceedings of the Annual Session of the District Assembly No. 48 of the Knights of Labor, Held at Druid's Hall, Cincinnati, Sunday, January 8, 1888* (Cincinnati, 1888), p. 8.

The vast majority of assemblies organized in 1886 and 1887 were made up of factory artisans (safe workers, carriagemakers, carriage painters, furniture finishers, cigarmakers, shoemakers, and so forth). However, separate and mixed assemblies were also organized by hotel waiters, coal cart drivers, musicians, actors, street pavers and rammers, steamboat workers, clothing cutters, and street car workers. Jonathan Garlock, *Guide to the Local Assemblies of the Knights of Labor* (Westport, Connecticut, 1982), pp. 381 – 84.

5. *Times Star*, June 15, 1886.

6. *Enquirer*, May 3, 1886.

7. *Commercial Gazette*, November 7, 1887.

8. *Enquirer*, October 25, 1886; May 16, 21, 30, June 1, 1887; February 18, 22, 1888; M. C. Lockwood, *Glimpses of Day. Sermons Preached in the First Baptist Church, Cincinnati, Ohio* (Cincinnati, 1892), see introduction (n.p.); *Minutes of the 85th Anniversary of the Miami Association of Regular Baptists* (Cincinnati, 1887), pp. 12 – 15.

9. *Thirty-Seventh Annual Report of the Cincinnati Chamber of Commerce for the Commercial Year Ending August 31, 1885* (Cincinnati, 1885), pp. 53 – 55; *Chamber Report — 1886*, pp. 59 – 69; *Chamber Report — 1887*, pp. 59 – 61; *Enquirer*, August 8, September 4, October 4, 1886; January 1, 1887; *Commercial Gazette*, August 28, December 25, 27, 1886; January 1, 1887.

10. Food prices were based on the changing cost of eight basic items. *Seventeenth Annual Report of the Bureau of Labor Statistics for the Year 1893* (Norwalk, Ohio, 1894), pp. 798 – 806. For changes in rent and wages see *BLS — 1885*, p. 138; *BLS — 1886*, pp. 220 – 21, 238 – 39.

11. See table 12.2. March, April, and May — the months when wage agreements were usually reached for the coming year — were generally the heaviest periods of unionization and strike activity.

12. *John Swinton's Paper* estimated that 30,000 men and women belonged to unions. The Bureau of Labor Statistics — which gathered only a partial list of all Cincinnati unions — placed their estimate at 18,700. *John Swinton's Paper*, quoted in Kaufman, *Samuel Gompers and the Origins of the American Federation of Labor 1840 – 1896* (Westport, Connecticut, 1973), p. 240n; *BLS — 1887*, pp. 217 – 18.

13. A brief summary of the diverging views of the CLU and the ACBT can be found in *Enquirer*, August 30, December 1, 12, 1886.

14. Steven Joseph Ross, "The Culture of Political Economy: Henry George and the American Working Class," *Southern California Quarterly* (Summer 1983) 65:145 – 66; Charles Albro Barker, *Henry George* (New York: Oxford University Press, 1955), pp. 455 – 81; Edward Rose, *Henry George* (New York: Twayne Publishers, 1968), pp. 119 – 22; Arthur Nicholas Young, *The Single Tax Movement in the United States* (Princeton: Princeton University Press, 1916), pp. 94 – 98; Louis F. Post and Fred C. Leubuscher, *An Account of the George-Hewitt Campaign in the New York Municipal Elections of 1886* (New York, 1887); Peter Alexander Speek, *The Single-Tax and the Labor Movement* (Madison: University of Wisconsin Press, 1917), pp. 24 – 108; Henry George Jr., *The Life of Henry George* (New York: Doubleday and McClure Co., 1900), pp. 459 – 81; Leon Fink, *Workingmen's Democracy: The Knights of Labor and American Politics* (Urbana, 1983), pp. 38 – 233.

15. The CLU's Committee for Political Organization was responsible for coordinating the early activities of the ULP. The committee also conducted an active correspondence with the New York CLU and ULP. *Enquirer*, November 19, 24, 1886; *The Standard*, February 26, 1887.

16. Robert Curl to Hugh Cavanaugh, October 30, 1886, "Letter Book of the Corresponding Secretary of Cincinnati Typographical Union No. 3," ITU No. 3 Headquarters, Cincinnati. Local and national dissatisfaction with KOL policies is explored in Morris, "Road to Trade Unionism," pp. 313 – 15; Gerald N. Grob, *Workers and Utopia: A Study of Ideological Conflict in the American Labor Movement 1865 – 1900* (Chicago, 1969), pp. 107 – 18, 128 – 29; Frank T. Stockton, *The International Molders' Union of North America* (Baltimore, 1922), pp. 45 – 47.

17. *Enquirer*, November 25, December 3, 16, 31, 1886; *Commercial Gazette*, December 6, 1886; *Iron Molders' Journal*, December 31, 1886; *John Swinton's Paper*, November 28, 1886; Kaufman, *Gompers and the AFL*, pp. 159 – 64.

18. *Enquirer*, December 1, 1886; also see Ibid., December 6, 20, 1886.

19. Morris Hillquit, *History of Socialism in the United States* (New York: Russell and Russell Inc., 1965, originally published in 1903), pp. 251 – 54.

20. A diverse group of Irishmen, including labor leaders Thomas Leonard, Hugh Cavanaugh, and James Molloy (all officers in the KOL), and Catholic priests Father John MacKay, Father T. V. Crowley, and Father F. H. Cusick, and politicians Michael Ryan, Joseph Carberry, and J. W. Fitzgerald, all held offices in the Irish Land League.

On Irish radicalism in the Gilded Age see Eric Foner, "Class, Ethnicity, and Radicalism in the Gilded Age: The Land League and Irish-America," *Marxist Perspectives* (Summer 1978) 1:6 – 55; Carl Wittke, *The Irish in America* (Baton Rouge: Louisiana State University Press, 1956), pp. 71 – 285; Thomas N. Brown, *Irish-American Nationalism 1870 – 1890* (Philadelphia, 1966), *passim*; Michael A. Gordon, "Studies in Irish and Irish-American Thought and Behavior in Gilded Age New York City," Ph.D. diss., University of Rochester, 1977.

21. Terence V. Powderly, *Thirty Years of Labor 1859 – 1889* (Columbus, 1889), pp. 169 – 202; Terence V. Powderly, *The Path I Trod* (New York, 1940), pp. 150, 181; Jacob Oser, *Henry George* (New York: Twayne Publishers, 1974), pp. 68 – 92; Foner, "Class, Ethnicity, and Radicalism," pp. 25 – 46; Barker, *Henry George* pp. 335 – 77; Speek, *Single-Tax*, pp. 24 – 87; *John Swinton's Paper*, October 17, 24, 31, 1886.

22. *Commercial Gazette*, February 24, 1887. The following discussion draws upon the speeches, arguments, and platforms of the December, January, and February ULP conventions.

23. *Enquirer*, January 17, 1887.

24. Ibid.

25. *Commercial Gazette*, December 20, 1886.

26. Ibid., January 14, 1887.

27. *Enquirer*, January 17, 1887.

28. Henry George, *Progress and Poverty: An Inquiry into the Causes of Industrial Depressions and the Increase of Want With Increase of Wealth . . . The Remedy* (New York: Robert Schalkenbach Foundation, 1955, originally published in 1880), p. 328.

29. For a more thorough analysis and explanation of George's theories, particularly his Single Tax idea, see Ross, "Culture of Political Economy," pp. 147 – 59; Henry George, *The Single Tax. What It Is and Why We Urge It* (Cincinnati, n.d.), pp. 1 – 12; Robert V. Andelson, ed., *Critics of Henry George: A Centenary Appraisal of their Strictures on "Progress and Poverty"* (Cranbury, New Jersey: Farleigh Dickinson University Press, 1979), pp. 15 – 393.

30. *Enquirer*, January 17, 1887.

31. *The Standard*, February 26, 1887.

32. *Enquirer*, January 17, 1887; December 20, 1886.

33. *Commercial Gazette*, February 24, 1887; also see *Enquirer*, February 22, 23, 24, 1887; *The Standard*, March 26, 1887.

34. *The Standard*, February 25, 1887.

35. *Enquirer*, February 23, 1887.

36. *Commercial Gazette*, December 20, 1886; *Enquirer*, January 17, 1887.

37. *Commercial Gazette*, January 14, 1887.

38. *Enquirer*, March 20, 1887.

39. Six of the nominees were born in Cincinnati, one in Indiana, two in Ireland, and one in Germany. *Enquirer*, March 20, 21, 1887.

40. All six Cincinnati-born candidates grew up among the city's shops and factories. The four candidates born outside the city had worked on an average of a little more than fifteen years in Cincinnati. Similarly, the majority of party activists had labored in Cincinnati for more than ten years.

41. *Enquirer, Commercial Gazette, Times Star*, December 19, 1886 – April 4, 1887. The "United Labor" column — printed in the *Enquirer* — was the most valuable source of information concerning the building of a party organization.

42. *Enquirer*, March 29, 31, April 2, 4, 1887.

43. Ibid., March 28, 29, April 1, 4, 1887.

44. Henry George to Terence V. Powderly, April 19, 1883, quoted in Kaufman, *Gompers and the AFL*, p. 154.

45. An examination of the lists of vice presidents — printed in newspapers — indicates that these positions were distributed among rank-and-file ward members.

46. *The Standard*, December 10, 1887. For a more thorough discussion of the relationship between religion and labor during the 1870s and 1880s, see Herbert G. Gutman, *Work, Culture, and Society in Industrializing America* (New York, 1977), pp. 79 – 117; Foner, "Class, Ethnicity, and Radicalism," pp. 6 – 55; Henry May, *Protestant Churches and Industrial America* (New York: Harper, 1949); Jean Quandt, "Religion and Social Thought: The Secularization of Post Millennialism," *American Quarterly* (October 1973) 25:391 – 407; Ross, "Culture of Political Economy," pp. 151 – 52.

47. *Enquirer*, April 16, 18, 1887.

48. Ibid., May 16, 1887. Powderly wrote of Lockwood: "Yours was the first voice in this country among God's chosen, which was lifted in defense of oppressed laborers." Lockwood, *Glimpses of Day*, introduction (n.p.). Foster was forced to resign his pastorate in 1890 because of "his advocacy of the claims of labor." "Minute Books of the Central Labor Council," 1, September 17, 1890, Proceedings of the Cincinnati Central Labor Council, Special Collections, UCL.

49. *Enquirer*, April 3, 1887.

50. *Enquirer, Commercial Gazette, Times Star*, March 20 – April 3, 1887.

51. *Enquirer*, April 4, 1887; Morris, "Road to Trade Unionism," pp. 317 – 18.

52. *Enquirer*, March 28, 29, 31, April 2, 4, 1887.

53. Ibid., March 30, 31, 1887.

54. Ibid., April 3, 1887; *Commercial Gazette*, April 3, 1887.

55. *Enquirer*, December 15, 1886.

56. Andrew J. Hickenlooper, "Personal Reminiscences," 2:624, CHS.

57. *Commercial Gazette*, April 3, 1887.

58. Ibid., April 3, 9, 1887

59. *Volksblatt*, April 1, 1887, quoted in Morris, "Road to Trade Unionism," p. 305.

60. Hickenlooper, "Personal Reminiscences," 2:624; *The Standard*, June 30, 1887; *Enquirer*, April 1, 1887; *Iron Molders' Journal*, June 30, 1887.

61. *Enquirer*, April 5, 6, 1887.

62. Ibid., April 10, 1887; *Commercial Gazette*, September 4, 1887.

63. *Commercial Gazette*, September 4, 1887; Zane Miller, *Boss Cox's Cincinnati: Urban Politics in the Progressive Era* (New York, 1968) pp. 76, 258n.

64. *Enquirer*, June 5, 1887; also see Ibid., May 12, 1887; Hugh Cavanaugh to Terence V. Powderly, October 21, 1887, Terence V. Powderly Papers (reel 23) Tamiment Institute, New York University.

65. *Enquirer*, June 4, 19, July 5, 1887; *Commercial Gazette*, June 4, July 5, 1887.

66. *Commercial Gazette*, July 5, 6, 1887; *Enquirer*, July 5, 6, 1887.

67. *Enquirer*, June 4, 1887.

68. *Commercial Gazette*, June 19, 1887.

69. *Enquirer*, July 3, 1887.

70. Ibid., August 30, 1887; also see Ibid., June 6, 1887.

71. Ibid., July 5, 6, 1887; *Commercial Gazette*, July 5, 6, 1887.

72. Henry George to C. D. F. Gutschow, November 25, 1887, Henry George Collection, Special Collections, New York Public Library; also see *The Standard*, August 6, 13, 20, 27, 1887; Barker, *Henry George*, pp. 496 – 502.

73. Rose, *Henry George*, pp. 123 – 24; Young, *The Single Tax*, pp. 119 – 21. Ethnic divisions can be gleaned from a careful examination of the names of United and Union Labor Party activists printed in Cincinnati newspapers.

74. *Commercial Gazette*, August 30, 31, 1887; *Enquirer*, August 30, 31, 1887.

75. *Enquirer*, November 10, 17, 1887.

76. Ibid., November 9, 1887.

77. Quoted in *Commercial Gazette*, November 12, 1887.

78. *Enquirer*, November 10, 1887.

79. Ibid., November 9, 1887; also see Hugh Cavanaugh to Terence Powderly, November 15, 1887, Powderly Papers, (reel 24), NYU.

80. *Enquirer*, April 8, 1888.

81. Ibid., April 14, 1887, April 8, 1888; *Commercial Gazette*, November 7, 1887; George Jr., *Life of Henry George*, pp. 465 – 501; Henry George to C. D. F. Gutschow, November 25, 1887, George Collection, NYPL.

82. Powderly, *Path I Trod*, pp. 34–66; Powderly, *Thirty Years*, passim; Grob, *Workers and Utopia*, pp. 34 – 118; Kaufman, *Gompers and the AFL*, pp. 109 – 12, 175 – 76, 206; Fink, *Workingmen's Democracy*, pp. 3 – 37.

83. *John Swinton's Newspaper*, August 7, 1887.

84. *Enquirer*, November 9, 30, 1886; January 1, February 7, July 10, 11, 14, August 15, 1887; *Commercial Gazette*, February 14, 1887; Morris, "Road to Trade Unionism," pp. 313 – 15, 319, 341, 351 – 66.

85. Quoted in Grob, *Workers and Utopia*, p. 140.

86. Quoted in Kaufman, *Gompers and the AFL*, p. 172.

87. Quoted in Grob, *Workers and Utopia*, p. 166. The philosophy and development of the AFL are detailed in the following: Ibid., pp. 74 – 78, 138 – 86; Kaufman, *Gompers and the AFL*, pp. 101 – 222; Quint, *American Socialism*, pp. 60 – 71; Harold Livesay, *Samuel Gompers* (Boston: Little Brown and Co, 1982); Samuel Gompers, *Seventy Years of Life and Labour: An Autobiography* (New York, 1925).

88. "Minute Book — CTU No. 3," 2, February 8, 1888.

89. Ibid., 2, September 2, 1888.

90. Ibid., 2, February 5, 1888.

91. Hugh Cavanaugh to Terence V. Powderly, March 3, 1888 (reel 25), NYU. For an analysis of the shoemakers' strike and the demise of the KOL, see James M. Morris, "The Cincinnati Shoemakers' Lockout of 1888: A Case Study in the Demise of the Knights of Labor," *Labor History* (Fall 1972) 13:505 – 19. Father Mackay's role is discussed in *Enquirer*, February 22, 1888; *Times Star*, February 20, 22, March 17, 19, 1888. The names of various shoemakers in Mackay's parish can be found in "St. Patrick's Census and Pew Accounts," Archives of the Cincinnati Diocese, stored at Mount St. Mary's Seminary, Cincinnati, Ohio.

92. *Enquirer*, March 29, 31, April 4, 5, 1888.

93. "Report of the General Secretary," in *Annual Report of the General Master Workman* (Cincinnati, 1888), p. 2; *Enquirer*, September 9, 10, 1888.

94. *BLS — 1888*, p. 80.
95. These statistics were compiled from data contained in the U.S. Department of Interior, Census Division, *Report on Farms and Homes: Proprietorship and Indebtedness in the United States at the Eleventh Census: 1890* (Washington, 1896), pp. 30–32, 51, 319, 373–74, 598, 605.
96. *Enquirer*, September 16, 1886; February 3, 1889; *BLS — 1888*, p. 80.
97. *Enquirer*, March 21, 26, May 15, 16, 17, 18, 1888; *Commercial Gazette*, March 21, May 15, 16, 17, 1888.
98. *Enquirer*, May 17, 1888. Delegates to the Union Labor Party convention in June 1887 wore buttons which read: "Organized to Protect our Homes, Flag, and Country." *Commercial Gazette*, June 19, 1887.
99. *Commercial Gazette*, May 15, 1888.
100. *Enquirer*, May 16, 1888.
101. *Commercial Gazette*, May 15, 1888.
102. Ibid.
103. *Enquirer*, March 21, 1888.
104. *John Swinton's Paper*, January 16, 1887.
105. *Enquirer*, March 21, 1888.
106. Ibid., March 26, 1888.
107. *Prospectus of the Technical School of Cincinnati, 1886 – 1887* (Cincinnati, n.d.), p. 5. The prospectus also includes a list of the school's trustees.
108. Ibid., p. 6.
109. Union Labor Party delegates passed the following resolution: "The foundation of a republic is in the intelligence of its citizens, and children who are driven into work-shops, mines, and factories, are deprived of an education which should be secured to all by proper legislation." *Commercial Gazette*, May 17, 1888.
For contemporary debates concerning the question of technical education for the working class see *Technical Education. Extracts From Addresses Delivered . . . in Cincinnati, Ohio, June 22, 1887* (Cincinnati, 1887); *Technical Education. Extract from Addresses* (Cincinnati, 1888); *Report of the Committee of the Senate Upon the Relations Between Labor and Capital, and Testimony Taken by the Committee*, 5 vols. (Washington, 1885), 1:406. Also see, *Prospectus of the Technical School of Cincinnati, 1886 – 1887* (Cincinnati, n.d.); *First Annual Catalogue of the Technical School of Cincinnati, Ohio, 1887 – 1888* (Cincinnati, 1888); International Pressmen and Assistants Union of North America, *Souvenir Album Convention Book* (Cincinnati, 1903), pp. 66–67.
110. *The Standard*, November 17, 1888. Frank Rist, August Bruck, Harry M. Ogden, and Joe Herzog assumed important positions within the Democratic Party. "Doc" Connolly, Tom Butterworth, John Schrage, and Union Labor Party councilmen Vorbroker and Brill moved into the ranks of the Republican Party. H. T. Ogden and W. Frank Smith assumed key positions of leadership within the Prohibitionist Party.
The final decline of the Union and United Labor parties is described in *Enquirer*, August 8, 14, September 4, 11, 14, 16, 27, 30, October 5, November 8, 1888; Morris, "Road to Trade Unionism," pp. 343–47.
111. For a discussion of labor participation in party politics during the early 1890s see Morris, "Road to Trade Unionism," pp. 342, 347–61; Barbara Musselman, "Trade Unionism in Turbulent Times: The Central Labor Council of Cincinnati and Vicinity, 1889–1894," M.A. thesis, University of Cincinnati, 1971; Barbara Musselman, "The Quest for Collective Improvement: Cincinnati Workers, 1893 to 1920," Ph.D. diss., University of Cincinnati, 1975, pp. 129–58.
112. Cincinnati Labor Council, *The Chronicle*, February 1892, p. 2.
113. For accounts of the general divisions within the labor movement see "Minute Books of the Central Labor Council," 1–3, June 20, 1889–December 31, 1895, UCL; Musselman, "Trade Unionism," *passim*; Musselman, "Quest for Collective Improvement," *passim*; Morris, "Road to Trade Unionism," pp. 347–72.

Selected Bibliography

Manuscript Collections

Cincinnati Historical Society [CHS]
    George S. Blanchard Scrapbook
    Henry Castles Collection
    Central Turners Records, 1850 – 1948
    Cincinnati Chamber of Commerce Collection
    Cincinnati Fire Department Records, 1819   1950
    The 1820 Cincinnati Data Bank
    William T. Coggeshall Scrapbooks
    Martin Davis Collection
    Julius Dexter Papers
    Joseph B. Foraker Scrapbooks
    Miles Greenwood Collection
    George Henshaw Collection
    Andrew Hickenlooper Papers
    Rufus King Papers
    Sidney Maxwell Papers
    Minute Books of the Iron and Machine Molders' Union No. 4, Volumes 1 – 2
    Letters of Augustus Roundy
    Peter Schmitt Collection
    Letters of George Valentine
    Vine Street Congregational Church Collection
    Timothy Whiting Collection
    Samuel Williams Collection

Cincinnati County Recorder's Office, Hamilton County Courthouse [HCC]
    Incorporation Records of Hamilton County (misfiled as "Church Records")
    Records of Partnership
Public Library of Hamilton County and Cincinnati [PLHCC]
    George M. Herancourt Collection
    George Puchta Collection
University of Cincinnati Library, Special Collections [UCL]
    Minute Books of the Franklin Reading Room and Mutual Instruction Institute
    Ohio Mechanics' Institute Collection
    Proceedings of the Cincinnati Central Labor Council
    Records of the Cincinnati Central Labor Union
Cincinnati. International Molders and Allied Workers' Union Headquarters
    Records and Minute Books of the Iron and Machine Molders' Union No. 4 (Volumes
       3–4)
Cincinnati. International Typographical Union No. 3, Headquarters
    Records of the Cincinnati Typographical Union No. 3
Cincinnati. Mount St. Mary's Seminary
    Archives of the Cincinnati Diocese
Columbus, Ohio. Ohio Historical Society
    Federal Manufacturing Schedules, Hamilton County, Ohio, 1850, 1870, 1880
New York City. New York Public Library, Special Collections.
    Henry George Collection
New York City, Tamiment Institute, New York University Library
    Terence V. Powderly Papers (Microfilm)

Newspapers and Journals

Cist's Weekly Advertiser, 1847–1849
Commercial, 1843–1883
Commercial Gazette, 1883–1890
Elevator, 1841–1842
Emancipator, 1877–1878
Enquirer, 1841–1890
Gazette, 1830–1890
Iron Molders' Journal (Cincinnati), 1866–1890
John Swinton's Newspaper (New York), 1883–1887
Nonpareil, 1850–1853
People's Paper, 1843–1845
The Scientific Artisan, 1858–1859, 1878
The Standard (New York), 1887–1888
Times-Star, 1840–1890

The Unionist, 1883
Western General Advertiser, 1844 – 1845
Working Man's Friend, 1836

Government Publications

Cincinnati, *Annual Reports of the City Departments of Cincinnati,* 1853/54 – 1890.
Ohio Adjutant General, *Annual Report of the Adjutant General,* 1877 – 1887.
Ohio Bureau of Labor Statistics, *Annual Report of the Bureau of Labor Statistics,* 1877 – 1905.
Ohio Commissioner of Statistics, *Annual Report of the Commissioner of Statistics,* 1857 – 1860.
Ohio Department of Inspection of Workshops, Factories, and Public Buildings, *Annual Report of the Department of Inspection of Workshops, Factories, and Public Buildings,* 1884 – 1892.
Ohio Secretary of State, *Annual Report of the Secretary of State,* 1865 – 1895.
United States Commissioner of Labor, *Third Annual Report of the Commissioner of Labor, 1887. Strikes and Lockouts.* Washington: Government Printing Office, 1889.
—— *Fourth Annual Report of the Commissioner of Labor, 1888. Working Women in Large Cities.* Washington: Government Printing Office, 1896.
—— *Tenth Annual Report of the Commissioner of Labor, 1894. Strikes and Lockouts.* 2 vols. Washington: Government Printing Office, 1896.
—— *Thirteenth Annual Report of the Commissioner of Labor, 1898. Hand and Machine Labor.* 2 vols. Washington: Government Printing Office, 1899.
United States Department of the Interior, Census Division, *Report of the Manufacturers of the United States,* 1840 – 1900.
—— *Statistics of the Population of the United States,* 1850 – 1900.
—— *Report on Farms and Homes: Proprietorship and Indebtedness in the United States at the Eleventh Census: 1890.* Washington: Government Printing Office, 1896.
—— *Report on the Social Statistics of the Cities.* 2 vols. Washington: Government Printing Office, 1887.
United States Senate, *Report of the Committee of the Senate Upon the Relations Between Labor and Capital, and Testimony Taken by the Committee.* 5 vols. Washington: Government Printing Office, 1885.

Proceedings and Transactions

American Federation of Labor, *Proceedings of the American Federation of Labor,* 1886 – 1890.
Cincinnati Chamber of Commerce and Merchants' Exchange, *Annual Report of the Chamber of Commerce and Merchants' Exchange,* 1849 – 1895.

Cincinnati Conference of the Methodist Episcopal Church, *Minutes of the Cincinnati Annual Conference of the Methodist Episcopal Church, 1852 – 1900.*

Cincinnati Industrial Exposition, *Annual Report of the General Committee of the Cincinnati Industrial Exposition, 1870 – 1888.*

Federation of Organized Trades and Labor Unions in the United States and Canada, *Report of the Annual Session, 1881 – 1885.*

International Typographical Union, *Report of the Proceedings of the Annual Session, 1853 – 1890.*

Iron Molders' International Union, *Proceedings of the Annual Convention of the Iron Molders' Union, 1859 – 1890.*

Knights of Labor, *Proceedings of the Annual Session of the District Assembly No. 48 of the Knights of Labor, Held at Druid's Hall, Cincinnati, Sunday, January 8, 1888.* Cincinnati, 1888.

—— *Record of the Proceedings of the General Assembly of the Knights of Labor, 1878 – 1890.*

Miami Association of Regular Baptists, *Minutes of the Miami Association of Regular Baptists, 1830 – 1890.*

Ohio Mechanics' Institute, *Report of the Annual Fair of the Ohio Mechanics' Institute, 1838 – 1870.*

Protestant Episcopal Church in the Diocese of Ohio, *Journal of the Proceedings of the Annual Convention of the Protestant Episcopal Church in the Diocese of Ohio, 1838 – 1890.*

Contemporary Published Works

American Protestant Association Liberty Lodge No. 2, Cincinnati, *Constitution, By-Laws, Rules, and Regulations of the Liberty Lodge of the American Protestant Association, of the State of Ohio, Instituted July, 1853.* Cincinnati: W. H. Longley, 1856.

Ameringer, Oscar, *If You Don't Weaken.* New York: H. Holt, 1940.

Barney, H. H. *Report on the American System of Graded Free Schools, to the Board of Trustees and Visitors of Common Schools.* Cincinnati: Daily Times, 1851.

Bishop, Leander J. *A History of American Manufactures from 1608 to 1860.* 3 vols. Philadelphia: E. Young, 1864.

Chambers, William. *Things As They Are in America.* London and Edinburgh: W. and R. Chambers, 1854.

Chevalier, Michel. *Society, Manners, and Politics in the United States: Being a Series of Letters on North America.* Boston: Weeks, Jordan, 1839.

Cincinnati Typographical Union No. 3, *Souvenir of the Fall Festival Labor Day, September 24, 1900.* Cincinnati: Sixth Street Printing Works, 1900.

Cist, Charles. *Cincinnati in 1841: Its Early Annals and Future Prospects.* Cincinnati: E. Morgan, 1841.

—— *The Cincinnati Miscellany, or Antiquities of the West: And Pioneer History and General and Local Statistics.* 2 vols. Cincinnati: Caleb Clarke, 1845 – 1846.

—— *Sketches and Statistics of Cincinnati in 1851.* Cincinnati: Wm. H. Morgan, 1851.

—— *Sketches and Statistics of Cincinnati in 1859.* Cincinnati: Wm. H. Morgan, 1859.

Constitution and By-Laws of the General Trades' Union of the City of Cincinnati and Vicinity. Cincinnati: N. S. Johnson, 1836.

Constitution, By-Laws, and Rules of Order of the Washington Council, No. 1 of the Order of the United American Mechanics of the State of Ohio. Cincinnati: 1847.

Drake, Benjamin and E. D. Mansfield. *Cincinnati in 1826.* Cincinnati: Morgan, Lodge, and Fisher, 1827.

Drake, Daniel. *Natural and Statistical View, or Picture of Cincinnati and the Miami County.* Cincinnati: Looker and Wallace, 1815.

Esselborn, Pauline Rehfuss. *Recollections of Pauline Rehfuss Esselborn 1844 – 1925.* N.P.: Private Printing, N.D.

Familton, James B. *The Printer's Apprentice: Or Job Printing Made Easy.* Cincinnati: L. E. Rogers, 1869.

Fireman's Protective Association. *History of the Cincinnati Fire Department.* Cincinnati: 1895.

Flint, Timothy. *Recollections of the Last Ten Years in the Valley of the Mississippi.* George R. Brooks, editor. Carbondale and Edwardsville: Southern Illinois University Press, 1968 (originally published in 1826).

Foraker, Joseph B. *Notes of a Busy Life.* 2 vols. Cincinnati: Stewart and Kidd, 1917.

Ford, Henry A. and Mrs. Kate B. *History of Cincinnati, Ohio.* Cleveland: L. A. Williams, 1881.

Gerstaecker, Frederick. *The Wanderings and Fortunes of Some German Emigrants.* Translated by David Black. Cincinnati: 1856.

Gompers, Samuel. *Seventy Years of Life and Labor.* 2 vols. New York: E. P. Dutton, 1925.

Goss, Reverend Charles F. *Cincinnati: The Queen City, 1788 – 1912.* 4 vols. Cincinnati: S. J. Clarke, 1912.

Greve, Charles. *Centennial History of Cincinnati and Its Representative Citizens.* 2 vols. Chicago: Biographical Publishing Co., 1904.

Gustorf, Frederick Julius. *The Uncorrupted Heart: The Journals and Letters of Frederick Julius Gustorf 1800 – 1845.* Fred and Gisela Gustorf, editors. Columbia: University of Missouri Press, 1969.

Hall, James. *The West: Its Commerce and Navigation.* Cincinnati: H. W. Derby, 1848.

Haller, William. *German Socialism in America.* Cincinnati: 1879.

Harpel, Oscar. *Harpel's Typograph or Book of Specimens.* Cincinnati: Oscar Harpel, 1870.

History of Hamilton County. Cincinnati: S. B. Nelson, 1894.

History of the Manufactures of Cincinnati: Being an Index to the Principal Manufactories. Cincinnati: J. C. Campbell, 1870.

Howe, Henry. *Historical Collections of Ohio.* 3 vols. Columbus: Henry Howe and Son, 1891.

[International Publishing Co.], *Leading Manufacturers and Merchants of Cincinnati and Environs.* Cincinnati: International Publishing Company, 1886.

Joblin, M. *Cincinnati Past and Present.* Cincinnati: M. Joblin, 1872.

Kenny, D. J. *Illustrated Cincinnati: A Pictorial Handbook.* Cincinnati: G. E. Stevens, 1875.

King, Rufus. *Report to the State Commissioner of Schools, On the History and Condition of the Public Schools of Cincinnati, December 1859.* Cincinnati: Robert Clarke, 1859.

[Leonard, J. W.], *The Centennial Review of Cincinnati: One Hundred Years.* Cincinnati: J. M. Elstner, 1888.

Lockwood, Melanchon C. *Glimpses of Day. Sermons Preached in the First Baptist Church, Cincinnati, Ohio.* Cincinnati: 1892.

Mackay, Charles. *Life and Liberty in America: Or Sketches of a Tour in the United States and Canada, in 1857–8.* 2 vols. London: Smith, Elder, 1859.

Mansfield, Edward. *Personal Memories: Social, Political, and Literary with Sketches of Many Noted People.* Cincinnati: Robert Clarke, 1879.

Marquis, A. N., ed. *The Industries of Cincinnati.* Cincinnati: A. N. Marquis, 1883.

Maxwell, Sidney D. *The Suburbs of Cincinnati.* Cincinnati: G. E. Stevens, 1870.

McCulloch, Hugh. *Men and Measures of Half a Century.* New York: Scribner's 1888.

Melish, John. *Travels in the United States of America In the Years 1806 & 1807, and 1809, 1810, & 1811.* 2 vols. Philadelphia: T. & G. Palmer, 1812.

Moore, Robert. *Autobiographical Outlines of a Long Life.* Cincinnati: R. Moore, 1887.

Morrison, Andrew. *The Industries of Cincinnati: Manufacturing Establishments and Business Houses.* Cincinnati: The Metropolitan Publishing Co., 1886.

Nimmo, Joseph Jr. *The Commercial, Industrial, and Transportation Interests of the City of Cincinnati.* Washington: Government Printing Office, 1881.

One Hundred Years of Presbyterianism in the Ohio Valley. Cincinnati: 1890.

Piatt, Donn. *Some Historical Notes Concerning the Cincinnati Fire Department.* Cincinnati: Private Printing, n.d.

Powderly, Terence Vincent. *The Path I Trod.* New York: Columbia University Press, 1940.

―――― *Thirty Years of Labor, 1859 to 1889.* Columbus: Excelsior Publishing House, 1889.

Reemelin, Charles. *The Life of Charles Reemelin.* Cincinnati: O. Weier and Daiker, 1892.

Roe, George M. *Our Police: A History of the Cincinnati Police Force. From the Earliest Period Until the Present Day.* Cincinnati: 1890.

Rosenberg, Nathan, ed. *The American System of Manufactures: The Report of the Committee on the Machinery of the United States 1855 and the Special Reports of George Wallis and Joseph Whitworth.* Edinburgh: Edinburgh University Press, 1969.

Smith, William. *Annual Statement of the Trade and Commerce of Cincinnati Including a General View of the Present Position and Future Prospects of the City.* Cincinnati: Gazette Co., 1885.

Stevens, George. *The City of Cincinnati.* Cincinnati: George S. Blanchard, 1869.

Technical Education. Extracts from Addresses Delivered . . . in Cincinnati, Ohio, June 22, 1887. Cincinnati: 1887.

Technical Education. Extracts from Addresses Delivered . . . in Cincinnati, Ohio, June 13, 1888. Cincinnati: 1888.

Thayer, George Augustine. *The First Congregational Church of Cincinnati, A Historical Sketch.* Cincinnati: Ebbert and Richardson, 1917.

Thomson, William. *A Tradesman's Travels in the United States and Canada, In the Years 1840, 41, 42.* Edinburgh: Oliver and Boyd, 1842.

Tocqueville, Alexis de. *Journey to America*. Translated by George Lawrence. New Haven: Yale University Press, 1960.

Trollope, Frances. *Domestic Manners of the Americans*. New York: Whittaker, Treacher, 1832.

Tunison, J. S. *The Cincinnati Riot: Its Causes and Results*. Cincinnati: Keating and Co., 1886.

Typothetae of Cincinnati, *Report of the Committee On the Cost of Printing. Presented to the Typothetae of Cincinnati, August 9, 1888*. Cincinnati: 1888.

Secondary Sources

Books and Articles

Arms, Richard G., "From Disassembly to Assembly. Cincinnati: The Birthplace of Mass-Production." *HPSOB* (July 1959) 17:195 – 203.

Atherton, Lewis E. *The Pioneer Merchant in Mid-America*. Columbia: University of Missouri Press, 1939.

Becker, Carl M. "Evolution of the Disassembly Line: The Horizontal Wheel and the Overhead Railway Loop." *CHSB* (July 1968) 26:276 – 82.

Berry, Thomas Senior. *Western Prices Before 1861: A Study of the Cincinnati Market*. Cambridge: Harvard University Press, 1943.

Cabot, C. E. "The Carters in Early Ohio. A Glimpse of Cincinnati in its First Quarter Century." *New England Magazine* (May 1899) 20:344 – 51.

Cahill, Marion Cotter. *Shorter Hours: A Study of the Movement Since the Civil War*. New York: Columbia University Press, 1932.

Cebula, James. *The Glory and Despair of Challenge and Change: A History of the Molders' Union*. Cincinnati: International Molders and Allied Workers' Union, 1976.

Cincinnati Typographical Union No. 3. *Centennial Booklet*. Cincinnati: Cincinnati Typographical Union No. 3, 1946.

—— 125th Anniversary Commemorating the Foundation of the Cincinnati Typographical Union No. 3. Cincinnati: Cincinnati Typographical Union No. 3, 1971.

Commons, John R., Ulrich B. Phillips, Eugene A. Gilmore, Helen L. Sumner, and John B. Andrews. *A Documentary History of American Industrial Society*. 10 vols. Cleveland: Arthur H. Clark Co., 1910 – 1911.

Commons, John R., David J. Saposs, Helen L. Sumner, E. B. Mittelman, H. E. Hoagland, John B. Andrews, and Selig Perlman. *History of Labour in the United States*. 4 vols. New York: Augustus Kelley, 1966.

Connaughton, Sister Mary S. *The Editorial Opinion of the Catholic Telegraph in Cincinnati On Contemporary Affairs and Politics 1871 – 1921*. Washington: The Catholic University Press, 1943.

Dannenbaum, Jed. "Immigrants and Temperance: Ethnocultural Conflict in Cincinnati, 1845 – 1860." *Ohio History* (Spring 1978) 87:125 – 39.

Downard, William L. *The Cincinnati Brewing Industry, A Social and Economic History.* Athens: Ohio University Press, 1973.

Duggan, Edward P. "Machines, Markets, Labor: The Carriage and Wagon Industry in Late Nineteenth-Century Cincinnati." *Business History Review* (Autumn 1977) 51: 308 – 25.

Executive Council, International Typographical Union, *A Study of the History of the International Typographical Union 1852 – 1963.* 2 vols. Colorado Springs: International Typographical Union, 1964.

Farrell, Richard T. "Cincinnati, 1800 – 1830: Economic Development Through Trade and Industry." *Ohio History* (Autumn 1968) 77:111 – 29.

Federal Writers' Project, *They Built A City: 150 Years of Industrial Cincinnati.* Cincinnati: Cincinnati Post, 1938.

Garlock, Jonathan. *Guide to the Local Assemblies of the Knights of Labor.* Westport: Greenwood Press, 1982.

Geier, Frederick V. *The Coming of the Machine Tool Age — The Tool Builders of Cincinnati.* New York: Newcomen Society of England, American Branch, 1949.

Gephardt, William F. *Transportation and Industrial Development of the Middle West.* New York: Longmans, Green, and Co., 1909.

Hamant, Nancy R. "Religion in the Cincinnati Schools 1830 – 1900." *HPSOB* (October 1963) 21:239 – 51.

Hunter, Louis C. *Studies in the Economic History of the Ohio Valley: Seasonal Aspects of Industry and Commerce Before the Age of Big Business: The Beginnings of Industrial Combination.* Northampton: The Department of History, Smith College, 1915.

Jordan, Philip D. *Ohio Comes of Age, 1873 – 1900.* Columbus: Ohio State Archaeological and Historical Society, 1943.

Keeler, Vernon. *The Commercial Development of Cincinnati.* Chicago: University of Chicago Press, 1938.

Lamott, Reverend John H. *History of the Archdiocese of Cincinnati 1821 – 1921.* New York and Cincinnati: Frederick Pustet Co., 1921.

Lippincott, Isaac. *A History of the Manufactures in the Ohio Valley to the Year 1860.* Chicago: University of Chicago Press, 1914.

Meyer, Henry W. *Memories of Buggy Days.* Cincinnati: Brinker, 1965.

Michael, Ann Deborah. "The Origins of the Jewish Community in Cincinnati 1817 – 1860." *CHSB* (Fall-Winter 1972) 30:155 – 82.

Miller, Zane. *Boss Cox's Cincinnati: Urban Politics in the Progressive Era.* New York: Oxford University Press, 1968.

Morris, James M. "The Cincinnati Shoemakers' Lockout of 1888: A Case Study in the Demise of the Knights of Labor." *Labor History* (Fall 1972) 13:505 – 19.

Musselman, Barbara L. "Working Class Unity and Ethnic Division: Cincinnati Trade Unionists and Cultural Pluralism." *CHSB* (Summer 1976) 34:121 – 43.

Neufeld, Maurice F. "Three Aspects of the Economic Life of Cincinnati From 1815 to 1840." *OAHQ* (January 1935) 44:65 – 80.

One Hundred and Fifty Years of Presbyterianism in the Ohio Valley, 1790 – 1940. Cincinnati: 1940.

Park, Clyde W. *The Cincinnati Equitable Insurance Company: Oldest Fire Insurance Company West of the Alleghenies.* Cincinnati: 1954.

Perko, F. Michael. "The Building Up of Zion: Religion and Education in Nineteenth-Century Cincinnati." *CHSB* (Summer 1980) 38:96 – 114.

Roseboom, Eugene H. *The Civil War Era: 1850 – 1873*. Columbus: Ohio State Archaeological and Historical Society, 1944.

Scheiber, Harry N. *Ohio Canal Era: A Case Study of Government and Economy 1820 – 1861*. Athens: Ohio University Press, 1969.

Spanheimer, Sister Mary Edmund. *Heinrich Armin Ratterman, German-American Author, Poet, and Historian, 1832 – 1923*. Washington: Catholic University Press, 1937.

Stockton, Frank T. *The International Iron Molders' Union of North America*. Baltimore: Johns Hopkins University Press, 1921.

Streifthau, Donna L. "Fancy Chairs and Finials: Cincinnati Furniture Industry, 1819 – 1830." *CHSB* (Fall-Winter 1971) 29:172 – 97.

Stritch, Reverend Alfred G. "Political Nativisim in Cincinnati, 1830 – 1860." *Records of the Catholic Historical Society of Philadelphia* (September 1937) 48:227 – 78.

Sutton, Walter. *The Western Book Trade: Cincinnati as a Nineteenth-Century Publishing and Book-Trade Center*. Columbus: Ohio State University Press, 1961.

Utter, William T. *The Frontier State 1803 – 1825*. Columbus: Ohio State Archaeological and Historical Society, 1942.

Wade, Richard. *The Urban Frontier: Pioneer Life in Early Pittsburgh, Cincinnati, Lexington, Louisville, and St. Louis*. Cambridge: Harvard University Press, 1959.

Weisenburger, Francis P. *The Passing of the Frontier 1825 – 1850*. Columbus: Ohio State Archaeological and Historical Society, 1941.

Wittke, Carl. "The Germans of Cincinnati," *HPSOB* (January 1962) 20:3 – 14.

——— *The Irish in America*. Baton Rouge: Louisiana State University Press, 1956.

——— *Refugees of Revolution: The German Forty-Eighters in America*. Philadelphia: University of Pennsylvania Press, 1952.

Zucker, Adolf, ed. *The Forty-Eighters: Political Refugees of the German Revolution of 1848*. New York: Columbia University Press, 1950.

Doctoral Dissertations and Masters Theses

Aaron, Daniel. "Cincinnati, 1818 – 1838: A Study of Attitudes in the Urban West." Ph.D. diss., Harvard University, 1942.

Abbott, Carl John. "The Divergent Development of Cincinnati, Indianapolis, Chicago, and Galena, 1840 – 1860: Economic Thought and Economic Growth." Ph.D. diss., University of Chicago, 1971.

Anderson, Celestine Estelle. "The Invention of the 'Professional' Municipal Police: The Case of Cincinnati, 1788 – 1900." Ph.D. diss., University of Cincinnati, 1979.

Baughin, William A. "Nativism in Cincinnati Before 1860." M.A. thesis, University of Cincinnati, 1963.

Brickner, Barnett. "The Jewish Community of Cincinnati: Historical and Descriptive." Ph.D. diss., University of Cincinnati, 1935.

Butler, Tod Jordan. "The Cincinnati Southern Railway: A City's Response to Relative Commercial Decline." Ph.D. diss., Ohio State University, 1952.

Chartener, William Huston, "The Molders' and Foundry Workers' Union: A Study in Union Development." Ph.D. diss., Harvard University, 1952.

Clark, Sister Mary Edward. "The Contribution of the Irish Immigrant to the Early

Growth and Development of Ohio 1758–1860." M.A. thesis, Catholic University of America, 1945.

Dannenbaum, Jed. "Drink and Disorder: Temperance Reform in Cincinnati, 1841 – 1874." Ph.D. diss., University of California, Davis, 1978.

Dobbert, Guido A. "The Disintegration of an Immigrant Community: The Cincinnati Germans, 1870–1920." Ph.D. diss., University of Chicago, 1965.

Farrell, Richard T. "Cincinnati in the Early Jacksonian Era, 1816–1834: An Economic and Political Study." Ph.D. diss., Indiana University, 1967.

Flack, Irwin F. "Who Governed Cincinnati? A Comparative Analysis of Government and Social Structure in a Nineteenth-Century River City: 1819–1860." Ph.D. diss., University of Pittsburgh, 1978.

Glazer, Walter Stix. "Cincinnati in 1840: A Community Profile." Ph.D. diss., University of Michigan, 1968.

Hamel, Dana B. "A History of the Ohio Mechanics' Institute, Cincinnati, Ohio." Doctor of Education diss., University of Cincinnati, 1952.

Hett, Christopher B. "Political Boss of Cincinnati: The Era of George B. Cox." M.A. thesis, Xavier University, 1968.

Jebsen, Harry. "Cincinnati's Protestant Clergy in Social and Political Reform 1865 – 1915." M.A. thesis, University of Cincinnati, 1966.

Kiefer, Kathleen J. "A History of the Cincinnati Fire Department in the Nineteenth Century." M.A. thesis, University of Cincinnati, 1967.

Koch, Herbert F. "The Panic of 1857 and Its Effects in Ohio." M.A. thesis, University of Cincinnati, 1951.

Larew, Marilyn Melton. "The Cincinnati Branch of the Second Bank of the United States and Its Effects on the Local Economy, 1817–1836." Ph.D. diss., University of Maryland, 1978.

Michael, Ann Deborah. "The Origins of the Jewish Community of Cincinnati 1817 – 1860." M.A. thesis, University of Cincinnati, 1970.

Miller, James R. "The Steamboat as a Factor in Transportation and Industrialization in Cincinnati 1800–1860." M.A. thesis, University of Cincinnati, 1967.

Morris, James Matthew. "The Road to Trade Unionism:" Organized Labor in Cincinnati to 1893." Ph.D. diss., University of Cincinnati, 1969.

Mostov, Stephen G. "A 'Jerusalem' on the Ohio: The Social and Economic History of Cincinnati's Jewish Community, 1840 – 1875." Ph.D. diss., Brandeis University, 1981.

Musselman, Barbara L. "The Quest for Collective Improvement: Cincinnati Workers, 1893 to 1920." Ph.D. diss., University of Cincinnati, 1975.

—— "Trade Unionism in Turbulent Times: The Central Labor Council of Cincinnati and Vicinity, 1889–1894." M.A. thesis, University of Cincinnati, 1971.

Neufeld, Maurice. "The Queen City of the West: Cincinnati From 1815 to 1840." M.A. thesis, University of Wisconsin, Madison, 1932.

Pierce, Donald C. "Mitchell and Rammelsberg: Cincinnati Furniture Makers 1847 – 1881." M.A. thesis, University of Delaware, 1976.

Rengering, William A. "Early Germans in Cincinnati and Biographical Studies of Four Representative Men." M.A. thesis, University of Cincinnati, 1951.

Rogers, Virgil A. "The Irish in Cincinnati, 1860 – 1870: A Typical Experience." M.A. thesis, University of Cincinnati, 1972.

Shaver, Diane. "The Mid-Nineteenth Century German Immigration Movement into the United States." M.A. thesis, University of Cincinnati, 1960.

Siegel, Nancy Ray. "A Matter of Public Welfare: The Temperence Movement in Ante-Bellum Cincinnati." M.A. thesis, University of Cincinnati, 1971.

Speiss, Philip D. "The Cincinnati Industrial Expositions (1870 – 1888): Propaganda or Progress?" M.A. thesis, University of Delaware, 1970.

Streifthau, Donna Largent. "Cincinnati Cabinet- and Chairmakers, 1819 – 1830." Ph.D. diss., Ohio State University, 1970.

White, Joseph Michael. "Religion and Community: Cincinnati Germans, 1841 – 1870." Ph.D. diss., University of Notre Dame, 1980.

Wing, George A. "The History of the Cincinnati Machine-Tool Industry." Doctor of Business Administration diss., Indiana University, 1964.

INDEX